CREATIVE DRAMATICS

An Art for Children

Creative Dramatics

AN ART FOR CHILDREN

Geraldine Brain Siks

ASSOCIATE PROFESSOR
UNIVERSITY OF WASHINGTON

HARPER & ROW, PUBLISHERS
NEW YORK, EVANSTON, AND LONDON

As you encourage the growth of artistic achievement through the medium of creative drama, you strengthen the cultural life of our nation and all nations. The inclusion of the arts in the education of children contributes to the enrichment of mankind.

—DWIGHT D. EISENHOWER

Contents

Foreword

his is a true story about children, creativity, and drama. It starts with a child and ends with a poem. This book could have been called *Gateway to Adventure,* for it opens for the reader (parent, teacher or leader of children in any capacity), avenues of understanding. It will not only enthuse but will show how the universal urge to create and the human instinct to dramatize can be kept alive, released and channeled so that the child's natural creative tendencies might bring to him and to others continual joy and awareness.

No book is an island. This one is no exception. It has grown from shared experiences. It is a part of the Seattle story in creative dramatics. In it Geraldine Brain Siks, its author, has touched upon the growth of the program in creative dramatics in Seattle and at the University of Washington. She has, however, made no reference to her role in the building of this program. Like other natives of the Northwest, including the grandmother described in this book (who I suspect is her own), Jerry Siks has "an eye and a yen for building" and "a love and a knack for teaching others how to build." People born and bred in the Northwest, even its adopted sons and daughters, are doers bent on doing. Dreams and plans, however, precede their spirited doing. Never out of sight of water, mountains, trees, flowers, sky and space, the inhabitants in their thinking and doing reach high, wide, and deep.

The Seattle story started with a dream envisioned and shared by a volunteer, Ruth Gonser Lease. She left Montana in 1941 with her husband and two daughters. She was a storyteller with a love and understanding of drama, so it was natural that she share this talent and enthusiasm during the war with youngsters who had come to Seattle from every part of the country with their parents who worked in the wartime industries. Uprooted from home soil, reservoirs of a multitude of impressions old and new, these children had a great need for expression. Creative dramatics met that need— so much so that Seattle Junior Programs gave assistance to expand the program. Then the Seattle Junior League, in 1946, adopted the program as a special project and, with the coöperation of Junior Programs, Public Schools, Park Board, Art Museum, City Council and the Council of Social Agencies, made creative dramatics available to even greater numbers of children.

As the program grew, so did the need for trained leaders. Hence in 1947 the University of Washington was approached by the Junior League. With the coöperation of Glenn Hughes, Executive Director of the School of Drama, and Lloyd Schram, Director of the Adult Education Division and Extension Services, creative dramatics was added to the curriculum, and a director was appointed to teach at the university. I had the good fortune to be that director.

Within a year the university assumed full responsibility for the program. The increase in the number of students on and off campus and during summer sessions necessitated a second teacher. An outstanding one was at hand—Geraldine Brain Siks. She had been closely associated with Winifred Ward at Northwestern University; for seven years as a creative dramatics specialist in the Evanston Public Schools; for four years as associate director of the Children's Theatre of Evanston. A mother of two sons, she was writing children's plays in whatever leisure time a mother of two growing boys can find.

To trace the development of the Seattle program from 1948 on by no means departs from the author of this book, for Geraldine Siks has played an active role in every episode of the story: the inclusion of creative dramatics as a requirement for education majors and recreation majors in 1950; the establishment of a B.A. degree in the area through the General Studies Division of the university; the creation of a basic academic field in children's drama for elementary education majors in 1955. Each step was accompanied by further increase in the number of students—a healthy cross section of all the schools within the university.

In 1948 Ruth Lease and others interested UNESCO in the activity, and that organization recommended informal playmaking for the children of Europe. By 1950 students from Austria and other European countries began to arrive, followed by others from Japan, the Philippine Islands, Hawaii, and Egypt. When the first arrivals from other lands returned home, they carried with them copies of *Creative Dramatics in Home, School, and Community,* coauthored by Mrs. Lease and Mrs. Siks.

The community aspect of its title was no idle phrase, for with the increased emphasis on leadership training, creative dramatics had spread beyond the immediate scene into the state. In libraries, classrooms, leisure-time programs and camps, Sunday schools and state institutions, teachers were sharing this art with children and young people. Many of their experiences have been included in this present book.

In 1948 Margaret S. Woods, an extension staff member at the university, initiated a summer program in creative dramatics for children in the Fauntleroy community of Seattle. Under Mrs. Wood's guidance this program grew steadily. It became a city-wide program sponsored by the Seattle Council of the Parent-Teachers Association and during the summer months of 1957 brought creative dramatics to children in twenty-five schools throughout the city. This program also offers creative arts experiences to preschool children throughout the year.

With community interest at a high peak, Alice Jean Lewis, a former university staff member, turned her thoughts to children with speech and hearing problems. As a result a unique pilot project in this area has been developed, known as the Integrated Creative Arts Program for Speech-Hearing Handicapped.

All this time Ruth Lease was working out plans for the establishment of a program that would make the creative arts as free and accessible to children as public libraries and museums. The dream was realized in January, 1957, with the establishment of the Seattle Creative Activities Center.

The creative dramatics program at the University of Washington began in the community. The university has never forgotten this source nor its own status and responsibility as a state-wide institution. For ten years it has strived to realize on a wide level a triple objective: to offer instruction in the philosophy and techniques of creative dramatics; to offer experiences in informal playmaking to children through groups set up under faculty leadership for student observation; *and,* to constantly interpret this art for children to interested individuals and community groups through speeches, workshops, demonstrations, and publications.

In its realization of these objectives, the program is greatly indebted to the author of this book. In writing it she has drawn upon her experiences in all three areas: teaching, guiding children, and working with community leaders and teachers in a variety of situations. She writes as she teaches—with warmth and authenticity, imagination, and understanding. Knowledge alone would be dull and confining. Enthusiasm without knowledge, asinine if not dangerous. But when knowledge *and* enthusiasm motivate action, the result is rooted in reality and can soar high.

It has been my privilege and my delight to teach side by side with Geraldine Siks for almost ten years. Unchangeable in basic integrity, she is ever changing and growing in her pursuit of greater understanding of children and drama. Under her guidance, as revealed in this book, creative dramatics is more than an activity; it becomes an art for children.

AGNES HAAGA, Director
Creative Dramatics

University of Washington, Seattle

Preface

reative Dramatics: An Art for Children came into being in answer to many questions asked by students, teachers, and children's leaders. It was written to share creative adventures which classroom teachers and community leaders have guided children into experiencing. It was also written to share the fun, friendliness, beauty, and bucklin'-to that children have enjoyed as they have worked and played together. But the book was written primarily as a result of enjoying and believing in children and drama.

This is a textbook for creative dramatics courses which offer training in creative leadership. It is also a book for elementary teachers, children's leaders, and parents who wish to share this art with children. The book emphasizes philosophy while it concentrates on basics in guiding. It begins by considering a child in relation to the way he grows and develops as a unique personality. It points out the need for art experiences that will foster a child's personality growth and development. The premise on which this art is based is then explored, first by considering creativity, and next by delving into drama as an art. The fundamentals of drama are discussed to provide an insight into dramatic content and structure.

Because this art depends largely on sound creative leadership, the qualities and responsibilities of a good leader are examined. With these four chapters serving as a foundation, the book branches out to consider dramatic material for beginning and advanced groups of children.

The creative process is investigated in detail. Specific emphasis is centered on how to guide. Pitfalls are pointed out in the hope that leaders will profit by avoiding them. After the creative process is discussed, the book focuses on guidance at specific age levels with particular stress on classroom correlation. It includes a detailed emphasis on how to guide little children, proceeds to guidance for 7- and 8-year-olds and then for 9-, 10-, and 11-year-olds. Questions and activities are included at the end of each chapter for the purpose of strengthening a leader's understanding. A selected bibliography and a selected list of material are included. Nearly a hundred photographs of children at different age levels are used throughout the book to illustrate basic guidance principles and methods.

The book has been designed for use in four different ways: (1) It has been planned for a beginning course in creative dramatics. Students may read the book from beginning to end throughout a quarter or semester, to become introduced to the philosophy and techniques of the art. (2) It has also been planned for use in an advanced course in creative dramatics. Used in this way the entire book should be studied chapter by chapter. Chapters 3, 4, 5, 6, and either Chapters 7, 8, or 9, should be studied in detail, depending upon the age level at which the student is concentrating. (3) The book may be used in education, recreation, sociology, religious education, or library classes for supplementary reading. The entire book may be assigned for rapid reading, or students may gain a stronger insight by studying Chapters 1, 2, 3, 4, and either 7, 8, or 9. And (4) the book may be used by classroom teachers, children's leaders, and parents as reference for techniques and material.

Originally this book was designed for the classroom teacher in the elementary school and the emphasis in the age-level chapters is still slanted specifically toward classroom correlation. However, as the book developed, the basic truth of the art revealed itself. Once the leader understands children, drama, and the art of guiding, she is prepared to share this art with children wherever she meets them, whether it be in a classroom, in a community program, or at home. The leader need only select material that is correlated with a specific situation wherein she is teaching. The basic principles, techniques, and philosophy remain the same.

Many people have helped with this book. It would not be possible to mention all the colleagues, students, parents, friends, and children who have contributed in various helpful ways. To each one I am grateful. For specific acknowledgment I express my gratitude to my own teacher, Winifred Ward, for her loyal friendship and inspiration during twenty years. I am deeply indebted to Glenn Hughes, Executive Director of the School of Drama, University of Washington, who has directed a kindly eye and encouraging attitude toward the development of creative dramatics as an art. Professor Hughes made it possible for me to gather experiences with children in classes sponsored by the university, and to obtain many of the photographs used in this book. To Professor Agnes Haaga, Director of Creative Dramatics at the university, I wish to acknowledge many contributions both directly and indirectly. During the years it has been my privilege to work with Miss Haaga, I have gained much in the way of wisdom, encouragement, and specific techniques which are interwoven in the pages of this book.

Miss Haaga read the manuscript and offered pertinent suggestions. To the late Ruth Lease I am deeply grateful, particularly for her inspiring belief that several creative dramatics books need to be written. For many specific suggestions I thank Margaret Woods, Extension Assistant Lecturer in Creative Dramatics. Whitie Marten, Supervisor of the Still Photography Production Unit of the University of Washington, and his staff deserve a special tribute of thanks for the fine photographs of children which illustrate the book (all photographs except as otherwise indicated).

To my sister Hazel Dunnington, Assistant Professor of Speech at Central Washington College of Education, I express sincere gratitude. Mrs. Dunnington was the critic of this book. She read it chapter by chapter, showing me how to strengthen many of its weaknesses, and helping me to work out questions and activities.

I wish to thank the following school administrators and teachers in addition to the teachers whose contributions appear in the book: Superintendent E. W. Campbell, Director of Elementary Education Dorothea Jackson, and principals Katherine Maxwell and Lester Roblee of the Seattle Public Schools; Superintendent Dr. Ray W. Howard, Director of Instruction Adah Miner, and principals Jordan Moe and James Dunn of the Shoreline Public Schools; Superintendent Dr. George B. Brain and Principal James Zylstra of the Bellevue Public Schools; Superintendent Charles A. McGlade, Assistant Superintendent T. H. Muncaster, and Principal Lyle Messinger in the Everett Public Schools and Barbara Hill of the Wenatchee Public Schools. In the Kohler Public Schools of Kohler, Wisconsin, I thank Principal Harold L. Paukert, and at San Jose State College Dean C. Grant Burton, Dr. Harold Crain, Professor John Kerr, and Harold Hancock.

Community groups have assisted in different ways. Acknowledgments are due the Seattle Public Library and the library staff at the University Branch, especially Katherine Porter, Children's Librarian, Seattle Junior Programs, Inc., Professor Kenneth Carr, and Alice Jean Lewis; Dr. John Reich and W. R. Martini of the Goodman Memorial Theatre of the Art Institute of Chicago; and Emily Pribble Gillies, Nancy Taf: Smuck, and Reverend Russel Weberg for help in religious education.

For the kindness of colleagues in other countries I express my appreciation to John Allen and Yolande Bird of the British Centre of the International Theatre Institute, Peter Slade of Birmingham Drama Centre, Leon Chancerel of Paris, and Bjorn Moe of Copenhagen.

The excerpt of President Eisenhower's on page v is from his telegram of August, 1957, to the Children's Theatre Conference delegates on the Thirteenth Anniversary Meeting, Tufts College, Boston, August 18–24.

It is a pleasure to thank Lousene Rousseau whose advice and criticisms of the manuscript have been invaluable.

To my mother and members of my family who helped in inestimable ways I am grateful, especially to Lillian Brain for help with my manuscript. While I have been writing, my husband Charles and my sons Jan and Mark have proved to be creative cooks and critics.

Lastly, I say a special thank you to hundreds of boys and girls whose creative experiences are shared with you herein.

G. B. S.

January, 1958

CREATIVE DRAMATICS

An Art for Children

FIG. 1.1.   A beginning. (*Photograph by Charles J. Siks*)

CHAPTER 1

A Child and His Art

To live would be an awfully big adventure!—J. M. Barrie

This is Timothy Paul McCubbins (Fig. 1.1). He was named to honor his grandparents, but the only name he knows is Tim. He is almost 18 months old, and he is already very much a person. Day after day he eats, and sleeps, and adventures in the world around him.

How will Tim get on as he grows older? What kind of man will he grow up to be? What dreams will be his to dream? What will he do for others? What little niche will he fill? How will he live this glorious thing called life?

No one knows, really. His home and his parents are going to have a lot to do with the way Tim turns out. Tim's teachers are going to leave imprints in many different ways. Tim's playmates, the people, the towns where he lives will weave patterns in his living. Even the world in its struggle for right and might will affect Tim's life. And Tim will affect the lives of those with whom he lives in many different ways.

Carl Sandburg has poetically said:

There is only one child in the world
and the child's name is All Children.[1]

When every child makes his entrance into the world he comes with hope. A little child, like a young tree, cannot go untended. A child needs help in growing up and upward. Parents, teachers, and youth leaders must care about every child who comes their way. They must care enough to find ways of helping children grow to live good lives.

HOW DOES A CHILD GROW?

Growth remains a miracle and a mystery. We cannot see growth but we see the results of growth. It is now generally accepted that a child grows into a whole personality by having his developmental needs satisfied. These basic growth needs are physical, mental, social, emotional, and spiritual. An individual's needs remain constant throughout life although they change in degree with age, maturity, and learning.

The great challenge to parents, teachers, and youth leaders lies in understanding basic human needs, and in finding ways to meet them.

Physical Needs. Tim's parents, like most parents, are quick to recognize a child's physical and physiological needs. They satisfy needs for food, liquids, and proper elimination, and for clothing, shelter, and proper temperature. Most parents and teachers strive to meet a child's needs for fresh air, sunshine, and exercise. They take a child out-of-doors and give him opportunities to play; to release his energies in ways that satisfy him. Most adults provide oppor-

[1] Edward Steichen (compiler), *The Family of Man*, The Photographic Exhibition published for The Museum of Modern Art, Simon and Schuster, in collaboration with The Maco Magazine Corporation, 1955.

tunities for a child to change from vigorous activity to less vigorous activity. They generally provide for periods of rest and sleep.

On the whole, adults are rather touching in the way they strive to help a child grow physically; yet physical needs are generally the easiest of all basic needs to satisfy.

Mental Needs. Just as every child needs to exercise his muscles, he also needs to exercise his mind. As soon as Tim learned to crawl he started exploring his environment. He found he could open kitchen cupboards. He discovered something to eat inside cereal boxes and wrappers. When he found paper wrappers on soap he tore them off to find what was inside; then he wondered about what he'd found.

The magic words of childhood are *how* and *why*. A child does not mean to be destructive when he tears something apart. His mind is at work and his fingers follow fast. He is curious about the world around him. He wonders about the sky, the sun, the grass, and the earth. He wonders about darkness. He wonders why the moon changes shapes, what a star is, and how it twinkles. Every child wonders about such wonderful things as shadows and wind, sun and snow, rain and rainbows.

How does one explain the curiosity of a child's mind? Every child has a basic need to know, to learn, to seek knowledge. He gains a strong sense of intellectual security in the realization that he knows. Equally as important, he needs to let others know that he knows. He wants to express and reveal his knowledge. "I can do . . . ," "I know how to . . . ," and "Do you know?" are familiar statements made by boys and girls throughout childhood.

Social Needs. Every girl and every boy needs to love and to be loved. A child needs to know that someone really cares about him, and he needs to care about someone too. Every child needs approval.

He needs friendly help in learning how to behave toward persons and things. A child blossoms in an environment where he is given approval for little accomplishments and kindnesses. He needs to be reassured often that he has contributed or helped even though in small ways. A child needs grown-ups who show him by example how to live kindly and happily with others.

Every child needs the warm companionship of friends. One of a child's basic needs is the feeling that he belongs; that he is one of a group; that he is liked for being himself. There are times when a child needs to be the most important person in a group. He needs to be the center of attention. Not only on a day when others light candles and sing "Happy Birthday," but for moments on others days.

A child needs to learn that others need to feel important too. He needs to learn to take turns and share moments of glory before he will enjoy the friendliness of friendship.

Emotional Needs.   Every child has feelings. Sometimes Tim feels happy and sometimes he feels sad. Sometimes he feels frightened and sometimes he feels mad. Sometimes he feels lonely. Sometimes he feels glad. As he grows older he will experience in varying degrees such feelings as jealousy, hate, and a desire for revenge. There will be times when he will have feelings of doubt, secret feelings of disappointment and defeat. He will suffer through feelings of embarrassment, sorrow, guilt, and carefully camouflaged pain.

A child needs to know that all feelings are very natural, but he needs to learn to channel his feelings in ways that are acceptable to himself and others. He needs to work off his feelings in constructive ways rather than having them hushed up inside his surging self. He needs to learn that he will not be allowed to hurt himself or others when he has these strong feelings. He needs help in learning how to release and control his feelings.

All children need the uplifting feeling of success and they need to cope with the downhearted feeling of failure. Sometimes from failure comes a bigger success. A child needs experiences similar to those of building block towers. He needs to build towers that stand, and towers that topple, for life is made up of experiences that tower and topple one's emotional self.

Spiritual Needs. There are millions and millions of children in the world. One of them is Tim. In many ways he is like all children. In other ways Tim is like no one else in all the world. He is different from everyone who ever was or ever will be.

Each child is an individual. He comes into this world with a spirit of his own. Tim has a dynamic, outgoing, forceful spirit, while the little girl next door has a gentle, delicate, almost dreamy spirit. Each one is normal. Each child is a pattern unto himself.

The spiritual side of an individual is in essence his personality. It is the quality which gives him distinction and sensitivity. Because adults do not readily recognize the spiritual needs of a child, they have, in far too many instances, neglected its development. A child's spirit is as intangible as love is intangible. It has been spoken of as a gift or talent, as imagination, as a poetic attitude. It has been referred to as a child's bent, his knack, his aptitude, his potential, and his self. It is the spirit of a child which gives him identity.

A child needs to be guided patiently as he develops his creative spirit. He needs someone who believes in him and shares many experiences that discipline and satisfy his spiritual self. Just as it takes time for a grain to send forth a shoot, a stalk, an ear, and a grain in the ear, so it is with a child's creative spirit. Just as surely as a grain of wheat brings forth wheat, so will a child's creative spirit bring forth his own special gift if it is nourished. Often a child's creative spirit shows up strongly. He needs help in exercising, enriching, and developing it. Often a child's creative spirit is hidden away in emotional depths. He needs help in arousing and discovering it so it may be developed.

These are basic needs of growing children. A child needs beauty and love every bit as much as he needs food and exercise. He needs quiet just as he needs laughter and shouting. He needs to be alone just as he needs to be with others. He needs to work as well as to play. All components of growth are equally important if he is to develop a wholeness of personality. For a child *to live* is quite a different thing than for him *to exist*. He needs to be guided in his growing so he reaches for his best. He needs to find his way to enjoy and contribute to the world in which he lives.

ART EDUCATION FOR CHILDREN

One of the most significant trends in recent years is the emphasis on creative arts programs for children. This has come about because of the effectiveness with which creative arts experiences contribute to freedom for growth and personality developmnt. Viktor Lowenfeld, a leader in this field, explains the underlying reason for this educational trend: "If children developed without any interference from the outside world, no special stimulation for their creative work would be necessary. Every child would use his deeply rooted creative impulse without inhibition, confident in his own kind of expression. . . . What civilization has buried we must try to regain by creating the natural base necessary for such free creation."[2]

The philosophy on which art education is based is clearly stated by Victor D'Amico, who says: "The concept of child as artist implies that every child is a potential creator endowed with those sensibilities that characterize the artist. The concept transcends the idea

[2] Viktor Lowenfeld, *Creative and Mental Growth*, The Macmillan Company, 1949.

of art as performance or as product and looks upon art as a way of living—the means of enjoying and enriching life through experience. The teacher who regards the child and art in this way possesses the key to every child's creative growth."[3]

Brooks Atkinson, in reappraising Robert Edmond Jones's *The Dramatic Imagination,* says: "First: food, clothing and shelter. Second: art. The man who is hungry and cold cannot give much thought to anything else. The immediate necessity of staying alive consumes all his energy. But once he is relieved of the primary essentials, he inhabits a sphere of society where only art can give his life meaning. Art mediates between the day's work and eternity: between the prosaic facts of life and the grand truths of the universe, 'the proving of things unseen,' in the language of the Old Testament."[4] Man has always had a kinship with beauty. Present-day man, like primitive man, appreciates beauty and has a natural desire to express his strong impressions, but he needs encouragement and stimulation.

Our American civilization has unknowingly suppressed this natural impulse. As a nation we are characterized by a materialistic philosophy. There is a noticeable absence of cultural living among the masses of our peoples. For many, perhaps most, arts are a luxury rather than a necessity. Our environing world pictures the likeness of ourselves. We have only to look at our homes, schools, communities, and institutions to see a reflection of our civilization.

Educators and child psychologists recognize the need for experiences in childhood that strengthen a child's sensibilities and encourage strong expression. It is because of this underlying need that art

[3] Victor E. D'Amico, *Creative Teaching in Art,* International Textbook Company, 1942.
[4] Brooks Atkinson, "Fine Case for Art," *The New York Times,* July 1, 1956.

education is being included in school and community programs with renewed stress. The importance of guiding children into cultural experiences is vital if boys and girls are to appreciate, experience, and create beauty. When art experiences are woven into a child's school program they help him acquire a philosophy of living while he is gaining knowledge and discipline in skills. The two must go hand in hand. Humanities and skills must be developed together for children growing up in an electronic age. A child needs skills to meet the realities of living. Skills become his wings, his abilities to do. But along with skills a child needs imagination, and a philosophy that guides his flight. He needs to find enjoyment, scope, awareness, and adventure in his daily soaring and doing.

The responsibility for the quality of art education rests squarely with parents, teachers, and youth leaders. The purpose of this book is to make clear this responsibility. It sets forth a philosophy of the art of creative dramatics and presents many different ways of sharing it with children.

WHAT IS CREATIVE DRAMATICS?

The best way to understand creative dramatics is to experience it, and to observe children experiencing it. Let us begin by watching a group of 9-, 10-, and 11-year-olds.[5] They meet on a Saturday morning in a basement room of a public library.

A Beginning Experience. It is a first class meeting, and a new experience for all the children except Julie, Ann, and Scott. These three arrive early to help the teacher. Scott moves benches into the center of the room and arranges them in a large square. The girls set up a record player, and spread a blanket on the floor inside the

[5] This is a composite account, from students' observation reports, of a class at the Seattle Public Library under the sponsorship of the School of Drama of the University of Washington.

square. The teacher and children sit on the blanket and talk and laugh together while they wait for the others. Whenever a child arrives he is greeted warmly. Some of the newcomers appear to be at ease. Others are tense and shy. They survey the room anxiously and notice a large group of adults seated along one side of the room.

When all the children arrive the teacher introduces herself. In a friendly way she explains that her name is the same name as a color. She tells them that it might be Miss Blue or Miss Orange, but it happens to be the same color as a pussywillow and an elephant. The children quickly guess her name to be Miss Gray. She warns them in a spirit of fun not to call her Miss Elephant. The children laugh and begin to relax.

Miss Gray asks the children to take a good look at the adults. She wonders if one of the old members would tell the others why the adults are visiting. Scott explains: "They are going to be teachers and they want to see how much fun creative dramatics is so they can teach it too."

The teacher explains that the visitors are friendly people. She suggests the children pretend the observers are a part of the library, like illustrations in books. The children respond to this idea. They smile and relax a little more.

Miss Gray then speaks slowly but with spirit: "As Scott told us, creative dramatics is fun. It's fun because of you, every one of you. It's your ideas, your experiences, and your way of sharing with others that makes creative dramatics exciting and fun. We never know what good idea you might think of and share. I've had a list of your names for over a week, and I've been wondering what each of you would be like."

The teacher looks at the children closely and smiles. "You know, I think we look quite a bit alike. Each of us has eyes, a nose, and a mouth, and everybody has hair on his head. I see black hair and brown, yellow hair and tan, and reddish, whitish and—."

The children look at each other and laugh and talk among themselves. Then they listen again as Miss Gray continues: "Last night when I was wondering about you, I remembered when I was 9 years old. That was the summer my family moved to a farm away out in the country. We had a great big hay barn there. My sisters and brother, and the neighbor boys and I thought the barn was the most wonderful place in all the world to play. Sometimes we made tunnels, and caves, and even thrones in the hay. We pretended to be pirates, and wizards, and kings, and queens, and all kinds of exciting people. Sometimes we climbed high up to the rafters and became wicked old witches waiting in the sky to cast spells on one another. Whenever we saw someone we jumped to the hay in a wild rage. We bounced through the hay as we flew after our victims and cackled evil spells upon them."

Julie's hand is waving. "Could we make up a play about witches?"

"How many would like to?" asks Miss Gray. Several hands go up eagerly. A few children call out in strong approval. "Maybe we will," the teacher says. "We'll decide as soon as we know each other better. You know, when I used to make up plays I had a little *secret dream* about this. I thought the most wonderful thing that could ever happen would be for me to grow up to be an actress."

"An actress!" Ann calls spontaneously. "That's just what I want to be, only I want to be a singing actress. I dream and dream about it."

"You keep right on dreaming, Ann. Keep on singing and creating too. This is the way to make a dream come true, or to cause you to dream a new dream."

Miss Gray turns to include all the children. "Has anyone else been dreaming dreams as Ann and I have? Not about being an actress, but about doing something else? Who has been dreaming daytime dreams?"

The children appear to be thinking. Some raise their hands. Some are hesitant. After a minute or two Miss Gray speaks: "Sharing dreams is one of the friendliest ways to get acquainted. You already know a little about Ann and me. Suppose each one of you introduces yourself by telling your name, and sharing *one thing* you've dreamed of being or doing."

The teacher smiles and nods to each child in turn. She makes it easy for each one to speak. These are their dreams:

"My name is Julie—it's really Julia Alice, but I like to be called Julie. I'd like to be the best ballerina in the world."

"I'm Scott. I've dreamed of being a mountain climber, not *just* a mountain climber, but one of the best."

"I want to be a ballet dancer too. I'm Phyllis."

"I'm Helen. I want to be a scientist and discover new cures, you know—like polio shots only something else."

"I'm Mary Lou. I don't know yet."

"I want to own a horse ranch someday. I just love horses. My name is Kathy."

"I'm Tommy. I like horses too, but I would like to ride along the Antonio Trail."

"David's my name, and I've thought about this before. I'd like to be a clown and make people happy because it's important for people to be happy."

"I'm Joan. I would like to go to Africa and help Dr. Schweitzer if he thought I could."

"I'm Joy—a piano teacher."

"I want to marry a farmer so I can live on a farm. My name is Carol."

"I'm Floyd. I want to be a flyer."

"I want to be a stewardess. I'm Sally."

"I'm Bob. I want to play a trumpet in the university band."

"I'm Mark and I want to be a mounted police."

"My name is King. I want to be a champion ice skater."

"I'm Marjorie. I want to be a puppeteer. Ann and I put on a puppet show for little children in our neighborhood. Once we were on television."

"My name is Dee-Dee—it's really Judith. I want to be a champion swimmer. First I want to swim across Green Lake, then across the Straits of Juan de Fuca, and then across the English Channel!"

"You really have been dreaming, Dee-Dee!" Miss Gray says. "How many like to swim?" Most of the children do. The teacher praises the ideas: "These are wonderful dreams. The world needs pilots and stewardesses just as it needs sportsmen, entertainers, farmers, housewives, and doctors. If you really care enough about making your dream come true, you can do it by working hard and dreaming. Now in creative dramatics we may cause our dreams to come true this very day. Suppose we ask Julie or Ann or Scott, one of the children who has been here before, to explain what creative dramatics is."

Ann is first to speak. "Well, to me creative dramatics is playing so you feel you are really in the places you pretend. You get to be all kinds of characters, and you get to create them in your own way."

Scott says, "Creative dramatics is creating. All you've got is your imagination and yourself. It's hard sometimes to make it real, but that's where the fun comes in."

Miss Gray speaks with enthusiasm. "Let's see how strong our imaginations are right now. Let's take Dee-Dee's dream and make it

come true first. Let's imagine this whole room is Green Lake, and we'll all go swimming with Dee-Dee."

Dee-Dee smiles. The children are eager. Julie's hand goes up. "I think these benches could be the raft at Green Lake. We could dive in or jump in from here."

"Fine!" says the teacher. "Let's stand up on the raft and see if everyone has room to jump."

The children get up from the floor and stand on the benches facing out in the room. "Before we jump, let's face in toward the raft. Why do you *like* to swim?" the teacher asks. The replies come quickly.

"Cause it's fun!"

"The water feels cold and good."

"I think it's fun to swim under water. I keep my eyes open."

"It feels good when you get the rhythm and cut through the water."

"I like to swim on my back."

"It's fun when I make speed. I like the side stroke best."

"I think it's fun to dog-paddle."

Miss Gray speaks up. "You really know why it's fun! How are we going to get the good feeling of water and rhythm in this imaginary lake?"

The children think. "In our arms," says Ann using gestures.

"That's right. Is that the only place?"

"In our legs?" Dee-Dee asks a little hesitant.

"That's right too," Miss Gray nods as she moves her arms and legs in the motions of swimming. "But where else do we get that good feeling that comes with swimming?"

"In our whole selves—all over," Julie volunteers as she moves her hands downward from her shoulders to her knees.

"Good—but is the feeling only on the outside of ourselves?"

"Outside and *inside!*" says Scott as he remembers from earlier experiences. "You have to feel it in your stomach and in your bones."

Everyone laughs. "We're not laughing at you, Scott, we're laughing because it *sounds* funny, but you're exactly right. Whenever you create you get the feeling of whatever you're doing right *in your middle*—way down deep inside. You have fun whenever you really *feel* whatever you're creating. That is a secret of creative dramatics."

"You kind of get the feeling inside your heart too, don't you, Miss Gray?" Ann asks.

"Yes, Ann, inside your heart too. Now we're getting the idea. You *think*, and *feel*, and *put your heart* into your swimming or whatever it is you're creating."

"Can we swim now?" Scott asks enthusiastically.

"Yes! When I give a signal everyone jumps in and swims with his own strong feeling, twice around the lake. On your marks! Get set! Go!"

All of the children jump off the benches (Fig. 1.2). Most of them are confident. The teacher joins in the swimming with obvious enjoyment. Two girls start to swim but lose courage and stop. They giggle and whisper to each other. Miss Gray notices them. She calls out in a friendly way, "Joy and Mary Lou, watch us from the raft and see how each one is swimming in his own way. See if you can tell how Bob feels."

Bob is lying flat on the floor struggling to pull himself forward. Miss Gray swims to one end of the lake. She moves out of the imaginary water and turns on a record player. A recording of Poldini's "Valse Serenade" sounds. The children stop and listen in surprise.

"There's a park concert going on. Swim to the music of the band," Miss Gray says with enthusiasm. She increases the volume. The rhythm and surge of the music spur most of the children on. Their

Fig. 1.2. "Ooooh! The water feels cold and good." (*School of Drama, University of Washington*)

swimming becomes spirited. One boy torpedoes through space with his arms against his body. He runs with quick steps to give the feeling he is diving and rising. Bob swims to the surface and enjoys the rhythm of the Australian crawl. Phyllis moves her feet in a short skipping rhythm as she walks backward giving the feeling she is swimming on her back. Several children swim with free side strokes. A few dog-paddle. One steamboats. Two splash each other. All are having fun. By the time the children have gone twice around the room most of them are ready to return to the raft.

Miss Gray is excited and pleased. "You're *good* swimmers! Let's ask Joy and Mary Lou which swimmers had fun."

"Everybody did," Joy says shyly.

"Yes," says Mary Lou quickly.

"You're right," Miss Gray says encouragingly. She asks if any swimmer wants to tell just how he had fun. A few children describe their swimming. Bob explains that he was swimming on the bottom of the lake until he had to come up for air.

"Who would like to *show* rather than *tell* while the rest of us watch?"

Several children jump in and swim again as the band music is played. "This is the way to have fun! See how each one is feeling and swimming in his own way," Miss Gray calls enthusiastically. When the swimming is over, several children comment briefly with praise and descriptions of what they saw swimmers doing.

"Now that we've had fun with Dee-Dee's dream, we can do something very special by using our imaginations. Does anyone have an idea what we might do with Green Lake for a different kind of fun?" Miss Gray asks.

The children are somewhat puzzled by this question. "We can freeze Green Lake into the smoothest ice pond in the land," she explains.

Suddenly King calls out, "I get it. If we do we can skate. That's *my* dream. Let's do it."

Miss Gray leads the children into a short discussion of skating and of the good feeling that comes with the rhythm of skating. When the children are ready she suggests that each child choose a pair of skates from an imaginary trunk. While the children put on skates in pantomime, the teacher goes to the record player. She makes an exciting announcement, "The Park Band is ready with music just made for skating. Listen and see if you can feel yourself skating to the rhythm of the music."

The music sounds. Its lilting rhythm creates a strong festive mood. King is eager. When the music stops he calls out, "That's the 'Skater's Waltz'! They played it for the Ice Follies. Could we pretend we're skating in an ice show?"

"A splendid idea, King," says the teacher. "Each one think of *one special way* of skating; the way you feel the happiest when you are on skates."

Joy raises her hand slowly. "May I watch? I've never skated on ice skates."

King has a suggestion: "Have you ever roller skated?" Joy nods. King continues, "Well it's a lot like roller skating, only the feeling's a hundred times smoother when you glide."

"Suppose you try and see if you enjoy it. If not, you skate to the edge," Miss Gray suggests. "Suppose everyone move down to this end of the lake. When the music strikes up, skate out in all this space. *Feel* you are sharing the fun of skating with everyone who has come for the ice show. Get the *feeling* inside yourself and *enjoy* it."

The music starts. The beauty and force of the waltz rhythm bring all of the skaters out into the room. Joy and Mary Lou skate side by side but are hesitant. Miss Gray glides in between them and takes each one by the hand. The three skate together with spirit and fun. After skating once around they stop and watch the others.

Interesting ideas appear. Tommy skates backward. Julie and Ann skate together. Phyllis and Carol dance and twirl. David gives the feeling that his skates keep turning in, then they appear to be turning out and he sits down with a bump. Miss Gray calls to the skaters to stop and watch David clown. After they watch him she asks everyone to watch King. King skates beautifully in large circles around the room. Other children are singled out in pairs or groups for a few moments of spotlight recognition.

As the morning continues the children play imaginary pianos with Joy and imaginary trumpets with Bob. At the close of an hour the playing comes to an end. Miss Gray promises that on the following Saturday they will become puppets with Marjorie and Ann.

"Will we go mountain climbing too and do everybody's dreams like we did today?" Scott asks.

Miss Gray promises they will. The children respond eagerly. King's hand goes up suddenly. "I'm going to write a play about this so we'll know whether everybody's dreams come true."

"A play," Miss Gray says with strong approval. "King, that's wonderful."

"I'm going to try to write one. I've never written one before."

"We'll be waiting for it, to see what happens," Miss Gray says warmly. "Maybe someone else will write a story, or a poem or draw a picture about his dream. This is the way good things begin. People dream, and then they carry out their dreams. This library and every book on the shelves were first dreams before they became real. So keep dreaming and keep watching for dreams that people have made come true. We'll see you next week for more fun together."

All of the children hurry away except King. He sits on a bench

and makes a note of each dream. "I'm going to have my play take place ten years from today."[6]

"That's good," says the teacher.

"I think I *will be* a champion skater 'cause I'm going to skate twice a week for ten years. That ought to do it, don't you think?"

INTERPRETING CREATIVE DRAMATICS

When children are caught in the magic of creative dramatics something unexplainable happens that gives soul and spirit to a group experience. In the words of 7-year-old Judy, creative dramatics is "sharing thoughts and stories, and it makes you feel so good inside!"[7]

Creative dramatics is *an art for children.* It may be defined as *a group experience in which every child is guided to express himself as he works and plays with others for the joy of creating improvised drama.* Improvised drama means children create drama extemporaneously. They create characters, action, and dialogue as they are guided by a leader to think, feel, and become involved in the issue at hand.

No Scripts. When children create they do not use scripts. In this art the medium through which a child expresses is his whole self in relationship to other people and ideas. The idea from which a group creates may be a story, a verse, or an experience. It may be from literature, from life, or from children's imaginings. Children are guided into planning, playing, and evaluating for the pleasure and joy of creating together. When a child becomes involved in his creating he speaks freely for a character as he expresses himself.

[6] "The Meeting," by King Cole, by permission of the eleven-year-old author whose *real* name is King Cole. See Chapter 9, p. 353.

[7] Ruth Lease and Geraldine Brain Siks, *Creative Dramatics in Home, School, and Community,* Harper & Brothers, 1952.

No Technical Aids. In creative dramatics there is neither a need nor a place for scenery, costumes, lights, properties, make-up, or a stage. Occasionally a property or a lighting effect may be used to motivate or heighten a mood. Children are guided to use their imaginations to create illusions. An 11-year-old girl, describing the way her queen was dressed in "The Knights of the Silver Shield," said, "I wore a long golden dress and a cape of scarlet satin with white ostrich plumes over it. My crown was a band of gold with a big diamond right in front. When I walked into the great hall I felt just like Queen Elizabeth." This spontaneous description typifies the thinking and feeling that every child experienced as he costumed himself vicariously for this royal ceremony.

Creative thinking is always being encouraged; it is not being limited by the use of paper crowns or improvised costumes. Children enjoy the challenge of imagining, and describing settings and costumes. They like to create illusions with the furniture on hand such as chairs, tables, benches, or whatever happens to be available within a room.

No Audience. There is no formal audience in creative dramatics. The only desirable audience is a part of the group chosen to enjoy, appreciate, and evaluate the playing. When an audience comes in from the outside, whether it be observers, parents, or other children's groups, some children are always concerned with the audience. An audience situation tends to divide the thinking of a children's group, for a few individuals become more interested in the audience than in the play they are creating. Whenever this happens a child fails to create, for he is not wholeheartedly involved. With the inhibition of even a single child, the creativity of the group is impaired. When group spirit weakens it not only lessens creative expression, but it misleads an audience by the impressions they receive.

An audience that expects to see a play similar to a formal play may laugh when children become doors, trees, wind, or whatever may be required for a story. Audience laughter is often misunderstood by children who are creating, and illusions are broken. From all considerations it seems wise to keep creative dramatics in the intimate realm where it belongs, free from onlookers. If an audience of prospective teachers or leaders comes to observe, individuals should be instructed to refrain from talking, laughing, or calling attention to themselves. It should be remembered that a creative experience is seldom the same with an audience as it is when children are entirely free from the emotional presence of others.

When a creative experience becomes set or formalized it moves out of the realm of creative dramatics. It may become a creative project or a formal play where dialogue and action are set. In situations such as this, children are often ready to enjoy sharing with an audience.

Basic Requirements. The four basic requirements for the art of creative dramatics include a group of children, a qualified leader or teacher, a space large enough for children to move about freely, and an idea from which to create.

Chief Objective. We are now in a position to see that creative dramatics emphasizes participation rather than product (Fig. 1.3). Its chief aim is experience; experience that fosters child growth and development. The way in which a child expresses himself provides a gauge of his development and reveals his needs. This art encourages the growth of individual spirit in the presence of a group. It provides for self-realization and coöperation in an atmosphere of spirited group play (Fig. 1.4).

VALUES TO AN INDIVIDUAL

"Why do you like creative dramatics?" a father asked his 9-year-old son. The boy was having difficulty deciding between baseball and creative dramatics which both met on Saturday mornings.

"'Cause it's fun," was the boy's quick reply.

"Fun?" questioned the father. "You mean to tell me it's more fun than the Little League?"

"Well—it's a different kind of fun. Remember when I was Little John and Rusty was Robin Hood? Well, I don't like to brag, but everybody said I was *good* when I kept Robin moving so fast with my quick lunges."

FIG. 1.3. "Little mouse, please help us pull big turnip." (*School of Drama, University of Washington*)

"Who's Robin?" asked the father.

"You mean Rusty? He's that new boy in our school with red hair. He used to be my enemy but now he's one of my men."

When children are fired with enthusiasm and their playing reaches a high mood of belief, the values that come to an individual are many. Whenever values become the chief object of pursuit an experience is in danger of becoming like a wild-goose chase, dull, plodding, and uninspired. *Values come through the fun of experiencing dramatic moments which are strong in belief* (Fig. 1.5). Among the values most evident in contributing to child growth and personality development are the following.

Develops Confidence and Creative Expression. *Freedom for an individual is a relationship between himself and others.* In creative

FIG. 1.4. "Reach for a cloud and sail to Spain!" (*School of Drama, University of Washington*)

dramatics a child is given many opportunities to develop confidence and use his creative powers. He expresses himself in group discussion as he helps in planning. He expresses himself through his playing, and in the many times he praises or evaluates others. He gradually learns to enjoy rather than fear the opportunity to stand up and share his ideas, opinions, and views. A child whose expression find

neither a place nor an appreciation by others is unhappy and far
from free.

*A child expresses himself for the same reasons that men of all ages
have expressed themselves, because he has something to say.* In this

FIG. 1.5. "Olé! He's the very one for the bullfight in Madrid."
(*School of Drama, University of Washington*)

art each child is encouraged and motivated to reach within to express
his feelings and beliefs in his own honest way. Individuality is constantly encouraged, recognized, and developed.

Beauty is a universal feeling with mankind. A group of 6-year-olds
talked about beautiful things they had seen in the summer.[8] Each
one drew a large colorful picture of "The Most Beautiful Thing I
Can Think of." When they finished drawing each child described

[8] Lake Forest Park School, Shoreline Public Schools, Seattle, Washington.

his picture. For the next several days the children enjoyed playing their different ideas of beauty. Beauty was recognized in such replies as these: "A mother deer in the woods," "Easter bunny hiding baskets," "My Toni doll," "Diamonds in rings are so beautiful," "Peter Pan flying in the air," "Some swans I saw," "Boats on a lake," "A beautiful rainbow," "Living under a tree," "Pretty flowers," and "The inside of a ferry."

On the first snowy day of winter a group of second graders watched snowflakes and became snowflakes making the world white and clean.[9] After they had enjoyed expressing themselves in strong rhythmic action the teacher asked, "What else is as white as the snow?" After thinking quietly for a minute these seven-year-olds had these impressions to share: "Whitecaps rolling upon mixed green waves," "White side walls on tires," "White jets streaming through the blue sky," "White chalk making squares for hopscotch," "White chalk playing tiddley winks on the blackboard," "Girls wearing white blouses," "Boys wearing white tennis shoes," "Paste pasting paper," "White pages turning in a book," "White lines on a highway," "White milk in a glass," "Salt coming out of a shaker," "Sugar," and "White paper waiting to be written on."

In a summer class a group of 10- and 11-year-old girls and boys created a play from the story of "The Conjure Wives."[10] In an exciting discussion the children talked about the beauties of the summer world. They shared ideas of things they had seen, such as "A Peace Rose in full bloom," "Robins flying," "Tall branchy pine trees," "Healthy people," "A steep waterfall," "Green grass," "A little baby laughing," "Galloping horses," and "White-capped waves." They then discussed evil spells that witches might cast on the eve of mid-

[9] View Ridge School, Everett Public Schools, Everett, Washington.
[10] School of Drama, University of Washington, Seattle, Washington.

summer. The children darkened the room and became swiftly moving witches. The boys as well as the girls cackled wildly as each witch pantomimed a spell to the background music of "Danse Macabre" (Fig. 1.6). The leader as Wicked Witch Woman called to her sisters, "Come, my wicked sisters! What evil did ye do this night? Speak!" One by one the witches answered with such evil chants as these: "He, he, he! I put poison in the Peace Rose and every blooming flower. Whoever smells a flower will sleep until next summer."

FIG. 1.6. "He! He! I changed green grass to black, black ashes!" (*School of Drama, University of Washington*)

"Sisters, hark! Listen to the robin. He no longer sings but crows like a rooster. A crowing robin. Ho! Ho! Ho!"

"See the forest—trees without needles—bare trunks and branches like skeletons on the hills."

"I let all the disease germs loose so no one will be healthy. I rule the world. I have made it weak."

"Sisters, see the waterfall. I've sent it flooding the lands."

"He, he, he, he! Galloping horses hop like rabbits. He, he, he!"

"Sisters, hark! Red-capped waves, red-capped waves, red-capped waves! Hark!"

A younger group of second and third graders had a similar experience in which they expressed themselves as big bad giants.[11] With strong pantomime each giant tramped through the world causing one kind of trouble. When the teacher, the Great Giant of the Sky, halted the giants, she commanded each one to report his doings. In loud voices, the giants called across the world, and reported such terrible deeds as these: "I was tramping on houses like a giant hurricane."

"I was a giant wind. I lifted up trees and houses and cars and threw them in the air."

"I blew everybody's hats and coats off and papers and books out of their hands and everything went in a hubbub."

"My giant was fire. I burned up the world."

After the destruction, a sensitive little girl said, "Let's be good giants now." With equally as much enthusiasm and power the good giants went to work. The fire giant called out, "I'm dropping down giant seeds so they'll grow into trees by tonight." The wind giant said, "I'm putting a new car in everybody's garage." The hubbub giant said, "I'm dropping down new shoes for the children."

Develops Social Attitudes and Relationships. Creative dramatics by its very nature is a group art. It calls for teamwork (Fig. 1.7). It requires coöperation in planning, playing, and evaluating. It provides a play situation where children experience basic rules in living with others. They learn to take turns, respect one another, avoid interruptions. Each child is given opportunities to be both a leader and a

[11] *Ibid.*

member of a group working together in some form of concerted effort for the success of a scene or experience. A child constantly yields to discipline as he joins with others to create and express.

Children learn how to relate to one another as they communicate their thoughts and feelings in group experiences. When a third grade group was playing "The Rabbit Who Wanted Wings," the teacher[12]

Fig. 1.7. "Watch my trained elephants!" (*Lake Forest Park School, Shoreline Public Schools, Seattle, Washington*)

helped the group evaluate the playing of the Little Rabbit, Mother Rabbit, Mr. Owl, and Mr. Groundhog. She then asked the children what was the strongest thing in Father Rabbit's character.

"Well, Jim's rabbit hopped like a rabbit, and wiggled his ears like a rabbit, but he didn't make me feel worried," said Susan.

"What feeling did he give?" pursued the teacher.

"He seemed more like a rabbit acting silly the way he hopped and looked at us," Susan said honestly.

[12] Polly Jepsen, Bryant School, Seattle Public Schools, Seattle, Washington. Mrs. Jepsen is now Assistant Professor of Education, Los Angeles State College.

"I thought so, too," spoke up one of the boys.

"You know what I think we'll do?" asked the teacher to check the strong thinking which she felt was symbolized in waving hands. "We might give Jim another turn to be Father Rabbit. How many would like to?"

About half the hands went down. "I thought we got to play this time," said one of the boys who had been in the audience.

"Most of the time we do," the teacher continued. "Last time Jim wasn't quite in character. I know Jim can create a very worried Father Rabbit because Jim has been worried himself many times. Jim is one of the best thinkers I know, when he thinks. How many would like to give Jim a chance to try again?"

Almost every hand went up. Jim was challenged. When the scene started every child was involved. The little rabbit hopped to his home. Father and Mother Rabbit came out and looked him over curiously. Father Rabbit folded his paws and said in a husky, threatening voice, "Begone, young man, and never darken my doorstep again!" (Fig. 1.8).

The children cheered Father Rabbit. In this instance Jim and others realized that to gain attention and win respect one needs to express in his own honest way. The entire group had experienced democracy in action for the hearts and minds of every child had been aroused. Moments such as this happen often in creative dramatics and help children learn how to get along and enjoy others.

An elementary principal was impressed with the unusual way a classroom teacher shared creative dramatics. Year after year he placed children with her who had been classified as "failures" and "problems." Year after year this teacher helped these children grow into boys and girls with spirit, confidence, and noticeably improved social attitudes. One year she was given 14 such children among a group of

Fig. 1.8. "Begone! Do you understand?" (*Photograph by Royal C. Crooks; Bryant School, Seattle Public Schools, Seattle, Washington*)

36. At first the teacher was discouraged. Then she began to wonder: Why is Billy missing school and complaining of frequent headaches? Why can't Helen read? Why does Lawrence give his friendship grudgingly and "bully" others?

As the teacher worked with the children she recognized basic emotional cravings and social hungerings in each child. She shared creative dramatics even more than she had in other years. She was sincere and hard-working as she realized how vital this year was for each child's welfare. She was skillful in unifying learning experiences and found ways to integrate creative dramatics with music, language arts, social studies, physical education, fine arts, and experiences such as open house, pet day, and spring festivals. She provided creative experiences every day where individuals had opportunities to express ideas and feelings.

After several months this group was ready to play an entire story. When they were ready to put a story together for the first time the teacher started to choose the characters. Billy's hand went up. "May I be the curtain?"

"Why do you want to be the curtain?" the teacher asked.

"The curtain's important. We can't have our play until the curtain gets it started," Billy replied thoughtfully. Shy Billy's dignified way of starting each playing on time and in the proper spirit was important.

Creative dramatics gives every child many opportunities to feel important to others. When this same group was playing favorite characters from a reading book they had completed, Helen, a Negro girl, said, "I think 'Snow-White' is the prettiest story I know. I'd like to be Snow-White when the wicked queen talks to the magic mirror."

"Would you like to be the queen or the mirror so you may talk?" the teacher inquired.

"Oh, no," Helen replied. "I want to be Snow-White picking daisies in the castle garden. I want the castle window to be open a little, so I can hear what the mirror says."

The group planned and played the scene as Helen described it. When the mirror chanted its rhyme and said, "Snow-White is lovelier far than thee," Helen stopped her picking. She listened and smiled with a feeling that was felt by every child.

"Helen looked just like Snow-White," Lawrence said as soon as the scene was over.

"I felt just like her, too," said Helen, radiant from this happy experience.

With similar experiences day after day and week after week a transformation gradually took place among these individuals and the group. Near the end of the year this class was chosen to be filmed for an educational documentary, to share a program with a Parent-Teachers' Meeting and to experience other honors that came to them. In each instance individuals reacted with joy, stability, and group pride. The principal, many parents, and the teachers who had known these children from earlier years were curious to learn how the changes had been effected. They didn't understand fully when the teacher said, "Through the art of creative dramatics." But the children who had experienced the good year of growing, sharing, and belonging understood. When they created an impressive Award's Day in their room the last day of school, every child received recognition. It was particularly significant to the teacher that Helen was given the award for having read the most library books during the year. Everyone was happy when each child cast a secret ballot and voted for Lawrence, the former bully, as the person who made the most effort to improve himself.

Develops Emotional Stability. Drama deals with emotion. The real purpose of emotion is to guide and inspire right conduct. Drama's purpose is to stir and release inner feelings in a legitimate lifting way. In creative dramatics children's emotions are exercised when they become both good and evil characters. In their playing they often experience lowness and loftiness in exciting story conflicts. In so doing they release emotions in a healthy way (Fig. 1.9).

In a kindergarten class little children delighted in playing "Three Billy Goats Gruff." They played it again and again for they enjoyed the conflict. After several playings they created dialogue freely. When one of the trolls warned Big Billy Goat Gruff that he would eat him up, the goat called out, "Come ahead! You're a mean old bully. You've been mean to us so I'm going to poke you to pieces."

A vigorous make-believe fight resulted with all the goats egging on Big Billy Goat Gruff. After the playing the children laughed and talked about the fight. David, one of the boys who had been

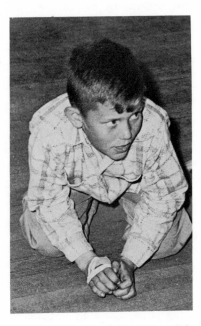

FIG. 1.9. "Honest, Hucky! It's devil fire sure enough!" (*School of Drama, University of Washington*)

watching, said, "Johnny's goat sure talked in tune to the troll."

"How do you feel about the troll now that he's gone away from the bridge?" the teacher asked.

"I feel like dancing," said one of the boys. "I do, too," called several others.

"I feel kind of sorry for the troll," said a little girl.

"Why?" asked the teacher.

"'Cause the troll can't hide under the bridge any more and he doesn't have any friend's house to go to."

Good literature is concerned with strong truths of living. When children experience good literature in creative dramatics they often release feelings and attitudes that have been bottled up inside. In so doing each child gradually gains an understanding of desirable and undesirable motives in relationship to living. A group of fourth, fifth, and sixth graders enjoyed playing Raymond Macdonald Alden's "The Knights of the Silver Shield."[13] When they created the knight ing scene the teacher asked if anyone had an idea how Roland felt when he walked toward the throne to be knighted. Several hands went up. "I know his feeling," said a boy. "It's like you feel when everyone is watching you—the way I felt when I walked on the stage in the school auditorium to get my Cub Scout Lion Badge."

"I felt the same way when I was flower girl for my cousin's wedding," one of the girls volunteered.

Another girl spoke out with strong feeling. "I think Roland feels scared and happy at the same time. I felt that way in Adoption Court last week. I wanted to be adopted because my new mother and daddy are so nice, but I was scared with the judge and all those people

[13] School of Drama, *op. cit.*

staring at me—and it was quiet—but it meant so much it was worth it—that's the way it is with Roland."

When a sixth grade class played this same story, Henry, an un-attractive and unpopular boy, was eager to be Sir Roland in the gate scene. It is here that Roland resists the temptations of three disguised giants. Henry created Sir Roland with depth of feeling and power of language. When the scene was over the teacher commented spontaneously: "Sir Roland, you were magnificent."

"Henry even looked like a knight," one of the boys said.

"Wow!" said another. "How could Henry ever do that?"

Henry, who had been moved by this creative experience, spoke freely releasing feelings that had been buried inside for a long time. "I've had experience," he said speaking straight from his heart. "Ever since I was little, I've been called names like Pimples and Guppy—and names worse than these. I used to fight back, but I always got the worst of it. I finally learned to control myself and say a quick prayer for the guys who sounded off. Prayer is strong—knights know that. I read in one of our books where a page spends a whole night praying before he takes the oath of knighthood. I was thinking of that when I was Sir Roland."

This experience appeared to be a turning point in Henry's life. Many of his classmates who had known him since kindergarten and who had been mean or indifferent toward him changed their attitudes in this unexpected moment. Two years later Henry came back to see his sixth grade teacher. In an unassuming way Henry divulged that he had been elected president of the junior high school student body. He was to make an acceptance speech the next morning and he wondered if the teacher had time to listen and evaluate.

Develops Bodily Coördination. It is a law of human nature for a child to be active. In creative dramatics a child's body is the medium through which he creates (Fig. 1.10). He yields to strong discipline as he coördinates his body, his mind, and his emotions to become a variety of characters. Every creative dramatics experience includes some form of rhythmic movement. With many different experiences a child releases energies and gradually develops coördination and poise (Fig. 1.11).

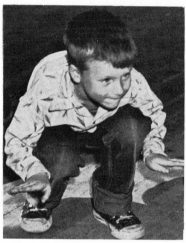

FIG. 1.10. "Ducky - daddles, the sky's a-falling!" (*School of Drama, University of Washington*)

FIG. 1.11. "I'm the strongest man in the whole world!" (*Lake Forest Park School, Shoreline Public Schools, Seattle, Washington*)

Contributes Toward a Philosophy of Living. Greatness happens in creative dramatics because children are great, and drama has the capacity for greatness. Greatness happens in big and little ways. It happens in moments of laughter. It happens whenever children become involved in exciting moments and express strong and spontaneous feelings. These are the moments that live. They are remembered. In the words of Keats, "A thing of beauty is a joy forever: Its loveliness increases."

Creative dramatics stimulates a child's awareness. It causes him to learn to look and listen, and from this to see, hear, and feel (Fig. 1.12). It strengthens his sensibilities and builds a receptiveness to the world that surrounds him—to the world of people, nature, things— to moods, beauties, wonderings (Fig. 1.13). A sensitive child expresses and uses his creative impulse freely and confidently. When children create from good literature they live the lives of many different kinds of characters. In dramatic ways they experience fundamental and universal truths in living. There is something within the folk and fairy tales and stories by great authors that reaches a child, for the inherent truth touches his imagination and his soul. Children are very susceptible to beauty and emotional intensity. When a child identifies with a character he examines the character's motives, relationships, attitudes, and ways of communicating. In so doing a child wonders about his own way of living. Because he can feel and understand feeling, he is free and secure. He is not puzzled or ashamed if his reactions differ from those engendered by unreasoning tradition, ignorance, and prejudice. He learns how to think through his reactions. He cogitates and thinks upon things far greater and more glorious than his immediate sphere of living. He strengthens his social and aesthetic attitudes and appreciations. In indirect but vivid ways creative dramatics introduces children to a philosophy by which to live.

A classic illustration occurred when a group of fourth, fifth, and sixth graders created a play from *The Sorcerer's Apprentice*.[14] After an exciting discussion of sorcery and magic each child became Willi-

[14] *Ibid.*

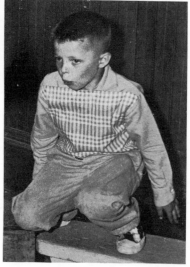

FIG. 1.12. "There's a tree on our street that looks just like this." (*School of Drama, University of Washington*)

FIG. 1.13. "This is the way a horned owl really sounds." (*School of Drama, University of Washington*)

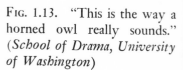

bald who was "not an ordinary sorcerer." Each created good magic to serve mankind. Some of the sorcerers spoke aloud and shared ideas such as these: "I am creating seeds that will grow into money trees. There will be a money tree for everyone in the world."

"My potion is bubbling over into a mountain of ice-cream. There will be mountains and mountains, brown and white, chocolate and vanilla so everyone will have enough ice cream."

"I am making a potion of smoke. Wherever the smoke goes people will breathe it. Once they do they will feel kind and good. There will be no more wars. Mine is a potion of peace for the whole world."

After these and other ideas had been discussed a boy by the name of Charles asked to play Willibald and start the scene. It was planned that Willibald, who was secretive about his magic, would call his faithful spiders out from the walls of the dungeon. The spiders would draw his secret plan from him. When the group was ready Charles, as a powerful sorcerer, stirred his imaginary potion with elaborate gestures. He moved to the center of the dungeon and called in a low eerie voice, "Come, my faithful spiders. I am making the greatest magic of all times."

From four different corners of the room the curious spiders crawled. "What are you making, master?" called one.

"Why have you called us from our sleep?" asked another.

"Why? Why? Why?" called the others.

Willibald smiled and gestured. "I am making a potion of smoke. The smoke will float out of the world. Whenever man smells smoke he will quit working."

"Quit working? Quit working?" questioned the spiders.

"I do not see how this will help mankind," said a spider.

"It will ruin mankind," said another.

"Hark!" said Willibald. "I will explain. Man *hates* work. Everywhere I go I hear men say, 'I have to go to work.' 'If only I didn't have to go to work.' 'I hate my job—it's the worse kind of work. It's work, work, work!' "

"But how will you help?" asked a puzzled spider.

"I will take work away from man. He will have nothing to do but sleep all day and be lazy. Soon he will have nothing to eat, no heat for his house, no lights, no gas for his car. His clothes will wear out and he won't get any more, for no one will be working. Man won't be able to work in his garden 'cause that's work too. He won't be happy."

"So this is your plan?" asked a confused spider.

"I still don't see how it works," admitted another.

"Ha, ha! I'm not an ordinary sorcerer. Man will begin to say, 'I want to work! If only I could go back to work!' Now do you see how I will help mankind?"

The children were fascinated with Charles's idea. They temporarily forgot Willibald and discussed the concept of work. It was decided among the children that people should choose work that they enjoyed rather than choose to work at something they hated. They thought people should prepare themselves for work rather than take whatever they could get to earn a living. One boy suggested that adults worked too steadily and never thought it important to take time off to play. Each child shared an idea of the kind of work he thought he would look forward to doing for his life's work.

CREATIVE DRAMATICS IN EDUCATION

Children go to school to grow and to learn so they may live happily as citizens in a democratic society. We have considered specific ways in which creative dramatics contributes to child growth and development. We have recognized ways in which John Dewey's accepted principle of *learning by doing* is put into action. We have been aware of pupil-planning, pupil-participation, and pupil-evaluation in each creative experience. We have seen William Kilpatrick's theory functioning and emphasizing that *an individual learns what he lives* and *to the extent that he lives an experience*. Experiences that are creative, exciting, vital, and dramatic contribute to permanent learning. Dramatic experiences based on literature and life are wide in scope and provide a variety of opportunities for children to get close to realities that cannot possibly be reached firsthand (Fig. 1.14). In a spirit of strong belief children travel vicariously through time and space to broad worlds and enjoy rich experiences (Fig. 1.15).

As we continue we will recognize further ways in which creative dramatics affects learning and meets educational needs of children. Four fundamental educational principles that creative dramatics constantly emphasizes will be observed. (1) It provides for self-realization in unified learning experiences; (2) it offers firsthand experiences in democratic behavior; (3) it provides for functional learning which is related to living; and (4) it contributes to learning which is comprehensive in scope.

VALUES TO THE COMMUNITY AND WORLD

Parents, teachers, and youth leaders have always been part pioneers. In this electronic age they become even more vital as pioneers. Whether they realize it or not they are pioneering in the richest of all frontiers—in the development of children and youth. The quality and force of pioneering always depend on the belief, vision, and courage of its leaders. Youth leaders must, first of all, believe in a child and in all children. They must believe in the art of living and in drama as an art to enrich living. They must believe in the values

FIG. 1.14. "We learn about the religion of the Arabs." (*Ronald School, Shoreline Public Schools, Seattle, Washington*)

FIG. 1.15. Arabs pray for rain. (*Ronald School, Shoreline Public Schools, Seattle, Washington*)

that come from keeping alive a child's creative spirit and in channeling his energies into dynamic dramatic experiences.

Leon Chancerel, a world leader in children's drama, sounded this challenge at the First International Conference on Theatre and Youth:[15] "There is in children a thirst for the marvelous and even more, a need of laughter and emotion. *It must be fulfilled.* The impressions of childhood always remain. It is necessary that they be worth while. Children who do not laugh become disillusioned men. Those whose hearts are not touched become men with hearts of stone. It is not to men that it is necessary to teach love, but to children."[16]

A community can grow with its children and youth. When the dynamic power of childhood is channeled into strong creative community programs the community as well as the children benefits. Children join in creative activities that utilize their time, energies, and deepest resources of power. They develop a community spirit and a feeling of responsibility toward the town or place in which they live. "Juvenile delinquency and vandalism can be lessened in communities everywhere if leisure-time youth programs are challenging enough to bring children from the streets. Creative dramatics offers an active program whereby children are given a chance to 'blow off steam,' where feelings are expressed rather than suppressed, and where boys and girls find pleasure working together. . . .

"An up-and-coming community that wisely tunes itself to the tempo of youth and provides worthy recreational programs benefits by a society that is worth while and wholesome."[17]

[15] International Theatre Institute, UNESCO House, Paris, France, April, 1952.

[16] "Report of The First International Conference on Theatre and Youth." United States National Commission for UNESCO, 1952. Unpublished.

[17] Lease and Siks, *op. cit.*

The greatest periods in the history of the world have been those in which man's creative powers have flowered in the arts, in exploration, and in religion. Cultural and spiritual forces are far more unifying than political ones, for they speak the language of men's hearts. Drama has been a cultural force since the days of the Greeks in the fifth century B.C. The play spirit has been a strong and fundamental force in children since the world began. When these two forces are brought together there is tremendous child power. The power of people lies not in machines but in the hearts and minds of all mankind.

Through the art of creative dramatics children and youth can be guided into developing a strength of spirit such as the world has never known. The art of creative dramatics is a childlike way to help children discover the real world in which they live, to discover the friendliness of others, to discover the magic and love that are deep within their souls. If children in homes, schools, and communities throughout the world are brought into the realm of creative art experiences where they can laugh and talk together, play and work together, think and feel together, then they can live together.

Questions and Activities

1. You have a friend with whom you correspond twice a week. Recently you have mentioned creative dramatics in every letter. Your friend has asked you to explain. Write a one-page letter explaining the philosophy and nature of this art for children.
2. Draw up a PTA program to consider the importance of creative arts in elementary education. (Consider both pros and cons.) Consider also how creative dramatics stimulates both (a) the growth and personality development of children, and also (b) enhances learning in subject areas.
3. Explain in a short paragraph your understanding of Brooks Atkin-

son's "Art mediates between the day's work and eternity." Hand your statement to another person in class for evaluation.

4. Analyze in semioutline form the basic growth needs of children that were met in "A Beginning Experience" in creative dramatics. Include specific illustrations including children's comments and questions to verify your analysis.

5. Observe a creative dramatics class. Analyze it from the viewpoint of values to the individual children.

6. Write a short editorial for your school or community newspaper based on the philosophical statement: "The power of people lies not in machines but in the hearts and minds of all mankind."

7. As you reflect on your childhood, what basic growth needs do you feel were satisfied in your growing-up days? What needs were not met as satisfactorily as you feel they should have been? Write a three-page impression of your childhood to answer these questions.

8. Eight-year-old Bill comes home from school and talks enthusiastically about creative dramatics. Bill's mother is curious. She calls you on the telephone to find out the *what* and *why* of creative dramatics. Work in pairs to plan five-minute telephone conversations to share in class.

9. Be prepared to contribute to class discussions that are motivated by each of the following questions or statements:

    a. What are the basic requirements for a creative dramatics program?

    b. "Creative dramatics emphasizes participation rather than product. Its chief aim is experience."

    c. "In creative dramatics the only desirable audience is a part of the group chosen to enjoy, appreciate, and evaluate the playing."

    d. "Values in creative dramatics come through the fun of experiencing dramatic moments which are strong in belief."

    e. What values may creative dramatics contribute to children?

    f. "Creative dramatics is educationally sound."

    g. "The greatest periods in the history of the world have been those in which man's creative powers have flowered in the arts, in exploration, and in religion."

10. Start a creative dramatics notebook or file for yourself in which you include pictures, quotations, personal observations, etc., of (a) children and children's personality growth and development and (b) your own personality growth.

CHAPTER 2

Creative Imagination

*Know you what it is to be a child? It is to be something
very different from the man of today. It is to have a spirit
yet streaming from the waters of baptism; it is to believe in
love, to believe in loveliness, to believe in belief; it is to be
so little that the elves can reach to whisper in your ear; it
is to turn pumpkins into coaches, and mice into horses, lowness into loftiness, and nothing into everything, for each
child has its fairy godmother in its own soul.—Francis
Thompson*[1]

ight-year-old Carol had a secret from everybody in the world
full of people. No one except her toy giraffe knew. It was a secret
about pretending. She had promised to share her secret with her
friends in the creative dramatics class on Saturday. Most of them
were 8-year-olds, too, except for the few who were seven.

When Saturday came, Carol tied a pink ribbon around the blue
giraffe's neck. She carried it proudly as she skipped down the side-

[1] Reprinted from *The Works of Francis Thompson,* Vol. III: Prose by Francis
Thompson, by permission of Burns, Oates and Washbourne, Ltd. Copyright 1913 by
Sir Francis Meynell.

walk. She remembered the fun in creative dramatics. On the very first day they pretended a branch of autumn leaves was a fairy wand. Each one waved the wand, and wished to go to a special place. Carol could still feel herself floating on a piece of dandelion fluff gliding up to the moon with all the others. She remembered how real it seemed when they stood on the moon and looked for beautiful things in the nighttime world below.

All at once Carol started marching down the sidewalk. She was thinking of the day they played they were marines and went to Korea on a big ship. She remembered how Gene who was a marine sergeant gave signals for marching, and turning, and stopping.

Suddenly Carol stopped marching. "We can't be late today," she said to her giraffe, and she ran the rest of the way to class. When Carol opened the door into the library room she saw the children and teacher sitting on a blanket on the floor.[2]

"Carol's here," called Gene who had been watching for her.

"Good morning, Carol," greeted the teacher cheerfully. "We've been waiting for you, and we've been waiting to hear your secret."

Carol held the giraffe behind her as she slipped off her coat. As she joined the others she said, "My secret is Blue Queenie, and here she is!"

The children were surprised. They seemed to be expecting something different. "Did you say your giraffe was named Blue Queenie?" the teacher asked curiously.

"Yes, she's Blue Queenie and she's magic. My secret is that Blue Queenie takes me to fairyland every night after I go to bed."

"To fairyland?" whispered a little girl under her breath.

---

[2] This is a composite account, from students' observation reports, of a class at the Seattle Public Library under the sponsorship of the School of Drama of the University of Washington.

"Magic?" asked another.

"Could Blue Queenie take us to fairyland too?" asked Gene.

"Oh yes, she could, Gene," Carol said earnestly. "If it's all right with Miss Smith."

CREATIVE VENTURE IN FAIRYLAND

The teacher smiled. "I think it's wonderful. It isn't every day that we have a magic giraffe visit us, let alone take us to fairyland. Who is ready to go with Blue Queenie?"

The children's hands fairly flew into the air. Carol's eyes flashed with excitement.

"What do we do?" asked the teacher, looking at Carol. "Will Blue Queenie lead us away to Fairyland?"

"Oh, no," said Carol. "Blue Queenie has her own magic way." She then held the giraffe at arm's length, looked it straight in the eye and spoke to it firmly: "One-ery, two-ery, two-ery, three, Blue Queenie, we need a magic key. Pff! Pfff! Pfffff!"

As she spoke, Carol looked upward and reached into the air high above her head. Suddenly she caught an imaginary key. In her excitement she called to the others. "Look, keys are flying down. Hurry and catch one. They're magic."

The children and the teacher hurried to their feet. In the fun of make-believe they too could see imaginary keys. Each one reached and caught one.

"Now do we go to fairyland?" the teacher asked.

"Oh, no. We have to find the door to fairyland," Carol said. Again she spoke firmly to her giraffe, "One-ery, two-ery, three-ery, four, Blue Queenie, we need a magic door. Pff! Pfff! Pfffff!"

While the children watched, Carol stepped out in front of them, and pantomimed a large arched doorway. "See. Here is the door to fairyland. You have to unlock it with your keys. Blue Queenie and I will lead the way."

Carol stepped back. She put her imaginary key into the imaginary door, turned the key, pushed open the door, and stepped through.

"Fairyland's beautiful," she said looking around to see its beauty as she spoke.

Each child and the teacher unlocked the door in turn. As if by magic each one seemed to be transformed into the loveliness of fairyland as he stepped through the door.

"See how pretty the flowers are," Carol said. "And smell the blooms."

"And listen to the way the birds are singing," called Gene. He was caught in the magic, too.

The teacher sensed a good opportunity to lead the children to the story she had planned to share with them. "Yes, listen to the birds," she said. "I think I hear a little gray bird singing. He sounds as if he were far away in the northland. Carol, do you think Blue Queenie with her lovely magic could get us up to the snowy northland?"

Carol was surprised and pleased by the question. Her eyes sparkled as she said, "Blue Queenie has to think."

The children watched with rapt attention. Carol took the giraffe's hind leg and scratched its ear. Suddenly a big smile spread across Carol's face. She held the giraffe in front of her, and said hopefully: "One-ery, two-ery, two-ery, two, Blue Queenie, we need a big snow shoe. Pff! Pfff! Pfffff!"

Immediately down from the northland came imaginary snowshoes, two for each child and two for the teacher. By this time everyone was laughing and in a strong spirit of pretending. They put on their snowshoes and walked with big rhythmic steps toward the northland. When they were about halfway down the room Gene called out in fun and alarm, "Blue Queenie, we're in trouble. There's a snowslide ahead of us. What'll we do?"

Carol announced seriously that her giraffe had to think. The children watched entranced. After a minute of deep thought, Carol called out, "One-ery, two-ery, two-ery, tay, Blue Queenie, we need a great big sleigh. Pff! Pfff! Pfffff!"

Almost immediately the children saw an imaginary sleigh arriving. They watched with wonder as Carol described its coming. Gene called to a boy near him, "Come on, Steve, let's sit in front and drive the reindeer."

With little confusion the children found partners and joined in a long line behind these two. They started singing "Jingle Bells." To their own gay rhythm the sleigh glided magically over the high imaginary snowslide and up and down the full length of the room. When they came to the far end of the room the teacher called to Gene, "Slow your reindeer down. We're almost to the northland village."

The children came to a stop and the teacher moved to the center of the room. "Look," she said with active pantomime. "There is only one fire in all the cold, snowy northland, and here it is. Let's sit around it and warm ourselves while we hear a beautiful story about this fire."

Then the teacher told the old Indian legend, "How the Robin's Breast Became Red." The children listened intently. When the story was over they were in a strong mood for creating. The story itself and the delight of Blue Queenie had fired their imaginations. They wanted to become the white bear first of all. They talked about how they thought he looked and felt. Each one found an imaginary cave and became the big selfish polar bear. Each one paced and growled. The teacher became a convincing bear to encourage several hesitant children to enter into the playing. Using a big bear-like voice the leader's bear talked to some of the growly bears about their mean feelings toward the villagers.

When the children changed back to themselves they discussed how the bear would feel when he saw the hunter's son fall asleep. Then each child became the bear and pounced on an imaginary fire. Some bears rolled. Others lunged toward the fire and pawed it with their sharp claws. All of the bears growled and each one enjoyed this vigorous selfish action.

The teacher then turned the children's thoughts to the little gray robin. Boys and girls told why they thought the little robin liked the hunter and his son. The children shared ideas about how they thought the robin looked and felt when the bear put out the fire. Then each child became the little robin searching for a tiny coal and fanning his wings patiently when he found one.

"I would like to be the robin all by myself, and light up the clumps of grass," Emily said after she had been warmly praised for her convincing little robin.

"All right, Emily, the rest of us will be clumps of grass," the teacher said including all of the children. Then she spoke slowly, "How do you suppose we could ever be a clump of grass?"

The children thought as they considered this idea.

"We could curl up like this," said one of the boys as he proceeded to draw himself up into a close little huddle on the floor.

"We could use our arms for blades of grass like this," said a little girl who stood with her arms outstretched.

"I'm going to be a clump of grass like this," said Steve as he stretched out full length on the floor, thrust his legs into the air, and balanced himself by putting his hands on his back and rested his elbows on the floor.

"These are beautiful clumps of frosty grass," said the teacher. "Suppose the rest show us rather than tell us how you will feel like frozen grass. Find your own place, get yourself rooted in the ground, and freeze like a clump of grass outside a village hut."

The children moved about freely as each one found a place in which to create his idea of frozen grass. The teacher watched, and gave the children time to embody their ideas. When she saw that they were settling down into all kinds of different creations of grass she spoke in a hushed voice: "This is the most beautiful northland I've ever seen. You have frozen into such beautiful clumps and clusters. I can hardly wait to see how each one will feel as it flares up into a flame when the little robin brings a tiny spark."

Gene broke the magic spell for a moment. He couldn't seem to get the feeling of being a clump of grass. "Could I be the bear and roll on the fire and really put it out?" he called.

Gene was alert. He was ready to put the story together. The teacher understood his request. "Yes, Gene, you be the bear, and Emily will be the bird. Everyone else will be a clump of grass to help the northern people, and I will be the hunter's son who falls asleep."

After the group decided where the hut and fire were to be, each character took his place and the play was ready to begin. The hunter's son started the action by calling the little bird, talking to it, and giving it a crust of bread. While the bird ate the bread crumbs, the boy told the bird how sleepy he was. The boy stretched and yawned and struggled to keep awake. The bird chirped anxiously, but even so the boy fell asleep. The little bird flew near the boy and chirped loudly trying to wake him. The white bear growled fiercely. He had kept close watch. In a powerful savagelike way he moved to the fire. He lunged on the fire, pawed it, and rolled over and over the coals while the little robin chirped fearfully (Fig. 2.1). Then the bear growled triumphantly and walked away.

When the bear was out of sight the robin flew to the fire, pecked among the coals, and fanned her wings patiently. She went closer and closer to where the fire had been. Suddenly she spotted a little light. She fanned it until it grew brighter and singed her feathers. Then she took it up in her beak, and flew to a clump of grass, and then to another, and on and on to each one.

One by one each clump of grass began to move as if it were burning slowly (Fig. 2.2). Little by little the clumps flared up into a mass of strong, swift, swirling movement. The little bird flew to the hunter's son and woke him. The bear crawled back toward the clearing. All three watched the flaming, flaring sky. While the flames were at high peak the teacher called, "Curtain."

"It's beautiful!" Gene said. "Just beautiful."

"It's like big bonfires going higher and higher." This from Emily

There was general approval and exhilaration.

"Blue Queenie took us to a wonderful fairyland today," the teacher said when she realized it was past time for the children to leave. "We'll talk about it next Saturday. Watch for little birds, and listen to their songs when you share crumbs with them, and look to see if you have something as magic as a giraffe around your house."

The morning had been lovely from Blue Queenie's arrival to the flaming fires. The children were still talking about this experience when they returned the next week.

"Blue Queenie and I kept seeing beautiful fires in fairyland all week long," Carol told them. "I wrote a little poem about the way they looked. I would like to share it if there's time."

"There's always time for sharing," said the teacher. "We'd like to hear your poem right now."

FIG. 2.1. "Grrr! I'll put an end to the fire now!" (*School of Drama, University of Washington*)

FIG. 2.2. Slowly the frozen grass flared into a flame. (*School of Drama, University of Washington*)

Carol unfolded the paper which she took from her pocket. "It's called 'Colors.' This is the way it goes."

> Dark blue as a bottle of ink—
> Brown as a cow,
> White as a bucket of paint.
> What shall I think of now?
>
> Blue as forget-me-nots—
> Red, red, red as a rose,
> Yellow as a daisy chain.
> And pink, pink, pink as my nose.
>
> Green as a clump of bushes—
> Blue as the sky,
> White as a picket fence.
> And brown, brown, brown as my eye.
>
> Purple as a slender mountain—
> Green as the garden wall
> Black as clouds of rain.
> But gold, gold, gold is best of all.[3]

WHAT IS CREATIVE IMAGINATION?

It's sparks and flares and flashes of independent thinking. It's what Carol and Emily and Gene and all fired-up children have. Their creative imaginations symbolize the birthright that comes into the world with every child. It is as mysterious and as wonderful as a child's heartbeat. It is powerful for it springs from a rhythmic source. It is delicate for it roots in sensitivity. It is original because it originates from within. In some unexplainable way a child has a flash of vision. He seeks fulfillment. In a free, inspired way imagination takes form. With almost divine confidence, expression is born.

All children are creators. They paint, draw, speak, write, sing, and

[3] By permission of the 8-year-old poet, Carol Heitlinger.

dance with joyous abandonment. They create in an almost reckless way. They are crude and confident in their freshness. They are vital. They are expressive. This does not mean that every child will grow up to be an artist. It does mean that when a child makes his entrance into the world he comes with a gift of imagination, with the power to create, and a desire to express himself.

Hughes Mearns, a foremost professor and teacher of creative arts, explains: "The great truth for both teachers and students to realize is this: A gift exists in each one of us, some sort of gift; but we must find it for ourselves. . . . The creative spirit is something more than a product in clay and canvas; it is dancing, rhythmic living, a laugh, a flash of the mind, strength of control, swiftness of action, an unwritten poem, a song without words; it is life adding its invisible cells to more and more abundant life."[4]

Ruth Sawyer believes that creative imagination is common in all mankind, but is held in diminishing degrees of consciousness and strength. Mrs. Sawyer says: "I believe children to be the freest, most universal creators. Left unhampered, a child begins very young to put into everyday life a series of masterpieces of creative thinking and doing. He is everlastingly bringing about that spiritual change in each object and idea with which his imagination plays. He works with direction; he strikes at the core of what he would express; he has nothing to discard, for he has accumulated nothing unnecessary. It is as if he were always saying: 'This I like. This I will make—sing —play—be!' "[5]

As early as fifth century B.C. the Greeks recognized the significances of man's creativeness. In Sophocles' beautiful *Antigone* the chorus of Theban elders voiced this when they said:

[4] Hughes Mearns, *Creative Power*, Doubleday & Company, Inc., 1929.
[5] Ruth Sawyer, *The Way of the Storyteller*, The Viking Press, Inc., 1947.

> Many are the wonders of the world,
> And none so wonderful as Man.[6]

In striking poetry they described remarkable ways in which man had conquered land and sea, language and thought. They honored man's wise inventiveness as they spoke solemnly, concluding:

> All-fertile in resource, resourceless never
> Meets he the morrow.[7]

WHY SHOULD IMAGINATION BE DEVELOPED?

For a child to exist, to be alive, is mystery in itself, but it is his ability to create and express himself that sets him apart from all other living creatures. Creativeness is the fundamental purpose for which human beings were put on this earth. Growth is the purpose of all human existence. In order to realize himself, an individual must develop his mind, his body, his imaginative faculties in whatever directions they may turn. Unless a child's creative powers are developed they remain dormant and are of little use to him. There is almost always a child or a few children among a group whose imaginations are noticeably strong. These children find ways of using and developing their powers for themselves. On the other hand, the greatest number of children throughout the country need constant encouragement to keep alive and develop their imaginative faculties.

Alex Osborn, a leader in the field of stimulating creative imagination at the adult level, emphasizes that "all human beings, to a greater or lesser degree, possess the imaginative faculty. Whether this talent can be enlarged by training is questionable. The point is that

[6] *Antigone,* translated by R. Whitelow in *Ten Greek Plays,* translated by Gilbert Murray and others, Oxford University Press, 1930.
[7] *Ibid.*

the student *can* be trained to use more productively the talent which he innately possesses."[8]

In each generation in our society we are concerned with the freedom of each individual. We are concerned with a child's right to live a good life. From the beginning of time man's everlasting challenge has been with the elements, his fellow man, and himself. When an individual is secure he feels free from without and free from within. A child who gradually develops his creative capacities along with other basic aspects of his development feels free and competent to meet, rather than fear, the environmental forces of daily living. He becomes a resourceful confident individual who is able to find a way to meet circumstances.

If a child is to become a free individual, free from outer and inner fears, he should be encouraged to use his imagination day after day. He should be motivated into *doing* something constructive to meet situations. He should not be allowed to become *passive* in accepting circumstances as he finds them. To allow a child to become passive is to allow his greatest gifts to go undiscovered. Life for too many individuals becomes a routine of mere existence rather than vital with abundant living. A creative child generally becomes a confident and capable individual. If his imagination is developed he continues, all his life, *to use his vision in five basic areas of living.*

In Improving Physical Environment. Imagination helps an individual transform his environment. It helps him refurnish his home and surroundings. If a child is to be secure in the area of concrete objects he must learn to be a maker of things rather than to be always dependent on someone else. He must be given opportunities for dreaming and doing. Whether a child makes a dress for a doll, builds

[8] Alex F. Osborn, *Applied Imagination*, Charles Scribner's Sons, 1953.

a tree house, paints a picture, creates a play or a puppet show, or figures out how to make a motor run, he is using his creativity and applying it in physical ways. He gradually develops a power to touch and transform things that make up his environment.

To be able to "make something out of nothing" is to experience the joy of living. Life becomes rich to those who enjoy the creation of such things as colorful kitchen curtains out of empty potato sacks, beautiful flower gardens out of unsightly back yards, unusual lawn furniture from empty nail kegs, attractive headdresses out of kitchen scouring pads, rare handbags from fishing creels, extraordinary children's toys from discarded cartons, charming theatres from old buildings, and singular centerpieces from arrangements of weeds and wheat straws.

In Meeting Unexpected Situations. Life by its very nature is unpredictable. In the lives of everyone there are unexpected happenings that must be met with a sudden change of plans. When an individual knows how to meet a problem by figuring out an alternative plan he feels secure within himself. This ability contributes much both to his emotional stability and to the security of others with whom he lives when he saves a situation from becoming an emotional calamity.

When a child learns how to use his imagination he becomes resourceful. He gradually develops a perceptive attitude toward solving problems, meeting emergencies and unexpected happenings. He gains a security of attitude as he remains calm and figures out what to do.

When families work together and solve unexpected problems, they strengthen family spirit. Families have found thorough enjoyment in joining forces and solving such universal problems as cleaning the house in 15 minutes for out-of-town guests, arranging an indoor picnic when rain disrupts outdoor plans, planning creative children's parties, solving the ticklish problem of remaining neighborly while keeping the neighbor's dog from trespassing through a flower bed, figuring out how to stretch a dinner for four to satisfy eight hungry people when old friends stop by at dinnertime, and creating unusual and inexpensive gifts for wedding, birthday, graduation, and Christmas presents.

In Expressing Ideas and Opinions. Freedom for an individual exists when he knows how to communicate with others. A creative individual has the power to visualize, to picture, to size things up for himself. With an ability to perceive he is free to express his opinions, to contribute to a plan of action, and to consider values. In an imaginative way he is able to communicate and get his ideas across to others so they are accepted and discussed.

A child who is lacking in imagination has few ideas to share. He generally resorts to borrowing ideas and opinions from others. He accepts and conforms for fear of speaking out and not being able to explain or clarify his convictions. An individual with imagination feels secure. He forges ahead for he has ideas and knows how to express them.

In Enjoying Solitude. A creative person enjoys being by himself from time to time. He finds enjoyment in moments of solitude wherein he refreshes and satisfies his creative spirit in ways that are satisfying to him. He may read, paint, listen to music, work in a garden, walk or exercise in the outdoor world. He does not shun being alone, but uses this time to enrich himself spiritually.

The creative person finds ways of enjoying himself. He enjoys creating in a way that satisfies himself. Whether a mother makes a cake, a father fashions a workbench, a little girl makes a potholder, or a boy builds a bird feeder, each experiences the surge of self-motivation and self-enjoyment.

The unhappy person too often depends entirely on commercialized amusements for his pleasure. He lacks sufficient vision and drive to stir himself into doing something that synchronizes his whole being. Fortunate is the individual who nourishes and exercises his imaginative faculties in childhood and sustains his creativity and attitudes throughout life. Far too many adults reach the middle and later years of life complaining that time hangs heavy because there is a sameness to each long day.

Contrast this attitude to that of a cheerful grandmother who served with spirit in one worthy community project after another. When she received a county fair catalogue she became excited about exhibiting flowers. She encouraged others to do so and was indirectly responsible for an extensive and showy floral exhibit. This grandmother found real challenge in creating "historical arrangements." For several weeks she let her imagination play upon several possibilities. The day before the fair she gathered three long stalks of thistles with lavender blossoms. She arranged them among a cluster of golden wheat straws. She placed them in a large buffalo horn, and called the arrangement, "Westward Ho." For another entry called "Peace," she placed a beautiful Peace Rose in front of a framed scroll of the Japanese Treaty of 1953. An exhibit created by another grandmother was two black lanterns filled with bouquets of bright red salvia. A message attached to one of the lanterns read: "One if by land, and two if by sea."

In Strengthening Social Relationships. Henry Thoreau recognized that "To affect the quality of a day for others is one of the greatest of all arts." When an individual opens his heart and uses his imagination to find little ways of brightening the lives of others, friendship flourishes. Happiness begins with individuals and spreads to others. This is the true spirit of living. It is dependent on a creative attitude of concern with and for others. It is the attitude that Ralph Waldo Emerson voiced when he said, "Live, let live, help live."

A mail carrier established friendly relations between a florist's shop and people on his mail route in an imaginative way. The mailman praised the florist's unusual flowers. The florist, in turn, gave the mailman a choice flower each morning to wear in his cap, such as a lavender carnation, a daffodil in December, and other unique floral specimens. People on the route were impressed with the mailman's flowers. They were motivated to frequent the florist shop and they made a point of ordering from this florist whenever they had an occasion for flowers.

In quite an unexpected way a garbage man built a strong friendship among his customers. Happy over the birth of his first child he decorated the hood of his truck with pink paper streamers. On either side of the truck he printed in big letters: "It's a boy." He was surprised and humble with gratitude the following week when many of his customers came to meet him with gifts for his son. This unexpected gesture impressed him so strongly that he found ways of giving his customers unusual service.

A doctor endeared himself to many mothers in a community when the news spread that he had prescribed a lollipop for a lonesome little boy who refused to eat. The boy had been left with a neighbor during the night when his mother was taken to a hospital for an emergency operation. The next day the child was so lonely for his mother that he refused to eat or drink. The doctor was consulted in the evening. When the little boy was given his choice of colored lollipops, his loneliness was forgotten for the moment. By the time he had finished the lollipop he was hungry, and asked for his supper.

A young businessman improved his business relations when he created a slogan that appealed to the imagination of his public. In all his advertising he used the slogan: *I Live to Dye.*

A neighbor created a lasting friendship by giving a creative Christmas present to a working mother and her three young sons. The present was a large piece of paper, cut in a circle and painted to resemble a pie. On the back of the paper was written this note: "On the twenty-fifth day of each of the next 12 months, you shall have a home-baked pie for dinner." These neighbors convinced others in their community of the unbelievable value in a pie for establishing a good-neighbor policy.

IMAGINATION IN THE HOME

Lin Yutang, in *The Importance of Living,* says: "It has seemed to me that the final test of any civilization is, what types of husbands and wives and fathers and mothers does it turn out? Beside the austere simplicity of such a question, every other achievement of civilization—art, philosophy, literature and material living—pales into insignificance."[9]

Children grow quickly. In a few years the children of today will be the adults of tomorrow. Children whose attitudes and imaginations have been nourished will find ways of building happy relationships in family and community living.

Imagination Builds Understanding. By the power of imagination a parent is able to put himself in the place of a child. It helps him to better understand the feelings a child has. It helps him to find ways of opening doors into a child's world and of keeping the doors

[9] Lin Yutang, *The Importance of Living,* The John Day Company, Inc., 1937.

of understanding open throughout childhood and youth. A mother was at sixes and sevens with Jeff, her 4-year-old son. She couldn't seem to understand his behavior patterns. She and her husband had commented often that they wished Jeff was more masculine in his behavior like the boy next door.

One day Jeff came hurrying home from nursery school. "Mommy," he said excitedly. "You be the sun and I'll be a tulip and I'll grow."

"The sun," his mother said sharply. "I *can't* be the sun."

"I'll be the sun," Jeff said undaunted. "You be the tulip and you grow."

"No, this is stupid," his mother said putting a firm and abrupt end to Jeff's childlike desire.

In the evening Jeff's mother attended a Family Life Meeting and heard an inspiring speech on discovering a child's creative spirit. The mother said she lay awake a long time that night wondering about Jeff, and feeling regretful that she had failed to join in his playing of the tulip and the sun. She said she decided she would make a renewed effort to try to discover what Jeff was like.

The next morning Jeff was up early. He was excited when he found a bright red geranium had blossomed in the back yard. He hurried in to the kitchen and said, "Mommy, that flower talked to me."

The mother said she would have rebuffed such an idea on a previous day. Instead she asked curiously, "What did it say?"

"It just talked," Jeff said. Then he skipped out the door and looked at the flowers, apparently happy with his mother's friendly interest. In telling about the experience the mother said she was deeply touched by her son's belief that flowers could communicate. She said she suddenly remembered how wild mountain flowers had seemed to speak to her when she went fishing with her husband before they were married. She said she recalled how she used to hear songs in the wind, find "books in the running brooks, sermons in stones, and good in every thing."[10] She said while she was reflecting, Jeff skipped into the house and announced that the flower had talked again. "Do you know what it said?" he asked.

"What?"

"It said, 'Happy Christmas.' "

The mother said she was taken aback in surprise until she realized that Jeff and the geranium were remembering the joy of Christmas on a warm May morning. From that day on this mother and her young poet son understood, appreciated, and enjoyed each other.

Imagination Dissolves Emotional Tensions. By being *aware* of the way a child receives impressions from his environment, a parent may find imaginative ways to channel them into satisfying expressions of feeling. A young father took his 5-year-old daughter Stephanie to a city zoo one evening. It was feeding time for the animals, and a hungry lion paced back and forth in his cage. Stephanie was intrigued with the lion and his growling. "What's the matter with the lion?" she asked.

"I guess he's mad," the father explained.

"Why is he mad?" Stephanie continued.

"Well I suppose his dinner isn't quite ready, and he wants it now."

"He sure is mad!" the little girl said. Not until the lion was fed and calmed down was she content to leave this fascinating scene.

The next morning before breakfast Stephanie was impatient to have someone untie a knot in her shoelace. Her mother was late in preparing breakfast, and her father was shaving. The mother became irritated by Stephanie's persistence. The father could hear dissension

---

[10] William Shakespeare, *As You Like It,* Act II, Scene 1.

mounting in the kitchen. As he listened to the yelling and shouting he became angry too. All of a sudden an idea flashed through his mind. He dropped on all fours and crawled into the kitchen in the convincing character of an angry lion, even to his lathered mane. His wife and little girl were startled by his lifelike characterization. The wife screamed with laughter and Stephanie joined in the fun of becoming a lion too. Soon they were all laughing at each other. The shoelace was untied. The father had his breakfast, was at work on time, and was in a pleasant mood all day. So were the mother and Stephanie. For several weeks whenever any tension mounted in this home, it was released with a loud lion growl. The word "lion" had a magic effect on this little family, and probably always will.

Another mother was *aware* of a disturbing problem among the three younger children in her household. When the furnace rumbled one evening an older brother told his younger brothers that a blue bear had come to live behind the furnace which was painted blue. Every time the furnace rumbled the blue bear grew bigger in the minds of the children. They were afraid to play in the basement and couldn't be persuaded to go down with the parents to look behind the furnace.

The mother figured that if the bear got in the basement by the power of imagination, he could perhaps be lured away by the same power. She tried while the three children watched fearfully from the stairway door. With exciting pantomime and convincing language the mother lassoed the bear, and struggled to pull him out the basement door so the zookeeper could come by and get him. By a strange coincidence a truck drove down the alley shortly after the bear had been left outside the backyard gate. After the truck had gone the boys went to the basement with their mother. They looked anxiously to see where the bear had lived behind the furnace. Now that he was gone, they played without fear. Several weeks later when the family visited the zoo, the children were disappointed not to see a bright blue bear in the cages with the brown bears and grizzlies. The boys' father assured them that if the bear had been such a beautiful blue he had probably been sold to a circus.

Imagination Enriches Living. Family living becomes enjoyable and enthusiastic when parents help children develop creative attitudes toward work and play. Parents do not set aside a special time for children's creative activity; rather they make it a part of whatever the children are doing at home. *A parent uses the magic of indirection and positive thinking.* A friendly parent recognizes a child's strong interest, and stirs his imagination in this direction until the child becomes a creative thinker.

Work can be fun for a child when he approaches it with spirit and enthusiasm. Daily chores such as cleaning one's room, sweeping walks, weeding gardens, gathering garden vegetables, and mowing a lawn may become pleasant experiences when a child has a positive attitude toward accomplishment. Friendly "words from mother or father may work like magic in turning a lawn mower into a large mowing machine or into a high-powered combine moving across the wheat fields of Montana. Johnny maneuvering the lawn mower may suddenly become the owner of a large ranch, or he may become a hired man or a chief engineer operating a new machine, or if he prefers he may be a team of work horses pulling the machine around the alfalfa field. He may want to be a gardener who takes great pride in keeping his own yard as neat and clean as the city park."[11]

When girls are approached in a friendly, imaginative way they enjoy helping with housework tasks such as sweeping, dusting,

[11] Ruth Lease and Geraldine Brain Siks, *Creative Dramatics in Home, School, and Community,* Harper & Brothers, 1952.

cleaning, and ironing. "If mother will find a small white apron and perhaps a headdress for her daughter Ann and suggest that Ann be Rosie the cleaning lady or Bridget the maid, she will see how easily work can turn into play. Giving a word of praise to Bridget when any task has been nicely done is important for an appreciative mother to remember. 'Sure, and the kitchen's pretty as a picture, Bridget. I couldn't have cleaned it better myself.' "[12]

Wise parents are alert to children's self-initiated desires for play. They realize the importance of encouraging children to follow creative pathways. They encourage rather than discourage. They approve a child's creative desires such as wanting to make a playhouse in a corner of a bedroom or an outdoor shed, or wanting to build a tree house in a back-yard tree. Parents encourage a child's worthy idea, offer few suggestions, and provide objects or discarded materials that may heighten a child's creative thinking. A parent uses care in not dominating or overdirecting a child's creative play. On the other hand, a parent encourages, enjoys, and appreciates with enthusiastic comments of approval now and then. A trunk or large box of old clothing and discarded materials is a rich source of motivation for almost every child.

Children enjoy creative parties. Children become stimulated to create pantomimes and share dramatic scenes and skits when interest is motivated and guided. Such themes as cowboys and Indians, Mother Goose characters, pirates, circus animals, sports festivals, and scavenger hunts have provided exciting, creative birthday parties. A mother and her young daughter created great enjoyment and neighborhood enthusiasm when they shared Un-Birthday Parties and Mad Hatter Teas. The children and mothers enjoyed the delight of nonsense. They experienced Yellow Teas, Pink Teas, Rabbit

[12] *Ibid.*

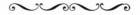

Teas, Squirrel Teas, and a variety of Mad Hatter ideas. At each tea each child arrived with a contribution either in the way of an appropriate refreshment, decoration, or idea for entertainment.

Parents who are aware and put their imaginations to work on everyday problems find innumerable ways of enriching family living. One mother was disturbed with the confusion that resulted whenever she took her four little children grocery shopping. By watching her children and using her imagination she solved this problem in an enjoyable way. The children, who ranged in age from 2 to 7 years, were fascinated with playing train. One day when they were chugging around the yard the mother called, "Toot! Toot! All aboard! Train leaving for the grocery store!"

The children in their spirit of play chugged toward her, single file like the cars of a train. The 7-year-old was the engine, and the mother skillfully managed to become the caboose so she could maneuver the train from the rear. Together they chugged down the street in a happy line. The engine whistled whenever they came to a crossing. The train chugged quietly down the lanes in the grocery store while the caboose-man did the shopping, and gave each car a package to carry. In a pleasant way this mother avoided the problems of walking five abreast or of losing a child. The friendly little train was a refreshing sight to store clerks, and other shoppers who found themselves watching for the times the train would come into the village.

Imagination Prepares for New Experiences. When parents guide a child in *playing out* and *imagining* a new experience that child generally enjoys rather than fears the experience. A parent uses imagination to *dramatize* and *focus* the situation with strong and realistic feeling. The mother or father assumes the role of the new person the child is to meet such as a barber when a child gets his first haircut. "Together they create the situation and make it as realistic as possible. They act it out again and again until the child feels confident and secure when he encounters the situation in reality."[13] Roles are switched so a child understands both his own feelings and those of the person he is to encounter.

Parents and little children have enjoyed playing out and preparing for new experiences such as a child's first trip to the corner store alone, to the dentist, to nursery school, to a birthday party, to kindergarten, to Sunday school, or for his first ride on a school bus, or going to a restaurant with relatives, or for a tonsilectomy or a visit to a hospital. In a similar way parents have guided little children into learning how to answer a telephone, answer a door, thank someone for a gift or a compliment, and take a message to a neighbor down the street.

Parents have guided older children into playing out new experiences such as first trips alone on a plane, train, boat, or bus. Situations have been acted out so a child has enjoyed announcing his selections at a recital, introducing a guest or a speaker, awarding a prize or announcing a program, leading the flag salute, applying for a job, selling greeting cards, and giving a speech of acceptance when elected to an office and giving a speech when defeated for an elective office.

IMAGINATION IN THE SCHOOL

A teacher who is with a group of children day after day for a school year will go far either in nourishing or in neglecting the development of a child's creative spirit. Emotion is one of the strongest foods for nourishing sensibilities and helping appreciations to grow. When a child is aroused by experiencing great music, litera-

[13] *Ibid.*

ture, or art he *lives* deeply in his own inside world, and these moments don't entirely fade away. They stay with a child, for they become a part of his being. Those moments become his innermost secrets and he cherishes them. There should be many of these moments for children in school.

Encouraging Creativity. John Dewey explains that sensitive awareness to environment is the beginning of aesthetic appreciation. He believes that all people have the hidden power to see and enjoy harmonies and beauties in the environment, but in modern man the capacity for alertness is developed only in relatively few individuals.[14] Since awareness is the strongest motivation for creation, a teacher who helps a child develop awareness enriches his appreciation and creative expression.

Teachers find that as children are encouraged they become increasingly creative and give forth with often startlingly delightful expression. A second grade teacher took her children to an art museum. After seeing exquisite art objects and paintings the children decided they would like to have their own art museum. They arranged a corner of their room and called it "Our Art Museum." The teacher kept the children reaching for beauty and fineness of expression by exhibiting only a child's best during the weekly showings.

A third-grade teacher motivated expression with Robert Louis Stevenson's "Happy Thought." With an increased awareness that, "The world is so full of a number of things . . ." the children decided to have a mailbox for the "King of the World." A large carton painted yellow and blue served to collect creations. The teacher made it easy for sensitive, shy children to express by suggesting that each creation be marked whether it was to be shared with the kingdom or kept in confidence for the king alone.

[14] John Dewey, *Art as Experience*, Minton, Balch & Co., 1934.

An abundance of creative expression came from boys and girls in a 9-, 10-, and 11-year-old class (Fig. 2.3) who were motivated by an exciting discussion on how creativity made America. A large, colorful sign was posted which stated: Creators—Who?—You! The first creation to be developed was a telemhone (Fig. 2.4). It was described by the girl who devised it as "a gadget to help people realize they should talk only one minute on a telephone for friendly calls, and two minutes for an emergency."

Among other creations that appeared over a period of nine weeks were two outstanding body designs for new automobiles, two short stories, the beginning chapter of a book, two one-act plays, an original cartoon, a puppet show, a musical instrument made from a collection of empty beverage bottles filled with different amounts of water, and six poems including "The Rainbow":

> One day when I was herding the cows
> Near the railroad tracks,
> I looked above.
> The rainbow was like a field of flowers in the sky.
> I wondered again—
> What was at its end?
> A pot of gold or just a fairy's hut?[15]

A Talent Time Program motivated by a television program challenged a sixth grade class to share talents every Friday afternoon. This program built strong rapport and brought recognition to individuals for dancing, singing, story writing, sharing plays, clay modeling, woodcarving, soap carving, and for organizing a small orchestra.

Developing Awareness Through the Senses. An ancient Persian poet emphasized the need for beauty in living when he said: "If

[15] By permission of the 10-year-old poet, Maria Liisa Miettunen.

FIG. 2.3. "The name of my play is *Elf's Mystery*." (*School of Drama, University of Washington*)

FIG. 2.4. "A telemhone? What's it for?" (*School of Drama, University of Washington*)

thou hast two pennies, spend one for bread; with the other buy hyacinths for thy soul." One of the most exciting ways for children to gather "hyacinths" is through sensory awareness. "Hyacinth-time" is a way in which some classroom teachers begin and end each school day. An awareness question is asked at the close of the day. When the children return the next morning they either take a few minutes to share "hyacinths" or each child writes or draws his idea. "Hyacinths" are later shared or posted for all to see. A teacher asks only one hyacinth question a week or a day, depending on the group. A child's awareness and thinking are sharpened by limiting his expression to a single word or a single thought which paints a clear picture of his impression.

By Sense of Sight. Questions including the following have been asked to stimulate awareness in seeing: What was the most beautiful thing you saw on your way to school today? What was the biggest thing you saw this week? What was the littlest thing? What do you see when you look up in the sky? What do you see when you look out your bedroom window? What have you seen that was so beautiful you would like to have others see it right now? What do you see that tells you it is spring? What is a beautiful sight for you in the fall? What is yellow? What is blue?

In answer to, "What is green in springtime?" a group of 7-year-olds had these replies: "grass," "rhododendron bushes," "rhubarb leaf," "raspberry leaf," "pine needles," and "little green frog in the green, green clover."[16]

In a sixth grade class, among the answers to the biggest things they had seen, children were delighted to find noticeable differences in their impressions. Among their big things were these: "a hole in my jeans," "Ink on my new sweater," "Mt. Rainier," "church when

[16] View Ridge School, Everett Public Schools, Everett, Washington.

the choir sang 'The Lord's Prayer,' " "an apple orchard with ripe apples on every tree," "Puget Sound from the bluff above Golden Gardens," "squash on my plate when I had dinner at my friend's," "a truck which almost sideswiped us," "the sky," "my Winnie Mae model when I got it together," "Dolly, my horse," and "a bouquet of flowers in a new, modern house."

Poetry, including, "I Have Magic Eyes," by Madeline Dixon, Sara Teasdale's "Night," and Elizabeth Coatsworth's "Swift Things Are Beautiful," has motivated searching for loveliness and an eagerness to share.

Children enjoy painting, with words, the first pictures that come to their minds when they hear a single word. Words that have appealed to children include "mother," "friend," "Thanksgiving," "home," "fun," "winter," "fire," and "pink."

Imaginations are exercised when children are asked to describe, by association, something they have seen. For instance, a class of second graders was asked, "What did the snow look like when you first saw it this morning?" One little boy said, "Like a torn blanket." A little girl said, "It looked like a great big white tablecloth for Christmas dinner."

By Sense of Smell. "The best smell for me is when my mother bakes bread," said a fourth grade boy. "I like the smell of gasoline better," said another. "My grandmother smells just like roses," said one of the girls. "I like the smell of the stuff the barber puts on my hair." These were among the favorite smells of 9-year-olds.

Other questions which have been asked to develop awareness in smelling include the following: What do you like best to smell at night? What does your house smell like when you first walk in? What smell do you like to smell in winter? What good smell have you smelled when you have walked down a city street? What have

you smelled that would make a good perfume? What food smells better to you than it tastes? What smell makes you feel happy? When has your nose given you a warning of trouble or danger? What is your nose telling you now? What one thing do you think people buy because of its smell? What is a good smell in spring? What is a favorite smell for you in summer? What smell do you like to smell in the fall?

By Sense of Taste. Walter de la Mare's "Bunches of Grapes" and "Cupboard" always motivate children into expressing what they like to eat. Questions such as the following stimulate interest in the sense of taste: If you were really hungry and could have one thing to eat, what would you choose? If you could make a make-believe sandwich and put three things you like best between two slices of bread what would you choose? What food that comes out of the ground do you like best to taste? What food do you like best to taste which you may pick off a tree? Of all the sour tastes, which do you like best? Of all the sweet tastes you've tasted, which is the sweetest for you? What soft taste is pleasant for you? What is the most unpleasant taste you have had? When has your tongue given you a warning about something you started to eat? What is your tongue telling you now?

By Sense of Touch. A group of third graders found great delight in thinking about the sense of touch. They started by sharing pleasant touches to their hands, to their feet, and then to their whole selves. In answer to the last question the children expressed such pleasant things as "warm water in my bath," "cold water in a shower," "my winter pajamas," "my nylon nightgown," "the wind blowing against all of me," "when I get into daddy's bed after he gets up," "rolling on grass," "covering my whole self except my eyes and nose with sand," "snowflakes on my face in a snowstorm," "swimming in a mountain lake without my bathing suit."

Polly Boyden's "Mud" and A. A. Milne's "Sand-Between-the-Toes" stir children with the special delight that comes with the sense of touch. For further stimulation, such questions as the following may be asked: What have you touched that makes you feel like being kind? What have you touched that makes you shiver? What is the smoothest thing you have ever touched? What is the roughest thing you have ever touched? What have you touched or what has touched you that warned you of trouble or danger? Close your eyes and hold out your hand and see what you think your hand is touching now. Children's imaginations are exercised when a teacher touches each child's hand with a variety of objects, each with a different touch surface. To emphasize the sense of touch children are asked to close their eyes. Objects that have aroused strong feeling include a clothes-brush, a chestnut burr, a pine cone, an inflated balloon, a ball of fur, a sprinkle of salt from a shaker, a feather, a pearl necklace, and a puff of air.

By Sense of Hearing. "Have you ever thought how much people are like radio and television receivers? We receive messages with our eyes and ears, with our tongues and noses, and with our hands and feet and whole selves. Have you ever stopped to think how wonderful it is to listen and really hear messages?" A fifth grade teacher motivates awareness with this approach. She asks children to close their eyes, and discover what their ears tell them. She then proceeds to open and close a door, tiptoe from one end of the room to the other, and rub her hands together in a rapid, circular movement. Children recognize the first two sounds readily, but they seldom guess the last sound. They become intrigued by what they hear, be-

lieving the sound to be such things as "a tiny electric motor," "water moving," "material swishing," and a "dog panting."

The following questions have been used to encourage children to listen: What for you is a pleasant sound at night? What do you like to hear in the daytime? What is the quietest sound you have ever heard? What is the loudest sound you have heard? What have you heard that is as quiet as a caterpillar crawling? What sound is as welcome to you as a drink of cold water when you are thirsty? What is a friendly sound of spring? What sound do you like to hear in winter? What sound in summer do you like best? What does the rain sound like? What does the wind sound like to you?

Building Appreciations. When children become sensitive to beauty in nature they become more sensitive in their relationships with human nature. They develop understanding, tolerance, and respect for the thoughts and feelings of others. The third grade teacher who encouraged children to put their expression in the king's mailbox asked them to make a list of things that made them "as happy as kings." An 8-year-old boy's list included: "a boat with me in it on the water," "when a fish jerks my line and I catch it," "my dog," "when I caught the ball and put the other team out," "when I go to Grandma's farm," "riding my two-wheeler," and "breakfast."

The happiest thing for an 8-year-old girl was: "when I pull a tooth and put it under the rug and find a fairy penny the next morning."

Rupert Brooke's "The Great Lover" was a favorite poem of a sixth grade teacher. When he shared it with his class an inspiring discussion followed. This led to the desire for each child to make a list of things he had loved. An 11-year-old boy's list included: "a little fawn by the side of the road," "when I hit the bull's-eye," "the way I feel after I've done a hard job for the first time," "when I go hunting with my dad," "a double rainbow," "catching my first 8-pound salmon," "earning my bronze medal in sports," "watching wild ducks fly," "getting chosen to be lieutenant for the school patrol," and "swimming under water."

A girl's list of "Things I Have Loved" included: "having a horse like Midge," "camping this summer where it was so pretty and peaceful," "ice-cream sundaes with hot fudge and nuts," "when mom tells me the house looks nice after I've worked so hard to clean it," "when Rosie, my dog, comes to meet me after school," "winning the fishing derby for catching the most fish," "singing in a choir and alone," "having a friend like Judy," "baby chicks," and "my horse blanket 'cause we had to sell Midge."

IMAGINATION IN COMMUNITY LIVING

Recently 12 cities were honored for being outstanding cities in America. Why were they so honored? Why did the peoples of these cities and their bordering communities work with zest, spirit, and vision to make their cities beautiful, productive, and vibrant with good will? Why did the peoples in these cities forge ahead with initiative and action while great numbers of peoples in thousands of other cities and towns remained passive in an acceptance of things as they were?

We don't know. But we can believe with James Stephens that in these communities there must have been leprechauns, leprechauns with crocks of gold. James Stephens discovered that "A community of Leprechauns without a crock of gold is a blighted and merriless community."[17]

What is a leprechaun but a spirit, a spirit of vision and delight? A

[17] James Stephens, *The Crock of Gold*, The Macmillan Company, 1936.

spirit of initiative and action? A spirit of power and belief? We have recognized this spirit in community leaders who use vision to awaken others to action in community development programs. We have seen how one individual fires other individuals into beautifying a town or city by starting a campaign to improve the appearance of back yards, front yards, vacant lots, parks and parking lots, and railroad stations and airports.

We have watched recreational leaders work near-miracles in developing social, recreational, and cultural programs for children, youth, and adults. We have watched leaders develop natural resources to strengthen community activity, spirit, and incomes. We have seen educational leaders forge ahead with new learning programs which are sound and stimulating. We have watched land being cleared for new churches and synagogues because leaders with religious faith and zeal have awakened within peoples a need for religious living.

We have watched abandoned barns and community buildings take on new life when people gather together to sing, to make music, to put on plays, to dance, to paint, to work with clay. We have seen basement rooms, grange halls, libraries, and recreation halls spring to life when spirited individuals have shared creative dramatics with children and youth. Art festivals have sprung up in communities here and there because individuals believed in cultural values and found ways to share art experiences. When we consider what spirit, belief, and imagination can do for the peoples of communities we are inclined to agree with James Stephens that "A Leprechaun is of more value to the Earth than is a Prime Minister."[18]

CREATIVE IMAGINATION FOR THE WORLD

"Where there is no vision the people perish." These words spoken

[18] *Ibid.*

centuries ago by a wise king are as meaningful today as when they were first spoken. One of the most tragic facts about our culture is that few people heed this truth. In each generation there are individuals with vision who find ways of satisfying human needs. But if these numbers could be multiplied, millions of peoples throughout the world who are suffering from hunger and cold would have food, clothes, and homes. As we think upon these needs we recall other familiar words, "Man cannot live by bread alone." Some few there are who respond to this call in each generation, but altogether too few in view of grievous human needs.

When we pause from reading daily papers headlined with disturbing news of world affairs we often wonder how fundamental issues will be resolved. We wonder what might be done to solve illiteracy among millions. We wonder how masses of peoples could be taught basic skills in reading and writing. We wonder how persecuted peoples could be reached so they may think and act for themselves rather than be ruled by a tyranny that dictates their lives and thoughts.

Every human being has feelings. Whether a child is born in Cairo, Kyoto, or Calcutta he has a life to live. He, too, thinks and feels and has needs and dreams similar to those of a child born in Cincinnati. When one considers how short the span of human life is upon this earth the need for reaching children and youth becomes urgent. Human objectives become vital throughout the world. The art of creative dramatics has proved its worth in being one way to keep alive creative spirits of children while it builds attitudes of tolerance and good will.

From childlike imaginations of Blue Queenies, talking geraniums, and telemhones to the adult vision of United Nations, Houses for Hiroshima, Care Packages, and Atoms for Peace is but a step in the development of creative power. If children in towns, villages, and cities throughout the world were guided into vivid creative art experiences in their growing years there would ultimately be a renaissance in mankind such as the world has never known. Teachers, youth leaders, and parents must be dedicated and yet be bold for:

> A child, more than all other gifts
> That earth can offer to declining man,
> Brings hope with it, and forward-looking thoughts.[19]

Questions and Activities

1. A. You are a member of a committee that has been asked to prepare a bulletin board display to motivate creativity (1) of children and (2) of adults.
   B. You are a member of a committee that will evaluate the displays (1) from the creative standpoint and (2) from the standpoint of stimulation.
2. List three community groups that could motivate creative programs for children in the community in which you live. List four ways in which your community or neighborhood could be enriched, improved, and beautified.
3. Exercise your imagination and have fun as you answer the following questions which have been enjoyed by people from 9 to 90. (Allow yourself 10 to 15 minutes for answering.)

You

a. What would be a good adventure for you today? ....

b. What thought always causes you to soar high in spirit? ....
....

c. Write down the first picture that flashes in your mind when you hear the word "happy." ....

d. When and where have you felt beauty in silence? ....
....

e. What is a secret? ....

[19] William Wordsworth, *Michael.*

f. How high is up? ....

g. How deep is down? ....

h. What smell do you like to smell best? ....

i. What is home? ....

j. Why is a smile? ....

k. What is sadness? ....

l. What is a friendly sound by night? ....

m. What is a friendly sound by day? ....

n. Where is treasure? ....

o. What is the best thing you have ever tasted?............................

p. What have you heard today that made you laugh? ....

q. What have you touched this week that made you wonder? ....

r. Describe in one word a little girl you know. ....

s. Describe in one word a little boy you know. ....

t. Ask a question you have wondered about. ....

    ....

u. Who are you? ....

4. In your notebook or file include a section entitled "Hyacinths." Include one sensory impression each day.

CHAPTER 3

The Art of Drama

All the world's a stage,
And all the men and women merely players:
They have their exits and their entrances;
And one man in his time plays many parts.
—William Shakespeare

Children play. Wherever we find children, we find play. Whenever their physical needs are satisfied they seek expression through play. They channel energies and emotions. They communicate with playmates in an atmosphere of mirth and fun. They pretend. They try on life. They represent many different persons, things, and events in their play. Play is as natural to a child as eating and sleeping. It is a fundamental force in growing. When a child is involved in a strong spirit of play he gives of his true self. He expresses freely. To most children play is magic. It is action. It is spirited. It is belief.

An Old Art. So it is with man. The play spirit remains. The impulse to dramatize surges through human blood. "Wherever and whenever humans have progressed beyond the mere struggle for physical existence, to gods and recreation and self-expression, there has been theatre in some sense: an inevitable place for acting, dancing, dialogue, drama, in the ordered scheme of life."[1] The play spirit is basic in the art of drama, for without it art does not come into being. If we trace back the records of mankind we find that drama had its beginnings in religious expression and gradually progressed toward aesthetic themes.

From *The Story of the Theatre* we learn that "Primitive man, wherever his home, whatever his era, employs dancing and music (the foundation of drama) in the worship of his deities. . . .

"The origin of Greek drama was in the ceremonial worship of Dionysus (Bacchus), god of wine and fertility. . . . Rising from orgiastic ritual during the sixth century B.C., it developed in the course of a hundred years into a magnificent combination of poetry, acting, and pageantry. . . . Its motives were religious, patriotic, educational, and aesthetic. Devoted in its early days to mythology, it came soon to embrace recorded history, and finally to interpret and evaluate contemporary life."[2]

In the art of theatre we find a distinction between the player and the spectator. Many peoples are stirred by the expression of a few actors, players, dancers. Drama moves its spectators with the magic of belief as they experience life in a vicarious way.

Alexander Dean believed that "Art is man's interpretation of life expressed in a way that can be universally recognized and understood. . . . The purpose of all art is to arouse the emotions . . . to stir us emotionally and intellectually in the same manner in which the artist was moved when he received his inspiration to create from nature."[3] Some of the greatest interpretations of life, the greatest masterpieces in literature have been expressed in the form of drama.

[1] Sheldon Cheney, *The Theatre*, Longmans, Green & Co., 1930.

[2] Glenn Hughes, *The Story of the Theatre*, Samuel French, Inc., 1928.

[3] Alexander Dean, *Fundamentals of Play Directing*, Rinehart & Company, Inc., 1941.

When we consider a child's many compelling drives, passions, yearnings, and desires, we recognize the need for bringing him early into a world of beauty and ideas. One of the most natural and child-like ways is through the art of drama, an organized form of the art of play. Hughes Mearns tells us that "A higher appreciation of art always follows dramatization, whether it be of literature or of history or geography."[4] Children who play at being birds enjoy the beauty of birds with a little deeper joy. "And those . . . children who danced and sang in the imaginary valley . . . all their days will feel the nearness of those mountains which they have once been themselves, and they will be the better for it."[5]

CHILDREN'S DRAMA

The concept of children's drama as an art includes both creative dramatics and children's theatre. To gain a clearer understanding of this broad art, let us first observe children's theatre.

Children's Theatre in Action. It is Saturday morning. We go to a theatre where a play is to be presented for children. We arrive early and sit in the large auditorium. Soon children begin to arrive, children of all ages. Older children bring younger ones. Some come alone. Groups come together. A few mothers bring their littlest ones. Some of the children talk and laugh together. We hear two little girls talking about *Cinderella* for this is the play they are to see.

Music begins to sound. It is Ravel's "Tavana." Children begin to listen. As the house lights dim a hush comes over the audience. Footlights brighten and the curtains open slowly. At once we see Cinderella. She is barefoot, and in ragged clothing. As she picks cinders from the fireplace ashes, she stops her work and smiles for she seems

[4] Hughes Mearns, *Creative Power,* Doubleday & Company, Inc., 1929.
[5] *Ibid.*

to be thinking a happy thought. Suddenly we hear the angry voices of the sisters and stepmother. We cringe when the sisters find the dress Cinderella has been making, and the selfish stepmother rips it to shreds.

We feel the poignant yearning in Cinderella's heart when she asks to go to the ball. We understand her sobbing when her sisters laugh, and mock her, and lock her in the kitchen with no way to fetch pumpkins from the field.

Like a beautiful dream itself, we see a fairy godmother spring lightly from the cinders. With a touch of her magic wand we see Cinderella's ragged clothing change before our eyes. Her dress becomes a beautiful gown trimmed with jewels, and she steps into the prettiest pair of glass slippers in all the world. We are excited when tiny mice and rats scamper across the kitchen floor drawing a pumpkin behind them. We marvel when a handsome golden coach and proud footmen suddenly appear outside the window.

Then, as if in answer to every child's secret wish, we soon find ourselves experiencing a castle ball, dancing the dance of all dances, a prince with a princess (Fig. 3.1). Suddenly we hear the fairy godmother's warning—12 gongs on a tower clock. We feel Cinderella's fear as she rushes away and loses her glass slipper. We feel the anxiety of the prince as he examines the glass slipper and announces he will search the kingdom over until he finds the princess.

We are moved to hearty laughter when the vain and ugly stepsisters and the stepmother try desperately to fit into the slipper. We experience a moment of high elation when Cinderella's foot fits the glass slipper, and brings from her pocket the very one to match it. We feel a surge of joy when trumpets sound announcing that the prince has found his bride. We are deeply touched when Cinderella asks if her stepmother and stepsisters may live in the castle, and we hear the prince agree. When we see Cinderella and the prince ride away in the royal carriage we feel in our hearts that they will "live happily ever after."

Fig. 3.1. "You are here. It isn't only in my dream." (*Photograph by Goodman Memorial Theatre; courtesy Goodman Memorial Theatre, Art Institute of Chicago*)

As the curtains close upon fairyland, we applaud heartily along with the children. The magic of the theatre has happened. Young spirits have been fired. *Cinderella* has kindled the beauty, truth, and laughter that is a part of every child. Faggots have burned brightly. We hear children laugh and talk among themselves. Most of them leave the theatre with their better selves shining forth. Many carry the play with them. What they received from the play they will, perhaps, never talk about. We are certain as we remember our childhoods that rich dramatic moments such as these become eternal. Once these moments have become a part of a child they remain to spring forth at unexpected moments in living.

When the auditorium is empty the curtains open. We meet the director and the cast. We learn that *Cinderella* was written by the outstanding children's playwright, Charlotte Chorpenning.[6] Players and technical crews are young adults studying theatre. The director explains that the cast has rehearsed for four weeks under his direction. Technical crews, under his supervision, have built scenery, made costumes, planned lighting, and created magical effects. We recognize that considerable expense has gone into producing this play. We learn that it is to be shared with other children's audiences that afternoon and on the following Saturday.

Children's Theatre Defined. Children's theatre is an art for children. It may be defined as a group theatre experience in which each child participates vicariously as a member of an audience (Fig. 3.2). A child sits in an audience along with many other children to enjoy a play. The play, written by a playwright, is produced by the combined efforts and imaginations of director, actors, and technical artists. In some children's theatres the actors are adults, in others they are children. In either case they memorize the dialogue of the play, and are directed by a director who synchronizes the production.

The chief goal of playwright, director, players, and technical artists is to produce good theatre for an audience (Fig. 3.3). A director's constant objective is toward a finished product, a play that will come alive for an audience of children. Mrs. Chorpenning believed that "Good theatre is a near thing to life itself to feed an in-

[6] Charlotte Chorpenning, *Cinderella*, The Children's Theatre Press, 1940.

Fig. 3.2. "What's going to happen now?" (*Photograph by James O. Sneddon, Office of Public Information, University of Washington, School of Drama Production; courtesy Seattle Junior Programs, Inc., Seattle, Washington*)

born urge for growth through experience. . . . A play can give the child an immediate experience in the final outcome of something he just saw happen. . . . When a child from four to forty watches a

FIG. 3.3. Young King Arthur. (*School of Drama Production, University of Washington; courtesy Seattle Junior Programs, Inc., Seattle, Washington*)

play, the whole orchestra of his Self is playing—senses, nerves, glands, muscles, memories, intelligence, intellect, spirit. The experience builds into him dreams, desires, urges, new memories, perceptions— conscious and unconscious—that may flower in the next hour or in the far future."[7]

Children's Drama Clarified. Children's drama is made up of formal drama which is called "children's theatre" and informal drama which is called "creative dramatics." These two forms are in harmony as they provide for enjoyment and child growth. Children's theatre provides strong impressions. Creative dramatics provides for strong expressions. A child must have both. He must take in and he

[7] Charlotte Chorpenning, *Twenty-One Years with Children's Theatre.* The Children's Theatre Press, 1954.

must give out. The cycle must be completed if a child is to grow harmoniously. Children's theatre and creative dramatics complement each other in bringing beauty and expression into a child's life.

UNDERSTANDING FUNDAMENTAL DRAMA ELEMENTS

To create is to cause something to come into being. A housewife makes a cake. A carpenter builds a house. An artist paints a picture. A musician composes music. A playwright writes a play. Every artist must know how to create with the elements of his art. He must understand the fundamental aspects that go into the making of whatever he sets out to fashion or form.

A housewife must know what basic ingredients go into the making of a cake. She must know how to mix the basic ingredients of sugar, butter, eggs, milk, flour, leavening, salt, and flavoring. She must know the amounts of each ingredient, and the ways and order in which they are mixed to result in the kind of cake she wants. In one mixing she may make an angel food cake, in another a butter cake, or a coffee cake, or maybe a pancake. In each instance, certain basic ingredients are put together, but they vary in amounts and in ways of mixing.

So it is with a play. Basic elements blended together in an aesthetic way cause the miracle of a play to come into being. If a creative dramatics leader is to help children create a play she must know what makes a play. A leader must know and understand the fundamental drama elements that go into the making of a play. She must understand play structure.

What Makes a Play? A play is a portrayal or interpretation of life. It is clearly focused, revealing an almost exaggerated, heightened insight into some issue of living. If we look below the surface of a play and analyze it, we find that every play has certain fundamental elements interwoven in its dramatic structure.

The three narrative elements which narrate or tell the story of a play are *characters, plot,* and *theme.* In a play these elements are presented through *action* and *dialogue.* What the characters do and say are motivated by the *emotional conflict* between characters involved in the story or situation. The unique way in which a play unfolds and reveals itself determines its *style* and *form.*

Characters. A play begins with characters. In most plays characters are people; in children's stories they are often animals, birds, beasts, or fish who have basic characteristics of human beings. In folk and fairy tales characters are frequently such fascinating things as talking sausages and singing bones.

In analyzing dramatic elements a leader first determines who the main or hero character is—the person to whom the story belongs. This character is the protagonist, the one who generally takes the initiative in solving the problem and thus leads the action forward. The leader gets acquainted with this character by finding out what he looks like, what he is like as a person, and what he does throughout the story. She determines why he does what he does by studying his motives, actions, reactions, and relationships with others as he becomes involved in the struggle of the situation or story problem.

The character or characters who work against the leading character are referred to as the antagonist or opposing characters. It is frequently the antagonist who causes the story problem. These characters are analyzed in a similar basic way as to appearance, personality, and purpose.

Characters who serve to assist main characters are called supporting characters. The leader lists those characters who join forces with the hero and those who oppose him. These characters are studied to determine their purpose—to see whether they are involved in the action or serve largely to create atmosphere for the play, and to determine whether they function individually or as a group.

In early experiences a leader chooses stories that are limited to protagonist and antagonist characters, rather than stories that are complex with many supporting characters.

Analyzing Characters in *Cinderella.* We discover quickly that Cinderella is the heroine or leading character. In appearance we find her to be beautiful, young, dressed in ragged clothing, and going barefoot. Later we see her in the finery of a princess. In personality Cinderella is gentle, loving, and true. Her every thought and action are motivated by love which gives us an insight into her purposes throughout the play.

Main characters who join with Cinderella are the fairy godmother, the prince, the queen, and royal servants. In analyzing the fairy godmother we wonder first about her appearance. Is she young or old, light or earthy? Since she first appears from among the cinders of the fireplace, is she perhaps firelike in her movements with radiant warmth and brightness? Or, since she has close companionship with mice, rats, and lizards is she more likely to be an earthy fairy of the woods with a crooked tree branch for her wand of magic? In personality and purpose the fairy godmother is revealed to be "as good as a good fairy."

The prince is handsome, young, and princely. One story version tells us he wears "a small golden crown and a suit of white velvet trimmed in gold." His purpose is genuine love, which motivates his actions and words.

On the list of opposing characters are the selfish stepmother and the two jealous sisters. In appearance each is different. Each goes to extremes in attempting to make herself beautiful by outward adornment which results in colorful, gaudy, clashing garments, and outlandish hair-dos. The characters may be fat or thin, for each varies in the extreme approach she uses to beautify herself. In personality each one is ugly and awkward, for her thoughts and motives are ugly, jealous, and self-centered. The chief purpose of each of these three is to prevent Cinderella from going to the ball, from seeing the prince, and from trying on the glass slipper.

Supporting characters who heighten emotion by creating atmosphere are the fairy godmother's cortege and the royal servants.

Plot. The plot is the story of the play. It tells what the characters do. It is the sequence of events that unfolds as the leading character becomes involved in a problem which he struggles to solve. A good plot follows a dramatic line in which there is a beginning, a middle, and an end. The beginning reveals the problem. The middle sets forth the complication and entanglement. The end builds to a climax wherein the problem is solved. In most instances, but not always, the hero solves his problem with the assistance of others.

To analyze plot, the leader considers the dramatic line of action. The order must be arranged in a tight relationship of basic episodes. Order varies with stories, but two basic patterns are found in cause and effect and in problem and solution. To establish the dramatic line the leader looks for the initial incident that touches off the story problem around which the entire play revolves. A good play often camouflages a story problem. Related incidents may be presented at the outset which introduce characters or setting, and only hint toward the problem rather than reveal it sharply at the outset; thus an audience gradually discovers the problem for itself.

Once the story problem has been determined, basic episodes are lined up and listed. Each episode is arranged in the order in which it complicates and intensifies the problem until a final episode is

reached. This is generally the climactic episode which solves the initial problem. Thus a plot is analyzed, except for a possible brief episode of resulting action. When a leader has clearly analyzed a plot she can formulate the problem, complication, and solution, each in a clear statement.[8]

Analyzing the Plot of *Cinderella.* In *Cinderella* the problem may be stated in the following way: Cinderella, who is prevented from going to the prince's ball by her cruel stepmother, is befriended by her fairy godmother who sends Cinderella to the castle in fine array.

The complication may be stated as follows: In rushing from the ball Cinderella loses her glass slipper, which the prince finds, whereupon he vows to search the kingdom until he finds the beautiful princess whose foot the slipper fits.

The solution may be stated in this way: Cinderella, who is prevented by her stepmother from seeing the prince, befriends a royal servant who invites her to try the slipper; thus Cinderella is revealed to the prince who claims her for his bride.

Theme. A story, like a play, has something to say. The theme is the truth of a play. It is what a play says in terms of human, universal truth. Its message is generally a fundamental truth or a few closely interwoven truths. It is for this reason that a good play and a good story carry a strong emotional impact. They awaken the truth within a child.

It is largely because of these underlying truths that our finest folk and fairy tales have stood the test of time. They are as meaningful in terms of human living today as they were when they were first told or written. They are fresh and appealing to each new generation, for beneath their delights they are concerned with the same

[8] *Ibid.*

basic truths that children experience generation after generation in good living.

The theme lies in why the characters do what they do. Their actions are motivated by their ways of living, by the truths within them or the violations of basic truths. The theme gives meaning to a play. Its power lies not so much in what children hear, but in what they *feel* as a play comes alive for them.

It is essential for a creative dramatics leader to discover what a story is saying in terms of truth. She is then in a position to guide children indirectly into feeling the impact of truth as she helps them explore a character's emotions and actions. In Hans Christian Andersen's delightful old tale, "The Emperor's New Clothes," there are no long lectures on truth. But in the comedy and fun of this charming satire we find the story to be saying, "Honesty is the best policy," or "To thine own self be true." Closely interwoven we find "Selfish pride and vanity go before a fall," "Selfishness and greed lead to self-humiliation," and "A little child shall lead them."

One of the most beautiful of all fairy stories is "Sleeping Beauty." Here we find another truth which is fundamental in living. Love is made tangible and real to children through such reaching moments as a baby's christening, an evil spell brought on by jealous rage, a deep and sorrowful sleep, and a final rejoicing in great happiness. Children are always touched by the beauty of this story. They are not perhaps aware of the specific truth that gives it great magnitude, but they do feel the power of love. If we examine the story to find its essential truth we discover that it says, "Evil and jealousy may put beauty to sleep, but love will reawaken it."

Analyzing the Theme of *Cinderella.* Again looking at *Cinderella,* we marvel at the array of special wonders that are gathered together in a childlike way to reveal a basic truth in living. In this once-upon-a-time experience we find a truth so basic in living that we perhaps overlook it until we begin to ponder. What *Cinderella* says is, simply, "Do unto others as ye would that they would do unto you." Or, to state this truth in different ways we may say, "The meek shall inherit the earth," "Beauty is what beauty does," "The truth will out," and "Love conquereth all."

Action. "Drama" comes from the Greek word meaning "to act or to do." Above all, drama is action. The action shows the way a plot unfolds, the way a story happens. A good leader thinks in terms of action because children think in action. A good play unfolds in episodes that are vivid and clear in action, emotion, and rhythm.

"Don't tell it, show it," are familiar words from Charlotte Chorpenning.[9] Action may be shown in pantomime, in rhythmic movement, or in incidents charged with emotion. In a children's play there should be economy in the number of incidents required to reveal a story. A leader analyzes action in relationship to characters and plot. Basic scenes which are essential to establishing problem, complication, and solution are listed. Rhythmic movement and pantomime are analyzed within each scene.

Analyzing Action in *Cinderella*. In *Cinderella* three basic scenes are required to establish the problem. These include: (1) Preparation for Ball, (2) Departure for Ball, and (2) Fairy-Godmother Scene.

Rhythmic movement and pantomime in Scene One include dressing, preening, parading in front of mirror. In Scene Two rhythmic action includes arrival of coachman, departure for ball, and sweeping cinders. Scene Three includes the magic entrance of the fairy godmother, transformation of Cinderella's clothing, the rhythmic transformation of mice, rats and lizards, and Cinderella's dancing for joy as she departs for the ball.

[9] *Ibid.*

Three basic scenes which heighten the complication are: (1) Ball Scene, (2) Cinderella's Arrival, and (3) Cinderella's Departure.

Rhythmic action in Scene One at the ball includes the dancing of the guests. The chief emphasis is on the exaggerated dancing of the stepmother and stepsisters in an effort to impress the prince. In Scene Two, with Cinderella's arrival there is noticeable rhythmic movement in bowing, curtseying, and in the dancing of Cinderella and the prince. In Scene Three, with Cinderella's hasty departure there is rhythmic movement in the ticking of the tower clock, swift movement of Cinderella, hurrying and rushing of guests, and resulting confusion until the prince finds the slipper.

Scenes required to work out a solution to the story include: (1) Slipper-Trying Scene and (2) Prince Finds the Princess.

Rhythmic movement and pantomime center around the exaggerated actions of the stepsisters as they make an effort to fit the slipper. Strong rhythmic movement climaxes the play when Cinderella tries on the slipper and dances joyously when the prince claims her for his princess.

Dialogue. Dialogue is conversation between two or more persons, the talking that takes place between characters. Action, as we have seen, is what characters do. Dialogue is what they say as they become involved in the emotion of a situation. In a play dialogue is set forth in speeches, but in a story there may be little if any dialogue woven into the narration.

A leader first determines whether a story is primarily a dialogue or an action story. Dialogue stories may be thought of as those in which dialogue not only advances the play but adds much to the charm and individuality of the characters. Such stories as *Winnie-the-Pooh, The Wind in the Willows,* and *Alice in Wonderland* are heightened by unusual dialogue of the characters. When an experi-

enced group is ready for the challenge of creating extensive dialogue a leader may choose a dialogue story; however, most children's groups prefer stories where action is strong with some dialogue interwoven.

In analyzing dialogue, a leader determines the function of dialogue in the story. Is it essential to the unfolding of the problem? That is, does the development of the plot hinge on what characters say? Is the theme developed by dialogue? In what ways is the atmosphere of a play strengthened by dialogue?

After a leader has analyzed the place of dialogue in a story, she studies dialogue in relationship to characters. She discovers dialogue which is true-to-life and natural for characters in a particular situation. She then searches for dialogue opportunities that will offer creative challenge in voice cadence, rhythm, chanting, vocabulary, and content.

Analyzing Dialogue in *Cinderella*. Dialogue true to life is spoken by Cinderella, for like many fine human beings she is "good and pious and guided from heaven." Equally as true to life in feelings and words are the stepmother and stepsisters, whom the Grimm brothers described as being "fair of face but vile and black of heart."

Announcements by royal servants offer rich opportunities for dialogue strong in rhythm, chanting, and voice cadence. Outstanding opportunities for creative dialogue are found in the conversation of the fairy godmother and the fairy creatures. How might a fairy godmother talk? What words might a fairy use which are different from those used by a human being? Might a fairy talk in some sort of magic way? How might a little mouse feel and talk when he suddenly becomes a handsome white steed? How might a footman speak who had recently been a white rat?

Emotional Conflict. Drama is caused by conflict. Conflict arouses emotions. Feeling is a vital quality in motivating the action of the characters. The emotional conflict in most children's plays is between two sets of characters who oppose each other in a specific issue or problem. Characters who emphasize worthy values in living generally triumph over those motivated by evil intent, character weakness, or dishonorable gains.

In many children's stories the conflict develops quickly. This is essential in stories which are to be created into plays. Such is the case in "The Three Billy Goats Gruff," where the selfish troll prevents the hungry goats from getting food. The conflict develops immediately into an emotional clash which rises to a battle to resolve the basic issue. A similar conflict occurs in "Little Black Sambo." Here the happy little jungle boy immediately encounters a clash with greedy tigers who want to eat him up. Rather than running away, which would mean certain death, this young hero meets his conflict by being brave and facing his foes. He remains calm as he figures out how to save himself from four successive encounters with the tigers. This is high drama in emotional suspense for little children. "Sambo outwits the tigers over and over. He is happy and completely triumphant, the envy of all young hero worshipers."[10]

In the story of "King Midas" the emotional conflict lies within the character of the king. Midas is greedy in his desire for gold and fails to recognize and appreciate his many worthy values. Throughout the play he experiences two forces in steady opposition. Gradually through much suffering he is brought to a right relationship in his attitudes of living.

In analyzing emotional conflict a leader looks for the two basic forces that oppose each other within the play. She looks for the strong emotional feelings that each main character experiences.

[10] May Hill Arbuthnot, *Children and Books,* Scott, Foresman and Company, 1947.

Emotional reactions of main characters in the basic scenes are then analyzed.

Analyzing Emotional Conflict in *Cinderella.* In this play Cinderella and those who assist her symbolize the good, whereas the stepmother and stepsisters symbolize evil. The conflict lies in the resulting actions which are motivated by love on one hand and by hate on the other. It is the blending of actions, reactions, and interaction which arouses feelings and causes emotional suspense as one experiences the play.

Form. Form is the way a play evolves and reveals itself. It is the way a play is styled—the way it is structured to reach an audience. Every play has its own unique form, though it may be recognized as a basic type of drama. Tragedy and comedy are the oldest and most distinctive forms of drama. "Another important classification of the drama is based on the author's style of writing, his method of depicting characters, and the way he brings out his theme. In realistic drama, life is pictured as it actually is—often ugly, sordid, and unhappy, although not necessarily so. . . . In romantic drama, life is shown as we should like it to be. The language is beautiful, frequently poetic; the characters are usually of the nobility or other high social positions; and the setting is in an ideal spot, faraway in time or space, where dreams can come true."[11] There are many variations of basic drama forms including melodrama, farce, satire, folkplay, allegory, fantasy, and sentimental comedy.

Children's plays follow closely the basic forms of children's literature. These include hero and historical tales, realistic stories, fairy and fanciful tales, humorous stories, informational stories, and animal tales.

[11] Katharine Anne Ommanney and Pierce C. Ommanney, *The Stage and the School,* McGraw-Hill Book Company, Inc., 2d. rev. ed., 1950.

In analyzing the form of a play or story a leader first determines its basic form and then analyzes further to discover intangible qualities that give distinctive style to its basic form. These qualities may be recognized in underlying rhythms, moods, and atmosphere. In the hero tale of "William Tell," a forceful, steady rhythm rises in tempo to a stirring climax. This indicates to a leader that the story fairly marches with purpose, and should be shared with strength, force, and seriousness (Fig. 3.4). On the other hand there is in "Pi-

FIG. 3.4. *William Tell.* (*Photograph by Dansk Foto Reportage; courtesy Dansk Skolescene, Copenhagen, Denmark*)

nocchio" a lively, staccato rhythm. The story hurries and scurries in a merry, puppetlike pleasantness from one unexpected skirmish into another. A leader analyzes the unique form of a story so she may be true to its intent when she shares it with children.

Analyzing Form in *Cinderella*. *Cinderella* is basically a fairy story. It is romantic in nature, for it pictures life as children would like it to be. The story reveals itself in an almost dreamlike atmosphere in which evil clashes with goodness and justice triumphs and is rewarded. The story moves with distinctive romantic rhythm. It unfolds in irregular patterns of brightness and shadow, and has overtones of color, sparkle, and delight interwoven with ugliness, earthiness, and despair.

UNDERSTANDING FURTHER DRAMATIC TERMS

Rhythmic Movement and Pantomime. Rhythm and movement are basic in the art of drama. Rhythmic movement is an inclusive term which refers to spatial movement, body movement, and pantomime. Spatial movement refers to rhythmic action which a child uses when he moves through space (Fig. 3.5). Spatial movements basic to a child are walking, running, hopping, jumping, and leap-

FIG. 3.5. "Slow down! I see Madrid!" (*School of Drama, University of Washington*)

ing (Fig. 3.6). "Body movements are swinging, bending, stretching, pushing, pulling, twisting, striking, dodging, shaking, and bouncing"[12] (Fig. 3.7).

"Pantomime" is a term used interchangeably with rhythmic movement meaning to communicate thought and feeling entirely with action. Pantomime refers to both body and spatial movements. Or it may include finer rhythmic movements expressed with arms and fingers (Fig. 3.8).

Dramatic Play. Dramatic play is a child's natural way of playing, of dramatizing and pretending. For instance little children frequently play at pretending to cook, to iron, have a tea party, care for a baby, sell groceries in a store, fly an airplane, or be an airplane. Older children often enjoy pretending to be cowboys, Indians, horses, queens, beauty operators, pirates, or to dramatize such exciting events as a circus, rodeo, dance recital, horse race, boat race, or a battle of one kind or another. Dramatic play is a child's way of entering into experiences that interest him.

"Dramatic play" is a term which refers to creative playing centering around an idea, a situation, or a person, place, or thing. It generally utilizes the dramatic elements of characterization, action, and dialogue. It seldom has plot. It unfolds spontaneously. It is fragmentary and fun.

DEVELOPMENT OF CREATIVE DRAMATICS

Professor Glenn Hughes, in reflecting upon the development of creative dramatics, has said, "Although it is entirely possible that several thousand years ago a cave-mama employed the principles of creative dramatics in the rearing of her cave-child, it appears to be

[12] Gladys Andrews, *Creative Rhythmic Movement for Children,* Prentice-Hall, Inc., 1954.

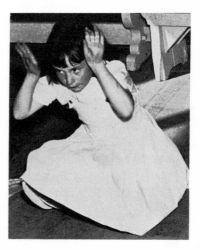

FIG. 3.6. "Whoa, Pegasus!" (*School of Drama, University of Washington*)

FIG. 3.7. "Come Bunny-lunny, we must tell the king." (*School of Drama, University of Washington*)

FIG. 3.8. "Lif-Laf-Luf! Wake up, broom! Fetch firewood!" (*School of Drama, University of Washington*)

certain that the first consciously organized application of these principles was carried out only a few years ago by Winifred Ward at
Northwestern University. It is from Miss Ward's pioneering that
creative dramatics has come to be an accepted technique."[13]

In the United States. Early in the twentieth century a renaissance in childhood education brought about a new philosophy of
teaching. New principles and procedures emphasized child growth
and development in relationship to learning experiences. Years earlier the poet, William Wordsworth, had voiced the essence of this
philosophy when he said, "The child is father of the man."

During this educational trend it was natural that Winifred Ward,
with her understanding of children and drama, would perceive the
art of creative dramatics for children. In 1924 she shared her idea
with Ralph Dennis, Dean of the School of Speech at Northwestern
University. Together they convinced the school authorities of the
public schools of Evanston, Illinois, of the worthiness of this art for
children and youth. Miss Ward was given an opportunity to experiment. She put her beliefs into practice with children in the Evanston
Public Schools and gradually developed a center for training children's drama leaders at Northwestern University. The significance
of this art as well as its development under Miss Ward's leadership
must be acknowledged by the rapid growth of creative dramatics
programs throughout the country during the past quarter century.
An intensive study of creative dramatics in the United States reveals
that no college or university was "offering curricular work in this
field prior to 1932 with the exception of Miss Ward's own course at
Northwestern University."[14] The Northwestern program remains

[13] Ruth Lease and Geraldine Brain Siks, *Creative Dramatics in Home, School, and
Community*, Harper & Brothers, 1952.
[14] James E. Popovich, "A Study of Significant Contributions to the Development

outstanding in the training it offers for creative dramatics leaders today. It emphasizes particularly the correlation of this art in elementary and junior high school curriculums.

A recent survey indicates that courses in children's drama are now offered at more than 200 colleges and universities throughout the country.[15] It is estimated that more than 4000 future leaders and elementary teachers are being trained in creative dramatics each year. In addition to the program at Northwestern, other institutions which offer opportunities for student teaching and observation of children's classes in their courses include the following: Universities of Washington, Pennsylvania, Minnesota, Texas, Denver, and California at Los Angeles; State Universities of Michigan, Ohio (Kent), and Illinois State Normal School; and Colleges of San Francisco State, San Jose State, Birmingham Southern, Adelphi, and Skidmore.

University of Washington Program. Among the many creative dramatics centers throughout the country one of the most comprehensive is the program at the University of Washington.[16] This program, which developed during the past decade, owes its beginning to the pioneering spirit of Ruth Lease. As a Junior League volunteer Mrs. Lease shared creative dramatics with many boys and girls living in housing project areas in Seattle during the past war. Because of the vital way in which this art reached children Mrs. Lease foresaw the need for training leaders. She presented her idea to Glenn Hughes, executive director of the School of Drama. During the fall

---

of Creative Dramatics in American Education," Northwestern University Library, unpublished thesis, August, 1955.

[15] Children's Theatre Conference, "A Directory of American Colleges and Universities Offering Training in Children's Theatre and Creative Dramatics," College Curriculum Survey Committee, American Educational Theatre Association, Agnes Haaga, Chairman, August, 1957 (mimeographed).

[16] School of Drama, University of Washington, Seattle, Washington.

quarter of 1947 the School of Drama added a course in creative dramatics to its curriculum. Through the coöperative efforts of the Seattle Junior League, the Drama School and the Division of Adult Education and Extension Services of the University, Agnes Haaga was appointed Director of the Creative Dramatics Department at the University.

Under the inspired and dynamic guidance of Miss Haaga the creative dramatics department grew. The University assumed complete responsibility for this program during the following year, though community endorsement and coöperation contributed strongly to its significant development. The College of Education recognized the values of this art and in 1950 made a course in creative dramatics mandatory for an elementary school certificate. The General Studies Department set up a program whereby a student could earn a B.A. degree in the area of creative dramatics. In 1955 a basic academic field for elementary education majors was established. The Schools of Social Work, Recreational Leadership, Nursery School, and Nursing included courses in creative dramatics in their curricula.

An outstanding feature of this training program is centered on active participation. Students experience and observe creative dramatics for two quarters before they are guided into teaching this art to children.

In the World. While creative dramatics was finding its way to children in the United States, similar programs were springing up in other countries throughout the world. In an international survey made by the International Theatre Institute of UNESCO, information was collected from 27 countries of the world.[17] Eighteen of these

[17] Geraldine B. Siks, "Theatre for Youth: An International Report," *Educational Theatre Journal*, December, 1955.

countries indicated either experimental or extensive emphasis on creative dramatics programs for children.

Peter Slade of Great Britain has done outstanding developmental work in the field of Child Drama in connection with the British Educational Drama Association (Fig. 3.9). His work at the Birmingham Drama Centre has been recognized internationally for its significance as an Art Form for children (Fig. 3.10).

Marie Dienesch and Leon Chancerel have pioneered creative dramatics in France, while other leaders have been at work in Germany, Austria, Canada, Australia, and South Africa. Thus we have leaders from all corners of the earth, unaware of each other, arriving at basic beliefs and practices in sharing this art with children.

John Allen of the British Centre, in an introduction to the international report, voiced a universal attitude toward creative dramatics:

The fact of the matter is that we are dealing with a new subject of study. Is it a new art? a new aspect of art? a new educational technique? Or a bit of all these? We do not know. . . . But it is clear that in many countries of the world the educational drama . . . represents, or shall we say, is the outcome of, an altogether new approach both to education and dramatic art. We are engaged in fact in applying the work of Froebel, Dewey, and Pestalozzi to the drama, and that of Stanislavsky, Copeau, and Granville-Barker to education. In many countries theatre for young people is edging into the educational system, trying to nuzzle out a place for itself in the school curriculum . . . and demanding of the conscience of society that economic barriers not be allowed to stand in the way of insistent education and artistic necessities.

What is wanted is a wider recognition that theatre for young people is here to stay; and that authorities throughout the world must give fuller opportunity to its study.[18]

[18] *Ibid.*

FIG. 3.9. All the dandelions get up and dance. (*Photograph by Victor Thompson; courtesy of Peter Slade; Children's Theatre, Rea St., Birmingham, England*)

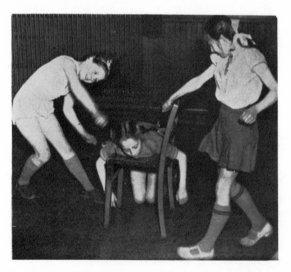

FIG. 3.10. "We chop off your head for disobeying the king!" (*Photograph by Victor Thompson; courtesy of Peter Slade; Drama Centre, Rea St., Birmingham, England*)

Questions and Activities

1. Dramatic activities in schools have been labeled by some as a "frill." Refute this charge in a one-page open letter to parents by explaining the development of the art of drama through the ages.

2. Complete the following statements to indicate your understanding of children's drama:

    a. Creative dramatics is an art for children in which they experience drama by ....

    b. Children's theatre is an art for children in which they experience drama by ....

    c. You have heard the comment, "What a dramatic moment!" Drama, in essence, is caused by ....

    d. "Rhythmic movement" is a dramatic term which means ....

    e. "Pantomine" is a dramatic term which means ....

    f. "Theme" as used in drama means ....

    g. The basic difference between dramatic play and playing a story lies in the ....

    h. Winifred Ward is credited with being the person who ....

    i. A striking aspect of the University of Washington creative dramatics' program lies in ....

    j. Creative dramatics is being shared with children in as many as ....countries throughout the world.

3. Choose one of your favorite children's stories which is recommended for creative dramatics. Analyze the basic drama elements inherent in the story.

4. Examine a catalogue of children's plays. List three plays that have been adapted from among children's favorite stories, and cite the chief conflict in each.

5. Be prepared to contribute to class discussions motivated by each of the following questions:
    a. Why is it essential for a creative dramatics leader to know and understand a story theme or themes before sharing the story with children?
    b. Why is it necessary for a leader to analyze the plot of a story to determine the cause and effect or the problem, complication, and solution?
    c. Even though a story may be strong dramatically, why is it equally important that it hold strong appeal for a group of children?
    d. Why is it important that children experience children's theatre and creative dramatics in childhood?
6. Record in your personal file or notebook the names of three children's plays, including the playwrights and publishers, and the titles of three stories that would make outstanding children's theatre plays.

Review Questions for Chapters 1, 2, 3

Dramatize a creative situation in which the class visits an educational television station. When the station director learns that you are studying creative dramatics he invites you to appear on a guest program. After the master of ceremonies opens the program and introduces you as a group, the following interview continues for 30 minutes. Class members volunteer to answer or to add additional information to an answer which needs further explanation. (M.C. indicates master of ceremonies. A. invites an answer.)

M.C.: Just the other day my 5-year-old daughter came home from kindergarten quite excited about creative dramatics. When my wife attended a P.T.A. meeting she heard the term "creative dramatics" used often. Frankly, neither of us knows what it means. Could you tell me and our viewers just *what is creative dramatics?*

A.:

M.C.: This sounds like fun! Is this the purpose of creative dramatics, or why does this art appeal to children?

A.:

M.C.: We all agree that children like to play, but what specific values does this art have in a school program? in a community program?

A.:

M.C.: I think we're beginning to get the idea. Tell us, just when, where, and by whom was creative dramatics started in this country?

A.:

M.C.: If you wanted to do further study in this art where might you go to make an intensive study of creative dramatics?

A.:

M.C.: Is this art enjoyed by children in other countries? Where?

A.:

M.C.: Most of our viewers are familiar with children's theatre plays. In what ways are these two forms of children's drama alike or different?

A.:

M.C.: Thank you for sharing new insights into this old art of playing.

CHAPTER 4

A Creative Leader

A great man is he who has not lost the heart of a child.—Mencius

Dear Miss Dickie,

Just think, this Saturday is the last time we will meet. You have taken us to such wonderful places in creative dramatics. I decided to take you to Fairy Land so you will have a happy vacation.

Are you ready? Fine, then let's start. First shut your eyes, then run ten steps and jump up in the air. See you're beginning to float up, up, up. Look! there's the rainbow. To get the rest of the way to Fairy Land we must walk over the rainbow.

Now we are walking on yellow dandelions. See how they glitter. And now we are walking through red sunset. Now we are on blue clouds and then on violets. We walk on green, green grass and then through ripe orange trees. Isn't the rainbow beautiful?

We are at the edge. Now we jump off. There! We are floating down to Fairy Land.

Goodbye. I love you.

Ruthie[1]

Miss Dickie was a creative dramatics leader who guided Ruth and other 7- and 8-year-olds into creative wonderlands. She be-

---

[1] Printed from manuscript by permission of the 8-year-old author, Ruth Carol

lieved that every Saturday was special—that each new creative experience was an adventure. With each new Saturday there came a new kind of splendor, sometimes great, sometimes less great. Much depended on the children, the weather, the day, the month, the season, and on Miss Dickie. Together the children and Miss Dickie experienced many rare moments such as the excitement of a circus, the surprise of an elf's birthday, the humor of a cat's tea party, the power of a giants' convention, and the beauty of a fairy queen's coronation. During these days Miss Dickie stirred imaginations, awakened beauty, and found ways of encouraging Ruth and every child to join in the fun of wondering and venturing into regions of delight.

Next to children, a leader is the most important factor in the success of a creative dramatics experience. With some leaders children forge ahead with spirit and splendor. With others they stand still and flounder. What is it that makes a good creative leader?

PHILOSOPHY OF CREATIVE TEACHING

The success of creative leadership rests squarely with the leader. Johann Goethe believed that "A teacher who can arouse a feeling for one single good action, for one single good poem, accomplishes more than he who fills our memory with rows on rows of natural objects, classified with name and form."

What is the most important quality of a good creative leader? Is it a matter of hard work, personality, several years of college training, a strong background in drama, or what? Though each of these is important, they do not fully answer our question. Rather we find ourselves asking, what makes a good doctor, a good minister, a good nurse, a good farmer, a good actor, a good carpenter, a good parent?

In scanning this panorama of people we see two farmers living side by side, one prospering while the other fails to prosper. We see two nurses enter hospital rooms; in the same amount of time one does all that is required for a patient while the other goes beyond and satisfies not only physical needs but lifts a patient's spirit as well. We see an actor in a theatre do a fair interpretation of a play, whereas another actor creating the same play moves an audience to glorious moments of enchantment.

What is it that causes an individual to be outstanding in whatever calling he follows? It would seem that those who succeed in their chosen fields have a basic philosophy in common. They have a friendly attitude toward humanity, and a creative attitude of enjoyment for their work. To return to our question, we find that every good creative dramatics leader has a genuine love for children and a deep belief and enjoyment in drama.

A person who wants to become a creative dramatics leader should examine her philosophy by answering such questions as these: Why do I want to become a leader? How do I honestly feel toward children, not just a few children, but all children? What, specifically, do I like about children? Why do I want to be with thirty or more boys and girls day after day, year in and year out? What is my earliest memory of drama? Why does drama hold a strong appeal for me? Why do I want children to experience drama in their growing-up days?

Attitude Toward Children. Socrates recognized, "One can teach only whom he loves." An adult who has a genuine love for children enjoys being with them. She cares about every child. She believes in and enjoys each one. She strives to understand every child who comes her way so she may guide him and cause him to reach for his true self. A leader's attitude toward children is fused in a mixture of love, adventure, discovery, beauty.

A good leader makes a steady effort to understand basic laws of human nature and to apply them. As far as basic principles in human nature are concerned all people are the same, yet each individual, each child, is different. A leader strives to recognize each child's individuality. She makes an effort to determine specific needs and interests of every child, particularly those who seem not to be so easily understood. This calls for hard work—patience, persistence, faith, awareness, love, and laughter. It makes digging for each child's best a pleasure, since she knows the results are moments of magic and human gold. A creative leader who has a warm friendly attitude toward children soon discovers with Grimm's little dwarf that "something human is dearer than the wealth of all the world."

It is a rare experience for adults to go adventuring with children. Teachers, youth leaders, and parents who shepherd a child or many children through nine months or many months and years of growing and living are fortunate when they realize the greatness of this experience. Children are comparatively new to the world in which they live. To an adult who is enthusiastic and ready to listen, children reveal ideas and beliefs that are refreshing and exciting.

The most gratifying part of creative guidance lies within a child. "If you expect children to come forth with beautiful and powerful thoughts and feelings, they will," says an outstanding theatre director who has recently become excited about sharing creative dramatics with children. A leader who believes in children realizes that every child has a rich reserve of creative power. A leader strives to spark a child's high voltage and harness it to a creative group experience that surges with feeling and belief. A leader never knows just what a child is waiting to express—a beautiful thought, something sad, ugly, exciting, powerful, mean, yearning—but waiting none the less. Children have deep depths and high heights, and wide worlds to

share whenever there is someone who cares enough to go adventuring with them.

Attitude Toward Drama. A good leader knows and enjoys drama from having experienced it. She seeks new and continuous experiences in this art. She becomes informed on the history and development of drama and theatre throughout the centuries. She becomes acquainted with the world's greatest plays, dramatists, playwrights. A leader acquires an attitude toward drama from many different experiences in this art. Until she experiences the beauty, magnificence, and power of drama she cannot hope to have an attitude that motivates her into finding ways to experience and share it. Attitudes are caught and gained from experiences.

A leader who enjoys drama is enthusiastic about sharing creative dramatics with children. She acts on her beliefs. Her creative attitude toward drama spurs her on with desire and determination to share drama with children. "We speak of a scientific attitude toward life, or of a philosophical attitude, or of a religious attitude. But of all conceivable attitudes the theatrical attitude is the most truly creative. . . . We are still lost in wonder before this magical art of the theatre. It is really a kind of magic, this art. We call it glamour or poetry or romance, but that doesn't explain it. In some mysterious way these old, simple, ancestral moods still survive in us, and an actor can make them live again for a while. We become children once more. We believe."[2]

Frequent comments from classroom teachers reveal the underlying need for leaders to know and understand the art of drama. The two following comments are typical:

"Creative dramatics is a luxury. I can't afford time for it in second grade where children need to learn so many skills."

[2] Robert Edmond Jones, *The Dramatic Imagination*, Theatre Arts Books, 1941.

"It's a pretty tough world children are growing up in and the question in my mind is whether we should concentrate on arming them with as much realism and subject matter as possible or soften it up for them with a goodly portion of sensitive, sweet, creative ideas in dramatic situations. I don't think children should escape realism when they are young. Why build up their egos and have them shattered later? And shattered they will be unless they know exactly who they are and what they are."

These teachers have admirable attitudes toward teaching basic skills to children. But neither understands the place or the need for creative arts in contributing to a child's well-rounded growth and personality development. Each comment points up a lack of the philosophy of drama and creative dramatics, a mistaken attitude, erroneous beliefs. Unless a teacher understands drama she cannot understand that creative dramatics integrates with living and learning; it is not brought in as something separate and apart. Art experiences always integrate and enrich life. All becomes purposeless if art becomes a pursuit for its own sake.

Until a teacher understands drama she may believe it to be "sweet," instead of realizing that drama looks sharply at life, and evaluates and interprets it. The experiences of creative dramatics are based on the very stuff of life with both its beauties and its conflicts. Creative dramatics leads children toward an understanding of life which in a large sense squares with reality.

Creative dramatics will find its way to children only when adults care enough about this art to find ways of bringing it to them. Teachers, youth leaders, and parents who believe in drama must be dedicated and determined. They must be as sincere in seeing that children experience creative dramatics as are teachers who believe in the beauty of music, dancing, and painting and share these arts with children.

BASIC QUALITIES IN CREATIVE LEADERSHIP

A good creative leader is forever becoming. She strives steadily to strengthen qualities and skills that contribute to the inspiration and effectiveness of her teaching. Leaders who consistently guide children into satisfying creative experiences are characterized by many fine qualities, three of which stand out most strongly—imagination, spirit, and greatness.

Imagination. Mary Poppins is magic.[3] She is so possessed with imagination that she causes suitcases, sidewalks, stars, and the east wind to take on new wonder for children. With Mary Poppins even the taking of medicine becomes strangely special, for whenever she pours a spoonful of medicine she pours a spoonful of suggestion as well. Mary Poppins has miraculous power not over medicine but over people. She always finds a way of accomplishing something significant with the littlest bit of magic.

A creative leader always uses imagination. *She finds an imaginative way to awaken the magic in others.* This is a secret of creative teaching and living. It lies within the teacher whether she is teaching at home, at school, or with children in a community program. Imagination is the key to indirection. It causes an adult to *suggest* with a childlike playfulness of surprise and delight, to nudge instead of nag.

An imaginative leader *searches with a creative attitude of mind until she finds an imaginative way to reach children.* She is never content to take ideas from others. She recognizes the necessity of utilizing her own unique individuality and imagination. She realizes

[3] P. L. Travers, *Mary Poppins,* Reynal & Hitchcock, Inc., 1934.

that no two leaders in the world are exactly alike and that she is most dynamic and effective when she is distinctively herself. An imaginative leader pursues until she finds an idea that she becomes excited about. She is not content with an idea that is usual, complex, or cumbersome. She radiates and fairly dances with delight when she thinks of something as simple as an apple blossom branch for a fairy wand to awaken wishes within children.

A leader with imagination always *recognizes beauty in simplicity*. A teacher who wanted to get her children into a mood to create from Rose Fyleman's fairy poetry went to a great amount of time and expense to purchase and costume six ceramic fairies. Another teacher in the same school planned to share fairy poetry with her children on the same day that the ceramic fairies arrived. The second teacher brought an imaginary "scarf of beautiful sunshine." She waved it gracefully as she shared it with the children. In a secretive way she told how she had discovered it on her window sill along with a "fairy message." This teacher and her children were soon off in a make-believe forest gathering "raspberry caps," "shiny leaf slippers," "shell necklaces," and "cobweb capes" to wear to fairyland. The children in the other room spent the same half hour without getting beyond examining ceramic fairies.

An imaginative leader is *aware and resourceful*. A leader with awareness senses beauty and significance in a child's expression. She visualizes and recognizes a way to use a child's idea so it leads a group into moments of high enchantment. A leader who is aware of the power of emotion guides children to create with feeling rather than to imitate with exactness, for she possesses a capacity to see, to feel, to believe. "To know is nothing at all," said Anatole France. "To imagine is everything."

A resourceful leader seeks the best possible place within a building for a group of children to meet. Or she finds a way to make the best possible use of limited space. She searches for stories and ideas that are "just right" for a specific group of children instead of using an experience that another leader has found to be right for her group. An imaginative leader is resourceful in finding creative ways to reach individual children and in meeting unexpected and unusual situations which frequently present themselves in creative arts experiences. An unimaginative leader is too frequently defeated, disturbed, and given to complaining. "It is always so much easier to be told exactly how to do a thing than to put one's own intelligence to work to solve each individual problem as it arises!"[4]

A good leader strengthens her imagination by using it. Jonathan Swift explains that "Vision is the art of seeing things visible." A leader forms a habit of visualizing ideas, for when an image is clear it can be seen and described. A class of college students, studying to become creative leaders, was shown a sheet of yellow paper. They were asked, "Of what does this color remind you?" One student wrote, "not a thing." Another wrote, "a piece of paper." Others answered, "lemonade," "butter on pancakes," "a little girl's pinafore," "October sunshine on Sunday afternoon," "a car I'd like to own," "a sweater I almost bought on the avenue," "lemon pie," and "mustard."

Three months later, after many creative experiences, these students were asked: "What have you seen today that caused you to look again because of its beauty?"

The not-a-thing student wrote: "Two mallard ducks were enjoying their morning meditation in the arboretum when they were suddenly interrupted by a convention of seagulls."

The piece-of-paper student wrote, "humility."

---

[4] Charlotte Lee. *Oral Interpretation*, Houghton Mifflin Company, 1952.

Spirit. *It is a leader's spirit that gives current, force, and a feeling of sailing forward to a creative dramatics experience.* Spirit is enthusiasm. Enthusiasm is passion. Passion is power. Enthusiasm stems from a Greek word meaning to be inspired or possessed with passion. It implies that a belief is put into action with strong force, confidence, and emotion. "It's the spirit that counts!" This old adage was never more applicable than it is in the teaching of creative dramatics. Whenever spirit is missing, an experience fails to become creative. It seems to drift, flounder in circles, and become stranded at low ebb. A leader's spirit may be characterized by physical vitality, but even more by emotional vitality, radiance, aliveness, intensity, and faith. Spirit is as intangible as the sunshine of sunshine.

When a leader is enthusiastic enough to fire children's creative spirits, something significant always happens. Vibrations of great human worth flow from vital individuals. "It takes real vitality to fire children's enthusiasm to the place where they become as excited at discovering America as Columbus was, and where they fight the Battle of Bunker Hill with a patriotic spirit second only to that of the British and the Americans in the days of the Revolution."[5] When a leader is prepared, and puts wholehearted enthusiasm into stimulating and guiding children she gets true enthusiasm and expression. When a leader is halfhearted as she approaches a creative experience, she either gets a halfhearted response or she is unable to capture and channel child power. A leader cannot expect the magic of creativity and group dynamics to happen if she holds back because she is emotionally insecure, lacks confidence or energy, or is unprepared.

A good leader cultivates a genuine play spirit. To do this she pre-

---

[5] Ruth Lease and Geraldine Brain Siks, *Creative Dramatics in Home, School, and Community*, Harper & Brothers, 1952.

pares material well in advance. She lives with her plan of procedure until she looks forward to sharing an experience with children. She acquires good health habits. She eats and sleeps properly and keeps herself physically and emotionally fit so she has energy and enthusiasm for firing children into expression.

A leader's charm, confidence, and power come in her spirited way of arousing children, and getting them to plunge into the fun of a creative experience. A creative teacher blooms with a wide-awake aliveness. She allows her creative spirit to surge with a steady pulsing rhythm which awakens ideas and keeps her alert for ideas forthcoming from children. She uses great care in feeding children only enough ideas to spark their creative powers. She is careful never to impose her ideas but to capture children's ideas so an experience becomes their true creation. It is a leader's vitality and spirit that make emotional contact with children's emotions. A leader with spirit arouses, energizes, and incites children into creative expression which causes the space of a room to be filled with power, feeling, animation, and aliveness. With each new experience in guiding children a leader realizes with Ralph Waldo Emerson that "Nothing great was ever achieved without enthusiasm."

Greatness. *A good creative leader is characterized by intangible qualities of greatness.* Aside from "being born great, or having greatness thrust upon you," how does a leader achieve greatness? A leader's greatness lies in the kind of person she is and strives to become. Greatness lies in the total of little everyday things. It's what a leader says and does, what she thinks and feels, how she acts and looks, and what she believes in. A good leader is aware of the fundamental truth, "You teach what you are." She honors living day in and day out, for she realizes she is essentially the same person whether she is in the classroom or away from it. Her way of living is reflected

and revealed in her appearance, language, attitudes, appreciations, sense of values, integrity, dignity, and humor.

A leader teaches children by example. Her influence on children is strong. She "gets what she gives" for "like attracts like." This fundamental truth indirectly guides a leader to give her best and keep her standards high. If a leader has a fresh clean, attractive appearance, and wears little touches of beauty and color, she soon finds children coming to class looking fresh and clean. She finds boys combing their hair and taking an interest in the way they look. It is not uncommon to find girls wearing flowers and bright colors just like those the teacher wears.

If a leader has power and conviction in her voice and speaks with beautiful diction, choosing words that honor language, she finds children responding to the beauty of communication. If a leader is kind, happy, hardworking, cheerful, honest, courteous, fair, and uses good taste and judgment, she finds her children reaching for these horizons. If, on the other hand, she is careless in appearance and speech, harsh in manner, and negative in attitude, her children tend toward careless and indifferent habits and attitudes.

Winifred Ward has discovered that children "are constantly forming attitudes—attitudes toward the teacher, toward one another, toward the subject, toward school, and toward many other things. And what people *feel* about anything is more important than what they *think* about it. For attitudes are the moving force of life."[6] A leader who realizes the magnitude of her influence on children evaluates herself honestly with the beginning of each new season— winter, summer, spring, and fall.

A leader achieves greatness with children when she enters into

[6] Winifred Ward, *Playmaking with Children,* Appleton-Century-Crofts, Inc., 2d ed., 1957.

their fun with genuine enjoyment and pleasure. A leader with a sense of fun has a childlike approach to their experiences. She has a spirit of delight that reveals itself in the way she motivates interest and causes each child to feel significant. A Den Mother for an active group of cub scouts expressed this feeling when she said, "Those lively little boys make me old, but keep me young."

In a spirit of fun a leader finds ways of encouraging each child to reach and realize his capacities. She is patient and understanding. She is careful neither to embarrass nor humiliate a child. Rather she respects and enjoys him. She finds ways of tuning into his world with imaginary antennae, more powerful than any machine ever made. The antennae work like a television or radio in one respect, for if a leader fails to tune in, she gets no reception. She tunes in largely with a wide-awake awareness of looking, listening, laughing, speaking, and playing. She is aware of the way each child enters into an experience. She is aware not only of what children say and do, but of what is beyond their words and actions. In this way she tunes into their hearts and minds, and finds ways of arousing ideas and feelings. Children enjoy a leader who causes them to venture into exciting realms of playing where they surprise themselves at what they are able to say and do. They cherish these moments. They admire forever a leader who causes feelings of courage, confidence, and beauty to surge within.

A leader's greatness is recognized in her artist's approach to guiding. Her sensitivity and awareness to the world of nature and human nature strengthen an aesthetic attitude which is interwoven in her guidance. She strives to bring a creative experience for children into the realm of the aesthetic rather than allowing it to remain for long an activity or an exercise. A leader is alert to significant moments in which she may tap creativity and open unexpected door-

ways. These may come about by an unexpected question she asks or when she captures an unexpected reply from a child, and builds it into a moment that soars with radiance, warmth, and wonder.

A significant way in which a leader achieves greatness is through a steady development of courage and faith. Like all human beings, leaders sometimes become discouraged. There are times when even with careful preparation a leader's guidance fails to spark children. There are times when she tries many different ways to reach a child, only to find after weeks of trying that she has apparently failed to find his real need. His behavior has a disturbing effect on an entire group of children when she is trying hard to cause the creative process to function. At times like these she wonders seriously why she is teaching, why she is spending her time and energy working with children.

It is in moments like these that a good leader grows and builds courage and faith. She thinks back to all those who before her have believed in children. She thinks back to the centuries of development in the art of drama. She considers the privilege it is to guide these very children, particularly the child who is in great need of understanding. She considers herself in relation to living. Like the Old Moon who spoke with Wynken, Blynken, and Nod, she asks herself, "Where are you going, and what do you wish?" With faith and courage she rights her attitudes and reinforces her challenge and pursuits.

A leader's righteous discontent keeps her striving to strengthen her guidance and her development as a person. She gains as much or perhaps more from her down-days as from her up-days. Whenever an experience with children reaches a low ebb, a good leader evaluates more keenly than when an experience reaches a creative height. When she takes stock of herself and her guidance she realizes the constant need for enrichment and relaxation in creative teaching. A creative leader who gives constantly of herself must gain new experiences to nourish her creative spirit. She must "Come out from under your four walls and roof. Declare a holiday."[7]

A leader needs to take time away from the work she enjoys. She needs to do that which for her conjures up new dreams—take a walk in the woods, a trip to the mountains, sleep a good sleep in a sleeping bag under stars, sit in the quiet solitude of church, listen to Beethoven or Bach, go to a theatre, enjoy a family reunion or a dinner party with friends, or find a comfortable corner in which to relax for a long while and enjoy *Huckleberry Finn*. She should seek the experience that refreshes. For as John Ruskin recognized, "There is no music in a 'rest'—but there's the making of music in it. And people are always missing that part of the life-melody." A creative leader soon realizes the wisdom in Mary Poppins' philosophy. Everyone needs to take a day off each week to do such exciting things as going to a zoo, admiring a sidewalk artist or visiting a rare friend like Mr. Wigg who has discovered the secret of laughter in living.

CREATING A CLIMATE FOR CREATIVITY

Who is responsible for creating a friendly environment so children feel free and secure enough to express themselves? Who is responsible for arranging a room and getting everything in order? For selecting experiences which fire children into moments to remember? For channeling children's energies and causing creativity to come into being? These are the responsibilities, but even more the challenges, of a creative leader.

Physical Environment. A leader first considers the physical environment of the room where children are to meet. If it is small, she

---

[7] Izaak Walton, *The Complete Angler*, T. N. Foulis, Ltd., 1925.

considers ways in which chairs, desks, or benches may be arranged to provide a maximum space for playing. If it is large, such as a gymnasium or auditorium, she considers ways to limit the playing area.

A friendly seating arrangement is planned to foster social and creative growth. When children sit in rows, and see only the backs of others' heads, there is little communication. They need to see each others' faces to catch each others' feelings. Sitting in a circle allows every child to see every other, and the unity and intimacy of a circle provide togetherness (Fig. 4.1). A semicircular or U-shaped

Fig. 4.1. "We can pretend we're sitting on the barnyard fence." (*Photograph by Brant Studio; Clyde Hill School, Bellevue Public Schools, Bellevue, Washington*)

arrangement allows children to see one another and provides an opening for playing. In crowded classrooms where desks are moveable, children may be guided into moving desks to the walls to provide an open space in the center of the room (Fig. 4.2). Or, in some instances where desks are not moveable, they may be encouraged to use the tops of desks or to use the space in aisles (Fig. 4.3). Some leaders have found a blanket or a discarded bedspread effective as a "magic carpet." Children enjoy the idea of magic and are more comfortable on a blanket than they are when they sit directly on a rough or cold floor. Care should be used so they do not face glaring light or openings that cause distractions.

Leaders frequently visualize a seating arrangement in advance, but invite children to do the arranging when they first arrive. In this way children's energies are channeled, and early comers are given a feeling of contributing toward the group experience. Little children enjoy arranging chairs or benches in a big square which

FIG. 4.2. "We get ready to play in an orderly way." (*Ronald School, Shoreline Public Schools, Seattle, Washington*)

they call "Our Play House" (Fig. 4.4). Part of the group watches others take turns playing on the patio, or the open space of the square.

Temperature and ventilation of a room are always regulated in advance. Children cannot create in an atmosphere that is overly warm and lacking in oxygen, or when they are cold and sitting in drafts from open doors or windows.

FIG. 4.3. "A bear!" (*Photograph by Royal C. Crooks; Bryant School, Seattle Public Schools, Seattle, Washington*)

When equipment of any kind is to be used, the leader should set it up and operate it in advance. A creative mood may be broken or completely lost if she stops to look for a recording or to find out why a machine fails to function at a moment when it is needed.

Remembering Names. *A creative leader makes a strong effort to learn each child's name at a first meeting.* A child's name is his symbol of identity. He not only feels honored but he feels kindly toward other persons who remember his name after a first meeting. A leader remembers a name by (1) pronouncing it clearly, (2)

writing it out, (3) associating it visually, (4) using it in speaking to or about the child, and (5) listening when others call a child by name.

Fig. 4.4. "Hum-Hum likes our play house." (*Photograph by Royal C. Crooks; View Ridge School, Seattle Public Schools, Seattle, Washington*)

When a child introduces himself she makes certain she gets his name correctly, both in pronunciation and in spelling. If a blackboard is available she writes or prints his name on the board when he introduces himself. This gives her an opportunity to look at the child, to say his name, and to associate his name with something characteristic of his appearance or personality. After she has written his name, she asks others to repeat his name. In this way each child is given a moment of recognition, and his name is associated with him. During every meeting, but particularly during a first meeting, she uses a child's name whenever she speaks to him. Many leaders have found that they are able to remember as many as 80 different children's names after first meetings at the beginning of a new year at school or in children's programs.

Friendly Atmosphere. A leader builds a friendly atmosphere by gaining the confidence and trust of every child. Many classroom teachers and creative leaders send a friendly letter to each child a few days before a class is to meet. A letter is written in a friendly way to arouse curiosity and personal interest, even though it is generally done in mimeographed form. The following letter written by a second grade teacher caused every child to arrive at school with enthusiasm and wonder:

A Summer Day

Dear_____,

Do you like surprises? I have a surprise for you and everyone in the second grade this year. The surprise is a little friend. His name is Pip.

Pip and I had fun this summer. We went camping. We wonder what you did that was the most fun for you. Maybe you would like to tell us, and everyone in the second grade. There will be 31 new friends when school starts on Monday.

I will wait for you by the front door. Pip doesn't know where he will wait yet. Who do you think Pip is?

Your new teacher,

Miss Post

On a first day and every day when children arrive for school or a class a leader greets the children in a friendly way. She talks with individuals rather than at them. She looks at a child while he speaks and she listens to what he says. When she speaks she strives to speak in a friendly, calm voice which communicates sincere feelings. A good leader is interested in what individuals do, and say, and share, and she is interested in those individual children who refrain from doing, saying, and sharing. A personal approach reaches a child's inner self for his "head will not hear until the heart first listens, and what the heart understands today the head will understand tomorrow."[8]

After a first meeting a leader always greets a child personally, calling him by name. A child, like all human beings, likes to be singled out in a personalized way, if for only a moment or two. A good leader is always alert for something specific within each child which she may approve or commend. It may be something comparatively insignificant such as a smile, clean face or fingernails, the way a child walks, skips, or enters a room, the way his hair shines, the way he thinks of others, his eagerness to share something he has made or brought. But to the individual child approval means a warm friendly feeling. It causes a child to feel a sense of worth, a sense of belonging, and a sense of striving.

A sixth grade teacher noticed a boy's haircut. The boy was extremely sensitive and found it difficult to relate to the other children. When he came up to the teacher's desk she nudged his elbow and in a quiet friendly way said, "Neat." The boy smiled in a disarming way. Several days later when the teacher wore a colorful blouse, the boy found an appropriate moment to comment. In a quiet way he smiled and said, "Neat." By the small approval of the boy's haircut the teacher caused him to feel significant, and he gradually gained status among his classmates.

[8] James Stephens, *The Crock of Gold*, The Macmillan Company, 1936.

The friendliest classrooms are those in which each child feels significant and important to the group. A good leader builds a feeling of group spirit and teamwork by causing individuals to feel that group problems, decisions, and experiences are to be solved and experienced together. A leader encourages individuals to share ideas. She always reaches children in a group by approaching them individually in a subjective way. She is sincere, and may say in effect: "All week long I've been waiting to share something special with every one of you. We've got to decide on something important." Or, "When this letter came this week, I wanted to call every one of you, but I waited to share what it says until today when we were all together to hear the exciting news." Or, "I've been eager to see you, because *you* are the best ones I know to help with our problem. I know every one of you will have an idea about this."

CREATIVITY AND DISCIPLINE

A creative child is a disciplined child, for he is a thinking child. He frequently disciplines himself when he pursues an idea with keen interest. More frequently he needs the steady discipline of a parent or teacher to cause him to do that which he strives to do, but is unable to do entirely with self-guidance. When we study the lives of great leaders in all areas of human endeavor we find that creativity and discipline function hand in hand. Leonardo da Vinci uttered the cry, "Oh God, you sell us everything for the price of an effort." Thomas Edison voiced this truth when he explained that he had found 20,000 ways in which the lamp would not light, but vowed he would work until he found one way that would cause the lamp to light. Ralph Waldo Emerson expressed a human need for discipline when he said, "Our chief want in life is for someone who can make us do what we are capable of doing."

Children Need Discipline. Children need strong discipline. When several gather together individuals frequently find difficulty in adjusting to others. Some relate to others with unusual behavior patterns for many different underlying reasons. A child may reveal his needs by interrupting, talking loudly or at length without thought of others, or by being disrespectful in other ways. Or he may be motivated by the freedom of space. He may run, shout, or climb on furniture without controlling his desires. When one child begins such behavior it often serves to invite action from others. One teacher says: "My experience has been that children do love to pretend. However, when they know they are going to make a play, it is like turning on a green light for almost any type of behavior. They get too excited, become discourteous, and then I lower the boom. I find it much easier to maintain that good balance in art work or in writing stories where each child works independently than in dramatic activities. Therefore, I lean toward those mediums of creativity and avoid the confusion and chaos of creative dramatics."

And yet children prefer order to disorder. They prefer togetherness rather than apartness. They enjoy creating independently, and they enjoy working together. Life offers rich experiences in both kinds of creative living for those who know how to relate to and work with others. A child needs to be guided into group experiences where he develops habits of both leadership and "followship." He needs many experiences so that he becomes prepared for voluntary teamwork and coöperation. Perhaps it *is* easier to "lower the boom" and guide children into working independently; but how will they learn to work and play together and so experience the core of creative social living, if they are not guided into many group experiences?

Freedom and Control. A leader, like a ship's captain, is the person who is responsible for steering the ship. It is her responsibility to motivate and channel children's energies, excitement, and ideas. She uses a positive approach. She is always prepared. She approaches children with zest, vitality, belief. She channels their ideas into discussion and expression. In most instances, with enthusiastic guidance, children have neither time nor inclination to resort to undesirable behavior for recognition. Their needs and interests are satisfied. However, in early experiences when every child is endeavoring to find his niche within a group, there is often an immediate necessity for law and order. Once this situation arises a leader must meet it with discipline. There will be no peace until there is law. Children cannot create in an atmosphere of confusion.

Establishing Group Laws for Order. The very moment the need for order presents itself a leader introduces order. She nips in the bud the first sign of disorderly and discourteous behavior. She approaches the situation in a friendly, firm way. It is vital that children experience a feeling of freedom and enjoyment in a group, but it is equally vital that they experience a secure feeling of discipline.

Dorothy Baruch, an outstanding child psychologist and teacher, has made an intensive study of discipline. She says:

In its derivation, the term "discipline" has to do with following a leader. The disciples of Christ were followers of Jesus. The disciples of Hitler were his followers.

But the quality of leadership in these two instances had very different effects on the motives and actions of the followers. The leader himself, the quality of his being and of his essential personality enter into the picture as does also the relationship between the leader and the led.

Parents can lead by either the Whip or the Word. So also can teachers. But the Word demands much more of sharing, of living together. It calls on us and the child for building mutual understandings and confidence.[9]

There are many different ways to introduce children to the need for group laws. One experienced leader asks the children to make their rules for creative playing at the very first meeting. She explains that all games and all living are governed by basic laws of order and explains the concept of order by the analogy of traffic lights, which children readily understand. She draws from the children the basic rules for listening when someone is speaking, for raising hands when they wish to share ideas, and of coöperating when they plan and play together. In this way each individual is aware of specific ways in which he disciplines himself in a group experience.

Most leaders find that children conduct themselves in a comparatively ideal way at a first meeting. It is generally at second, third, or fourth meetings that individuals may try unusual behavior patterns to attract attention. This is the psychological moment when many leaders prefer to introduce order. A leader stops the playing and discusses the need for group rules. A few basic rules are introduced, discussed, and listed.

One group of 7- and 8-year-olds arrived at basic social rules by discussing ways in which they could have fun when they met together. From their suggestions they abbreviated their rules into the following rhyme which they repeated at the beginning of each creative session:

> We have fun when everyone
> Listens, and thinks, and pays attention.

"Good Audience" Emphasized. Many leaders have discovered that children enjoy disciplining themselves when rules are intro-

[9] Dorothy Walter Baruch, *New Ways in Discipline*, Whittlesey House, 1949.

duced within the realm of drama. Whenever a need for order arises a leader explains that she believes the children need to use some secret magic. She explains that a secret helper could cause them to become a "good audience." The words "magic" and "secret" are rousers of curiosity and imagination. She asks, "How might we work and play together as a good audience?" Most children have had audience experiences, and a child feels important when he contributes an idea. From the discussion the leader clarifies the concept of good social behavior. She helps children realize that the secret of being a "good audience" is the same as that of being a good friend. She helps them see that friendly people think, feel, and listen when someone is speaking. She helps them see that friendly people like to share and enjoy working and playing with others. She explains that anyone in a group can make noise and run around the room like a noisy boy or girl, but that it takes real thinking and feeling to work and play and share together like good friends.

The leader may ask children to suggest a magic word that will be their secret helper. After several suggestions they vote upon the word that holds the highest appeal for the group. With young children the leader often clarifies this concept by explaining that a red light is a magic helper because it stops people from crossing a street when cars are coming. She asks them to think of a word that will help them stop and think just as they stop and think when they see a red light. One group of realistic 5-year-olds chose the word "Stoppity-Stop." It was not too imaginative, but it held meaning for the children. A group of 6-year-olds chose the magic word "Ten-Shun," suggested by a boy whose father was an army sergeant. Another group of first graders, motivated by the desire to be quiet, chose the word "Squeak" which they associated with a mouse.

Older children have chosen such magic words as "Freeze," "Bip,"

"Presto," "Mouseparia," "Zing," and "Cigam"—the latter chosen after a boy suggested that they spell magic backwards.

Maintaining Discipline. A law is effective only when it is enforced. Once rules have been made a leader must be firm in guiding children to respect them. After a magic word has been chosen she helps children make it function. She suggests that the children get up and move about the room and encourages each one to talk and think only of himself instead of others. After a minute of this kind of experiencing she calls the magic word, watching to see how quickly the children stop for attention. In some groups children decide that whenever the magic word is called they will return to their desks or places in the group. Other groups prefer to have the magic word stop them wherever they happen to be when the word is called.

In one beginning group of 5- and 6-year-olds a magic word was introduced and tried out for a first time. Two little boys found great glee in disobeying the signal. "It doesn't work for us," Floyd called as he and Charlie ran freely around the room. The leader waited until the two boys stopped running. She gathered the children about her and gave a careful explanation: "A magic word only works when you help it work, because the magic is inside of you. When a red light over a street turns red, it is signaling to you to think. If you forget to think, the red signal can't stop you. A magic word or a red light is a quick signal for you to think. Let's try again and see if Floyd and Charlie can catch the magic signal and be good thinkers just like the rest of us."

After this explanation the magic worked.

Most creative leaders who set up social rules and enforce them in a friendly, firm way find that children discipline themselves after two or three sessions of enforcement. One kindergarten teacher said, "Since I have shared creative dramatics with my kindergarteners I

find I am satisfying children's real needs and wants. I am firm about using the magic word. I can safely say that with eight different kindergarten groups during the past four years I have had no noticeable discipline problems after the first three weeks of school. Before I discovered creative dramatics some children used to cause trouble and confusion for an entire school year. It was really my fault because I didn't know how to guide them to satisfy their human hungers."

Guiding Children with Strong Needs. A creative leader always shares satisfying creative experiences that meet children's needs. She is particularly aware of the needs of the shy child and the child with aggressive behavior patterns. Each child needs patient understanding and guidance. The shy child needs to change his self-consciousness into self-confidence. He may prefer to be with a group but to remain on the fringes rather than participate actively. A leader makes it easy for him to participate according to his needs and growth. She may join him in watching from time to time, or she may suggest that he watch as a character or person who fits into the framework of the play situation. She encourages him to join in the playing but neither insists nor forces him to enter in until he is ready. Occasionally, she may take his hand and draw him into the fun and exuberance of group play without his realizing that he has made this step which he feared.

An aggressive child needs to channel his energies, ideas, and attitudes into pathways that bring group recognition and appreciation for him. A leader always urges better work from a child who is capable of stronger thinking, feeling, and experiencing. She helps an aggressive child realize the need for taking turns, for participating in minor roles for the enjoyment of a group experience.

"Tell a child what he wants most to hear, and see how he blossoms," says a creative leader who builds strong rapport with every

group of children. Every child needs and wants to hear that he has contributed something worth while when he has put forth his best effort. A child lives close to the truth of things and he knows when he has reached for his best. He grows in confidence when a leader praises him or draws specific praise of him from others. A leader is honest in helping a child see how he is relating to a group. She frequently voices a situation by asking questions such as these: "What should John do if he wants to share his idea?" "Why are we waiting instead of playing?" "Why are we going to give the 'audience' a chance to be the players this time?" "Who knows why we should take turns?" "Who knows why Stacy gets to be Miss Muffet this time?"

Every day is vital in the growth of a child. An outstanding creative teacher says: "As I begin each day I watch for ways in which I can honestly praise each child, not just a few children, but every child. As I say good-by to the children at the end of the day, I give each one a psychological pat on the shoulder. I make a point of capturing in one or two significant words, a moment which has had real meaning for each child."

CLASSROOM TEACHER OR CREATIVE DRAMATICS LEADER?

Children are always the first consideration. Ideally they will benefit from both a creative classroom teacher and a special creative dramatics leader. A classroom teacher, like a parent, is in a splendid position to guide indirectly. She knows and understands the many individual needs, desires, and interests of every child. She becomes alert to rare moments that suddenly occur during a day. She is in a position to capture these moments for brief creative interludes. Experiences such as these may evolve in no more than four or five

minutes, but they serve to add spice and savor to every child's creative living and learning.

A classroom teacher is in an ideal position to encourage individual expression in ways that allow each child's creative spirit to assert itself. She may encourage individuals to follow particular pathways and pursuits that will both satisfy them and also contribute to the enrichment of group experiences. She can utilize time in a skillful way by vitalizing learning experiences. She can integrate social studies, language arts, and other arts with creative dramatics, which culminates in exciting functional learning. Every child needs a steady individual challenge throughout a school year.

A special creative dramatics leader generally has a true appreciation and understanding of the art of drama and is in a position to bring new and refreshing experiences to children. She may work closely with the classroom teacher, and integrate and correlate learning for the children. Above all, she should maintain the creative approach toward integrated learning experiences. A special teacher who understands the creative process generally has the skill to keep a creative experience creative. She is careful to see that children do not merely represent or accurately depict scenes or episodes to meet factual learning. She knows how to keep the joy, excitement, and spirit in creative experiences while they learn facts and gain experiences in communicating with others. She generally knows how to arouse children's creative spirits and channel energies into authentic dramatic expression.

In most schools the responsibility for creative dramatics lies entirely with the classroom teacher. If she is to be successful she must first believe in the need for every child to express himself in creative dramatics; otherwise she will fail to share this art. She will let one day pass into the next, and each month will pass by without sharing.

Creative dramatics demands a belief and a dedication of one's energies and attitudes. It calls for a certain sense of humility and a steady pursuit. A teacher who cares for children and believes in the beauty of drama will find ways of sharing creative dramatics. She will help boys and girls "keep in their souls some images of magnificence."[10]

Questions and Activities

1. Recall a teacher from childhood whom you admired. Write a brief profile of this teacher. Recall a teacher from childhood you did not admire. Write a brief profile to explain why you did not admire this teacher.
2. You are applying for a position as creative dramatics teacher. You are asked to make a one-page profile of yourself including (a) qualities within your personality that you believe will contribute to strong teaching, and (b) qualities that you realize you need to strengthen.
3. As an enthusiastic leader of creative dramatics you have been concerned over the tendency of many teachers to feel that "creative dramatics is a luxury in second grade" and that since "it's a pretty tough world" children should learn "to face it." How would you answer these teachers? Discuss for ten minutes in buzz sessions. Although each group selects a spokesman to report to the class, others within the group share the responsibility of presenting the ideas discussed.
4. Use Mary Poppins' magic with children in the following everyday experiences. List the first three ideas that come to mind for an imaginative approach to each.
    a. Introduce yourself to a new group of children so they will re member your name, and gain an insight into your personality.
    b. Guide children to clean up the schoolroom in a friendly fun way.
    c. Celebrate a child's birthday in 15 minutes in a special creative way.
    d. Guide 30 children into unusual adventure on the playground in

[10] Jones, *op. cit.*

a cluster of autumn leaves, in a sandy place, in freshly fallen snow, in shadows, on pavement.

e. Guide children to create a Halloween party with just themselves and the space of the room.

f. Motivate children to rest in a way that invites relaxation.

5. Discuss the term "climate for creativity" in relation to a classroom situation or a community program situation. Consider (a) teacher's attitude and preparation, (b) physical environment, (c) remembering children's names, and (d) "magic word" for group discipline.

6. Work in pairs to plan a parent-teacher interview in which the teacher uses a friendly, creative approach to gain insights into a child's home environment.

7. Discuss the following statement, "Discipline is essential to creative expression. . . . Children cannot create in an atmosphere of confusion."

8. In your notebook or file, concentrate on that which will foster your own personal growth.

CHAPTER 5

Material for Creative Dramatics

We are such stuff as dreams are made on.—William Shakespeare

In the foothills of the Cascade Mountains there stands a sturdy homesteader's house, weathered and beautiful, built nearly a hundred years ago by a pioneer family and a spirited little grandmother. The men were farmers. They knew how to clear land, till, plant, and harvest. They knew very little about building houses. But the merry grandmother had an eye and a yen for building, and she had a love and a knack for teaching others how to build.

So she drew up a plan. While the men and boys felled tall trees, she scouted for a building site, singing as she went. She studied the lay of the land, listened to the wind, watched to see the way it rustled through the trees. She looked northward to the hills, and southward to the river valley. At last she found a place which she knew was right for building.

"We must build a firm foundation from strong timbers," the grandmother said, explaining her crude but sound plan. "Then we'll put the up-sticks in." At the end of each day's work they studied the plan together. "This one thing we'll do on the morrow," the grandmother smilingly said.

Little by little they built their house. It has stood these many years as a symbol of those who built together with spirit, dreams, and a plan.

MAKING A PLAN FOR GUIDING

A good creative dramatics leader is like a builder. She works forward ahead of her youthful creators in a way not unlike the grandmother and the pioneers. She selects material with an eye and a yen for satisfying children's needs.

When the pioneers homesteaded the land, their main goal during the first summer was to clear land and build a home. Their specific purpose was "to do one thing each day." In this way they gradually achieved their main goal. In creative dramatics the main goal is for enjoyable creative experiences that foster child growth and development. The specific goal of each experience is to meet the strongest needs of a group through a specific form of satisfying dramatic expression. Thus through a steady emphasis on basic dramatic elements children are gradually introduced to the fundamentals of drama.

Determining Needs of Children. How does a leader determine strong group needs? First of all, she considers the specific group of children she is going to guide—their ages, the number of boys and girls, and the situation in which she is meeting them. She asks herself questions such as these: What does this group of children need most as a group and as individuals? Do they need to break down social-emotional barriers and get involved in action? Do they have a greater need for sitting and expressing themselves through discussion? What do they need most from this creative experience which may be achieved through dramatic expression? By the end of this session, what should each child experience dramatically with true enjoyment?

Children's Needs at a First Meeting. First meetings are mighty. They build friendly attitudes, friendly relationships, and high interest—or they fail to. At a first meeting with a group of children unknown to one another each child needs to become acquainted with others. They need to learn the names of each of the children, and to discover a little about one another. Each child needs opportunities to express himself so others may discover what kind of person he is. Shy children need help in being brought into a group so they feel welcome and secure. Aggressive children need help in learning to respect and consider others. Every child needs to learn what kind of person the leader is.

A second strong need for most children is a need to move, to channel physical energies into expression. Children need to express themselves by *doing* something that is interesting, satisfying, and fun.

For children entering a new creative dramatics experience, a third need is to discover what this art is like. Before they come to creative dramatics they wonder about it. They need to experience it, to discover it by doing it. Since a play is made up of many basic drama elements they should discover only one or two elements at a time. Most groups which need to break down social-emotional barriers need to begin with drama's simplest and most basic form, rhythmic movement. Early experiences need to be simplified so children become involved quickly and have fun together.

A leader can clarify goals by writing them out. She may use a form similar to the form used by Miss Gray for a first session:

GOALS FOR A FIRST MEETING IN CREATIVE DRAMATICS

I. To Meet Basic Social Needs in an Atmosphere of Enjoyment
   A. To get acquainted with each other
      Children with leader
      Children with each other
      Leader with children
   B. To discover chief characteristics, needs, and interests of each child
      Observe each child's expression and way of expressing
      Observe each child's behavior and interaction with others
   C. To set up social rules when need arises
      Lead children into understanding why rules are needed
      Draw basic rules from group for listening, raising hands, and respecting each other with courteous attention
II. To Meet Basic Physical Needs With Creative Expression
   A. Guide each child into releasing energy
   B. Encourage individual expression in a variety of rhythmic movement experiences
III. To Introduce Children to the Art of Creative Dramatics
   A. Explain creative dramatics briefly or invite explanations from children
   B. Guide children into strong dramatic expression by encouraging rhythmic movement, pantomime, and individuality[1]

SELECTING MATERIAL

Material must be wisely chosen. A leader is always scouting and searching. She listens for ideas that interest children, ideas that are dramatic, ideas with hopes, dreams, wonderings, ideas with fun and flavor. She is alert for experiences in literature and life that will tug at the hearts and heads of growing children. She realizes the need

[1] See Chapter 1, pp. 8-19.

for exposing them to good literature rather than expecting mediocrity to motivate them into sharing their best.

Once goals are clarified, material is selected that will meet specific goals and at the same time hold high appeal for a group of children. Material for early sessions may be based on an idea, an experience, or a short verse which will arouse them into creative expression. A child will become involved in an experience and turn his imagination loose only when something excites and interests him. Material is the vehicle that arouses individual expression and causes creativity to assert itself. Material for beginning and early experiences is generally based on ideas from literature or life which stimulate expression in rhythmic movement.

Rhythmic Movement. Every living thing has rhythm—a graceful swallow, a swiftly darting king salmon, a willow tree. Every child is a rhythmic being, each with his own unique rhythm and pace. A child's rhythm begins with the beat of his heart which sends the surge of life through his entire being. He breathes, eats, sleeps, walks, thinks, feels, talks in rhythmic patterns.

The poet Langston Hughes points out that all "Rhythm comes from movement. . . . There is no rhythm in the world without movement first. . . . Thousands of years ago men transferred the rhythm of the heartbeat into a drumbeat and the rhythm of music began. The rhythms of music start folks to feeling those rhythms in their minds and in their bodies. . . . Deep inside of men and animals there are other rhythms that we cannot explain, but that are a part of life."[2]

Rhythm is the basis for expression in all the arts. It starts with the individual. Each artist expresses through a medium unique to his art. A painter expresses rhythmically in space with line and

[2] Langston Hughes, *The First Book of Rhythms,* Franklin Watts, Inc., 1954.

color. A musician expresses rhythmically in space with sound. A writer expresses rhythmically in space with words. A child expresses rhythmically in space with movement.

A child's body is his instrument of expression. He expresses thoughts and feelings when he runs, jumps, leaps, hops, rolls, dances, stamps, hits, dodges, and moves in many different rhythmic patterns. Without being aware of it, he may move upward, downward, or outward in the space at hand. He may move forward, backward, around and around. If he is angry, happy, fearful, or sad he may express with intense movement of his whole body. At other times and in different moods he may express only with his head, his shoulders, his trunk, his arms, legs, feet, or fingers. Because rhythmic movement is a child's natural way of expression, it becomes a natural way to introduce children to creative dramatics.

RHYTHMIC ACTION MATERIAL

Simplicity is the keyword in selecting material. Children, like all artists, express when they have something to say. Material must provide purpose. It must cause children to want to express.

Rhythmic action material should be limited to a single idea. For a first meeting an idea should encourage children to introduce themselves in a friendly, easy way. It should invite independent thinking and cause a child to want to share his idea. It should be an idea which leads to active expression.

Idea Based on Interests. A single idea is always based on a strong interest of children of a given age level. Little children are almost always interested in the real world around them. An idea may be chosen from among such interests as pets, playing, outdoor animals, growing things, grown-up people, toys, trips, and families.

Seven- and eight-year-olds are generally interested in faraway

places and wonderland. An idea may be chosen from among their many interests, such as wishing, imagining, playing, secret dreams, surprises, magic carpets, and riddles. Older children enjoy creating from ideas based on some aspect of adventure such as sports, hobbies, heroes, travel, camping, discoveries, achievements, favorite books, coded messages, and treasure maps.

Analyzing Rhythmic Movement. After an idea has been selected for interest, it is analyzed for rhythmic movement. Suppose an idea of "Summer Fun" has been chosen because of its appeal after summer vacation. The leader lists a variety of possible rhythmic movements that may be expressed from summer fun experiences, which may include going to a beach, camping, picnicking, fishing, parading, horseback riding, traveling, bicycle riding, going to a circus, building a camp, or visiting a national park.

When using a broad idea such as summer fun the leader analyzes material further, exploring several avenues of the idea. She becomes enthusiastic as she explores, and she is prepared to share a strong creative experience when she meets children. In analyzing rhythmic movement she visualizes children experiencing this interest. For instance, when she visualizes little children at a beach she sees them in action. In her mind's eye she watches their delight in wading, splashing, sailing boats, building sand castles, running in and out of waves, picking up shells, listening, digging clams, finding beach treasures, and stretching out in the sun. In visualizing older children going camping she may see them packing duffel, hiking up a steep mountain path, stopping to see the beauty of the outdoor world, finding a camp site, setting up camp, building a fire, chopping wood, cooking supper, eating, fishing, rowing on a lake, singing by firelight, sleeping under stars, and dreaming.

FOCUSING MATERIAL FOR CREATIVE EXPRESSION

Again simplicity is the secret of planning material so it arouses expression. A leader simplifies material by focusing children's thinking to one area of thought. Focus to free becomes basic in planning material. To focus means to tighten, to limit, to reduce to a clear-cut idea.

Focus to a Question.   Once an idea seems right for a group, it is focused to a single question which invites expression. Such a question might be this one: What one thing did you do this summer that was so much fun you would like to do it right now?

Let us analyze this question so we may understand how it has been focused to free a child for expression. It is subjective. It is asked with a *you* viewpoint which relates the material to the child. It asks, "What did *you* do?" It is a limited question which invites one response and challenges a child to think. It asks, "What *one thing?*" It causes a child to recall a single experience that held high interest for him. His reply provides an insight into his interests. Limiting the question also provides time for 20 or 30 children to reply. It prevents one or two children from dominating by giving lengthy accounts of summer experiences. It provides an indirect opportunity for each child to discover a bit about each other child.

The initial question is focused toward action by using an action verb. In the question, "What did you *do?*" the verb *do* immediately awakens images of doing, of experiencing through action. If the question had been stated without a close focus on action, it might have asked, "Where did you go this summer that was so much fun you would like to go there this minute?" In answering, a child might reply, "to my grandmother's," "to North Dakota," "to Neah Bay." With replies such as these, a leader needs to ask further questions to focus a group's thinking toward ideas that may be expressed in rhythmic movement. By focusing further, children often spend the greater part of 30 or 40 minutes discussing rather than doing. To children drama is action, and they are eager to do. Close focusing of material at the outset is essential. If this art is to involve children, it must lead them quickly into a spirit of active fun which sparks creativity.

Focusing Children's Replies. A leader has two choices in the way she shares rhythmic material with children. She may (1) encourage individual rhythmic expression from every child in group ensemble, or (2) focus group thinking to one child's idea which invites individual rhythmic expression in group ensemble.

If she follows the first way of sharing, she will stay on the beam of her original focus. For instance, the focus in this instance was on summer fun. After each child shares his idea of what he would like to do, she guides him into expressing his idea through rhythmic movement. For example, she may say, "Let's pretend we're right back in summer. We'll pretend this room is the whole world, and you are in the very spot where you were having fun this summer. You won't say a word, but you will show with your whole self how much fun you are having, doing just what you did this summer." She encourages the children to move out into the space of the room. She encourages each child to express his idea simultaneously with others. She watches closely. After this initial experience in rhythmic movement, she focuses children to watching one another in smaller groups. She may guide them into a half-and-half arrangement, in which half of the children will play again to share their pantomimes with the other half who watch. Or she may invite them to share in smaller groups of five or six, or in some instances she may recognize the need for having children share in pairs. When children watch each other she discovers areas of interest that hold high appeal for the entire group. She remembers these interests to recall later for further experiences in rhythmic movement.

If she follows the second way of sharing material, she invites each child to answer the initial question, after which she focuses group thinking to one idea. Miss Gray used this plan in the first day experience on dreams.[3] After children had expressed individual ideas, she focused thinking to Dee Dee's idea of swimming. This material was familiar to all the children. It provided security for many of them, for they were guided into expressing with thought and feeling. Each child expressed from the same basic idea, and thus felt secure in creating within this limited idea. This plan also allowed the leader time to analyze further ideas. In successive meetings rhythmic experiences were centered around mountain climbing, puppet shows, playing in a band, and ranch life. When a leader has analyzed material, she guides with security and with questions that draw strong creative expression.

MUSIC FOR CREATIVE RHYTHMIC EXPRESSION

Music has power. It arouses feelings that surge through old and young alike. Marching music almost always quickens the blood, stirs imaginations, and causes an irrepressible urge to move into action. Lullabies are soothing in their gentle rhythm and have a quieting effect. Music stirs many different feelings.

Dancing in its broadest sense is rhythmic movement. Dancing and rhythmic movement are generally heightened both in enjoyment and expression when they are accompanied with some kind of rhythmic beat—a chant, a beating upon drums, a clapping of hands, a song, instrumental music, or a recording of music.

[3] See Chapter 1, pp. 8–19.

Music or rhythmic accompaniment may be used in creative dramatics in the following ways: (1) to motivate or heighten a mood by suggesting a specific environment; (2) to provide a strong rhythmic pattern; (3) to arouse thinking and feeling; and (4) to tell a story. Many leaders have found the recordings of basic rhythms in *Rhythmic Activities* to be of particular value in providing rhythms for a variety of creative dramatics experiences.[4]

A leader selects music with as much care as she selects other material, and uses it only when she believes it will heighten a creative experience. Beginning leaders often use recordings too frequently, instead of using different ways to provide variety in motivation or rhythmic accompaniment.

Some events are always associated with music, such as a parade, circus, rodeo, sports events, fairies' parties, festivals, castle balls, witch dances, magic spells, and most ceremonies. Material that centers in an imaginative realm may be heightened by music which provides a distinctive mood as well as a rhythmic pattern. Whenever music is introduced for an imaginative experience, such as being snowflakes, it should be introduced in an imaginative way. For instance, if children have been guided to think, feel, and wonder about snowflakes, a beginning leader might say: "I'll put on some music, and you be snowflakes." Contrast this to a statement that weaves the music into the mood, such as: "Whenever it snows the snow fairies make music high in the sky. Listen and you may hear it. Soon a snow fairy will touch you, and see how you feel as you come snowing down from the sky." Or, if snowflakes have been shared in a more realistic way, the leader may say: "Whenever snowflakes come

[4] *Rhythmic Activities*, RCA Victor Record Library for Elementary Schools. Notes for teachers prepared by Lila Belle Pitts and Gladys Tipton, Radio Corporation of America, RCA Victor Division, 1947.

dancing or twirling, the wind blows through the treetops and makes music for them. Listen. When you hear the wind music, and feel the wind touch you, you be a snowy snowflake coming down in your own happy way."

Realistic experiences which are not associated with music are often more effective when done quietly without musical accompaniment.

FIRST DAYS WITH CREATIVE RHYTHMIC MOVEMENT

A Kindergarten Experience. A kindergarten teacher was aware of strong community interest in a Labor Day parade. During the first week of school when she asked how many had gone to the parade, she found that every one of the 29 5-year-olds had been there. Enthusiasm developed quickly. They decided to have a parade of their own. The teacher challenged each child to close his eyes and "see the prettiest thing parading down the street this very minute." A lively march tune sounded while the children thought.

Replies were spontaneous. Enough rhythmic action material was provided for Parade Time every day for two weeks. The first day they paraded as drum majorettes and big elephants. On following days they enjoyed parading as "new Dodge trucks," "galloping white horses," "big girls like bride dolls throwing flowers," "fire engines with a bell ringing," "clowns on roller skates," "a truck full of pretty flowers," "the queen of the float," "the army with real guns," "my brother and the Boy Scouts," and "a band with a man throwing drum beaters up in the sky."

Seven- and Eight-Year-Olds' Experience. A fluffy white dandelion in seed created a strong mood for wishing among one group of 7- and 8-year-olds on a first day. The children were well informed on dandelion magic. One little girl explained, "If the seed flies to the fairies, your wish comes true, but if it gets caught in a tree the fairies never know what you wished for. All my wishes have been caught in trees, but I keep wishing." The children became excited and asked if they might wish for one new thing to play with. The leader guided them into rhythmic movement by asking, "Would you be happy if the fairies brought you this?" She pretended to bounce an imaginary ball, to ride a scooter, and to show a rainbow across one end of the room. After the children guessed, each one pretended to bounce a ball, to ride an imaginary scooter in a parade around the room, and to make a roomful of rainbows. The leader guided the children into a short discussion on how to make actions speak.

She then suggested: "Let's pretend each one picks a dandelion seed and makes a secret wish. Let's pretend it comes true the minute the faraway fairies sound wishing music. Each one may show how you feel when you play with the special thing the fairies bring you."

The children stood in a big ring as round as a giant dandelion. Each one thought of his wish. Then the leader started a recording of "Fairies"[5] and moved inside the wishing ring and watched. The children expressed such actions as jumping rope, riding a bicycle, playing a piano, flying like a hummingbird, swinging, batting a baseball, jumping on a pogo stick, riding a pony, and pouring tea from a new tea set. For six sessions these children experienced rhythmic movement as they played "Fairy Wishes Coming True."

First Day with Nine-, Ten-, and Eleven-Year-Olds. *Adventure* was the keyword for a first meeting with a group of 9-, 10-, and 11-year-olds. After a short discussion the question was asked, "If you were experiencing the highest adventure of your life this very minute, what would you be doing?" Strong ideas for action were found in such individual replies as "exploring a pirate ship at the

[5] *Ibid.,* Vol. 1.

bottom of the ocean," "rescuing someone and applying artificial res-
piration," "singing in a Rodgers and Hammerstein production,"
"appearing as a ballet dancer on television," "digging for dinosaur
bones," "catching a 30-pound king salmon," and "riding to outer
space in the saddle-jet-helicopter that I am designing." Three sessions in rhythmic action were experienced from ideas that came forth
at this first meeting.

Unifying Creative Experiences. In each of these beginning experiences an initial focused question motivated the expression and enjoyment that followed. A creative experience must be unified. The
initial question or questions must be related to the material from
which children are to create. Unless the leader ties an experience
together she may find two or more different moods developing, none
of which is strong enough to invite creative expression.

A beginning leader asked a group of 20 6-year-olds to tell how
many brothers and sisters each one had. When they finished she
asked each child to tell what kind of pet he would like to be. Because of the time required for 20 little children to share comments
about brothers, sisters, and pets, the children became tired and restless. They were not at all interested in becoming pets. They wanted
to go outside and play. Had the teacher focused the initial question
to pets she could have motivated a desire for rhythmic expression
early in the period. Children would no doubt have been eager to
become such pets as "our kitten climbing up our big birch tree," and
"a shiny goldfish swimming around our pool."

ANALYZING GROUP NEEDS AFTER FIRST MEETING

Children are children. They reveal much about themselves in a
first creative dramatics experience. A friendly leader who breaks
down barriers finds many little doorways opening up into individual

worlds. She gains insights into different personalities. She almost always finds children who are happy, friendly, coöperative, children who are leaders, children who prefer to follow. She may find boys and girls bubbling over with knowledge and ideas they wish to share. She may find a surging rhythmic spirit of aliveness, freshness, eagerness.

On the other hand she may find a slow, silent group broken only by one or two dynamic individuals. Many children may be shy and tense. Others may hold back while they wonder what this new experience is to bring; one or two may be dominating or demanding.

Every group of children is different, since a group is made up of individuals. At the end of a first session an alert leader has a general picture of the group as a whole. She analyzes further, considering (1) individual needs, and the needs basic to children of a given age level; (2) the number of children in a group, number of boys and number of girls; (3) previous experience of individuals; and (4) group temperament.

Number and Sex.   The number of children is a strong factor in determining the nature of a group, for each child affects and influences others. Fifteen children generally provide an ideal group. This is particularly true in a leisuretime program where a group meets once a week for 40 minutes or an hour. In classrooms a group may include 25 or 35 personalities.

An all-girl or an all-boy group provides quite a different group experience from that provided by a mixed group of boys and girls. A leader always considers the composition of a group. She watches to see how individuals relate or fail to relate to one another. She is alert to determine whether boys or girls dominate a group, not alone in numbers, but in leading the group in initiating ideas, action, and interests.

Previous Experience. When children know how to create characterizations, they often fire others into strong expression in a much shorter period of time. Children with experience ask to create stories into plays much sooner than most beginning groups. A leader watches for previous experience to reveal itself, since this factor often influences the attitude and spirit of an entire group.

Temperament. "I have the liveliest children this year." "I've never had such a quiet group." "My children are the dancingest children I've ever had. At the slightest suggestion they want to dance." "You should listen in for a couple of hours in my room. My children are young philosophers. They want to ponder and discuss." "Mine are more like politicians. They want to talk all the time."

These comments made by teachers in a lunchroom on the third day of a new school year indicate how quickly alert teachers sense group temperament. When a leader is sensitive to this peculiar group faculty she catches an intangible quality that characterizes an entire group. She watches for signs of this temperament, which often provides a clue to the current of power within a group.

INTRODUCING CHARACTERIZATION

Characterization is basic in creating plays, for a play is always concerned with characters. Some leaders prefer to introduce characterization at a first meeting. Others prefer to introduce it only when children express themselves freely and confidently in rhythmic movement. To characterize means to create a person or thing different from oneself. When a child characterizes he takes on a new role (Fig. 5.1).

Selecting Material for Characterization. A beginning experience should be limited to creating one or two characterizations with strong feeling. Material selected for characterizations should meet the following basic requirements: (1) Characterizations should be well-defined and essentially true. (2) They should be involved in a situation which appeals to children. (3) They should be far removed from a child in age and characteristics.

True Characterizations. Life, like drama, is made up of forceful, purposeful people bent on doing good or doing evil. Children like to create characters who are well rounded and true to life. Children of all ages enjoy being animals. They find a peculiar enjoyment in being wild forest animals, trained circus animals, and friendly pets at home or in a zoo. They enjoy turning into bumblebees, spiders, and creatures who live in the sea.

Fig. 5.1. "Henny-Penny, wait for me." (*School of Drama, University of Washington*)

Children find delight in pushing past the boundaries of time and space and creating people who are older than they are and who are unusual in personality. Children often hunger to play characterizations of figures whom they fear in actual life. Most children of 6 years and older enjoy being giants, witches, and wicked fairies and wizards. They find real glee in occasionally being robbers, thieves, and plundering pirates. Children should have opportunities to become both good and evil characters in situations that are wholesome and strong. They should have opportunities to discuss characters' attitudes, motives, and relationships before creating. Characters should always be well defined and solid in substance. Creating from trivial characterizations or from characters from mediocre and low standard literature is as dangerous as leading children entirely toward always creating one-sided characters, either good or evil.

Characterizations in Interesting Situations. Vivid characterizations always appeal to children if they are involved in a situation that a child enjoys, understands, or wonders about. Events from real life and literature which are colorful and exciting generally hold high appeal.

A situation must always provide purpose. A child needs to recognize purpose before he expresses. He is somewhat lost when he is simply guided into becoming a lion doing whatever a lion does. "Let's be lions," a beginning leader often says. She is generally disappointed when few if any children create convincing lions. On the other hand when a leader explores with children the many different things a lion does in a given situation a child begins to form images that stimulate expression. He enjoys being a lion walking down the street in a circus parade, or a lion in a circus doing a daring act. He finds purpose in creating a hungry lion at the zoo waiting for dinner. Children enjoy being lions in a jungle stalking for food.

When an older child is guided into being a pirate he needs a specific situation from which to create. There is excitement and challenge in creating a pirate commanded by a pirate chief to, "Come aboard, matey. Show one thing that proves ye've sailed the stormy seas."

Characterizations Far Removed from a Child in Age and Characteristics. It is difficult for a child to create a straight role, though occasionally straight roles are enjoyed if the character is in a situation that is strong in conflict and purpose. The characterizations of

Little Black Sambo, Heidi, and Tom Sawyer are straight roles, but in these stories each character is involved in an exciting situation. On the whole, and particularly for beginning experiences, children enjoy creating characterizations which are noticeably different from themselves. They enjoy creating characterizations that encourage the use of the whole body. Characterizations that have held high appeal for beginning experiences are animals, creatures, and insects, rain, wind, snow, and fog, witches, giants, gnomes, and elves, and a variety of show people such as those found in a circus, carnival, and rodeo.

CHARACTERIZATION FOCUSED TO DRAMA GOALS

A leader always keeps drama goals in mind when she selects material. When the drama goal is characterization, she selects material that will meet this goal with strong emphasis. One vivid satisfying experience in characterization is worth a dozen weak, half-hearted experiences. When every child gets involved in the fun of being someone different from himself, creativity and characterization function hand in hand.

To understand how vital it is to select material that meets the goal of characterization, let us examine the kindergarten teacher's first-day experience with Parade Time. The specific drama goal for this session was characterization in rhythmic movement. The simplicity of the situation provided enthusiasm and rapid direct involvement of the children. The situation, which was high in appeal, limited the children to creating the two characterizations of drum majorettes and elephants. These characterizations, particularly the elephants, were far removed from the children's real selves. Each characterization provided a variety of rhythmic movement in marching, working with imaginary batons, lumbering along like heavy, proud elephants, and swinging trunks in a variety of purposeful actions. Each character paraded with feeling and with purpose in making people happy (the other half of the group). The situation provided a framework for coöperation. It kept the children organized. It provided fun and a feeling of enjoyment and success both as a group and individually.

Let us suppose, on the other hand, that the teacher had not been as keenly aware of the specific drama goal of characterization. She might have selected the children's first three responses which were majorettes, soldiers, and boy scouts, which are similar both in rhythmic movement and in characterization, and not as far removed from a child's self as elephants. Children, young children particularly, express with a singleness of concept. They select a vivid aspect of a character, and image it in their expression. At a first session children would probably create little difference between a marching soldier, a marching boy scout, and a marching majorette.

INTRODUCING SIMPLE PLOT, CONFLICT, DIALOGUE

Material that has a simple plot with a strong conflict is always exciting to children. It involves them quickly with strong emotional feeling. Many leaders introduce children to characterization in a situation that has conflict, rather than one on a high emotional plane. In either case, beginning experiences should be limited in characterization but strong in emotional conflict and action.

"Hickory Dickory Dock" is a classic example of beginning conflict material for little children. Characterizations are limited to clocks and mice and emotion is centered on fear which comes from unexpected noises. This emotion, which has been experienced by almost every child, causes children to create with strong feeling. They enjoy creating curious little mice who scamper on quiet feet looking for food as they come to the big clock in a "locked-up cupboard." They enjoy creating different kinds of clocks with different kinds of gongs, strikes, rings, and sounds to scare the mice. The mice enjoy waiting until a clock really scares them, before they scurry away. Little children enjoy playing this conflict over and over again. They like to take turns, first being the mice, then being the clocks. They delight in the emotional reaction which always comes whether they are playing or watching others play. Some groups have created this experience in an outdoor setting. A family of curious forest mice venture into a tent and are frightened by the sudden ringing of an alarm clock.

Older children enjoy creating conflicts which are well defined in simplicity for beginning experiences. A favorite experience for most groups is a picnic situation which offers strong characterization. Children are guided to create individualized characters centering around a family reunion, a pioneer picnic, or a community gathering where there will be people of all ages. They are guided into spreading a picnic table and gathering around to enjoy eating picnic food. Strong feeling of enjoyment is stressed before a surprise of sudden fear is introduced.

"What might happen to the merry picnickers which would frighten them and send them scurrying for shelter or safety?" Such a question often brings forth ideas of an unexpected thunder and hailstorm, a swarm of bees, a black bear crashing through the trees, or the cry of an approaching cougar. Individuals who think of the ideas often enjoy creating the conflict. They may create either in pairs or in small groups to surprise the gathering of picnickers.

After the picnic scene has been created with strong reaction to the conflict, dialogue is introduced as a new drama goal. When children have reacted with strong feeling in pantomime, they generally express dialogue naturally and freely.

Many groups enjoy putting their earlier characterizations into sudden conflicts. Forest animals may encounter a sudden storm, pirate crews may be surprised by a sudden attack from an enemy ship, cackling witches brewing evil may be alarmed by a sudden shower of rain or a forest fire, elves and fairies enjoying a festive dance may be thrown into a fearful panic by the sudden appearance of a wizard or giant.

When children are guided to experience conflicts such as these, each child creates his interpretations of the same character. The character who introduces the conflict may be created by the entire group in mass ensemble. Each child is encouraged to create in his own individual way. Then one or two children are chosen to create the character who introduces conflict within the context of the situation. In this instance, children who create freely and forcefully should be chosen. It is essential that a strong feeling of conflict be created so that characters within the situation will react strongly. If the conflict is a storm, or an enemy attack, it may be more effectively represented by an appropriate musical recording. "The Storm" from Rossini's *William Tell*, "Cloudburst" from Grofé's *Grand Canyon Suite*, and "Infernal Dance of Kastchei" from Stravinsky's *Firebird Suite* offer strong mood and forceful rhythm that motivate intense emotional reaction.

When children are guided into conflict material, the leader watches for moments wherein they react spontaneously with dialogue. Thus she introduces expression in dialogue in a natural rather than an unnatural situation.

STORIES TO BEGIN ON

Hans Christian Andersen tells us in "The Marsh King's Daughter," "The storks have a great many stories which they tell their little ones, all about the bogs and marshes. They suit them to their age and capacity. The young ones are quite satisfied with kribble, krabble, or some such nonsense, and find it charming; but the elder ones want something with more meaning."

A leader gains from the stork's advice. She watches a group of children to see how the material she is sharing satisfies and challenges. She evaluates each experience in order to determine the kind of experience a group needs. With children and drama in mind, she selects material which she believes to be right for their ages and capacities for the moment at hand.

After children have created strong characterizations in simple conflicts and have created dialogue naturally and freely, they are ready for a short story. A beginning story which is to be created into a play should be limited in characterization, strong in action and conflict, and should have a simple, forward-moving plot.

"The Three Billy Goats Gruff" is an excellent first story for little children to create into a play. Its characterizations are limited to goats and a troll. It presents a conflict in the problem of hunger which cannot be satisfied because of the troll. It provides for strong feeling in character and opportunities to speak in dialogue in a natural, understanding way. It provides for a good energy release in a make-believe fight. It provides a forward-moving plot which builds quickly to a satisfying climax. Many little children enjoy playing this over and over again, taking turns to become the four basic characters of the three goats and the troll. They often enjoy becoming other goat families on the hillside to warn the Gruff family, and to react strongly during each goat's experience on the bridge. Some children enjoy creating a bridge that moves in rhythm whenever the goats go trip-tropping across.

"A Tailor and a Bear" is an excellent beginning story which meets the basic requirements. It holds high interest for almost every group of children from 6 years of age through junior high school.

LONGER STORIES

After several experiences in creating plays from short stories most groups are ready for a longer story. A leader evaluates closely to determine whether she believes a group is ready for the coöperative experience of creating a play that evolves in more than one clear episode. When a group is ready, a story may be selected that requires two or three acts or several episodes to develop the plot. In a story of this kind there are generally several characters who need to be individualized. The conflict that develops generally calls for strong dialogue throughout the play.

A group that has gradually been introduced to the fundamentals of drama over a period of time should enjoy the challenge of creating a longer play, such as adventures from "Robin Hood" for older children (Fig. 5.2). When younger children are ready they always enjoy creating "Henny-Penny" (Fig. 5.3). If, on the other hand, children have been guided into creating from material that was too advanced or was lacking in appeal they may not be ready to create from a long story. Whenever a leader senses a situation of this kind she should share exciting and satisfying experiences in basic rhythmic movement and characterization. Children need to enjoy and learn how to create a characterization before they will enjoy creating from a long story.

Fig. 5.2. "Hark ye! Watch my arrow hit its mark!" (*School of Drama, University of Washington*)

Fig. 5.3. "Hurry, Foxy-woxy!" (*School of Drama, University of Washington*)

MATERIAL MUST APPEAL TO LEADER

A leader must like whatever material she is going to share. She must enjoy a story and be enthusiastic about sharing it before she can make it come alive for others. Telling a story is likely to remain mechanical and lifeless unless a leader feels a strong sense of emotion when she first reads it. If a leader does not enjoy one story she is far wiser to choose a story that she does like, even though the first story satisfies all other criteria. She cannot become involved in sharing and guiding creatively unless a story arouses a strong stimulation for her.

A leader must enjoy all material that she shares with children. If she has never been enthusiastic about going to a parade or a circus she should not choose this kind of material. If she has never enjoyed outdoor sports she will not become enthusiastic just because she decides it is good material to lead an older group into rhythmic action. She should always select material that she can become excited about.

SPECIFIC GOALS AND MATERIAL FOR A NINE-WEEKS' PROGRAM

Miss Smith was the leader who shared creative dramatics with Carol, Emily, Gene, and the group of lively 7- and 8-year-olds.[6] These children met for one hour each week on Saturday mornings. When Miss Smith completed a nine weeks' program with this group, the specific goals and material were developed as follows:

SESSION ONE

Group Goals: To get acquainted, and discover what each child is like in individual characteristics, needs, and interests.

Drama Goals: To introduce children to creative dramatics by channel-

[6] See Chapter 2, pp. 47–56.

ing their energies into expression in creative rhythmic movement.

Material: Rhythmic movement and pantomine based on children's wishes. Initial Question: When you wave a fairy wand and make a wish, what one special thing do you wish to do?

Music: "Fairies" (Schubert), *Rhythmic Activities,* Vol. I, RCA Victor Record Library for Elementary Schools, 1947.

Session Two

Group Goals: To channel physical energies and strengthen group spirit by giving individual recognition to 12 individuals who have told their wishes, but not yet created from them.

Drama Goals: To encourage individual expression in rhythmic movements of galloping, climbing, dancing, swimming, and flying.

Material: Based on children's specific wishes of "going to the land of horses," "climbing down the rainbow to the lost city of gold," "dancing with fairies and elves at their party," "swimming with mermaids," and "flying to Never-Never Land with Peter Pan."

Music: Variety of rhythms selected from *Rhythmic Activities,* Vol. I, *op. cit.*

Session Three

Group Goals: To satisfy mental as well as physical and social needs by disciplining children's thinking, social rules, and individual expression.

Drama Goals: To introduce characterization in rhythmic movement with strong emotional reaction in pantomime.

Material: Nursery rhyme, "Ride a Cock Horse to Banbury Cross." Characterizations limited to *people* riding to Banbury Cross, and the *fine lady* they see.

Music: "Jaglied" and "Fairies," *Rhythmic Activities,* Vol. I, *op. cit.*

Session Four

Group Goals: To strengthen group spirit by providing an opportunity for strong emotional involvement and release which contributes to group success. To guide the shy children (Donna, Lillian, Fay) into the playing. To discipline the two aggressive children by guiding them to contribute to the success of the experience.

Drama Goals: To introduce a short story which is strong in emotional conflict but limited in characterization, dialogue, and forward-moving plot. Emphasis will be on strong characterizations involved in conflict.

Material: "The Conjure Wives," an old tale retold by Frances G. Wickes. Source: Winifred Ward, *Stories to Dramatize.*

Music: "Danse Macabre," by Saint-Saëns.

Session Five

Group Goals: To satisfy spiritual needs by encouraging children to indirectly discuss the story theme as they plan the characterization of the Voice, and develop the final episode.

Drama Goals: To encourage creative expression in the characterization of the Voice, and in the transformation of the selfish sisters from witches to owls. To emphasize emotional reaction in transformation scene.

Material: Completion of story, "The Conjure Wives." Emphasis on theme: Selfishness transforms one into ugliness and loneliness. Emphasis on utilizing children's ideas of the Voice, and emphasis on fear of Wives.

Music: Same as used in previous session.

Session Six

Group Goals: To provide an exciting creative experience that fosters well-rounded growth with specific emphasis on coöperation and strong emotional release.

Drama Goals: To present a short story, limited in characterization, forward-moving plot, strong action, and worthy theme. To develop this story over two sessions by emphasizing characterization, reaction, and strong feeling.

Material: "How the Robin's Breast Became Red," by Flora J. Cooke. Source: Winifred Ward, *Stories to Dramatize.* Emphasis on characterizations of bear, bird, and hunter's son.

SESSION SEVEN

Group Goals: To provide a new creative experience which fosters well-rounded growth in encouraging creativity, coöperation, and physical and emotional release.

Drama Goals: Same drama goals as set forth in Session Six. New story introduced to be created over a period of three sessions because of the unexpected yet satisfying creative experience provided by "Blue Queenie." Since children created strong characterizations and played the climactic scene with beauty and strong feeling it seems advisable to introduce a new experience.

Material: "A Tailor and a Bear." An old tale. Emphasis in first session on story theme and characterizations of the tailor and the bear.

Music: "Of a Tailor and a Bear" by Edward MacDowell, *Listening Activities,* Vol. II, *op. cit.*

SESSION EIGHT

Group Goals: To satisfy social and spiritual needs by providing opportunities for children to plan and play together in groups of four to create the opening scene.

Drama Goals: To create opening scene with strong characterizations and strong expression in emotional reaction, interaction, and dialogue.

Material: Same story as used in previous session. Emphasis on opening scene including sudden entrance of bear into

tailor's shop and tailor's reaction as he plays for bear to dance.

Music: Same as above.

SESSION NINE

Group Goals: To provide an experience for well-rounded growth by creating final scene, and coöperating to create entire story with success. To include every child in final experience and provide experience in teamwork and group success.

Drama Goals: To create reaction of villagers and to create the Keeper's entrance and resulting reaction. To put entire story together weaving episodes into one complete whole.

Material: Same as above.

Music: Same as above.

CREATING ORIGINAL PLAYS AND STORIES

Often when leaders search for stories they are tempted to make up stories of their own. Leaders, both beginning and experienced, should be warned against this. A story is generally of little worth if it has been created chiefly to provide rhythmic action and a variety of characters. The best stories throughout the years have been told or written because the tellers or writers had something to say, something to share which found its way into being. Whenever a leader contrives a story it is likely to fail to reach children. Children may listen and play the story, but they sense the superficiality. A contrived story is artificial; it is a substitute for the real thing. Children need stories that have met the tests of good literature, stories which in some unique way like "Epaminondas" and "Peter Rabbit" touch children's souls. Leaders soon recognize the necessity of sharing only the finest and best in literature with children.

Shall children create plays from stories, or shall they create original plays? Some leaders feel that it is a greater creative experience for children to create original plots. True, this experience offers a tremendous challenge to children. It is one kind of experience for a leader to guide children to create a play from a good piece of literature. It is quite a different experience to guide children to create an original play. If a leader considers the challenge a director has when he directs players into creating a play from scripts she will perhaps recognize a similar challenge in guiding children to create from a story. On the other hand, when she guides children to create an original play, the chief requirement is for leader and children to have a good understanding of basic dramatic elements.

The answer to the question appears to lie with the leader. If she has a thorough understanding of dramatic elements and play structure, she may be in a position to guide children into an experience that is satisfying and thrilling. In so doing, she uses care in encouraging each child to contribute. Too often, one or two children dominate a discussion when a group is attempting to develop a plot. A leader must strive to keep every child reaching for ideas that will contribute.

One experienced group of 9-, 10-, and 11-year-olds created an original play called "The Road to Happiness,"[7] motivated by Rachel Field's "Roads." The children were asked the following question: If you could follow one road, where would you choose to go? They replied with such ideas as Alaska, Finland, New York, Washington, D.C., a road to our summer cabin, a road to hidden treasure, and a road to buried dinosaurs. An 11-year-old girl was the last to answer. She said, "This probably sounds funny but I think everyone is looking for the road to happiness." This idea had an electrifying effect on the group. An exciting discussion took place, and the children

[7] School of Drama, University of Washington, Seattle, Washington.

decided that happiness comes from doing something for others. With this theme in mind they arrived at the following plot which they enjoyed making into a play:

A boy and girl start out to find the Lake of Laughing Water because their grandmother is unhappy. She has told them an old legend which reveals that an enchanted lake is hidden in the hills near their home. The children start out on their journey to find the lake. They meet a little bird with a broken wing. They tie up its wing and take the bird with them so they may care for it.

They see a house in the woods and stop to inquire about the lake. An old witch lives in the house. She almost lures them to eat berries which will bring them under her spell, but they are saved by the little bird whom they have befriended. The children and bird hurry away from the witch and see a king's carriage coming through the forest. They stop the carriage to ask the king about the Lake of Laughing Water.

The king is worried because the queen is unhappy. When the king and queen hear the legend they decide to go with the children. The children have never seen a queen before. They pick flowers for her, and ask her how to take care of the bird's broken wing. Once the queen begins to help she finds she is no longer unhappy. She decides that they should all return to the castle where they may fix the bird's wing in the right way.

While the children and the bird join the king and queen in a royal banquet, the boy tells the legend. When the queen hears the story she decides that they must go to the grandmother's hut to take her with them in their search for the lake. The next day when the carriage arrives, the grandmother hurries out to meet it. She is so happy to see the children, but the children cannot understand what has happened to cause their grandmother's great happiness. The grandmother invites the king and queen to come into her little hut to have some bread and fresh mountain water.

The children hurry to get the water which is in a spring just outside the door. The bird goes with them. When the bird gets a drink he bursts forth in the most beautiful song that has ever been heard. The king and queen and grandmother hurry out to the spring. The children decide that the spring is the Lake of Laughing Water. The king tells them that happiness comes in doing for others. He asks if he and the queen may come every day to eat home-baked bread and to drink fresh mountain water. The grandmother is overjoyed. The children tell the king that everyone should think of a way in which they may help the ugly old witch to think of others, too. The king says they will not give up until they have found a way. As he and the queen drive away in the carriage the little bird sings his beautiful song. The grandmother and children wave happily until the carriage is out of sight.

ANALYZING MATERIAL

Before a leader can guide children into creating and expressing from material, she must know and understand material from a drama viewpoint. For this reason she analyzes carefully. If material has been selected for the specific purpose of motivating expression in rhythmic movement, it is analyzed from this viewpoint. If material has been chosen to encourage expression through characterization, it is analyzed from this viewpoint.

Whenever a story is to be shared the leader must explore it thoroughly, analyzing it in a way not unlike the way the pioneering grandmother studied and pondered. By digging and delving into a story, she begins to understand it. As she analyzes, she begins to enjoy it and becomes even more excited about sharing it than when she selected it. There is no short-cut way to prepare.

Editing a Long Story. To edit a story for creative dramatics means to tighten it dramatically. The chief need for editing most long stories lies in the plot. Many folk and fairy stories have a remote, narrative opening. For instance, in many versions of "Cinderella" the story begins where Cinderella's mother dies and her father remarries and proceeds with long rambling episodes in which Cinderella attends the castle ball on three different evenings. For creative dramatics a story must have an immediate opening, and episodes need to be dramatic.

To edit a plot, a leader chooses a point of attack which starts a story just as a play would begin its opening act. Basic episodes are focused into compact scenes which build in order toward the climax of the plot. The beauty, charm, and author's intent are always respected. A leader uses extreme care in neither adding main characters nor distorting the original story. Basically she adapts a story from narrative form into dramatic form.

Analyzing Story from Three Viewpoints. To prepare a story for creative dramatics, a leader analyzes it from the three following viewpoints: (1) basic dramatic elements, (2) basic moods and appeals to children, and (3) basic children's needs which it may satisfy.

ANALYZING DRAMATIC ELEMENTS

Name of Story: A Tailor and a Bear

Author: Jacob and Wilhelm Grimm

Sources: *Forgotten Fairy Tales* by Grimm

The Book House. Ed., Olive Beaupre Miller, Vol. III

Musical Recording: "Of a Tailor and a Bear," by Edward MacDowell, *Listening Activities,* Vol. II.

Adaptation of Story:

A Tailor and a Bear

Once upon a time there was a merry tailor. Day after day he sat cross-legged on a big table in his shop. He stitched, snipped, and sewed the finest clothes in all the land. People traveled from far and near to have the tailor make fine garments for them. Now the tailor had a special secret in his tailoring. He had a violin, and he loved music. Whenever the tailor was to make a gown for a queen, he would play music that sounded as if it were echoing through castle halls. Whenever he was to tailor a suit for a traveling minstrel the tailor would play music that sounded as if it were wandering over hills and countrysides. And while he played the tailor could see exquisite gowns and rare garments.

One morning the tailor sat on his bench and played a jolly tune for he was going to make a suit for a court jester. When he finished playing he put his violin beside him, and he started snipping with excitement. He could see a bright red suit trimmed with silver bells and sunshine ribbons. Suddenly the tailor was startled by excitement in the street. He heard cries, screams, shouts, running, and hurrying. He looked toward his door and listened trying to figure out what it might be.

All at once the door to his shop swung open. There coming into his shop was a big black bear. The bear growled and lumbered and glared around the shop as it came straight toward the tailor. The tailor was frightened. He jumped up from his table, and started to run. The bear came closer and closer in a savage rage. There was no way the tailor could get to the door and surely the bear would pounce on him and eat him. Suddenly the tailor thought of his music. Animals liked music. He knew they did. He snatched up his violin, tucked it under his chin, tuned it quickly, and started to play. At the first sound of music the bear stopped in his tracks and listened. The music was beautiful. The bear rocked from side to side, and slowly rose up on his hind legs and started to dance. Village folk had followed the bear to the doorway. They could not believe what they saw. They whispered to each other, each one ready to run if the bear should start toward the door.

The tailor was relieved, and without realizing it he played faster and faster. The bear could not dance to such fast rhythm. He grew angry. He dropped on all fours, started toward the tailor again and growled savagely. The tailor played slowly and calmly for he thought he knew what the bear wanted. The bear swayed until he caught the rhythm of the music. He rose up on his hind legs and danced round and round. His eyes shone and he growled with pleasure as he danced clumsily and heavily.

Suddenly a stranger pushed his way through the crowd at the door. He was the keeper of the bear, and had been searching frantically for the savage beast which he had trained to dance. The keeper rushed to the bear and seized him by his collar. He looked around to see if the bear had done any harm. When the keeper saw that all was well, he pulled on the bear's collar. The bear dropped on all fours and growled. He did not want to leave the beautiful music. The owner half pulled and half dragged the bear out of the shop, and the curious villagers followed them down the street. The tailor was excited with relief. He patted his violin gently, and put it on the table close beside him. He whistled for joy and picked up the jester's suit. As he set to work he made his needle fly, for he was so happy to be safe from the savage beast.

Form:

An old folk tale with a strong emotional impact which ends triumphantly in great relief. Story moves quickly in a merry way like a scherzo.

Themes:

"Music hath power to soothe the savage beast."

There's power in music.

Face your problems squarely rather than running away from them. There's danger in running away from trouble.

Keep a level head at all times, and you will think your way out of trouble.

Characters:

Excellent limitation of characters. Story requires three main characters to create exciting drama. It provides excellent opportunity to individualize village folk including such characters as a mayor, baker, cobbler, peddler, granny, and grandchildren. Villagers have strong purpose for they react to the fear of the bear.

Possible expansion of characters is recognized in the opportunity for customers to visit the shop at the outset. Customers will emphasize the importance of the tailor and may provide an immediate reason for his playing his violin.

Variety in characters is recognized:

Merry tailor who enjoys music and tailoring.

Wild bear who enjoys music and has been trained to dance.

Bear keeper who is worried when he realizes he has lost his bear.

Rhythmic Action:

Tailor: Opportunity for small rhythmic actions in cutting, stitching, sewing, showing garments to customers; jumping and running when bear enters; playing rapidly on violin, then more rhythmically and slowly; stitching with relief and enjoyment.

Bear: Heavy, clumsy, bearlike rhythm as bear enters; lumbering, menacing movements as he glares and searches room for music; swaying on all fours, dancing on hind legs, swaying round and round, clapping paws, bowing; suddenly sinking on all fours in savage anger when pulled away by keeper.

Keeper: Running, frantic searching, pulling and dragging bear.

Villagers: Rushing, running, shaking fists, following keeper.

Customer: Creative rhythmic movement depending on the kind of character. If a knight he may joust to show the tailor the kind of costume he needs. If customer is a princess she may dance to show the kind of costume she wants for a royal ball.

Scenic Action:

Action is set in tailor's shop.

Scene 1. Tailor enters shop, makes it ready, examines garments, tunes violin, and puts finishing touches on garment he is making.

Scene 2. Customer enters and orders a rare costume. Tailor plays a tune to get an idea for costume. Customer leaves. Tailor plays again.

Scene 3. Commotion in street is heard. Tailor listens. Door opens and bear enters searching for music which he has heard. Tailor reacts fearfully. Bear growls and approaches tailor. Tailor's fear heightens until he decides to play music to calm bear. Bear starts to dance, is angered at fast rhythm, growls, and starts toward tailor. Tailor plays more slowly. Bear dances with beauty, rhythm, and enjoyment.

Scene 4. Crowd gathers. Reacts strongly, fearfully, and with amazement.

Scene 5. Keeper arrives. He sees bear, pulls on rope, surveys room, pulls bear out of shop. Villagers react in relief and follow. Tailor reacts and sets to work with joy and relief.

Plot:

Straightforward and swiftly moving plot. The problem is established by the entrance of the bear. It is complicated when the tailor can't escape, and starts to play in rapid tempo. The tailor solves the problem of the bear's anger by playing slowly and calmly until the keeper finally arrives.

Emotional Conflict:

The tailor is frightened by the sudden entrance of a savage beast. Bear is in conflict with the music which apparently reached his ear from a distance and he was determined to find it. Keeper is in conflict with the fear that his bear has arrived in the village and done harm to the village folk, for he knows his bear is savage by nature.

Dialogue:

If group is ready for verbal expression there are opportunities for the tailor to sing, whistle, hum, talk to himself at the outset.

An opportunity for creative dialogue between customer and tailor when customer asks for a certain costume and tailor describes it with noticeable imagination.

An opportunity for tailor to react with strong dialogue when bear enters shop.

Bear's reaction may be done with strong reactions in savage growls and bear sounds.

Villagers may talk among themselves in quiet, hushed voices.

Keeper's dialogue will be natural and strong as he reacts with relief and anxiety as he finds the bear.

ANALYSIS OF BASIC MOODS AND APPEALS
TO CHILDREN

Realistic Appeal: The story appeals to some children because it presents

a possible situation. The bear is a real bear. He does not talk the way animals do in some stories. Rather he is savage and fierce. From time to time animals do escape from a traveling show or a zoo, or in some small mountain town. Now and then bears come into a village.

Fantasy Appeal: The story presents an unusual situation. The tailor is quaint and storybookish. He plays, sings, dances, and gets ideas for his tailoring through his music.

Music Appeal: Most children delight in music. They respond to various moods which music creates for them. They enjoy dancing to music, and are intrigued by the idea of a bear dancing to music and enjoying its distinct rhythm.

Tailoring Appeal: Color and unusual touches in clothes hold interest for some children.

ANALYSIS OF BASIC NEEDS WHICH STORY MAY SATISFY

Physical Need: Strong release of energy is provided in being a savage bear, a dancing bear, a heavy, clumsy, resisting bear. Satisfaction in finer coördinated movements is found in the tailor's actions of stitching and snipping, and playing violin in different tempos and rhythms.

Emotional Need: Splendid opportunity for every child to create the character of the tailor and react to the fear and panic that are experienced when the bear enters. Good opportunity for children to share similar frightening experiences when they are discussing the character of the tailor. Good opportunity to experience the emotional disturbance that the bear experiences in wanting the music to be slow enough for his dance. Strong reaction of fear and finally of relief in characters of villagers.

Mental Need: Strong opportunity for children to experience a real problem. Good opportunity for discussion which may be centered around questions: "What may tailor do when he first sees the bear? What would you do if you were surprised by an unexpected wild animal if you were alone at home?" Situation provides a good opportunity for children to discuss how to solve problems by observing, keeping calm, and thinking rather than becoming fearful and scared.

Creative Need: Strong opportunities for children to create a bear's dance, tailor's "costumes," unusual customers, unusual and interesting villagers.

Social Need: Opportunities for children to work in small groups to create action and interaction for villagers. Good opportunity for a group of four children to create customers as they work together. Such ·possibilities as a king with a herald and two servants, four knights, a family with a coachman, etc. Splendid opportunity for children to work in pairs to see how each pair may create the conflict scene between the tailor and bear. Strong opportunity for entire group to coöperate as they work together to create entire play. Each child encouraged to contribute in a specific way to the success of the group experience.

Questions and Activities

1. You, a creative dramatics leader, are going to meet a group of children for the first time. State the age group and number of boys and number of girls. Select a poem or an idea to be shared in this first meeting. List three ways this material meets the needs of these children. List the variety of rhythmic movements inherent within the material. List the focused questions you plan to ask during this first meeting to stimulate individual expression.

2. Discuss what is meant by considering material for creative dramatics from a *needs* viewpoint. Discuss what is meant by group and drama goals.

3. Divide the class into three buzz session groups. Each group will select a poem or idea that appeals to group members and is appropriate for creative dramatics at any age level. Each group will analyze the rhythmic action, and will plan three focused questions to stimulate individual expression based on this material. After 15 minutes, a spokesman from each group will share the rhythmic action anal-

ysis, and will ask one focused question to determine the degree of response each question brings.

4. After the above experience select a poem that you consider appropriate for creative dramatics at a specific age level. Analyze the dramatic elements in the poem. Focus the rhythmic action by planning three focused questions. State the questions in a way that will provide expression in three different kinds of rhythmic movement. Underline with red pencil the action verbs in each question.

5. Select a short story you like which is appropriate for creative dramatics for children of a certain age level. Analyze the dramatic elements in this story. Underline in red pencil the variety of characterizations this story offers a child for creative expression. If the story is limited in characters, suggest possibilities for multiplying characters or for adding new characters. Share your story analysis with a class member to read and evaluate with comments.

6. Complete the following statements:

a. When a leader meets a group of children for the first time it is essential that she guide with specific group and drama goals in mind because ....
....

b. In a first creative dramatics experience with a new group of children a leader guides to help children reach the following goals:
1. ....
2. ....
3. ....

c. In addition to dramatic content the four basic factors which determine a leader's choice of material to share with children include:
1. ....
2. ....
3. ....
4. ....

d. A leader selects a musical recording to heighten creative ex-

pression by considering it from the three aspects of ....
....

e. After a first meeting in creative dramatics a leader analyzes group needs from the five basic areas of child growth which include: ......
....

f. "Let's be airplanes!" This statement will provide stronger purpose for a child's creative expression when the statement suggests:
....

7. Include in your notebook or file favorite poems, favorite stories, pictures, and ideas you would like to share with children in creative dramatics. Emphasize quality rather than quantity as you select these materials.

CHAPTER 6

How to Guide Children to Create Drama

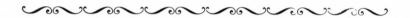

In all these dramas of the past there is a dream—an excite-ment, a high rare mood, a conception of greatness.—Robert Edmond Jones

*J*f a leader is to help children create drama, she must guide them so they "bring back this mood, this excitement, this dream."[1] To do this she must understand the creative process. She must know how to guide children so they become excited about expressing thoughts and feelings. She must know how to guide them to create drama as they play together. The greatness will then come through.

Understanding the Creative Process. The creative process is intangible. Beginning leaders find difficulty in realizing this. Rather they seek a set of well-defined, exact techniques. They look for a one-two-three method which may be geared to every session. They want specific directions like those which accompany machines. Children are much more wonderful and complex than the most complex machines. A child, unlike a machine, never remains constant. Each child, each group, each occasion is different. Every leader is different. For these reasons no two creative experiences are ever the same.

[1] Robert Edmond Jones, *The Dramatic Imagination,* Theatre Arts Books, 1941.

Five-Way Cycle. Although intangible, the creative process follows a basic pattern. It evolves in a five-way cycle. It consists of (1) motivating children into a specific mood; (2) sharing a story or idea; (3) guiding children into making a plan for playing; (4) guiding children into creating while they play; and (5) praising and guiding children to evaluate playing. Through evaluation children recognize the need for making a new plan for playing. The creative process then repeats the cycle. It is flexible. It is a continuous and interwoven procedure. It depends on children's expression and a leader's skill in channeling expression into dramatic action. To understand the creative process let us consider each of the five basic aspects in turn.

MOTIVATING: PLANNING MOOD

Just as a builder makes a plan to guide his building, a leader makes a plan to guide children into creating. A plan is made by considering a specific group of children in relation to a specific story or idea from which they are to create. *Planning a mood* is the first consideration. If a leader shares a story before children are in a proper mood, they may listen but fail to become involved in the story. All great art is created within the realm of mood. Creative expression comes from strong feeling and belief.

Determining Mood. Mood lies within an individual. It is thinking affected by feeling. It is a state of mind that an individual is in at a given moment. *A contemplative mood is basic in all arts.* This mood arouses an aesthetic attitude which causes individuals to *identify* and *feel with* an experience. This feeling of identification is called *empathy*. An experience must get inside a child before he can create from it. When a child gets involved he begins to think, feel, reflect, recall, and express. If he fails to get into a mood and identify, an experience never reaches him. It is like proverbial water on a duck's back—a surface thing, rather than a creative experience from within.

When 20 or 30 children gather together they are likely to be in 20 or 30 different moods. One child may be wondering about his mother who is working, another may be thinking about his puppy, another may be hoping others will notice his new shoes, while others may be in gay moods, mischievous moods, or—moods to begin.

A leader's first challenge is to clear the deck, so to speak, of many individual moods, and motivate children into one strong mood. This mood should lead children toward the story or idea. It should be a mood inherent in the material from which children are to create. The mood should arouse children into *thinking* and *feeling* and cause them to want to share and express. When this moment happens the creative process is set in motion.

What mood should be set? What mood will cause children to identify with an experience? How does a leader know what mood to develop before sharing a story? To determine this she examines the basic mood or moods of the story or idea. For instance, *dominating moods* are immediately recognized in the *universal ideas* of wishing, parading, adventuring, and dreaming.

In a good story an essential or basic mood generally dominates. When a child hears a story he identifies with the leading character. In most stories a leading character experiences a variety of moods within the story situation. A leader examines these basic moods to determine which is the *essential mood* that causes children to identify most strongly with the story. Basic moods are generally recognized in the following areas of a story: (1) opening incident, (2) leading character, (3) story problem, (4) theme, and (5) background and setting of the story.

Opening-Incident Mood. In "A Tailor and a Bear" the bear's sudden entrance creates a mood of surprise and alarm caused by the unexpected visitor. This is an universal mood. Almost every child has experienced it. If children are motivated to share experiences of times when they have been surprised by unexpected visitors a strong mood should develop. This mood will bring immediate identification with the tailor when the story is shared. An incident that opens a story should always be considered as a possible mood to develop.

Leading-Character Mood. The tailor is the leading character in "A Tailor and a Bear." If children are caused to wonder about *tailors* will a contemplative mood develop? Is a tailor mood a basic mood in this story? Would the story be essentially the same if the tailor were a weaver or a toymaker? Is it because the tailor is a tailor that a child identifies with his experience? Is it because the tailor does what he does in his sudden crisis that identification results? It appears that the tailor's occupation is not the essential factor that arouses mood.

When a leading character is an unusual personality this may be the basic factor that stimulates a contemplative mood. Such may be the case in a story about an elf, a fairy, a puppet, a witch, a machine, or an animal. A leading character is considered in relation to the mood the story creates by being a unique personality.

Story-Problem Mood. The tailor's problem is that of *keeping calm and thinking his way out of danger.* This is a problem almost every child has experienced. A problem mood always stirs feelings. When children share experiences that are similar to the key problem of a story they get into a problem mood. This mood generally leads to strong empathy when they hear the story.

Theme Mood. "Music hath power" is the underlying theme in

"A Tailor and a Bear." It is this essential truth which causes the tailor to create such beautiful garments. This truth causes the tailor and the bear to react as they do within the story. If children are brought into a music mood they will no doubt experience the power of music by listening to it. As they listen they begin to wonder. Wondering touches off both thinking and feeling. Wondering generally leads children into a mood far higher and more contemplative than a problem mood. A theme mood generally awakens feeling in a way similar to that invoked by an overture. It often causes children to think beyond realistic conflicts into wider realms. It appears that the theme mood in this story is the essential mood to develop within children.

Background-Mood. "A Tailor and a Bear" no doubt took place in make-believe land, or possibly in the days of traveling animal shows. A mood for make-believe land or medieval days is a possible mood for this story, but not a strong one. On the other hand a background mood may be a strong mood for a story that takes place in a distinctive setting or era. Stories which best lend themselves to background moods are legends, myths, and historical and adventure tales.

Antagonist-Mood. Very rarely is an initial mood developed for the antagonist or opposite character in a story. Such a mood lessens the suspense. It affects children in a way similar to that of hearing the answer to a riddle before hearing the riddle. It takes the edge off the emotional involvement. Suppose children have discussed bears before hearing "A Tailor and a Bear." When the story is told they do not experience the bear's sudden entrance with the same feeling of surprise and fear which the tailor does. Children are in a bear mood, quite different from the music-loving mood of the tailor at the outset of the story. An antagonist mood is seldom used as an

initial mood, but it may be used to remotivate children into creating from a story at a second or third class session, particularly if the children are to create the antagonist character.

MOTIVATING: PLANNING MOTIVATION

A strong mood always builds in two successive steps. It first gains attention and stimulates interest. It next arouses thinking, feeling, and a desire for expression.

Gaining Attention and Interest. In a good motivation these two steps are closely fused. Often they develop simultaneously. A skillful leader finds a *simple* way to capture children's attention; a *friendly* way to cause emotional walls to tumble; an *unexpected* way to cause imaginations and feelings to flourish. How does a leader plan a motivation? She is aware. She uses the very ways children use to motivate themselves into high spirits of thinking and feeling in their work and play. Let us look at simple, effective ways which may be used to capture attention and motivate expression.

Motivation by Sensory Stimulation. A child becomes attentive to something he sees, hears, tastes, touches, or smells. His senses are powerful antennae. They catch impressions. Children stop, look, and listen when their attention is focused on something they can see. The old axiom "One picture is worth a thousand words" is especially true with children. A single object, a picture, a slide, a film, or a book provides an immediate focus of attention. A distinctive sound captures attention in a similar way. A drumbeat, a recording, a whistle, a clapping of hands, a knock at a door, or an unusual voice generally gains immediate attention. Occasionally a story may lend itself to a mood better focused by one of the other senses.

Children may be easily motivated into a theme mood for "A Tailor and a Bear" through a sensory approach. They will quickly focus their attention by looking at an old violin or by listening to a musical recording.

Motivation by People. People are alive. One individual has tremendous power to motivate another individual. The old axiom could well be paraphrased "One person is worth a thousand pictures." Children focus immediate attention on a highly motivated individual. A dynamic child within a group or a child who comes to visit provides a natural focus of attention. A resource person may be invited for the specific purpose of sharing and stimulating interest. A visiting policeman builds a far stronger mood for safety than a badge or a picture of a policeman. A person from another country dressed in native costume arouses far higher interest than that which may be aroused by seeing pictures of foreign lands (Fig. 6.1).

When a person is not available, a leader considers the possibility of pantomoming a characterization to focus attention. Strong moods for stories have been built by leaders pantomiming an elf, a witch, a puppet, a circus clown, or an Indian chief. A pantomime breaks down barriers quickly, involves children in a spirit of fun, and motivates an immediate desire for active expression.

Unique ways of communication between peoples often serve to build a strong mood. A letter, a message, or an invitation may be used effectively. A letter from an elf, written on an autumn leaf, served to motivate a class of third graders into a delightful visit to fairyland.

How might children be motivated into a music mood for "A Tailor and a Bear" by using a people approach? A child or a visitor may be invited to share music. While children listen they may be motivated by a single statement: "Listen, and see just how this music makes you feel."

Motivation by Experience. An experience is exciting. It arouses

Fig. 6.1. A student from Japan builds a mood of beauty and wonder. (*School of Drama, University of Washington*)

interest. It means something is happening or has happened. Children may be motivated by immediate happenings in their environment such as recreational events, industrial developments, and seasonal happenings. An alert leader may utilize such experiences by planning an excursion, a walk, or a trip so children may experience firsthand. If this is not convenient, she may share an experience with the children. Or, she may invite a child to share an experience by suggesting: "John went to the circus last night. He is going to tell us about the most exciting thing he saw in the circus acts."

Immediate individual experiences such as a birthday, new clothes, a trip, a new pet, and other exciting events build a mood quickly when a child is invited to share. A leader should be alert to current seasonal happenings. High creative moods have been built from such seasonal occurrences as a sudden wind, a thunderstorm, a shower of rain, fog that appears unexpectedly, a first snowfall, a bird's nest, an arrival of polliwogs, an appearance of a rainbow, and a child's fascination with a shadow.

A leader who is alert to children's individual moods may hear a child or children singing. She may utilize this individual mood to build a group mood that centers around the power of music.

Motivation by Ideas. Ideas are stimulating. They arouse curiosities. An unusual statement, a quotation, a riddle, scrambled words, codes, puzzles, unexpected questions, and single words are effective ways to motivate children when using an idea approach. A single question may serve to barnstorm ideas. "What is the first thing you *see* when you hear the word *circus?*" Questions such as this generally bring forth a rapid flood of ideas that build a strong mood. Single words such as vacation, food, surprise, wish, Easter, Thanksgiving, Christmas, birthday, magic, treasure, and adventure have been used to build exciting moods for creative experiences.

To motivate a group of children into a music mood for "A Tailor and a Bear" the following riddle was asked:

> I speak to you.
> I speak to birds.
> I speak to beasts.
> I use no words.
> What am I?[2]

Seven- and eight-year-olds made the following replies: "Jesus," "the wind," "water like waves at the ocean," "God," "Mr. Nobody," "a teeny, tiny fairy." The replies were accepted enthusiastically as the leader said, "Everyone is right. Each of these speaks without using words. There is something more. Listen and something will speak to you right now. When it speaks you may do whatever it tells you." A little girl in the group played, "Baa, Baa Black Sheep" on her cello (Fig. 6.2). The children listened. Soon several children became sheep and lambs. A discussion about the power of music built a strong mood which led directly to listening to "A Tailor and a Bear."

Selecting One Way to Motivate. Creative guidance is highly individualistic. For instance, to get children into a creative mood for a circus, one leader might select a sensory approach. She might use a bright balloon or play a circus recording to focus attention. Another leader might stimulate interest through a person associated with a circus. She might invite a clown or a tightrope walker to visit a group of children. If this is not possible, she might create a convincing pantomime of one of these circus people. Another leader might be alert for comments coming from children when they gather for class. She may learn, by listening, that a child has gone to the circus or another child has helped feed the elephants. A leader would real-

[2] School of Drama, University of Washington, Seattle, Washington.

ize that a child's firsthand experience would be far more effective in motivating other children than her pantomime of a clown. Another leader might feel more secure in approaching a group with the *idea* of a circus. She might give each child an imaginary ticket

Fig. 6.2. Music speaks! (*School of Drama, University of Washington*)

and ask a single question: "This is a special circus ticket! It will take you to see whatever circus act you would like to see best of all. Which *one act* in a circus is the most exciting for you?"

After a leader considers several possible ways of focusing attention she selects one way which she believes will be strong in capturing attention and arousing children's interest.

Arousing Thinking, Feeling, and Expression. There's an art in asking questions. Much of the skill in creative guidance depends on a leader's ability to plan and ask questions. Creativity lies within a child. It must be drawn forth. After a leader has planned how to capture group attention and interest, she plans a searching question or questions.

A searching question is an open-end question which opens individual thinking and calls for expression. It is a question that is asked with who, what, when, where, why, or how. For instance, a question opens thinking when it asks: Why do you like music? What kind of music do you like best? When have you heard music that made you feel happy? These questions call for an explanation. They invite thinking and individual expression. A closed-end question is one which closes thinking. A closed-end question is generally asked with *do, is,* or *will.* For instance, thinking is closed when a question asks: Do you like music? Is this your favorite song? Will you sing for us? In each instance these questions may be answered with a *yes* or *no.*

A searching question is a subjective question. It relates each child to the desired mood. It is a *limited question causing a child to discipline his thinking and feeling before he answers.* A searching question may be focused in ways similar to the following:

What is the most exciting act in a circus for you? Tell us in one word.
If a tiny fairy hopped out of a flower in your backyard and granted you one wish, what one thing would you wish to do?
If you got a surprise package for your birthday, a tiny one or a great big one, what one thing would make you the happiest of all when you opened it?
If there were a knock at your door tonight, and you opened the door and found the most wonderful person in the world waiting to see you, who would that person be?

If you were on a mountain and could look far and wide, what to you would be the most beautiful thing you could see?

The effectiveness of a closely focused question may be compared to the effectiveness of an oil shaft. It drives straight and penetrates deep within the earth until it strikes an oil vein. The shaft causes oil to surge to the surface. Contrast this with a thousand surface strokes with picks and hammers. The latter fail to bring forth the rich resource from within. *One clearly focused searching question is worth a thousand unfocused questions.* A focused question causes a child to think, feel, and want to express. A leader must plan a focused question that will reach a child's creative depths. A focused question seldom, if ever, comes to a leader on the spur of a moment.

A mood must be kept within bounds. If children are going to create a play from a story over a period of five or six sessions an entire period may be used for motivating and enriching background. On the other hand, if children are to enjoy a creative experience in 40 minutes or an hour, a leader plans a way of building a strong mood in a comparatively few minutes.

MOTIVATING: GUIDING CHILDREN

"Children cannot create out of a vacuum. They must have something to say and be fired to say it."[3] Natalie Cole, an outstanding creative teacher, discovered this. Every creative leader soon discovers this for herself.

A Leader Creates Mood Indirectly. If a leader expects children to get into a mood she must first be in the mood herself. She may indirectly suggest a mood by her appearance. For instance, on a circus day she may wear a bright scarf or jacket whereas on a day for a witch story she may be dressed in black. An alert leader is

[3] Natalie Cole, *The Arts in the Classroom,* The John Day Company, Inc., 1940.

aware of the physical mood of a room. If a creative experience is to be centered in a gay mood, a brightly lighted room indirectly affects thinking. If an eerie mood is needed a slightly darkened room will indirectly contribute toward this feeling.

A Leader Is Alert to Children's Moods.   When children come to school or meet in an out-of-school program they generally arrive at different times. While children gather, a leader greets and enjoys each child personally. She is alert to individual moods. She looks for ways in which she may relate a child's mood to the mood of a story. She watches to see what children do, say, or bring to share. If a leader sees objects that are not related to the mood she will ask the children to save their "surprises" for a special sharing time. She may ask the children to put their objects on a "sharing table" or in an attractive "surprise basket" which she has provided in advance.

Children who arrive early may be encouraged to share experiences, to play a game, to ask riddles, or to join in an activity that is related in a specific way to the mood for the day. In a schoolroom a teacher often finds a mood developing early in a day. If this mood may not be developed at the moment it may be captured with an enthusiastic comment. Such a comment might be: "I see everyone is excited about the circus which is coming to town. Suppose we each store up our good circus thoughts. Save them until 2:00 o'clock today. The circus band will strike up then for everyone who is ready."

A Leader Motivates with Enthusiasm.   A leader motivates with enthusiasm and belief. What she says is important, but how she says it is vital to effective guidance. The tone of a leader's voice either communicates feeling and reaches a child, or it fails to. A leader uses her imagination and enjoyment of children in a creative way to arouse curiosities and feelings. Let us suppose a leader is going to share with children a recording of Edward MacDowell's "Of a Tailor and a Bear."[4] Rather than merely asking children to listen a leader becomes enthusiastic about motivating. A third grade teacher motivated high interest in listening to this music among her group of 30 third graders.[5] With a strong spirit of belief this teacher said: "Music is as old as the world. It speaks to everyone—to rich men, poor men, beggar men, and to you and me. Sometimes it invites people to dance, sometimes to sing, to march, to think a quiet prayer. Today we have a mystery melody. Listen and see what special mystery this music holds for you."

The children listened intently. They asked to hear the music three times. Then they shared ideas. One of the boys believed the mystery was concerned with a bullfight in Spain. One of the girls believed the mystery was about a beautiful ballet dancer who dreamed she was in a recital and suddenly forgot her dance. The children became excited and asked if they could write stories about the mystery in the melody. On the following day, after several stories were shared, the leader revealed the true mystery by telling the story. The children were in a "high rare mood" and created the character of the tailor with strong enjoyment and conviction.

A Leader Guides Rather Than Directs. A leader guides rather than directs children. This does not mean that she lets everything come and go in a willy-nilly way. Rather it means she is forceful in arousing interest and asking questions. She is alert in accepting answers. She accepts with a comment, a nod of approval, an enthusiastic repetition of a child's reply, a smile, a question that causes a child to think further about his idea, or an exclamation, depending

[4] Edward MacDowell, "Of a Tailor and a Bear," *A Library of RCA Victor Records for Elementary Schools: Listening Activities,* Vol. 2, Radio Corporation of America, RCA Victor Division, 1947.

[5] Polly Jepsen, Bryant School, Seattle Public Schools, Seattle, Washington.

on the child's reply. A leader is firm in guiding children to listen to one another. A leader is dynamic in accepting a reply, and moving on to another child. If a leader lacks force, an experience stands still. It bogs down or becomes dull rather than spirited and creative. The intangible qualities in creative guidance depend on a leader's ability to pace a group experience so it remains exciting and a rare experience.

A Leader Encourages Individual Thinking. Whenever a leader asks a question she encourages children to think. She gives them time to let the question reach within. She may suggest: "Suppose you close your eyes and really *think* about this. It's fun to dig down for your own idea. Sometimes you even surprise yourself with your idea."

A leader's sense of timing is vital in guiding children. She never rushes a child, nor does she dwell too long with one child. If a child isn't ready she encourages him to think further. If he is embarassed or insecure she may ask him in an understanding way if he prefers to keep his idea a secret. She then asks a child who is ready to reply.

A Leader Recognizes Creativity in an Idea. There is an art in listening. A leader listens carefully to each child's reply. She is alert to the way each expression may heighten a mood that is slowly beginning to develop. She captures a creative reply that strikes the chord of a mood. She commends it with conviction and appreciation in a way that stimulates others to think. In effect, a leader may say: "Julie, that's beautiful. Share your idea of mystery with us once more." Or, "Did everyone hear what David said? I don't think there's a bear trainer anywhere who has trained his bears to dance while they play 'Pease Porridge Hot.'" Or, "Floyd, how did you ever think of having a witch change a beautiful palomino into a donkey that kicks? We'll have an evil night to remember if each one thinks of an idea as strong as yours."

A leader's awareness of a rare bit of expression may be the high moment in the development of mood. Children's expressions are crude, unexpected, beautiful. A leader never knows what may come forth. She forms a habit of listening closely and of considering quickly the worth of a moment. When she captures an unusual moment of expression she often moves an experience into the realm of the aesthetic. When an unusual reply is heightened, it causes every child to think, feel, and wonder. Interaction takes place, and a mood builds high. Whenever a mood is strong it may be channeled into active expression. This was done when the leader suggested that the children *show* how the music spoke to them and made them feel. On the other hand, a leader may prefer to channel a mood directly to the story she is ready to share.

SHARING A STORY: PREPARATION

A story is an experience, real or imagined. It is something far more significant than words. It is an awareness, a presence of something universal and humanly significant. It may be a dream, a hope, a struggle, a funny or exciting happening. In creative dramatics the leader is the medium through which a story lives. It is not the personal self that she shares—rather it is the wonder, beauty, courage, laughter, or other qualities which the story awakens within her. These, in turn, she awakens within children. A story then becomes a creative experience and children are eager to create from it.

A Leader "Lives with" a Story. To share a story creatively a leader first makes the story her own. She begins to know it as an experience. This takes time. There is no short-cut easy way. After selecting a story, she reads it again for sheer enjoyment. She then edits and analyzes the story's moods, appeals, and drama elements. She begins to see it in her mind's eye. She sees it happening, unfolding in scenes and incidents. She sees it in a series of vivid pictures. She identifies with the characters, particularly with the leading character and she sees and feels the story in relation to this character. She experiences the story through the leading character's feelings. A story must become real and alive to a leader before she can make it live for others.

Ruth Sawyer, a rare storyteller, believes that a person makes a story her own by exercising strong discipline of the mind. "Intend the mind," Mrs. Sawyer says. "Call it meditation, for that is what it amounts to, this thinking through until the very essence of the object or idea is distilled, drawn out, and comprehended. Then, and not until then, can the creative imagination have full play."[6] To exercise this discipline means concentrating closely on a story, considering it visually and emotionally. It does not mean one or two quick readings or even a casual studying. Rather it means a holding of the mind to it with depth of concentration and emotional feeling.

A story, like a play, must begin and end with emphasis and interest. In editing a story a leader arouses interest with the very first words. She prepares an opening that will cause children to listen and feel a story mood immediately. Similarly, a story should end with enthusiasm and zest. A leader prepares an ending to tie a story together, to provide a complete and satisfying conclusion. A children's story generally ends on a triumphant note. Above all a story should end when the climactic action is over. It should not drag on and on with related but unnecessary explanations or philosophical references.

Equally as important is the preparation of the "middle" or "com-

[6] Ruth Sawyer, *The Way of the Storyteller,* The Viking Press, Inc., 1949.

plication" of a story. It is in the complication episodes that the highest emotional reactions generally occur. A leader determines the emotional responses each episode is to elicit. She proceeds to work for these responses as she tells the story aloud by feeling within herself the emotional intensity of each episode.

A Leader Visualizes Characters in Action. Let us suppose a leader is preparing the story "A Tailor and a Bear." She first sees the tailor's shop, the quaintness of it, its size, and space. She sees the very place where the tailor sits, sews, and fiddles. She sees the door leading to the street, and windows if there are any. She sees the tailor himself. She determines his age, size, shape, weight, and color of his hair and beard if he has one. She sees the way the tailor moves about, the way he stitches, the way he plays his violin. She becomes acquainted with him and knows him as a person. She discovers how he feels about his music, his tailoring, his customers, his fellow villagers.

She experiences the tailor's reaction to the commotion in the street. She experiences his sudden fear when the bear comes into his shop. She sees and feels the bear through the eyes and emotions of the tailor. She sees and feels the bear's hugeness, his rage and strength as he lunges forward, his pleasure when he suddenly hears the music. She experiences the quick succession of thoughts and feelings which the tailor experiences in this surprise encounter— fear, relief, fear, and great relief again. She sees and feels the anxiety of the villagers in doorways or at windows. She sees and feels the anxiety of the bearkeeper when he rushes into the shop to get the bear and to learn what destruction it may have caused. She feels the excitement of the villagers, and senses the great relief of the tailor when the bear is led away down the street.

A Leader Tells the Story Aloud. A leader tells a story aloud to discover how clearly she knows the story experience. She studies again the incidents that are not vivid and clear. She does not memorize dialogue as such. Rather she lives with the emotions and reactions of the characters. She reads the dialogue again and again and considers why its ideas were so expressed. Soon she finds she is speaking confidently for the characters, often using their very words.

A leader tells a story aloud many times. Each time she strives to strengthen a specific aspect which needs strengthening. When she is ready, she shares the story with another person to see how she brings the story to life. One beginning leader prepared a story for children by telling it aloud whenever she washed dishes. When she shared the story with children, she was startled by their response, for, as she said, "The dishes never did react. I was surprised when the children did."

SHARING A STORY: TELLING TO CHILDREN

Making a Transition. A skillful leader makes a smooth transition that carries children from a mood directly to a story. The transition may be a statement that relates the children to the story. Such a statement may be made in a way similar to this: "Everyone has had a different idea of the mystery in the music. There's an old story that solves this mystery, and I am going to share it with you now."

A transition may be a *suggestion* which builds a setting with word pictures. Let us suppose children are in a Christmas mood. A leader may *suggest:* "Suppose we travel down through the years and across the lands to the eve of the very first Christmas. Let us sit together on the hills of Bethlehem where the shepherds are watching their flocks. It is cold and we gather near a shepherd's fire. We hear the shepherds talking about the Roman soldiers. We hear little lambs bleating. . . ."

A transition may be a *statement that invites action*. When little children have been sitting for a discussion they may need to change position before hearing a long story. Let us suppose little children have been discussing new clothes to identify with "Little Black Sambo." To lead children into action a leader may suggest: "I have a brand new pair of shoes for every one of us. Each one put on his new shoes, and we'll go walking together. My new shoes will lead the way. As soon as you are ready, join in our new shoe parade! Let's see how you feel while your new shoes take you to a special place far out in a jungle."

Sitting to See and Listen. Children must see as well as hear a storyteller and a storyteller must see the faces of his listeners to tell how his story is living. A child who cannot see or be seen frequently does not listen. One child may quickly break a story mood and lessen the creative experience for an entire group. An imaginative leader achieves a good seating arrangement by considering it in advance. She may ask: "How may we sit so everyone may see as well as hear the story?" Or she may prefer to retain the mood which has been built by guiding toward a seating arrangement in her transitional statement. For instance, she may say: "Now that we have had such a long happy walk in our brand new shoes, let's sit in a circle as round as the sun. We'll sit in a great big circle in the shade of this big tall jungle tree." An older group which is to hear a witch story may be guided into a seating arrangement by a similar statement: "Come, sister witches, sit around this big brewing pot. All witches know the power of a circle. I've a tale to tell this night. Our evil must not be broken."

Avoiding Interruptions. A story is a creative experience. If it is

interrupted from time to time it fails to come alive. A leader avoids interruptions by building within children a desire to listen rather than interrupt. For instance, a leader may prepare for a familiar story by commenting: "This is such a favorite old story that many of you will know it. What will happen if you call out and tell others what is going to happen?"

From children's replies a good listening situation is quickly established. An outstanding leader who guides little children asks them how they may keep a secret if they know a story. When little children have "locked" their lips or "zipped" them closed they take great pride in listening without interrupting.

Sharing with Enjoyment. When a story lives for a leader she brings it alive for children. It is a leader's feeling and vitality that send the surge of life back into a story. It is knowing a story, and experiencing it through sharing that causes a leader to slow down or to speed up, to speak loudly or softly, to pause or to think quickly. A good storyteller fires and arouses others with the spirit of a story that has fired and aroused her.

PLANNING: MAKING A PLAN FOR GUIDING

A play, like a house, is built step by step. A play is put together character by character, incident by incident, scene by scene. Children are guided into creating a play by first creating a single character. Then another character is created. These two characters are then put together in a short scene or incident. Other characters are created, one at a time. Another scene is created. Finally an entire story is created into a play.

Before a leader meets a group of children she makes a careful plan. A child needs to picture a character in his mind before he can create the character. He needs to image a character by identifying with his feelings, and knowing why he does what he does. Character feeling is basic in creating, for emotion is vital in all art. If a child puts on a character from the outside only, he *reproduces* a character—he does not create. A reproduction is like a statue or a puppet. It lacks life, feeling, spirit, individuality. A child needs to be guided so he expresses a character's feelings from the inside outward to his body.

Planning Questions for Character's Feelings. A child creates a character when he understands that character in relation to himself. A leader guides children to the point of understanding by asking questions that are focused straight to the core of a character's feelings. She plans questions for each character which will cause a child to understand a character in a specific situation. Questions are often planned to help a child recall vivid experiences similar to those of the character. Let us examine "feeling" questions which guide children into understanding characters in "A Tailor and a Bear." We will consider questions that may be asked to help children understand the characters in their first appearances in the story.

Tailor

Once the tailor was just your age. What one thing do you think he must have enjoyed doing when he was a boy? Why?

Of all the musical instruments there are, why do you think the tailor chose to play the violin?

What musical instrument do you like best?

What kind of music or singing causes you to feel especially happy?

Why do you think the tailor became a tailor instead of a musician?

Why do you think the tailor played music to get ideas for his tailoring?

When have you been frightened by an unexpected sound or visitor?

What would you feel like doing if a bear came into this room right now?

Bear

When this big, shaggy bear was a baby bear in the forest, what outdoor sound do you think made him feel happy?

How do you think you would feel if you were suddenly taken away from your home to a very different place to live?

When the bear hears the beautiful strains of the violin why do you think he goes in search of this music?

Why does he dance with such enjoyment when he hears the music?

Who knows why the bear became angry when the music played too fast?

How do you feel when you "catch" the rhythm of marching music?

Villagers

Who is a villager?

When you grow up and live in or near a city or a town what would you prefer to do for an occupation or a profession?

How would you feel if just this minute we heard a commotion down the hall and a growling bear came rushing into this room?

Who remembers a time when you were frightened by an unexpected happening at your house or along your street?

How do you think a villager feels toward the tailor when the bear rushes into the tailor shop?

What do you think a villager might do? Why might each villager do something different in this emergency?

Keeper

What have you lost that you still remember?

How do you feel when you've lost something very important?

How do you feel when you hear that a wild animal has escaped from a zoo or a circus?

How do you think the bear keeper feels when he is searching for his bear?

Why do you think he is angry toward the bear when he finds him?

How do you think the bear keeper feels toward the tailor?

Planning Questions for Character's Appearance. *When a child* *explores a character's feelings he forms mental pictures of the character.* He generally transfers these pictures into his expression by using his body freely to create a character's outer appearance. When a child has discussed the tailor's feelings toward music and tailoring he generally pictures a tailor in his mind. A child who understands the savage, restless feelings of the bear almost always pictures the bear vividly in his mind. When a child is guided into becoming a bear he may use his entire body to create the bear's outer as well as inner character.

If children hesitate to characterize freely and convincingly, a leader recognizes the need for guiding children to consider specifically the character's appearance. To prepare in advance she plans several "appearance" questions. For instance, to plan the *appearance* of the tailor, a leader guides children with questions and suggestions similar to the following:

Close your eyes and see if you see a clear picture of the tailor in his shop. See if you see an old or a young tailor.

What does your tailor look like as he cuts and stitches fine cloth? Is he fat, thin, tall, or short? Is he happy or worried?

What kind of clothes has he made for himself?

How does your tailor move about his shop? How does he snip, and sew, and play his violin?

As soon as you see your tailor clearly, each one will describe *one thing* about the way your tailor looks.

How might you use your whole body to create the very tailor you picture in your mind?

Planning Questions for a Character's Actions. Often children need guidance to help plan a character's actions. A leader plans several "action" questions in advance. To do this she visualizes the character in action in the very space where the children are to create.

Questions such as the following may be planned to guide children to visualize a character in action:

When the tailor enters his shop, what do you think he does first of all?

What tools does he use in his tailoring? Where does he keep his tailoring tools when he works?

What might the tailor do to make his shop attractive for customers who come to see his rare garments?

What will the tailor do to get his violin ready?

How do you think the tailor feels as he opens his shop and starts each new day?

How might the tailor show his friendliness to other shopkeepers?

Planning a Clear Statement of Action. A good leader plans each playing sequence in advance. She plans a tentative statement of specific action. This may be planned in a way similar to the following:

Now we are ready to *be* the merry tailor.

Suppose you first move out into this space. Each one find an imaginary table where you may have your tailor shop.

Give yourself enough room to move about freely so you will not interfere with another shop.

See how you may use your whole self to become the tailor you have pictured in your mind.

We will begin where the tailor opens his shop and gets ready for the day in his own way. We will see how he enjoys his music while he tries to get an idea for a special garment he is going to make.

For the first time none of our tailors will talk, but each tailor will show how he *feels* as he creates in his very own way.

Planning for a Character's Dialogue. After a child creates a convincing character with strong feeling in pantomime, he is generally ready to express dialogue for the character. *Dialogue is always motivated by strong feeling.* Children often reveal their readiness

for dialogue by asking if they may "use words" or "talk this time."
A leader encourages dialogue only from children she believes to be
ready for dialogue.

To guide children into creating dialogue a leader moves a group
forward in one logical step. She suggests that she believes many of
the characters are ready to speak for they have strong feeling. She
makes a clear plan to guide children into creating dialogue:

Now that we have created merry tailors in pantomine, suppose we
hear some of the tailors talk so they may tell how they feel.

How do you feel when you are making something new which seems
to be going well?

How do you feel when someone surprises you with a visit?

I am going to be a customer who comes into a tailor shop where a
tailor is really being the merry tailor in our story.

When you hear my customer talk, stop and watch from your shop
window. I will speak to only one tailor who is thinking, feeling, and
being a real tailor.

If my customer speaks to your tailor, speak right up and answer his
questions just as the tailor would.

As soon as everyone opens his shop and gets his tailoring business
started for the day, I will enter a tailor shop.

When the leader introduces dialogue in this way she plans simple
questions which a character would naturally ask in a given situation. In this instance a customer might ask questions similar to the
following:

Good morning, my good man. I have traveled far. I am looking for
the shop of the famous tailor. Would you be good enough to tell me
where I may find his shop?

You are the famous tailor? Why do you play upon a violin rather
than stitching or snipping?

What is the most beautiful garment you have ever made?

I am servant to the king. I have come to order a beautiful gown for the queen. What kind of a gown do you suggest for the queen's birth-day?

After a leader has made a plan for guiding children to explore one character, she makes a plan to guide them into exploring the next character of importance. In a similar way she plans questions that will guide children to explore a character's feelings, appearance, and actions. She makes a plan for guiding children to create each character first in pantomime and then with dialogue.

Planning a Scene. After children have created two characters with true feeling and dialogue, they are ready to create a short scene wherein two characters meet. A leader makes a plan for guiding children to review the sequence of action. Review questions may be planned thus:

How does our story begin?
Who is the first person to visit the tailor's shop this day?
After the customer leaves, what does the tailor do?
Who hears the beautiful violin music?
What does the tailor do when he hears the commotion in the street?
How does the tailor feel when he sees the bear?
What does he do?
How does he happen to play his violin? How might he decide?

A leader summarizes a children's discussion of scenic action. She states a clear plan of action which emphasizes the specific drama goal of creating characters in scenic action. She makes clear to children how far a scene is to be played. For instance, a statement of action may be planned in some such way as the following:

It is going to be exciting to see how we bring the story alive for the first time, and make it seem as if it is really happening.

We will see how each character thinks, and feels, and talks as he does just what the characters do in the story.

We will begin where the tailor opens his shop. We will play to the place where the tailor is terribly frightened by the growling bear who is looking for the music.

Planning a Setting. The leader plans questions to guide children to create a simple setting for a scene. Questions such as the following may serve to guide effectively:

We are going to use this space for the tailor's shop. Who has an idea where the door to the street should be?

Who sees a good place for the tailor's table? Why should the table be as far away from the door as we may put it?

Why are the windows important when we play the story? Where should they be so we may see how the villagers feel?

What furniture is necessary to create this scene? Why?

Planning to Replay a Scene. A scene may be played and replayed as long as children are enjoying it, and are challenged to strengthen it dramatically and creatively. Each repeated playing should have a specific drama goal or goals so children recognize specific ways to strengthen a scene. In this way children are guided to reach for higher dramatic and creative planes.

After a first playing of a scene children are generally familiar with the sequence of action. If they have failed to develop action clearly in a first playing, it is discussed and evaluated. A clearer development of scenic action becomes the specific drama goal for the second playing. The leader states this simply to children before she guides them into playing.

Planning for Continuity and Teamwork. After children understand how a scene unfolds, they are generally ready to strengthen the continuity and tempo of a scene. This requires teamwork. A leader plans specific questions to cause children to see the need for tempo and teamwork as they develop a scene. Questions such as the following may be asked when a leader senses a need for guiding in this specific area:

What does it mean to have teamwork in a play? Who sees one way the players may work together to create this scene?

Could the tailor tell this story all by himself? Why not?

In what two ways do the customers help tell the story?

What happens if the customers wait too long before they visit the tailor's shop?

What happens if the customers decide to talk all morning to the tailor?

How fast do you think this story should move along? What may happen if it moves too quickly?

Planning for Conflict and Reaction. Most children's groups need to be guided into creating strong emotional feeling and reaction. Children seldom weave these elements into their playing with sufficient force until a leader guides them into strong expression. Drama comes into being only when characters act, react, and interact with strong emotional feeling. The leader considers different ways in which she may discuss feeling and reaction with children. She strives to help them understand how to weave these elements into their playing. She may explain by illustrating. Or she may lead a discussion using questions and suggestions such as the following:

How do you feel when a sudden knock comes on your door when you are home alone? How do you feel when someone calls, "Help"? What do you do?

How do you show your feelings when you are surprised or afraid?

In what other ways do you often show your feelings when you are with someone else?

A play must have as much feeling as real life. A play lives by feeling. A play becomes real only when every character shows how he feels about everything that is happening. This is called reaction.

Why should a character react to everything that happens during the

time he is in a scene? How may a character show strong reaction without speaking? In what ways might a villager show how anxious he is while he watches the growling bear?

What happens to a scene if a character reacts only when he speaks? What happens if only one character reacts? Why must every character react to everything he hears and sees?

We have created good characters, and we know how to keep the story moving. This time, let us see if every character makes us *feel* that he is really in the story every minute.

Planning for Use of Space. In early playings of a scene children are inclined to gravitate toward one another. They crowd in. They have a tendency to use a small place rather than to make use of all the space available. A leader plans specific questions to guide children to recognize the need for using space freely in which to create. Questions similar to the following may be used:

When you are at home do you always stay in one little place?

When you go to a store to buy a coat or a jacket, do you stand quietly in one place in the store? What do you do?

What do you think a customer might do before he gives an order to the tailor? What else might he do?

When you draw a picture on a sheet of paper do you put your entire picture down in one corner? How do you use all your paper to express your feeling?

Who sees how we might make a more interesting "stage picture" when we play this scene?

When you hear stirring band music what do you feel like doing?

When the bear hears the beautiful rhythm of the violin music do you think he will only keep time to it with the swaying of his head? What do you think a trained bear might do if he had this much room in the tailor's shop? Why?

This time when we play we are going to see how every character feels free to move. We will see how the characters work together to make an interesting stage picture in all this space.

Moving Action Forward. A leader guides a group forward to a new character or a new scene whenever she feels the group will benefit by going ahead. Little by little a play is created. The leader then guides children into the experience of creating the story from beginning to end. She does this by guiding children to review the sequence of scenic action.

Often, however, with beginning groups a point of satisfaction may be reached in the playing of the single conflict scene. A leader is always alert to children's interest in a story. She may find it wise to drop a story after children have created a single scene with satisfaction, and share a new story that offers different creative challenges.

PLANNING: GUIDING CHILDREN TO PLAN

Focusing on One Character. After a story is shared, how does a leader focus children's thinking on a single character? There are several ways. She may listen for spontaneous comments to see which character holds highest appeal for children. She may ask a focused question such as: "Which character is going to be the most *fun* to play?" or she may guide thinking to a specific character with an enthusiastic comment. Such a comment might be: "I see that everyone likes this story. Suppose we think first about the tailor." When a leader guides children to create the character who holds the highest interest for them, creativity reaches a high peak. A creative leader strives to follow the current and force of group feeling rather than to pull the group in a different direction.

Guiding Children to Understand a Character. A leader guides children to understand a character by first asking a "feeling" question. She allows time for children to think. If a single question strikes at the heart of a character's feeling, the leader draws replies, accepts replies, comments on replies, and channels replies. One question may be all that is needed to start children exploring a character. A leader may get an answer from six or seven children. She may find that every child has a desire to answer. If she feels the character is understood she may transfer the surging feeling into expression instead of spending further time in discussion. To guide children into expression she may explain in a way similar to the following:

This is exciting! It seems as if everyone understands how the big bear longs for the forest when he hears the music.

Rather than sharing any more experiences, each one of us will be the bear and show our feelings.

We will begin where the bear is sleeping in the warm sun by a hitching post in the village. Each bear will have his own space to sleep out here in the village square.

I am going to be the tailor in my shop over here. As soon as your bear hears the violin music, let us see how he wakes up, how he feels, and what he does.

For the very first time each one will show just how your bear *feels* without making even a sound. Is this clear to everyone?

If, on the other hand, a first question brings very little response, a different question should be asked. Children may respond immediately when the character is considered from a slightly different viewpoint. Creative guidance in exploring a character depends on a leader's skill in asking questions that arouse feeling and awaken imaginations.

PLAYING: GUIDING CHILDREN TO CREATE

Pantomiming a Character. Children are usually guided to create a character in pantomime for the first time. Pantomime demands clear sensory perception as well as strong inner feeling. When a child creates in pantomime he often finds his unique way of expressing while he searches for a way to communicate his feelings.

Creating in a Group. There's security in numbers. If space permits, a leader often guides every child in a group to create a characterization simultaneously. If the space is limited and the group is large, a half-and-half arrangement may be used. Half of the children may be guided to create while the other half becomes an observing audience. After the audience evaluates and comments on the players, the children in the audience become the players while the first players become the audience. If space is limited, small groups of four, five, or six children may create at one time while the remaining children watch. For instance, children who sit at one table, or in one row may have a turn at creating while the rest of the children become an audience. Each row or group creates in turn. Other ways to guide for variety are by pairs or in a one-by-one pattern. One confident child may be invited to show how he creates a character, another child is guided to join the first child, then another, and another until as many as ten or twelve children are creating simultaneously. In this latter plan each child receives an individual moment of recognition as he is chosen to join the others.

Choosing a Cast. A first playing of a scene sets a pattern of sequence. It is vital that a first scene be created with strong feeling rather than allowed to bog down. A leader casts a first scene by choosing children who have created the characters with security and enjoyment (Fig. 6.3). In successive playings of the same scene characters should be cast according to the needs of the children. Let us suppose a group is ready to play the opening scene in "A Tailor and a Bear." The leader casts four confident children to become the tailor, the bear, and two customers. In a second and repeated playings she may choose a confident child to create the tailor, and a

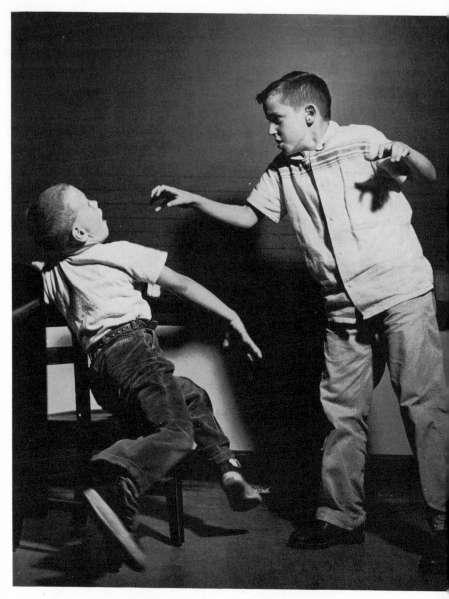

F<small>IG</small>. 6.3. "A Tailor and a Bear." (*Photograph by Royal C. Crooks; Bryant School, Seattle Public Schools, Seattle, Washington*)

child who needs recognition to become the bear. In choosing customers, one customer may be a secure child who enjoys creating and the other customer a less secure child who needs to gain confidence. The children will be challenged to create customers who are related in a direct way. A few possibilities may be suggested for customers such as two servants, a father and son, or a mother and a daughter.

An audience is always chosen with spirit to heighten its importance. A leader may suggest: "This time we are going to start the story. We need a good audience to see if we can make our playing real. Who would like to be the audience for the first time?" Or audience members may be selected individually before a cast is selected. For instance, a leader may invite children to become an audience in a way similar to the following: "For the first time we play we are going to have an *invited* audience. We are going to invite Jim, Monica, George, Irene, Mary, and Lois to be the first audience. Each one is a good thinker. They should be able to tell us what is strong in our playing, and what may need strengthening."

Guiding as Stage Manager. In early playings a leader often becomes a stage manager to heighten dramatic atmosphere and to get each scene started with spirit and zest. A leader uses dynamic theatre techniques of "curtain" or "cut" to start and stop the playing dramatically and effectively. When a cast has been selected and children have had an opportunity to discuss the scene, a leader moves the experience forward with the spirit of a stage manager. She speaks with directness and guides in a way similar to the following: "Characters in their places. Audience ready. Characters in character. Ready! Curtain!"

When a leader realizes children are not in character, she is in a position to build a more realistic mood by describing the setting with word pictures. For instance, for the story of "A Tailor and a Bear" a leader may describe the setting in a way similar to the following: "It is a warm sunny morning in a faraway village where a famous tailor lives. The tailor is coming to his shop to open it for the day. We are now ready to look into the shop of the tailor. Curtain!"

After children understand the role of a stage manager, one or two children may be chosen for this responsibility. One child may arrange and describe the setting. Another may be the manager who has the responsibility of starting and stopping the action of a scene.

PLAYING: LEADER CREATES WITH CHILDREN

It's a special delight for children when an adult joins in their play. A leader who creates with children not only enjoys herself, but causes children to get involved more quickly with wholehearted fun. By playing with children she is in an ideal position to guide them in a character role.

To Get Children Started. In first and early experiences a leader plays with children to get them started. She serves to break the emotional ice by playing freely and with enthusiasm. As soon as children create freely with enjoyment and spirit, she moves to the sidelines. She may remain in character ready to enter into the playing if the mood weakens.

To Encourage Shy Children. A leader may play with children for the specific purpose of encouraging the shy child or children. If she finds two or three children holding back, she joins them and plays with them. She may encourage them to become a character by sitting with their characters and communicating to them in pantomime. Or, she may invite a shy child to watch the others with her.

To Encourage Reaction. A leader often recognizes the need to create a strong characterization to motivate children to express active emotional reaction. She may create an antagonist or opposite char-

acter in a scene while every child within the group creates the protagonist character. She selects a characterization that carries strong
emotional conflict. Her characterization should provide force and
purpose for an entire group to work against with strong reaction.

For example, when a class of third graders created "A Tailor and
a Bear" each child was guided to create a convincing tailor. The
teacher created a convincing characterization of the bear. Her characterization caused a spontaneous reaction that made the children
to realize and understand the significance of emotional reaction
(Fig. 6.4).

FIG. 6.4. "A bear!" (*Photograph by Royal C. Crooks; Bryant
School, Seattle Public Schools, Seattle, Washington*)

To Draw Dialogue and Guide Playing. A leader may create a character for the specific purpose of drawing expression in dialogue from children's characters. For example, in "A Tailor and a Bear" one leader planned to become a customer for the specific purpose of talking to several different tailors in order to engage them in conversation.

A beginning group of fifth and sixth graders were guided to express dialogue in the characterizations of witches. The leader became Old Hill Woman who asked each witch what ugly thing she had brought for the evil brew (Fig. 6.5). When a leader becomes a key

Fig. 6.5. "Speak, sister, what ugly thing do ye bring for the brew?" (*School of Drama, University of Washington*)

character such as this, she not only draws dialogue but she keeps the playing organized and sustains a strong mood.

To Guide Indirectly for Continuity. When children put a long scene together for a first or second time a leader often assumes a minor role. From this position she may make a comment or ask a question in character to guide the children indirectly to keep the action moving forward. A leader reacts in character and speaks only if she feels the characters are uncertain as to action. For instance, one leader assumed the minor role of a court musician in the christening scene of "Sleeping Beauty" for this specific purpose (Fig. 6.6).

FIG. 6.6. "Your Majesty, I bring the baby princess three blue butterflies." (*School of Drama, University of Washington*)

To "Spotlight" a Child for Recognition. When a leader creates a character with children she is in a position to focus group attention on a single child who is creating a good characterization. For instance, if she becomes a customer visiting a tailor shop she may call out as follows, in order to focus group attention on a child: "Tailors, tailors! Look through your windows and see this fine tailor

shop. Listen to this tailor tell about the rare clothes he makes. He is indeed a rare tailor."

When a leader "spotlights" creative expression within the realm of a scene this gives recognition to one child and motivates stronger expression from others. Every child wants recognition. When a leader makes it clear that she is going to speak to only one or two characters, children strive with noticeable discipline to create and express with conviction.

PRAISING AND EVALUATING

"The sweetest of all words is praise." This truth, recognized centuries ago by a Greek teacher, is vital in living. Every human being, regardless of age, needs and wants praise. A few words of praise work wonders with a child. They raise his spirit, his confidence, his attitudes, his efforts.

A Leader Praises and Draws Praise. A skillful leader uses a positive approach in praising. She looks for something specific in each playing that can be praised honestly. When playing is over and "curtain" is called a leader makes an immediate comment of approval. A single comment may be similar to one of the following:

> Good! We carried the story through!
> For a first time, this was fine!
> Wonderful! We're having fun creating!
> What merry tailors!
> Excellent feeling! Let's talk about the bears!

The leader waits until the players are seated. Then she draws comments from children who were in the audience. In early sessions she may ask a general question to invite positive comments. A question similar to any of the following may be asked:

Now we are ready to hear from our audience. What was the best moment for you?

What did you see that made the playing so much fun?

When did the playing seem real?

Who has one fine thing to share about a character?

Leader Guides Children to Evaluate. After playing has been praised a leader guides children to evaluate playing. An evaluation looks at strong values and points out a specific way in which expression may be strengthened. For instance, a child may comment, "I liked Walter's bear." A leader guides children to evaluate by commenting: "Yes, Walter's bear *felt* like a bear when he first woke up. Who sees how Walter's bear could have been more like a bear when he was dancing?" Or, "Walter's bear was bearlike when he first woke up, but *why* did he seem to be more like a laughing boy in the tailor's shop?" Through a fair evaluation a child gradually understands how to create and sustain dramatic expression.

Leader Focuses Evaluation on Drama Goals. John Masefield discovered that "Great art flows from great encouragement." Children grow in their understanding of drama and dramatic expression only when a leader guides and encourages evaluation in relation to drama. After each playing the leader focuses evaluation on the specific drama goal children were striving for in their playing.

Evaluating Rhythmic Movement. In early sessions a drama goal is generally on rhythmic movement. When a leader invites comments a child may reply: "I liked the way Jewel was swimming." A leader replies with a comment that analyzes the child's expression in view of rhythmic movement. She may say: "Yes, Jewel enjoyed the water and made us *feel* the water in the rhythm of her swimming."

Another child may comment: "It was funny when Tommy held

his nose and jumped in." A leader replies with a focus on fundamentals of rhythmic movement. She may say: "You're right! Tommy did three fine things. He used his *whole self*. He used his *own idea*. He made us *feel* that the water was deep for he went down slowly until he sat on the bottom."

Evaluating Pantomime. When children participate in dramatic play or pantomime a child may praise somewhat like this: "I liked the way Lillian jumped with her jumping rope." A leader who is aware of the child's pantomime will reply by stressing a fundamental aspect of pantomime. She may ask: "Do you know why we watched Lillian so closely? It is because Lillian *saw* the jumping rope herself. She took hold of the handles and swung the rope over her head. This is a secret in pretending. When you *see* what you're doing, then others see."

Evaluating Characterization. When characterization is a chief drama goal children's comments may be made in this manner: "I liked Gene's tailor." "Hazel's tailor was good." A leader takes each comment in turn, and points out specific values in relation to characterization. She may reply: "Gene used his whole self to become a tailor. He was old and bent. Hazel's tailor was happy. In a strong character you must have both. You must be a character on the *inside* and the *outside*. This is a secret of creating too. You think, and feel, and become a character way down deep inside clear out to your fingers and toes and the top of your head. Then you make others feel and believe and your character is real."

When children begin to understand characterization, a leader guides them to evaluate. She asks questions that cause them to think and to analyze. Questions similar to the following may be asked:

Why did Susie's tailor seem to be the very tailor in the story?

Which tailor looked like a tailor from the top of his head down to his toes? Why?

What strong feeling did George's tailor have when the customer left the shop?

What did Jan's tailor show us when he not only played his violin but started to dance around his shop?

What happened to our story when Harriette's tailor laughed at the bear? Why?

Who noticed a special place in our story where a character surprised us by creating something we didn't expect?

Evaluating Dialogue. A leader focuses her initial comment directly to dialogue when this is the chief drama goal in playing. A leader comments, and asks questions similar to these to guide children to analyze:

Since this was the first time our characters have talked, what did you hear a character say that made him seem real?

When the customers talked to the tailor there was a strong place when it seemed as if the story were real. Who noticed that special moment in speaking?

Why do you think an old tailor should have an old voice?

What do you think of the tailor's shouting, "Yipes! A bear!"?

What might this tailor say which would have just as much feeling but would be more likely to be what the tailor in the story would say?

Evaluating Teamwork, Continuity, and Tempo. Whenever the drama goals are on teamwork, continuity, and tempo a leader focuses evaluation in this area. She makes a positive comment, followed by questions such as these:

For the first time we did well in putting this scene together. Where was teamwork especially strong?

In what one place did you feel a need for greater coöperation?

Who noticed a place where one character helped another character out?

How may the characters show good teamwork even when they are off stage?

What happens when everyone is coöperating except one person?

We succeeded in telling this part of the story. Was it clear to everyone in the audience?

Where do you think the story needs to move faster? Slower?

Who sees how we may keep the story moving without rushing it?

Evaluating Reaction and Conflict. A statement followed by questions focuses children's thinking to reaction whenever this is a chief drama goal. A leader may guide in a way similar to this:

This time we played to see if every character was feeling and reacting. How do you think we succeeded?

Why did everyone laugh when the tailor started to run?

Which character needs to react even more than he did this time? Why?

If, on the other hand, very little reaction takes place a leader first makes a positive comment on something worthy of comment such as characterizations, pantomime, or dialogue. She then discusses reaction by voicing the situation exactly as it developed and guides children into a discussion of reaction. After discussion the scene is replayed with reaction again being a specific goal.

Evaluating Use of Space. A leader focuses evaluation toward the use of space within the stage setting when this has been the chief emphasis in playing. Comments may be made somewhat in this manner:

There was a clear "stage picture" in our scene this time. What one thing made the picture so interesting to watch?

What one strong way did the tailor make use of his shop?

What was the best thing the bear did to make a good stage picture?

In what special way did the villagers add to the stage picture?

If, on the other hand, children have failed to make use of the space, a leader evaluates the situation just as it developed.

Evaluating Individuality and Individuals. A leader always remembers that a child is more important than the play he is creating. For this reason she is alert to the way individuals express and relate to others during discussions and playings. A child is guided and evaluated in relation to himself, not in relation to others. For instance, if a shy child volunteers with an idea, he may be praised strongly for it. If an alert child who is capable of fine thinking disturbs others, a leader helps him by saying in a firm but friendly way that the group needs his help too. From time to time a leader singles out three or four children who need recognition by asking them to share their pantomimes for the rest of the group. Confident children are challenged in similar ways with comments such as this: "This is going to be difficult to do for a first time, but I believe Mark and Ray and Paul will surprise us with the way they create this scene."

A leader strives to keep each child reaching for his best. A specific group goal often becomes that of giving particular emphasis to three or four children during a session. A leader uses care in giving every child individual "moments of glory," and a few children recognition which lasts longer than a glorious moment. In this way a few alert children do not dominate each playing session, but every child has his "day" over a period of several sessions.

A leader who praises creative ideas soon finds every child digging deeper for his own way of expression. Comments such as the following motivate every child within a group toward better creative thinking:

Dianne, you have such good ideas today. You have given us three good thoughts in a row.

Whenever Billy creates it is like a surprise. We never know what wonderful idea he is going to think of next.

Marilyn, that's a wonderful thought. You always think of something in your own way instead of borrowing thoughts from others.

Charlie, I wish I had a thinking cap like yours. Your idea will make our scene beautiful.

CREATING A PLAY

After an enthusiastic evaluation children are always eager to re-play. A leader challenges individuals to create by guiding them into vivid dramatic expression that causes the excitement of drama to find its way into their playings. Children may be guided to create from a story as long as interest is high. Many groups have enjoyed creating from a short story for two or three sessions. With a longer story children often sustain interest while creating episodes in two or three acts over a period of six or seven sessions. A leader evaluates each session closely to determine whether interest remains high or whether children will perhaps have an even greater creative experience by being guided into a new story.

The creative process with children is like creativity in all living things. It evolves in an unexpected way. It is often like a sunrise in design. It rises out of a state of quiet. It is ever-changing. Each moment is different. Suddenly the miracle happens. Ideas burst through with color, radiance, force, beauty.

Creative guidance is vital in firing children to this moment. For this reason a good leader plans carefully, and guides with spirit and belief. She is challenged to find ways to cause children's spirits to flame high with force and feeling.

Questions and Activities

1. Divide the class into buzz session groups. Each group will consider

the following questions, after which a group spokesman will present the conclusions of the group:

    a. Why is planning a mood so important in creative dramatics?

    b. Why should a leader plan a motivation when the guiding process is a creative one?

    c. What, in essence, is a leader guiding children to do when she motivates them into a specific mood?

2. Select a short story recommended for creative dramatics for children. Examine and list the basic moods in this story. Consider each of the five moods analyzed in connection with "A Tailor and a Bear" at the beginning of this chapter. Underline in red pencil the essential mood that will cause children to identify most strongly with this story.

3. Plan a motivation that will lead children to the essential mood of the above story. Include in the motivation (a) specific ways of gaining attention and stimulating interest, and (b) specific ways of arousing feeling and drawing expression. Write out a searching question that will relate a child to the desired mood and cause him to discipline his thinking and feeling before he answers.

4. Edit this story in preparation for sharing it with a group of children for creative dramatics. Give specific attention to the beginning, the end, and especially the "complications" of the story. Write out a transition or transitional statement you will make to lead children from the mood to the story.

5. Share this story (a) with your class group, (b) with a recreational group, (c) with children for whom you are baby-sitting, or (d) with children in your family. Evaluate special successes and special problems noted during the sharing. Consider especially "sitting to see and hear," "avoiding interruptions," and responses of children.

6. A. Plan questions designed to guide children to understand the main characters in this story you have told. Plan three to five questions which are focused straight to the core of the characters' (a) feelings, (b) appearance, (c) actions, and (d) dialogue.

B. Plan (a) how to weave reaction into the children's playing, and (b) how to guide children to use space freely.

7. Plan specific character roles you as leader will create when you guide children to create from this story. Plan roles (a) to get children started, (b) to encourage reaction, (c) to draw dialogue, and (d) to "spotlight" a child for recognition.

8. Plan specific ways in which you will praise and guide children to praise and evaluate each playing sequence. Focus attention on appropriate drama goals, and on individual expression and creativity.

9. Be prepared to contribute to a class discussion motivated by the following questions:

What do you think Masefield meant when he said "Great art flows from great encouragement?"

What evidences of Masefield's belief can you offer from personal experiences or from observations in children's creative dramatics classes? In the creative process what is the essential difference between praise and evaluation?

10. After you have enjoyed the fun of creating a play in class, analyze the instructor's role in guiding this experience from the five basic aspects of the creative process in guiding. Use a semioutline form. Include specific examples of guidance to substantiate your analysis and understanding.

11. Observe a children's class in creative dramatics. Analyze it from the viewpoint of the leader's role in guiding children to create. Follow a semioutline form as above. Cite specific examples.

12. Observe a children's class in creative dramatics. Analyze it specifically from the leader's role in motivating children into a mood at the outset, and in motivating children into a specific mood for creating each new character.

13. Observe a children's class in creative dramatics. Analyze it specifically from a leader's role in guiding by playing with the children Use specific examples to emphasize how and why the leader participated.

CHAPTER 7

Creative Dramatics with Little Children

The little ones leaped, and shouted, and laugh'd
And all the hills echoed.—William Blake

I t was summertime. Fifteen little children sat in a circle on a classroom floor. They smiled and wiggled as they sang:

> Happy birthday to you, happy birthday to you,
> Happy birthday, dear Susie, happy birthday to you.

Susie stood by the teacher in the middle of the circle.[1] "This is the happiest birthday cake I ever did see," the teacher said, as she smiled and looked at the happy little children around the circle. "What would you like to do with your birthday cake now, Susie?"

"Eat it," Susie said in fun.

"Fine! You're nice to share it with us. Suppose each one find a make-believe knife and make-believe plate and cut yourself a slice of Susie's make-believe birthday cake."

The children stood up quickly. They moved freely as they joined

[1] Hazel Dunnington, Central Washington College of Education, Ellensburg, Washington.

239

in the fun. Each one pretended to cut cake, and to eat it in rapid movements. They laughed and played with little squeals of delight. Susie and the teacher ate cake too. Then they sat on the floor in the middle of the circle to watch.

"You're sitting in the cake!" a little boy called out suddenly. The children laughed heartily at this funny idea. The teacher laughed too and waited until the children were seated and finished with their laughing. "Susie and I ate all the cake and 'licked the platter clean!' It's fun to play as though things really happen. Let's ask Susie what else besides cake she likes on her birthday."

"Presents," Susie said.

"How many like to get birthday presents on your birthday?"

The children responded eagerly. "How many like to give birthday presents to your friends?"

The children were equally as responsive. "Let's play that we give Susie the happiest birthday presents we know. This is what I would like to give Susie today. See if you know. If you do, raise your hand high. Your hand will show that you know."

The teacher pantomimed with enjoyment and fun. She galloped around the room on a frisky pony. A few of the children raised their hands. Others called out spontaneously: "It's a horse!" "It's a pony." "I know, it's a horse." "I'm going to get a horse."

The teacher brought the pony to a stop.

"Susie, it *is* a pony! Would you like this pony for your birthday?"

"Yes!" Susie said eagerly.

"Well, here he is. He's such a friendly pony. Come, ride him—he's yours."

Susie walked over to the make-believe pony a little hesitatingly. "Look," said the teacher as she pointed to the open space of the room.

"There are birthday ponies for every one of us. Here, Billy, here's a pony for you, and one for Jack, and one for Kevin."

One by one the children joined their enthusiastic teacher. She asked each child what kind of pony he would like to have. Some asked for black ponies, others for white and brown. One wanted a palomino, and one wanted a Shetland pony.

"We could have a parade," Kevin called out as he lined his pony up behind Susie's.

"Kevin, that's a fine idea. We'll have a birthday pony parade, and go riding with Susie. Maybe we will have some band music for our parade. Is everyone's pony ready?"

While the children were getting in line the teacher went to a record player and started a recording of "High Stepping Horses."[2]

The children stopped and listened with interest.

"It sounds just like a parade," Kevin said as the teacher pantomimed the riding of a rhythmic high-stepping horse and joined the children.

"Now we're ready for our happy birthday parade. Susie's pony will lead the way. Let's see how happy our ponies are."

Susie and the teacher led the parade around the room. Many of the ponies stepped high. Kevin's pony whinnied. Then several ponies whinnied. Some of the children laughed as they paraded together. Others really felt like frisky ponies.

"Oh, let's have happier high-stepping ponies," the teacher called. "Let's see how happy each pony is as he parades by Susie."

Each pony moved with stronger rhythm as he went by Susie. The ponies came to a stop behind Susie's pony.

[2] Clara L. Anderson, "High Stepping Horses," *RCA Victor Record Library for Elementary Schools:* Rhythmic Activities, Vol. 1, Radio Corporation of America, RCA Victor Division, 1947.

"Let's see how the ponies feel when the band plays this music," the teacher said as she started a recording of "Galloping Horses."[3]

"I feel like going like this," Kevin said and away he went galloping. The other ponies followed freely in a long line. After they galloped all the way around the room the teacher called, "Whoa, whoa, ponies. Whoa!"

The children slowed down, and the ponies came to a stop.

"My pony's puffing like a real horse," Kevin said.

"Let's have all our puffing ponies take a little rest on this green grass along the street," the teacher said as she indicated the space in front of them. Most of the children stretched out full length on the floor like children. Kevin stretched out like a pony. After a minute or two children began to sit up. Soon everyone was ready to play again.

"We have such beautiful birthday ponies. Let's watch Susie's and Aileen's and Larry's and Dick's. Watch to see how each pony gallops in his own special way. Watch how they gallop around the town." The teacher gestured toward the open space of the room. These ponies galloped and trotted like real ponies. Two ponies tossed their heads and whinnied as they all galloped back to the circle.

"Watch mine now," Kim called out as he started to parade alone.

"Whoa," said the teacher. "Stop your pony, Kim. We'll choose some more ponies to parade with you. Who wants us to watch his pony?"

The children were eager. They seemed to all talk at once: "I do!" "So do I." "Watch my pony." "See how mine goes."

The teacher waited until the children were quiet. "If you want us to watch your pony, raise your hand high," she said.

Every hand went up. The children were eager.

[3] *Ibid.*

"I know what we'll do. We'll have Kim lead all the boys' horses in a parade, and Aileen will lead all the girls' horses in a parade."

The ordered confusion of general movement into two different lines quickly subsided. Then the boys and girls took turns parading. The teacher called out with enthusiastic comments to praise individual ponies and ways of galloping. Several children praised each other's ponies too. When the parades were over the teacher suggested that each one tie his birthday pony to a make-believe fence. Soon everyone was sitting quietly in the circle again.

The teacher spoke in a low voice. "Let's close our eyes and think of another birthday present for Susie. If you could give Susie a present that would make her feel so happy inside what would your present be?"

The teacher waited for the children to think. "Raise your hand high as soon as you have a present to share," she said. Several hands started waving. The teacher chose David.

"This is what I'd give Susie," he said with a big smile.

David moved out of the circle and crawled on his hands and knees. He meowed in a little voice. The children laughed with delight as they realized what he was giving. Several called out: "It's a kitty!" "It's a cat." "I know what it is." "We have a kitty just like that only it's white."

The teacher quieted the children by suggesting: "Let's *listen* and *watch*. See if you can tell what *kind* of cat David is while he looks for a crumb of Susie's birthday cake."

David crawled slowly and quietly as he searched for something to eat inside the circle. Several children commented in a friendly way: "He's little." "He's soft," "He's a kitty—not a big cat."

The teacher was pleased. "David is a friendly little kitty, the nicest kind of birthday present for Susie. Just for fun, let's each one give

Susie a birthday kitty. See how much fun it is to be a hungry little kitty looking for something to eat because you are very hungry. Think how quietly a kitty walks on his soft kitty paws."

With this slight suggestion the children became convincing quiet kittens. They crawled in and out and around where the birthday cake had been. They meowed and enjoyed the meowing while each one looked for something to eat. The teacher and Susie watched the kittens. The teacher gave each kitten a gentle pat. Suddenly Kevin's kitty crawled away from the circle in great haste. He crawled on his hands and knees in a lively way.

"Kitties, kitties, watch Kevin's kitty. See if you know what his kitty is looking for," the teacher called enthusiastically. Kevin crawled faster and moved back and forth with quick movements. In a spontaneous moment Dick said, "He's after a mouse."

Several kittens joined Kevin's kitty. After they had had fun chasing a make-believe mouse, the teacher called: "Kitty, kitty, kitty, come, kitties."

The kittens crawled back. The teacher laughed as she said, "Susie will always remember such nice birthday kitties, especially the kittens who chased the mice. Now let's be ourselves again."

"I know what I'm going to give Susie," Kim said.

"I do, too," said Dick.

"So do I," called several others.

The teacher waited quietly. Soon the children were quiet. "You know what we'll do for Susie's birthday? We'll *tell* Susie what we would like to give her. Then we'll draw pictures of our presents for her. Let's hear what Kim would like to give Susie."

"Some baby chickies," said Kim. "We got some for Easter and they're soft like our baby's blankets."

Other birthday presents were shared and included "a dolly buggy," "a tea set," "swing set," "a puppy," "some stuff for a bubble bath," "an electric train," "a two-wheeler," "cowboy guns and a holster," "a baby," "ten fishing poles," "a hundred party dresses," "a rabbit," and "a pretty rock."

WHAT ARE LITTLE CHILDREN LIKE?

This happy group of little children was made up of boys and girls who were ready to enter kindergarten in the fall. Most of the children were 5-year-olds. A few were still 4, and two of the children were going to be 6 in December. Even though each child was different from every other child certain distinctive group characteristics and interests were evident. Fours, fives, and sixes are different. Each year of growth makes a noticeable difference in a child's behavior in these early years.

In referring to the growth and development of little children Gesell and Ilg have discovered the 4-year-old child to be generally outgoing and expansive. He is "constantly going out to meet the environment, making his thrusts in an almost harum-scarum manner. In contrast, the 5-year-old is self-contained, on friendly and familiar terms with his environment. He has learned much; he has matured."[4]

In a nursery school made up largely of 4-year-olds a leader may expect to find little children expressing themselves with strong, active, impulsive energies. At 5-and-a-half or 6 noticeable changes in behavior patterns appear with most children. "The young body of a healthy 6-year-old is supple, sensitive, alert. He reacts with his whole action-system. He does not only smile,—he fairly dances with joy. He cries copiously when unhappy, kicks and shakes with his grief.

[4] Arnold Gesell and Frances L. Ilg, *The Child from Five to Ten*, Harper & . Brothers, 1946.

. . . He uses body postures, gestures and speech to give expression to emotions and ideas which are taking shape within him."[5]

When a little child ventures out from his world of home and goes forth into a bigger world of society he generally goes to a nursery school, kindergarten, first grade, Sunday school or church school. When several little children meet together a leader becomes aware of basic group needs and interests. She analyzes behavior patterns in relation to the basic aspects of growth.

BASIC GROWTH CHARACTERISTICS OF LITTLE CHILDREN

Physical Characteristics and Needs. *A little child is active.* In playing "Happy Birthday" both boys and girls revealed a strong need for releasing energies through action. They galloped. They trotted. They ran. They crawled, and they stepped with high-stepping steps. A little child needs opportunities to bring his entire self into action. He needs experiences that invite the freedom and exuberance of whole body movements, and of movements which cause him to move freely in space.

A little child moves not unlike quicksilver in motion. *He needs a frequent change of physical position.* When the little "birthday" children were sitting and listening almost every child moved his arms and legs apparently without realizing it. One little boy, intent on the ideas of presents being shared, changed from a sitting to a standing, to a squatting position, and finally stretched out full length on the floor. Another child moved out of the circle and found delight in spinning himself around on the floor even though he appeared to be interested and had an idea to share when it was his turn.

[5] *Ibid.*

A little child *needs active moments followed by quiet moments.* During active play a leader needs to encourage strong wholehearted involvement so the child satisfies his energy needs with strong expression. A child who steps two or three steps like a horse or crawls two or three crawls like a kitten does not satisfy his basic need for projecting himself with action. He needs to be guided so he gets sufficiently involved to allow satisfaction physically, emotionally, and creatively. He needs time and space to use his body freely for expression.

A little child *needs to rest after strong involvement.* He may need to stretch out quietly for a minute or several minutes of complete rest. Or he may find it satisfying to sit still and share ideas. After a child's physical energies have been released, he often contributes many of his finest creative ideas in moments of quiet discussion.

Mental Characteristics and Needs. *A little child thinks independently.* He needs opportunities in which he expresses his own thoughts and ideas. A little child thinks in a visual way. He speaks in terms of pictures that are rich in imagery and not cluttered with details. He often needs help in disciplining his thinking. "Tell us in one clear thought," a leader often says to help a child clarify his thinking.

A little child has a short attention span. He can concentrate for a limited time on one idea before he becomes restless. For this reason children need brief discussions that emphasize feeling and lead directly toward action. A little child generally prefers to do rather than to discuss. He enjoys a variety of experiences.

A little child is curious. He receives new concepts by wondering, investigating, and observing. He becomes interested in words that symbolize concepts for him. A little child almost always enjoys using new words. He frequently exaggerates as he experiments with words and ideas. He needs to have ideas explained in vivid descriptive words that recall images for him. Often a single vivid word motivates a child into strong action.

Social Characteristics and Needs. *A little child wants to be with other children.* Fours enjoy being with other children but they prefer to play side-by-side, somewhat independently of one another. Fives enjoy playing with another child for short periods of time. Sixes begin to understand the sharing-attitude, although many sixes, like fives and fours, are strongly "I" centered. When little children gather together it is not uncommon to find a child "showing off" in ways such as yelling, running, shouting, pushing, or taking something from someone in order to call attention to himself. At the other extreme it is not unusual to find a little child preferring to sit alone and watch others play for several days or even weeks until he feels secure within a group.

A little child needs to be encouraged in a friendly way to join others, but he should not be forced into social patterns. With careful guidance each child will develop at his own speed and with the security he needs in a social situation.

Because almost every little child is self-centered in varying degrees in these early years, *he needs help in becoming a social being.* Each child needs to learn to take turns, to listen when someone else speaks, to raise his hand when he wishes to speak rather than interrupt, and he needs to learn to appreciate others. He needs guidance to repeat these actions over and over until he forms habits and attitudes of social awareness. He needs help to develop an attitude from "I" to "we." He needs praise in the presence of others so that he gradually feels secure and important to others. He needs approval with careful guidance when he comes forth with such comments as "Mine was best," or "Did you like mine the best?"

Emotional Characteristics and Needs. Most 4- and 5-year-olds are happy and in harmony with living. As a child approaches $5\frac{1}{2}$ or 6 he often becomes off key in his emotional living. He may be touchy, explosive, or given to extremes in emotional reactions. For many sixes life becomes stormy and frustrating for a time while new growth processes take place. Emotions are strong and close to the surface for most little children. When a little child is happy he is very happy and when he is cross he is cross all over. Whenever an emotional experience is recalled most little children are eager to share a viewpoint or an experience.

Most little children have real fears. They are afraid of unexpected sounds, animals that they associate with danger, sudden or unexpected happenings, cuts, hurts, darkness, storms, but most of all the fear of being left alone or away from the security of home and family.

Because little children have strong feelings they need opportunities to release emotions in a positive way. When a little child becomes confused he needs an understanding adult who voices and reflects his feelings, and helps him release his emotions in a satisfying way.

Spiritual Characteristics and Needs. A little child has a freshness of spirit. Each child needs praise and appreciation for creating and expressing in his own way. He needs a leader who frees him so he releases his true creative spirit. He needs help in being encouraged to be himself and express his own ideas. He needs appreciation for his sense of humor.

A 5-year-old girl arrived at kindergarten with the sudden announcement that her coat flew up a telephone pole and when she went after it she had lunch with Mrs. Telephone Pole. The teacher realizing the delicious nonsense replied: "I saw you and Mrs. Telephone Pole. What was it you were eating for lunch?"

The little girl was surprised. "Where were you?"

"I was coming down the street with a little pink cat who had a new hat," the teacher said in fun.

The little girl and the other children laughed heartily. It was quite a frequent thing for some child to tell a new story about Mrs. Telephone Pole during the rest of the school year.

WHAT INTERESTS LITTLE CHILDREN?

Little children live close to their environment. Their interests center around the real world in which they live. Their strongest interest is in home and family and the many intriguing activities and experiences of home. They are interested in pets, new clothes, toys, and playing. A little child wonders about grown-up people. He is particularly interested in what his mother and daddy do. He is fascinated with grown-up people who come to his house such as a milkman, a mailman, a truck driver who drives a truck bringing wood, coal, or oil. He often wishes he could go along with trucks and big people to exciting places in the country, town, and city.

Little children are interested in big machines that move with power and noise. They watch with fascination such powerful machines as cars, trucks, steamshovels, tractors, motorcycles, and bicycles. They find marked enjoyment in trains, planes, and boats, and they wonder about the faraway places they might travel.

Animals always interest a little child. He is interested in farm animals, forest animals, zoo animals, trained animals, and wild jungle animals that he hears about. He is interested in the way animals move about, the different things animals do, and in the unusual sounds an animal makes. He is fascinated with little insects too. Caterpillars, bugs, worms, grasshoppers all seem special.

Little children enjoy and are curious about the absorbing activities that come with each new season. Holidays and birthdays hold a singular interest. A little child responds to the wonder, beauty, and delight symbolized by such wonderful ideas as Santa Claus, the Easter rabbit, a glowing Jack-o'-lantern, a May basket, and a valentine.

A leader who is alert to children's comments and to objects they bring to share will discover new individual delights. Interests may often be motivated by television programs, community and family happenings, and by story and picture books that individuals have enjoyed.

INTRODUCING CREATIVE DRAMATICS TO LITTLE CHILDREN

Little children want to play, rather than make a play. The key to involving them lies in sharing simple, dramatic experiences that hold high appeal. An alert leader is aware of a little child's strong interests in his environment. These interests provide the essence of his play experiences in creative dramatics. There are many different ways to begin. Rhythmic movement satisfies their need for action and is basic in beginning experiences.

Begin with Rhythmic Movement. The following beginning experiences have been used with little children. Each experience invites free expression in rhythmic movement wherein a child remains himself. Each provides group fun, for it is based on a real life situation that holds high appeal for most little children. In each experience a mood was created before the focused question was asked.

Household Activities

Let's pretend our playhouse needs cleaning today. Let's see how we may clean it so it is spick and span and pretty. What one thing might you do to make our house clean and pretty? (Sweep, vacuum, dust, wash dishes, dry dishes, pick up toys, make beds, bring in flowers.)

Outdoor Activities

Our house is clean and pretty but our yard needs to be made beautiful. Who sees one way you might help to make it beautiful? (Mow the lawn, cut tall grass, plant flowers, water flowers, pick up papers, paint the steps, plant a tree, paint the house.)

Play Activities

We've worked hard and now it's time for fun. Let's pretend our playhouse has a big back yard where it's fun to play. It is just like a big playground or park where you may have fun doing whatever you like to play best. How will you play? (Swing, teeter-totter, rollerskate, roll on grass, ride a tricycle, slide on a slide, run races, jump, wade in a pool.)

Park Activities

Let's pretend we are a big happy family, and everyone is a brother or sister or cousin. I will be the mother, and we will go to the amusement park. We have only enough pennies for everyone to have one ride. When we get to the park what one thing will be the most fun for you to do? (Ride on a merry-go-round, ride on a motor boat, ride on an airplane, ride in a race car, ride a Shetland pony, ride on a train.)

Planting Activities

It's flower planting time. Who remembers what we do with tiny flower seeds which causes them to grow into beautiful flowers? (Dig the ground, plant seeds, cover seeds, water seeds, hoe the ground.)

May Hill Arbuthnot's *Time for Poetry* provides a rare legacy of poetry and verse rich in opportunities for creative rhythmic movement.[6] The following poems have been shared and enjoyed by little children: "The Swing," by Robert Louis Stevenson, "Merry-Go-Round," by Dorothy Baruch, "New Shoes," by Alice Wilkins, "Galoshes," by Rhoda Bacmeister, "Mud," by Polly Chase Boyden, "Who

[6] May Hill Arbuthnot, *Time for Poetry*, Scott, Foresman and Company, 1952.

Has Seen the Wind?" by Christina Rossetti, and "Down! Down!" by Eleanor Farjeon.

Begin with Characterization in Rhythmic Movement. The following experiences are centered in characterization where each child is guided to create a characterization that is noticeably different from his real self. These experiences have been used for early ventures in creative play and have held high appeal for most little children. In each one a mood was developed before the question was asked.

Transportation

Let's pretend we are going on a long, long trip to London today. We will go to see London Bridge. London is so far away we need to travel in different ways. We will travel in the same ways people travel to faraway places every day. What one way would you like to travel to London today? (Bus, train, plane, boat, taxi, car, bicycle, helicopter, on a horse.)

Pets

Goldie is such a friendly little fish. She watches us all day long, and makes us happy just by being with us. If you could have a pet of your own which would make you happy, what pet would you choose to live at your house? (Horse, dog, cat, turtle, bird, mouse, parrot, pig, duck, rabbit, monkey.)

Farm Animals

A farm is a friendly, busy place. All the farm people and all the farm animals are busy all day long. Bees are busy making honey, and lambs are busy making wool. If you could be a friendly farm animal which animal would you like to be best of all? (Cow, horse, chicken, sheep, rabbit, pig, dog, goose, turkey.)

Weather

See the pretty snowflakes floating down from the sky. If you were a snowy snowflake and could fly to one special place to make it pretty with snow where would you have your snowflake fly? (On our roof,

in a tree, on a telephone wire, on the schoolhouse, in the window, on the lawn, in the rosebush.)

Seasons

If you listen closely you will hear someone who is singing because it's spring. If you were a robin wanting to find the friendliest place in our town to build your nest, where do you think you would choose to build it? (In our cherry tree, in our birdhouse, in a tree by the church, in our garage by the roof, in the forest where the trees are pretty.)

Among poems that have motivated delightful experiences in characterization are the following: "Jump or Jiggle," by Evelyn Beyer, "Mrs. Peck Pigeon," by Eleanor Farjeon, "My Policeman," by Rose Fyleman, "First Snow," by Marie Louise Allen, "The Animal Store," by Rachel Field, "Holding Hands," by Lenore M. Link, "The Seals," by Dorothy Aldis, "Rabbits," by Dorothy Baruch, "Little Charlie Chipmunk," by Helen Cowles LeCron, "Boats," by Rowena Bennett, "Taking Off," by Mary McB. Green, and "Ferry-Boats" and "Trains," by James S. Tippett.[7]

Begin with Pantomime. Guessing games are always fun for children. Teachers have found pantomime games a delightful way to introduce little children to characterization. For instance, one kindergarten teacher shared a guessing game called: "Who am I?" After creating a mood she stated, "Watch and see if you can guess who I would like to be." She then created a strong pantomime of a happy ballet dancer. Immediately the children guessed. They were enthusiastic. They asked if they could be ballet dancers, too. Each child was encouraged to create in his own way as the children took turns being ballet dancers in small groups.

After playing this game with several different characterizations, children asked if they might share ideas. Mark, a sensitive little boy

[7] *Ibid.*

who had become intrigued with finger painting, was eager for a turn. When he was chosen, he seemed to grow taller and mightier with every step he took as he walked to the front of the group. Using both hands in full sweeping movements he appeared to be finger painting the entire space in front, above, and around him. When he stopped the children could not guess exactly who he was. With strong belief he said, "I was Jesus making finger paint up in the sky at sunset time."

After everyone had an opportunity to "finger paint a sunset," Charles was the next boy to have a turn. He walked up to the front of the group with equally as much conviction. With an imaginary gun he sighted carefully as he moved in a complete circle. Then he stood still, crouched for action with his eye alert in every direction. When the children were unable to guess, he said proudly, "I was General Custard looking for Indians just like he does on television."

A leader with imagination discovers many different variations of pantomime games. For instance, pantomime games may be developed around guessing what is inside imaginary Christmas or birthday packages, guessing who the surprise guests are at a creative Halloween party, and guessing favorite characters from Mother Goose or from stories a group has enjoyed.

Begin with Songs. Little children enjoy singing. Many of their songs are action songs that invite simple pantomimes or characterizations. After children have learned a song and enjoy singing it, they may be guided to create from it. Most leaders find it advisable to divide a large group into two groups. Half of the children sing while the other half pantomime.

A leader may guide in a way similar to the way one kindergarten teacher guided children to create from a song called, "Here We Go

'Round the Christmas Tree,"[8] sung to the tune of "Here We Go 'Round the Mulberry Bush." After the children had learned the song and were in a Christmas mood, the teacher asked, "What one thing do you like to do best around your Christmas tree on Christmas day in the morning?"

Immediate replies brought these different answers: "see my presents," "open presents and play with my new toys," "eat Christmas buns," "sing Christmas songs with all our family," "find out what Santa Claus brought," and "look in my stocking." The teacher guided the children into creating from each different idea in turn (Fig. 7.1).

These same kindergarteners were guided to create a happy reindeer Christmas party after they had learned to sing "Rudolph the Red-Nosed Reindeer" (Fig. 7.2).

Among the singing games that have been used to motivate pleasant creative expression are these: "The Farmer in the Dell," "Hippity Hop to the Barber Shop," "Ten Little Indians," "Yankee Doodle," "London Bridge," "The Muffin Man," and "Did You Ever See a Lassie?"

Teachers of little children will recognize many songs that offer splendid natural opportunities for beginning experiences in creative pantomime.

Begin with "Finger Plays." Little children the world around enjoy "finger plays." When they use their fingers to create short, simple "finger plays" they form vivid pictures in their minds. After they know and enjoy this activity a leader guides them to create from it by guiding them into a simple plan of action. Above all she guides them to feel the way the characters feel in whatever "finger play" they are enjoying.

[8] Orma M. Popke, Kohler Public Schools, Kohler, Wisconsin.

FIG. 7.1. "On Christmas Day in the Morning." (*Photograph by Dick Lemmerhirt; courtesy of Louis J. Charling, Kohler Company; Kohler Public Schools, Kohler, Wisconsin*)

FIG. 7.2. "Santa will never choose you, Rudolph." (*Photograph by Dick Lemmerhirt; courtesy of Louis J. Charling, Kohler Company; Kohler Public Schools, Kohler, Wisconsin*)

Begin with "Dramatic Play." When little children are motivated by an exciting or satisfying experience, they like to play this experience in their own way (Fig. 7.3). Opportunities for "dramatic play" are provided by community happenings, family happenings, group trips to a farm or fire station (Fig. 7.4), and by a child's involvement

FIG. 7.3. "Let's go!" (*Photograph by Edward A. Gilliland, Everett Junior College; courtesy of Bernice L. Rice; View Ridge School, Everett Public Schools, Everett, Washington*)

in "dramatic play." A kindergarten teacher soon recognizes that thrilling creative moments often develop during dramatic play.

One such experience occurred when three 5-year-olds built a "great big church" out of blocks.[9] They were pleased with their building and asked the teacher if everyone in the kindergarten could come to church "to worship." All the children and the teacher gathered in the spacious church except three young pilots. They were in a corner of the room testing the flights of their jet planes which they had made from tinker toys. "Are the pilots going to join us in church today?" the teacher asked.

"We'll fly around the church and guard it," one of the pilots answered. He started to circle around the church in strong rhythm. The other pilots joined him with convincing sound effects. When the pilots with their planes had circled three times, they stopped to

[9] Ann Browne Pirtle, Seward Public School, Seattle, Washington. Mrs. Pirtle was formerly on the creative dramatics staff at the University of Washington.

rest. "We'll sit up here on the hill and guard the church so the people won't be scared of anything," a pilot explained.

Fig. 7.4. "This is a real fire engine!" (*Photograph by Edward A. Gilliland, Everett Junior College; courtesy of Bernice L. Rice; View Ridge School, Everett Public Schools, Everett, Washington*)

The pilots sat quietly and listened while the church services began. Children sang songs, a few shared prayers, and the teacher read a psalm from a book a little girl had brought to share.

Illustrations of "dramatic play" which reached unusual creative heights are to be found in *Supplementary Materials for Use in Creative Dramatics with Younger Children.*[10]

Introduce Conflict Material. Whenever little children get involved in strong feelings of conflict they like to play an experience over and over again. Dramatic conflicts based on real life experiences which have proved satisfying include a family of mallard ducks being frightened by a fox (Fig. 7.5); a family of bluebirds being frightened by a hawk; a family of prairie rabbits being chased by a dog; a mother cat and new little kittens being chased by a dog; forest animals being frightened by a thunderstorm; and a snowman and his family being melted by the sun and the wind.

Mother Goose provides striking little dramas in a nutshell. "Mother Goose, not unlike Shakespeare, has proved her worth to the world. For years she has opened the first gateway to literature. Her rhymes, her jingles, her musical bits of poetry and nonsense which have been enjoyed for many generations have come down to us on their own merits of beauty, simplicity, and fitness."[11] "Little Miss Muffett," limited to two characterizations, provides a near-perfect drama for little children. When little girls identify with little Miss Muffett they thoroughly enjoy the beauty of the outdoor world while eating lunch. They are always surprised and frightened by the unexpected quietness of a spider who crawls curiously from somewhere

---

[10] Agnes Haaga and Patricia Randles, *Supplementary Materials for Use in Creative Dramatics with Younger Children,* University of Washington Press, 1952.

[11] Ruth Lease and Geraldine Brain Siks, *Creative Dramatics in Home, School, and Community,* Harper & Brothers, 1952.

behind. After children observe the crawling rhythm and silence of a spider they create spiders with strong empathy.

Drama centered around the fear of losing something "important" is found in "Little Bo Peep." Strong conflicts have been created in "Little Boy Blue," "The North Wind Doth Blow," "Humpty Dumpty," and "Six Little Mice."

FIG. 7.5. "Father Mallard, let's stop here. It looks safe." (*School of Drama, University of Washington*)

Poems that have provided moments of rare drama include Elizabeth Coatsworth's "Seagull and the Fish," Vachel Lindsay's "The Little Turtle," and Lillian Schulz Vanada's "Fuzzy, Wuzzy, Creepy, Crawly." In the latter, little children have delighted in becoming crawling caterpillars creeping for a quiet place to sleep. They have curled up in imaginary caterpillar blankets and shared unusual caterpillar dreams. When the caterpillars awaken from a long sleep and change into beautiful butterflies, children become excited about seeing the outdoor world for the first time through the eyes of a butterfly. They find peculiar enjoyment in flying like butterflies to the most beautiful place in the world, and sharing with each other descriptions of just where they have lighted.

Sharing Short Stories. Kindergarten and first grade teachers who understand creative dramatics guide little children into rhythmic movement, characterization, and short conflicts during the first three or four months of a school year. Most of these teachers find that children are then ready to create from short stories at the end of three or four months. Teachers have discovered that first stories for playing should always be *short stories, strong in conflict but limited in characterization.*

Winifred Ward has made a distinctive contribution by providing a collection of the finest stories for children to dramatize from literature.[12] Among the best stories in this collection for first story experiences for little children are those limited in characterization, such as: "The Tale of Peter Rabbit," "Little Black Sambo," "The Peddler and His Caps," "Teeny Tiny," and "Goldilocks and the Three Bears." Other fine short stories for playing include, "Why the Bear Is Stumpy-Tailed" and "The Lion and the Mouse."

Sharing Longer Stories. After little children have created several short stories into plays, they will be ready to enjoy longer stories. Longer stories generally provide several individualized characters who use dialogue. Among the favorites for playing included in Miss Ward's collection are "Why the Evergreen Trees Keep Their Leaves in Winter," "The Little Red Hen," "The Little Pink Rose," and "Ask Mr. Bear." Other favorite long stories include "The Three Little Pigs," "Henny-Penny," "The Big Turnip" by Tolstoy, "The

[12] Winifred Ward, *Stories to Dramatize*, The Children's Theatre Press, 195

Little Engine That Could" by Mabel C. Bragg, "Why the Bear
Sleeps All Winter" by Carolyn Bailey, *A Surprise for Mrs. Bunny*
by Charlotte Steiner, *Brownies—Hush!* by Gladys Adshead, *The
Noisy Book* by Margaret Wise Brown, and "Little Duckling Tries
His Voice," by Marjorie La Fleur.

When children are ready for longer stories two favorites which are
strong in drama are James Daugherty's *Andy and the Lion* and
Robert McCloskey's *Make Way For Ducklings* (Fig. 7.6).

FIG. 7.6. "Woof! I got that duck's tail feathers!"
(*School of Drama, University of Washington*)

Creating Climactic Episodes in Stories. Kindergarten and nursery
school teachers often share an entire story with little children in early
sessions. The story is shared because of its high appeal in dramatic
conflict and because it introduces children to good literature in a

splendid listening experience. The entire story is not played. Rather a teacher guides little children to create only one or two characterizations so they may play the highest dramatic moment in the story.

BASIC PRINCIPLES IN GUIDING LITTLE CHILDREN

The procedure for guiding little children is similar to the creative process in guiding older children. The chief difference lies in emphasis. *Playing* is emphasized with little children; whereas a play and drama terms are stressed with older children. Playing is introduced after a brief planning period. A plan-and-play-as-you-go process is most effective in meeting the basic needs of little children.

The five basic guideposts in guiding little children are: (1) analyzing material, (2) focusing thinking, (3) building mood quickly, (4) stating a clear plan of action, and (5) playing with children to guide and praise indirectly.

Analyzing Material. Simplify—simplify—simplify. Focus—focus—focus. These are a leader's two watchwords as she selects and analyzes material. One creative moment with strong empathy for a little child is worth a thousand unfelt moments in random movement.

A leader selects an idea that holds sure-fire interest for a group of children. After an idea has been selected, it is analyzed to determine its specific dramatic content, and its appeal to children.

Suppose a leader recognizes little children's interests in autumn leaves in early fall. To prepare this idea for a creative experience she "lives with" this material. She observes autumn leaves. She watches them in a way not unlike the way little children watch. She becomes aware of the variety of rhythmic movements of leaves. By close watching she sees that a leaf may float, whirl, flutter, dance, zoom, sail upward and downward, twirl, and fall. It may move swiftly or slowly depending on the wind and weather. The leader becomes aware of the quietness and beauty with which a leaf falls, or the merriness with which it flutters and dances. She considers why a leaf falls, and its real purpose in nature's plan.

After material has been analyzed, it is focused toward specific goals. A leader sets up goals to determine where and why she is guiding a group of children. Clear goals keep guidance focused with strong purpose.

Three clear goals are determined: group goal, drama goal, and a specific learning goal. Goals should always be written out to clarify focus. For example:

I. Group Goal
Strong physical and emotional release with creative thinking for every child.
II. Drama Goal
Expression in a variety of rhythmic movements with strong empathy.
III. Learning Goal
Mother Nature prepares for winter by sending leaves to make a cover for earth.

After goals are determined the leader visualizes children creating from the material. She may select rhythmic recordings to heighten mood. Or she may plan a specific kind of rhythmic pattern for movement such as chanting children's replies, sharing a rhythmic verse, or playing a piano.

A leader plans several playing sequences for each session. She visualizes children creating within the prescribed space of a room.

Focusing Thinking. Focus—focus—focus. Again, *focus* becomes a leader's guidepost in centering children's thinking on one idea.

She plans to capture attention and focus thinking in a way that appeals and functions.

The most natural and appealing way to focus children's thinking to autumn leaves comes on a day when leaves are falling and moving in exciting beautiful patterns. The leader may take the children out of doors or invite them to watch leaves from windows. While they are watching she focuses thinking further with specific suggestions: "Watch one pretty leaf and see how it moves. Watch to see how you think a leaf feels when it is free from a tree."

Building Mood Quickly. Feeling—feeling—feeling. This is the key to building mood. The leader strives to arouse each child's feeling. After thinking has been centered to one idea, she relates this idea to every child. She asks a focused question to arouse a specific feeling. In this instance, she may ask: "How do you feel when you are free to move in a great big room, or out on a great big lawn?"

She draws replies from three, four, five, or several children to heighten feeling within every child. She often emphasizes a reply by repeating a single word that conveys strong feeling. Suppose children have described a leaf as feeling "like sailing," "like a jet," "like flying on, and on, and on," "happy like a party," and "skipping-dipping." She captures these vivid words and uses them to guide children in their playing.

Stating a Clear Plan of Action. Clarify—clarify—clarify. This is the key in guiding little children to express in dramatic action. A leader must state a clear plan of specific action. A plan should include specific purpose for every child either as a player or an observer. If a child is to remain on the "inside" of a creative experience he needs to be involved in a specific way in each playing sequence. A leader organizes a large group of children by providing purpose for every child, and stating this purpose in the plan of action.

Suppose children have watched leaves, talked about different ways leaves move, and have had a brief discussion on how individuals feel when they move freely in space. A leader senses a little child's need for action. She transfers this mood into creative expression by stating a clear plan of simple action, maybe in a way similar to the following:

We have watched beautiful autumn leaves. Now we are going to *be* leaves.

The first time we play, the boys will be leaves, and the girls will be the merry autumn wind. Next time the girls will be leaves and the boys will be the wind.

Let's pretend there's a big, tall maple tree right here on this make-believe street. Let's see how each one of the boys uses his whole self to be an autumn leaf on one of the branches.

Now, suppose the autumn wind and all the breezes come up to this pretend hilltop with me. We will stand here on top of the hill. Each one may use your arms and whole self to swish and blow leaves in your own way. You may wish to have your wind hum or sing for the autumn leaves.

Now let's be the autumn wind and blow the beautiful leaves. See if you can blow a leaf off the tree. See how each leaf feels when you blow it free. See if you can guess where each leaf chooses to light.

Playing with Children. Fun—fun—fun. Praise—praise—praise. These are the keys in guiding happy creative playing with little children. A leader who plays and creates with children is on the "inside" of the magic realm rather than on the outside as a leader.

A leader who plays with little children is in an ideal position to guide indirectly a group and individuals by keeping an experience in a strong spirit of fun. A leader who enjoys playing is effective in keeping every child involved in a strong mood for playing and creating.

A leader, in character, may provide a rhythmic pattern of action which often heightens expression. For instance, as the wind she may "capture" comments from one of the children's winds, and build this into a rhythmic song or chant. Suppose a child's wind says, "Swishity-swishity-swish." The leader will recognize a splendid wind rhythm. She will give recognition to the child who thought of the idea by encouraging all of the winds to chant this child's idea. She will lead the chant with spirit and rhythmic force.

The leader who plays with children is in a position to draw free creative expression from a child. When a child becomes involved in the freedom and enjoyment of creating a character, the leader realizes he is in a strong mood for expression. She may utilize this moment by drawing further expression from the child. For instance, the leader as the autumn wind may call to a happy dancing leaf, "Little leaf, little leaf, I've been watching you from the mountain. You are the happiest autumn leaf I have seen all day. What makes you so happy today?"

A leader, in character, may encourage shy children with a gentle, physical touch and a few words of friendly encouragement. For instance, suppose a shy child becomes an autumn leaf for only a moment, and then sits on the floor. A leader, as merry Mr. Wind, may encourage this child with friendly, playful comments and by a gentle rousing into further action.

When a leader plays with children she is in a position to praise a child and focus group attention toward him for a brief moment of recognition while he is creating. For instance, as the wind the leader may move from one autumn leaf to another and call to the wind on the mountain in a way similar to this, "Autumn winds, watch and see how happy this autumn leaf feels, and this one, and this one, and this one, and see these two leaves dancing together."

When a leader is in character, she is in a strong position to control a child who needs help in disciplining his thinking. She is firm about guiding him in a friendly way. Suppose, for example, an aggressive child who wants recognition whirls like an autumn leaf in a rapid succession of circular movements. As the wind, the leader may touch him gently and guide in a way that is best for him. She may say: "Here is one of the liveliest leaves on the street. See how he moves. I will blow him into a clump of grass right down here so he will get a good rest for he must be getting dizzy. Come, little leaf, rest here until I blow you again."

Continuous Pattern of Guidance. When children are eager to play an experience over again, a leader guides them to do so. She utilizes a strong mood rather than breaking it with discussion or evaluation. She chooses a new group of children to play immediately. Or, as in this instance, children who were the wind became the leaves in the second playing of the same sequence.

A new creative purpose is introduced whenever a leader feels a new motivation is needed to spur children on to higher expression. She introduces a single focused question, and thus the creative process again begins its cycle. In this instance, the single question might be, "When the autumn winds blow the leaves from the trees, what do the leaves do to help Mother Nature get ready for winter?"

The leader captures children's thoughts and voices them as she injects new purpose into playing. "Everyone knows! Leaves make a warm cover for flowers and grass and hills and sometimes a warm nest for a squirrel. If you were a little leaf, and you had watched the beautiful world from high on a branch all summer, what special thing would you like to cover up for winter?"

A new organization of the group is made. Several children are chosen to be leaves, a few to be wind, and perhaps a few are chosen to be children watching leaves from a school window. A specific plan of action is stated. Playing takes on new interest, not only for the players but for the children who are watching with a pleasant sense of special importance.

Choosing Children in Groups. Kindergarten and first grade teachers generally choose children in groups for early creative playings. This plan not only facilitates guidance, but encourages the shy children to participate. If the leader always chooses from among volunteers, shy children do not volunteer. A shy child is generally happy to play when he is included in a group to which he belongs. If he is one of the Blue Table Friends or one of the People from Cherry Street who happen to be the children in the third row, he willingly joins with this group when it is chosen. Choosing by groups also provides a pattern of order. It disciplines an aggressive child to be patient while he watches others, as he realizes he will have a turn in time.

Changing a Pattern of Imitation. In early creative play children often imitate one another. Many will continue to do so unless a leader encourages creative thinking. In one kindergarten class, when a little leaf was asked where he was flying, he answered, "I'm covering up our camellia bush 'cause it froze to death last winter." The children who were watching thought this was funny. They laughed gleefully. The next two leaves answered in exactly the same way.

Whenever a leader senses a chain reaction in an imitation of thought, she motivates thinking with a suggestion or question. She may say, "What else might a leaf cover up?" In this instance, the leader as the chanting wind said, "I can see far and wide. I see so many beautiful things that need warm leaf blankets. I wonder if a little leaf is going to cover up something besides the camellia bushes." Several little leaves were ready with new ideas. One little leaf completely involved said, "I'm going to cover my daddy's car 'cause we haven't got a garage and it gets snow all over."

When a leader is aware of imitation in bodily expression she stresses creative thinking by emphasizing feeling. A leader often focuses attention on a child who is feeling. "Let's watch Eric's happy leaf. He is feeling like a leaf from deep inside himself, and he is being a leaf in his own way." Or, "I think I've seen a million leaves outside, and I've never seen two leaves just exactly the same. That is why Stella's leaf is so pretty. She is feeling like a leaf in a way different from any other leaf."

Praise Focused to Goals.   At the end of a playing experience the leader often emphasizes goals in a way that children can understand. She may ask "Who do you think had the most fun playing today?" Or, "Why do you think Hazel, Eric, Stella, and Lee had the most fun today?" Children are perceptive. They are quick to sense strong creative playing and group coöperation.

A leader focuses their comments to basic goals. She may emphasize: "Yes, they had fun because they really *felt* like leaves, they used their own ideas, and they used their whole selves to show how they felt. I think everyone had fun by playing together so nicely, too."

Leader Becomes an Audience.   A leader becomes a member of the group who is watching whenever she feels individual children are ready to create freely and forcefully. A child who is secure and ready for creative challenge is chosen to become a character in a strong guiding role. A leader casts little children in roles that call for initiative whenever she believes individuals are ready to enjoy rather than fear these moments of responsibility. She uses care in not dominating a group when she plays. She becomes sensitive to creativity and expression and allows a child to "blossom" as soon as he is ready.

Short Periods for Creative Playing. Creative thinking calls for strong concentration. When little children concentrate intently for 15 or 20 minutes they tire and need a change of experience. In a kindergarten or first grade, teachers have found that a short period of 20 minutes every day or three days a week is far more satisfying than an hour period once a week.

Because little children have short attention spans, a leader finds that the highest creative moments generally take place within the first 15 or 20 minutes of playing. If children do play for 45 minutes a high plane of creative expression is seldom reached after the first 20 minutes. When little children are tired, the creative spark is missing in their playing and the leader wisely brings the playing to a happy ending. If several children within a group have not had individual moments of recognition these children are chosen for the first playing whenever a group meets again.

In community or Sunday school programs class periods are often scheduled for an hour. In such situations the leader plans a different kind of activity for the last half hour. Creativity which has been motivated by playing may be channeled readily into creative painting, coloring, finger painting, or creating with clay. A creative experience may be enriched by sharing books and pictures or by an outdoor walk.

CREATIVE DRAMATICS IN THE SCHOOL

Creative dramatics has become an integral part of many kindergarten and first grade curriculums. It has been integrated in the lower elementary school program in areas of speech, nature study, science, language arts, social studies, and in the related arts of painting and music.

In Speech Classes. Teachers who understand speech therapy have

found creative dramatics an ideal experience to share with children who have emotional speech problems (Fig. 7.7). When a child is

FIG. 7.7. "Once I lost my jacket. Have you ever lost anything?" (*Photograph by Loren T. Cockrell, San Jose State College; courtesy of Harold C. Crain, Department of Speech and Drama, San Jose State College, San Jose, California*)

guided into the fun of playing he becomes involved in creating and forgets his emotional tensions. One kindergarten teacher says, "A child is at ease while he's playing and seldom stutters or gets a 'block' while his mind is entirely off himself. If he is guided to play often enough throughout a year, it has an almost miraculous effect on lessening his speech problem" (Fig. 7.8).

FIG. 7.8. "Lost your mittens? You naughty kittens!" (*Photograph by Loren T. Cockrell, San Jose State College; courtesy of Harold C. Crain, Department of Speech and Drama, San Jose State College, San Jose, California*)

In Nature Study and Science. What better way for a little child to begin to understand the outdoor world of nature than to play and create from his wonderings? "You can start creative play from almost anywhere if you are alert to little children's interests and delights," says one kindergarten teacher. "A little girl's discovery of a spider web in the doll corner or a little boy's exclamation over a seedling which has just sprouted are examples of moments which may lead directly to spontaneous high creative play."[13]

Skillful teachers have been alert to children's interests in the sky, weather, and in seasonal changes for motivation into playing. One kindergarten teacher introduced creative dramatics to her children in the fall shortly after school started.[14] On a warm autumn day she took them for a walk in a wooded pasture near the school. Each child gathered "signs of fall" and put his findings in a brown paper bag. As he did so, he became aware of the many seed pods flying in the air. The teacher caused the children to watch and wonder about the special way seed pods moved about. When the children were back in the room, the teacher guided them into further wondering. Soon each child became a seed pod flying quietly and freely in the autumn sky as he looked for a new home. The teacher became the sun and spoke to each little seed pod to see where it had planted itself (Fig. 7.9). Replies provided insights into a child's understanding of nature, and revealed a delight in creative expression. The following replies show both: "under a cool tree," "where a creek comes through the trees," "in the house in a pot," "on the side of a pond where ducks light," "in a rabbit's cage," "in a nice place where there is sun, water, and rain," "by our porch," "in a bird's nest," and "in an Easter basket."

With the coming of spring these children asked to play "seeds" again. By this time they were ready to enjoy creating from "The Little Pink Rose." They found great satisfaction in being not only seeds, but the sun, the rain, and many kinds of different flowers (Fig. 7.10).

[13] Pirtle, *op. cit.*
[14] Emma G. Mylroie, Lake Forest Park School, Shoreline Public Schools. Seattle, Washington.

FIG. 7.9. "Seeds" go to sleep for the winter. (*Lake Forest Park School, Shoreline Public Schools, Seattle, Washington*)

FIG. 7.10. "I am the sun. Please let me in." (*Lake Forest Park School, Shoreline Public Schools, Seattle, Washington*)

Another kindergarten teacher integrates strong learning experiences by correlating creative dramatics with nature study, singing,
and drawing.[15] She says, "There are many ways when you are
aware of children's interests. When a child brings a bird nest to
school it always leads to an exciting creative dramatics experience
on birds." Children are eager to share experiences about birds, bird's
nests, baby birds, the way birds fly and sing. They find great delight in figuring out how they might make a nest and become baby
birds inside tiny imaginary bird's eggs (Fig. 7.11). Little birds en-

FIG. 7.11. Four eggs in a robin's nest. (*Lake
Forest Park School, Shoreline Public Schools, Seattle, Washington*)

[15] Marie J. Pickett, Lake Forest Park School, Shoreline Public Schools. Seattle,
Washington.

joy hatching. The children find special joy in looking out from the nest to see one beautiful thing in the new world (Fig. 7.12). Chil-

FIG. 7.12. Little birds have hatched. (*Lake Forest Park School, Shoreline Public Schools, Seattle, Washington*)

dren especially enjoy guessing what mother bird brings to the baby birds for their breakfasts (Fig. 7.13). Mother and father birds often enjoy singing original songs to baby birds about a special place they have seen while they were flying. After playing birds, children always enjoy drawing pictures of birds, and singing songs about birds and springtime.

Fig. 7.13. "Baby robin, here's a ripe cherry." (*Lake Forest Park School, Shoreline Public Schools, Seattle, Washington*)

In Language Arts. Creative dramatics provides rich opportunities for a variety of fun experiences that contribute directly to growth in language arts. In creative play children speak, communicate, listen, and share with high intent. A kindergarten teacher says:

Creative dramatics is the purest kind of joy a child can have in kindergarten. It is rich experiencing in living. It stimulates a child's imagination and builds friendly attitudes toward others. It offers a natural way to unify a child's learning.

When a child creates and plays many different experiences he visualizes. He sees vivid mental pictures. New concepts become meaningful. Creative dramatics causes words to "come to life" for him. He lives in a wonderful world of beauty and enchantment after he learns to "hitch" words and mental pictures together. Through his play a child develops a vocabulary that he understands, and can use freely without hesitation. I have *seen* creative dramatics build reading readiness for many, many five-year-olds in a wonderful, happy childlike way.[16]

Visual and auditory discriminations are readily built through creative dramatics. A child finds much more enjoyment in being such active and impressive things as trains, cars, boats, and a variety of animals than he does in sitting quietly and making animal or machine sounds. A child's ability to discriminate grows through such satisfying experiences as becoming a train engine that moves fast or slow; a train with a light load or a heavy one; a train that has a big or a little engine; a train that whistles with a loud or soft whistle; a train that is near or far away; a train that is a "diesel, electric, or heavy freight."

Little children build an enjoyment and appreciation for good literature when they are guided to play delightful stories and verse after hearing them. Many first grade teachers have discovered that creative dramatics motivates reading as well as listening. When little children enjoy a story they often ask to play it. One first grade class was guided to play the favorite story after finishing each new reading book.[17] Before the children were ready to play they found it necessary to read the story again. After playing, these children

[16] Popke, *op. cit.*

[17] Lorraine B. Malphrus, Lake Forest Park School, Shoreline Public Schools, Seattle, Washington.

enjoyed drawing pictures and making a big book about "Our Favorite Story" (Fig. 7.14).

FIG. 7.14. "The children and the puppy and gray squirrel galloped to Sleepy Town." (*Lake Forest Park School, Shoreline Public Schools, Seattle, Washington*)

Several first grade teachers have introduced rhythmic movement and characterization to children through reading. When children finish a reading period they are guided to return to their desks "in character." A teacher often tests reading comprehension by guiding children to become specific characters, or to create specific actions such as the following: "Show us what Jane got for her birthday that made her the happiest." Or, "Return to your desk as the funniest person in the story." Or, "Be the person in the story whom you would like to have for your friend."

In Social Studies. By its very nature creative dramatics offers firsthand experiences in social growth. In addition, it offers rich experiences in dramatic play and pantomime for providing insights in a child's understanding of home and community life. Little children delight in pantomiming such games as the following: "This Is the Way I Helped Mother Today," "This Is What I Do to Help Daddy," "This Is the Best Thing I Had for Breakfast," "This Is What I'd Like to Be."

Treasured objects that children bring to school may motivate spontaneous dramatic play when a teacher is alert. Such was the case when 5-year-old Mike brought his milk truck to kindergarten. The teacher, aware of high group interest in the truck, guided the children into "playing milkman."[18]

Little children enjoy being a friendly policeman giving signals to "traffic and grown-up people." Experiences in safety are always heightened when teachers guide little children to become convincing trucks, cars, motorcycles, and real grown-up people crossing a street to shop or go to work.

A kindergarten group in Wisconsin revealed a strong interest in Indian life.[19] Children brought objects, and each child was eager to share his knowledge of Indian life. Early in the school year the children helped to build an Indian tepee (Fig. 7.15). Each child drew a picture on the tepee, for "Indians see such pretty things in the forest and the sky." Children strung beads and made feather headdresses. They were enthusiastic about becoming Indians gathering food, riding in canoes, having council meetings, and planning festive Indian dances. After several weeks of dramatic play, the children created climactic scenes from an exciting Indian story "Chee-Chee and Keeko" (Fig. 7.16).

Holidays are special days. They should be honored in a significant

---

[18] Pirtle, *op. cit.*
[19] Popke, *op. cit.*

way. Creative dramatics has brought many holidays "alive" for kindergarteners and first grade children. They have created Halloween parades by being witches, ghosts, jack-o'-lanterns, and cats. They

FIG. 7.15. "Keeko, you earn your feathers when you do brave deeds." (*Photograph by Dick Lemmerhirt; courtesy of Louis J. Charling, Kohler Company; Kohler Public Schools, Kohler, Wisconsin*)

have created ghost dances and witch parties. They have become rolling pumpkins changing into jolly jack-o'-lanterns.

Little children have created rare moments of devout thanksgiving when they have been guided to become grownups going to grandmother's for Thanksgiving dinner. After each child shares one thing

Fig. 7.16. Keeko sees a wildcat going after baby eaglets. (*Photograph by Dick Lemmerhirt; courtesy of Louis J. Charling, Kohler Company; Kohler Public Schools, Kohler, Wisconsin*)

for which he is thankful, children enjoy taking turns to pantomime a favorite food on the Thanksgiving table.

Christmas and Easter bring both beauty and delight. These days have been heightened when little children have played appropriate stories and verse.

Many kindergarten and first grade curriculums provide learning experiences centered on life on a farm. One kindergarten teacher shared a memorable farm experience with her 33 kindergarteners through creative dramatics.[20] Since the group was unable to visit a farm, the teacher invited a little "part" of the farm to visit the children. The visitor arrived in the delightful personage of a friendly red hen.

[20] Norma Roblee, View Ridge School, Seattle Public Schools, Seattle, Washington.

The children were delighted with their visitor. More than half the children had never seen a hen before. They listened to her talk in her pleasant humming way, and decided to name her Hum-Hum. Each day when Hum-Hum visited the children in their Playhouse the children learned something new about the farm where Hum-Hum lived. They learned about the other animal friends who lived on the farm with her. They found great enjoyment in becoming farm animals to keep Hum-Hum from "getting lonesome." They pantomimed activities of the farmer including such interesting work as driving a tractor, milking cows, pitching hay, driving trucks, and feeding pigs. They pantomimed the work they thought the farmer's wife would do. Children worked in groups and shared pantomimes for others to guess. They became the farmer's wife feeding chickens, gathering eggs, digging potatoes, pulling carrots and beets from the garden, picking apples and peaches, and "making cakes and pies and pancakes for dinner."

When Hum-Hum came to visit the children the farmer sent along some wheat for Hum-Hum to eat. The children were curious about the wheat and wondered whether it would grow. They planted several grains in a jar of water so they might see. When the roots and green stalks appeared they watched with great wonder. They were motivated to sing and pantomime in a new creative way one of their songs "Oats, Peas, Beans, and Barley Grow."

One day after Hum-Hum had been at school for a week she surprised the children with an egg (Fig. 7.17). The children were overjoyed. They urged the teacher to leave the egg with Hum-Hum so it would hatch into a little chick. The teacher explained that a hen has to want to be a mother hen before she will sit quietly on a nest of eggs all day and all night long. One of the boys volunteered to bring an electric heater to keep the egg warm. The teacher realized that a mood for baby chicks was beginning to build. She asked questions that caused the children to identify with a mother hen. After a short discussion Amy, one of the little girls, voiced the universal theme of motherhood when she said: "A mother hen loves her little chickies just as much as a real mother loves her baby, doesn't she?"

This was the moment the teacher had been waiting for. "How

FIG. 7.17. "Hum-Hum's laid an egg!" (*Photograph by Royal C. Crooks; View Ridge School, Seattle Public Schools, Seattle, Washington*)

many think Amy is right?" Every hand went up. "There's a wonderful story that tells how one mother hen felt about her little chicks. I would like to share this story with you right now."

With much enthusiasm the teacher told the story of "The Little Red Hen." When she finished the story, the children's hands were waving. The teacher invited their comments: "That lazy cat should

have helped!" "Little Red Hen was a good mother." "Little Red
Hen did all the work 'cause she liked her baby chicks."

These 5-year-olds had experienced creative dramatics since the
first week of school. They had created several short stories into
plays. The children asked if they could be Little Red Hen scratch-
ing for wheat. The Orange Table Friends were chosen to be the
first Little Red Hens to show how she felt and looked (Fig. 7.18).

FIG. 7.18. "Cluck, cluck, cluck." (*Photograph by Royal C.
Crooks; View Ridge School, Seattle Public Schools, Seattle, Washington*)

The children were highly motivated. Every child had a turn to be Little Red Hen before it was time to get ready to go home for the day.

The next day the children created the character of the cat. They found peculiar satisfaction in talking about lazy people. They decided that the cat was lazy and was having so much fun fishing that he wouldn't help Little Red Hen. The teacher became Little Red Hen to talk to the lazy cats, and to see how lazy each cat really felt (Fig. 7.19).

FIG. 7.19. "No, not I. I'm busy fishing." (*Photograph by Royal C. Crooks; View Ridge School, Seattle Public Schools, Seattle, Washington*)

The children asked to play the "first part" of the story. They decided the lazy cat should be fishing under a shady tree by the creek (Fig. 7.20). When Little Red Hen came by she asked him to help

Fig. 7.20. "Mr. Cat, will you please help me?" (*Photograph by Royal C. Crooks; View Ridge School, Seattle Public Schools, Seattle, Washington*)

in a "polite way" but the lazy cat was too "selfish." He thought a fish might swim away if he went away to help (Fig. 7.21).

On following days the children created a lazy pig. They decided he was having a picnic and was playing his violin so he wouldn't help Little Red Hen. Next they created a duck and a goose who wouldn't help because they were having fun "playing soldier." When Little Red Hen came to the mill, the children decided they

Fig. 7.21. "No, Little Red Hen. I'm tired and I'm busy." (*Photograph by Royal C. Crooks; View Ridge School, Seattle Public Schools, Seattle, Washington*)

needed a mill, a water wheel, and a miller. Little Red Hen felt happy after she carried her heavy load of wheat to the mill (Fig. 7.22).

The children created the entire story during a two-week period by playing for 20 minutes each day. They decided to make a farm mural before they played the story from beginning to end.

In describing this experience the teacher said, "A great value to the 33 children came in their convincing creations of farm animals, and their spontaneous expression in dialogue of animal's thoughts and feelings. The audience and Hum-Hum always felt as important as the children who were playing. It was a gratifying outcome of this creative experience when several children told of the fun they were having playing 'Little Red Hen' with their families."

FIG. 7.22. "Will you please grind this wheat into flour, Mr. Miller?" (*Photograph by Royal C. Crooks; View Ridge School, Seattle Public Schools, Seattle, Washington*)

An exciting circus was created by a combined class of first and second graders.[21] The first graders were motivated by a trip to the zoo, and the second graders by circus stories in their readers. The children shared experiences about circus and trained pets. They saw films on elephants, seals, monkeys, and circuses. They enjoyed learn-

21 Malphrus, *op. cit.*

ing circus songs and found great satisfaction in drawing circus pictures and writing circus stories.

When the day came to plan the circus, each child shared an idea of the one circus act he would like to see in their circus. After this initial discussion the children realized they had 19 circus acts. One of the boys concluded the discussion with this thought, "It would be a better circus if we had five good acts and could plan them and make them real." After several secret votings, the children arrived at five acts with a seal act receiving the most votes.

"What one thing might the best trained seal in the world do?" the teacher asked to focus each child's thinking.

After considering this, children shared the following ideas: "climb up on a step and clap his flippers," "bark for food," "count and speak," "dive and swim in a seal parade," "bounce a ball on his nose," "catch a fish in his mouth," "dance and sway to music."

"We'll have a circus to remember with such exciting ideas," the teacher said. "Now, how do you suppose we could change ourselves into a seal that really is a seal?"

The childern were ready with suggestions. Several showed how they would become a seal. Most of the children stretched out on the floor, but a few created seals from a squatting position. The teacher guided the children into taking turns to become seals in the specific actions the children had suggested. Children praised and evaluated one another's characterizations.

Each circus act was guided in a similar way. Trainers were then chosen for each act. Each child chose the animal or character he wanted to be. Children worked in small groups to plan surprise acts to share. They worked on the circus and circus activities for seven days, for 15 and 20 minutes each day in the classroom, and for many minutes at noon and recess. They were in a strong circus mood. They went out for recess in character eager to begin (Fig. 7.23).

FIG. 7.23. "Let's play tightrope walkers!" (*Lake Forest Park School, Shoreline Public Schools, Seattle, Washington*)

At last the circus day arrived. The circus took place in front of a colorful mural which the children had created together. Circus music played.[22] The circus man announced each act with great enthusiasm as he introduced each trainer. Heavy elephants marched in a circle and rose slowly up on their hind legs to "salute the American flag with their trunks" (Fig. 7.24). Seals bounced balloons on their noses (Fig. 7.25). Prancing ponies danced and jumped over a stick (Fig. 7.26), and a strong man lifted a baby elephant "as easy as a feather" (Fig. 7.27).

[22] "Ringling Brothers' Grand Entry," *Circus Album*, Ringling Bros. and Barnum and Bailey's Band, Columbia Records.

FIG. 7.24. "Ladies and gentlemen! Watch these elephants!" (*Lake Forest Park School, Shoreline Public Schools, Seattle, Washington*)

Questions and Activities

1. Bring to class a picture and/or a newspaper clipping which clearly indicates a strong interest of the 5- or 6-year-old. Relate this idea to creative dramatics in a brief statement concerning how the idea therein might be shared in a creative experience.

2. Divide the class into two groups. One group serves as a bulletin board committee, the other as an evaluation committee. Each member of the bulletin board committee contributes one idea which reveals either a characteristic, need, or interest of 5- and 6-year-olds. Ideas are shared with cochairmen who arrange an attractive and in-

formative bulletin board display. Each member of the evaluation committee makes a written evaluation of the bulletin board in view of (a) learning values and (b) attractiveness, creativeness, and projection. Written evaluations are summarized and reported by the cochairmen.

3. Participate in an experience with little children, or observe a little children's class in creative dramatics. As a result of this experience analyze the group of children from the standpoint of basic characteristics, needs, and interests.

4. Select a verse you like which is recommended for creative dramatics for little children. Analyze the dramatic elements of the verse, and underline the chief drama goal you will emphasize when you share this verse with children. What mood does this verse call for? Plan and write out a motivation.

Fig. 7.25. "Look! See the trained seals!" (*Lake Forest Park School, Shoreline Public Schools, Seattle, Washington*)

5. Select a short story you like which has been recommended for creative dramatics for little children. Analyze the dramatic elements and essential mood of this story. Plan a motivation, and outline a plan for guiding little children into consecutive "plan-and-play" sequences.

6. Plan to share a creative circus with a first grade group. List focused questions you will ask to guide little children to create an elephant, horse, and lion. List four different roles you as leader will play with first grade children in guiding them to create an exciting circus.

7. Divide the class into buzz session groups. Share with each group a

Fig. 7.26. "These are the best trained ponies in the world!" (*Lake Forest Park School, Shoreline Public Schools, Seattle, Washington*)

FIG. 7.27. "Watch the strong man lift an elephant!" (*Lake Forest Park School, Shoreline Public Schools, Seattle, Washington*)

song which little children enjoy singing. Each group plans how its song may be correlated into a delightful experience with creative dramatics. Each group creates from its song to illustrate this correlation for class members.

8. List three social study or nature study units little children experience in kindergarten or first grade which would be enhanced by integrated learning with creative dramatics. Study and outline one of these units. List points at which creative dramatics would provide unique teaching and experiencing values. State titles, authors, and sources of materials you would use in connection with this integrated learning experience.

9. After you have created from a little children's story in class, analyze the leader's role as she guided your group to create from this story.

10. Observe a little children's class in creative dramatics. Analyze this experience from the leader's role in (a) motivating children into a mood, (b) sharing a story, (c) guiding children to make plans, (d) guiding children during playing, (e) praising, and (f) guiding children to praise and evaluate one another's playing.

11. Include in your material file one idea, one verse, and one story that you would like to share with little children for creative dramatics. Recall incidents in your childhood which happened when you were 5 and 6. List several incidents, and include in your notebook.

CHAPTER 8

Creative Dramatics with Seven- and Eight-Year-Olds

And children's faces looking up
Holding wonder like a cup.
                    —Sara Teasdale

t was the first Saturday morning in a new year. Sixteen lively 7- and 8-year-olds gathered for creative dramatics.[1] All except two had played together for nine Saturday mornings in the fall.

"Happy New Year!" greeted the leader. "Let's begin the year by introducing ourselves to our new friends, Patsy and Jack."

When introductions were over, the leader said, "It's always a happy feeling to have new friends, and to have a new year. Many people celebrate a new year with special customs like singing or dancing. What did you do on New Year's Eve to celebrate in a special way?"

"We had company but I couldn't stay up that late."

---

[1] This is a composite account, from students' observation reports, of a class at the Seattle Public Library under the sponsorship of the School of Drama of the University of Washington.

299

"We went to church."

"Daddy blew his trumpet right at midnight, and everybody called 'Happy New Year' real loud."

"My grandmother was at our house. She had all of us go to the back door and open it, and then to the front door and open it way up. Then she said a little rhyme about letting the old year out and letting the new year come in. She said that was what they do in Ireland."

"Your grandmother knows," said the leader cheerfully. "People all over the world have special little customs. A friend of mine from Japan told about a custom that boys and girls in Japan do on New Year's night. Has anyone heard of a special Japanese custom?"

The children were curious but not a child ventured an answer. "They put a little picture of a treasure ship under their pillows," the leader explained. "If a boy or girl dreams that night, his treasure for the new year will be whatever he dreams about. Isn't that fun?"

"I know what I'd want my treasure to be," one of the boys said. "So do I," said another. "What if he dreamed an awful dream!" a little girl called out for everyone was talking excitedly.

"Freeze!" called the leader.

The children quieted down and listened. Patsy and Jack looked puzzled. "Who would like to tell our new friends what *freeze* means to us?"

Chan volunteered. "It's our magic word. It helps us to listen, and think, and work together."

"And to raise our hand when we have an idea to share," added Phyllis.

"That's right," said the leader. "Let's see how many have an idea of one thing you would like to find on a treasure ship. Think about it and see what would make you happy for a whole year. As soon as you have decided on one thing raise your hand high."

Soon every hand was waving.

"Good! We'll play New Year's treasure ships, but first we'll make a little plan. Who sees one way we may play our dreams?"

Jim volunteered. "We could go to sleep and when we start dreaming we could show our dreams in a quiet way just as though we were dreaming."

"I think we should show only one thing in our dream 'cause it's hard to guess if you do everything," Phyllis explained.

"You mean we really go to sleep?" Patsy asked.

Everyone laughed. "We almost forgot that you and Jack haven't played with us before, Patsy. Who would like to explain to them what we do in creative dramatics?"

Chan said, "We pretend. We pretend to go to sleep, and then we pretend we are really dreaming."

Lois explained further: "We get up and act out whatever we're dreaming or doing."

"Chan and Lois are right," the leader commented. "You pretend and show what you are doing with clear actions, for you first see in your mind what you are doing. There's another thing we always do when we are playing. Who knows what it is?"

When no one remembered the leader said, "You show your *feeling* with your *action*. You feel whatever you are doing and when you play you make your playing seem as if it is really happening. These are secrets of pretending. Do either of you have any more questions?"

"Do we all show our dreams at the same time?" Jack asked.

"That's a good question, Jack," the leader said. "Who sees how we might show our dreams at the same time so no one gets mixed in with another dream?"

The children looked around the room and started to consider this problem. Georgie's hand went up. "We could make a much bigger circle than this. When each one starts to dream he could play in the space just around him."

"A good idea! Does anyone else see another way?"

Robert came up with this thought. He gestured as he spoke. "We could pretend the ships are moving in this direction. When each one begins to dream he could get on his ship and move around the room like this." Robert gestured to show what he had in mind.

Jack was confused. "I don't know what he means."

"Suppose you show us what you mean, Robert. It's an excellent idea," the teacher commended. "Let's pretend you are asleep, and just beginning to dream a treasure dream. Let's see what you do, and how you feel when you show us your happy dream."

Robert closed his eyes for a moment. Then he got up from the circle. He started around the room moving freely from left to right. He was excited and happy as he became involved in his pretending. He appeared to throw something freely with first one hand and then the other. When he stopped, the children's hands went up quickly. They guessed several ideas of dreams before he explained. "I dreamed of a pirate ship with so much gold on it that I threw money to poor people and still had two chests for myself."

The children and leader responded enthusiastically to Robert's dream. "Robert, that's a wonderful treasure. No wonder you felt so happy and made us feel happy. It's going to be fun to see how each one thinks of treasure just as you did in your own way. Is Robert's idea of moving in your dream clear to everyone now?"

After a short discussion each child understood and was eager to begin. The teacher explained that she was going to be a grandmother and pretend that the children were her grandchildren.

The playing began. The teacher became a convincing grandmother. She heightened the mood as she spoke, "Here it is the first night of a brand new year, and all of my grandchildren have come to stay the night. I'll share treasure ships with them. Here, Rosie, here's a little treasure ship for you. Put it under your pillow and go to sleep. See what one thing makes you happiest of all. Sweet dreams."

The grandmother touched each child gently and tucked an imaginary treasure ship under each imaginary pillow. After a quiet moment in which every child was sleeping and thinking the grandmother started a recording of Gluck's "Ballet" on low volume.[2] "It sounds like the music of dreamland," the grandmother said quietly with anticipation. "I wonder if anyone has started dreaming yet."

This comment brought the dreams into action. Quietly but with exuberant feeling the children started pantomiming. Such happy, free expression! Some danced, some flew, some ran, one walked stately, another galloped. Each child was lost in living his dream. The grandmother watched closely while the children played joyously for two or three minutes. Then she turned the music down and spoke clearly: "My, how quickly the night has passed. I'll see if my grandchildren are sleeping on their pillows."

In a gleeful spirit of fun the children scurried back to sit in a circle. They were excited. Individuals called out spontaneously: "Could we do it again?" "Let's play again." "Please!" "This was fun!"

"Freeze!" called the teacher. When it was quiet, she said, "We'll

2 *Rhythmic Activities,* Vol. 1, RCA Victor Record Library for Elementary Schools, Radio Corporation of America, RCA Victor Division, 1947.

play again, but first let's hear about these happy dreams. I think I know what some of you were dreaming, but it's always fun to share. See if you can tell in one clear thought the treasure that your dream ship brought."

These were the children's ideas: "My ship brought a twirling little angel and we went flying around the world looking in people's windows to see nice things happening."

This was Lillian's dream. The children were impressed. Several praised her idea and then other dreams were shared.

"Mine brought Donald Duck to live with us."

"My ship was a ship of flowers. In the middle of it there was a money tree, and in the tree was a penguin."

"My big ship brought a rocket ship with hydrogen and I flew up to the moon."

"To the moon?" shouted Jack. "Oh, no! Boy! I should have thought of that instead of a motorboat."

"Each one is a good idea," said the leader. "How many would like to work hard and buy a motorboat someday?"

Several hands went up. "How many would like to go on a rocket to the moon?"

The boys' hands fairly flew into the air as they reacted with comments and exclamations. Several of the girls were excited too. "Maybe Gene will take us up to the moon today, but first let's hear about all of the treasures."

The children continued to share their dreams. "My ship brought 300 ballet dresses and 300 pairs of ballet shoes, and the prettiest dress of all was red, white, and blue."

"Mine brought a fairy in a little blue box."

"My ship was full of bricks and I was building a new house so we won't have to pay rent."

"My treasure was a puppy for my sisters and me."

"Mine was a queen's dress and a golden crown so I can be a queen whenever I want to be."

"My ship was a big ship. It brought a jet plane so I can be the pilot."

"My treasure was a new baby sister because we're going to have a baby in March."

"Mine was a pony and some hay."

"Mine brought a drugstore so I can make medicine and milkshakes for people."

This seemed funny to the children. They laughed heartily. "Would you like to share something from your drugstore with us right now, Gary?" the teacher asked. Gary was surprised. "Sure," he answered eagerly.

"Would you rather have medicine or milkshakes?" the leader asked as she included all the children.

"Milkshakes!" the children called unanimously, as they laughed. Several started calling out flavors and descriptions.

"Freeze!" said the leader, and she waited for each one to quiet down. "If we watch Gary closely we can tell just how he feels as he mixes a milkshake. I think it might be a good idea if Gene got his rocket ready so he can take us to the moon after we've finished our milkshakes."

The children were enthusiastic. Gene was pleased. He got up and moved to one end of the room and surveyed the space critically.

"How does it feel to taste a New Year's milkshake, Olive?" the teacher asked as she saw Gary hand the first milkshake to this little girl. "We'll see how these new milkshakes make everyone feel."

"I can taste the chocolate," Olive said as she smacked her lips. The children had fun sipping imaginary milkshakes through imaginary straws. They finished drinking the milkshakes quickly when Gene said the rocket was ready.

The leader and children joined Gene. Gene pointed toward the corner and said, "Everyone has to put a space suit on." The children started pantomiming. Some of the children knew exactly what they were doing. Others used vague general movements as they imitated actions.

Jack spoke up. "I'm not going to the moon unless this rocket has a pressureproof cabin."

"It has," Gene stated with strong belief. "It's a new pressureproof, streamlined rocket. We have to stay right behind each other 'cause we're going to zoom through space" (Fig. 8.1).

"Remember what Gene said," the leader called out. "Let's board the rocket now, and each find a place."

After some confusion in getting organized, the children lined up in a long line behind Gene. The leader was at the other end of the line. "Why are we going to the moon?" she asked as she climbed out of the rocket and faced the passengers.

"For the ride!" volunteered Chan.

"To find out what it's like up there," said Rosie.

"To see if the moon is different from the way it is down here," Jack said.

"These are all good reasons. We'll use all of them," the leader said with enthusiasm. "See how you feel when you go higher and higher and finally come to the moon. Then see what one new thing you find up there. Are we ready to take off, Gene?"

"No, I have two announcements to make. No one is supposed to talk except the pilot until we get back to earth, and everybody better watch out for deep holes on the moon. I'll give the orders like a pilot does."

The teacher climbed back into the imaginary rocket and joined the children at the end of the line. "Let's fasten our belts. Remember how you *feel,* and watch for one new thing on the moon. We're ready, pilot."

Gene sounded a smooth motor and a convincing siren. Then he counted backwards, "Five, four, three, two, one, zero! We're off!" he called. The children and leader followed Gene's quick running movements. They circled the room swiftly. After going around the room twice, Gene called, "We're coming to the moon. Make ready to land."

He slowed down his speed and made a smooth landing. He opened an imaginary door and called out, "Here's the moon." Gene moved out into the room walking with big steps and investigating curiously. Several of the boys were as involved as he. Several of the girls followed the leader. A few ventured off in space by themselves. Suddenly Jack ran around the room as if he were being chased. He jumped and dodged. Everyone watched

FIG. 8.1. "I have to check the instruments on my space ship." (*School of Drama, University of Washington*)

him. Several laughed heartily. Gene called out suddenly, "Rocket ship taking off for earth!"

The children hurried into line again. Jack was the last to get on the rocket. With similar sound effects Gene took off and circled the rocket back to earth. After they landed he said, "Now we'll get the reports."

"This was fun! Can we do it again?" Jack asked.

"Let's sit in a circle as round as the moon," the teacher replied. "We'll hear the reports before deciding whether to return."

When everyone was settled the pilot was asked to take charge. He got the following reports: "I saw tracks as big as I am, some kind of footprints like a giant's."

"I felt like I was walking on air when we got off the rocket."

"I saw the man in the moon." This from Phyllis.

"I found moon flowers," Lillian said.

Jack's report was saved until the last. "Mine is top-secret," he said. "I was almost caught by moon monsters. They are planning an invasion of the earth. I'm going to report this to the government."

"Be sure you do, Jack," the teacher said with a twinkle in her eye. "How many really felt they went to the moon?"

Several of the boys expressed strong belief. Some of the girls said they didn't really feel as though they were going through space. "I did," Jack spoke out. "I really saw green moon monsters."

The teacher commented on their replies. "Jack has already learned the secret of having fun just as many of you have. If you really *feel* and *see* what you're doing, you make others feel and believe."

Patsy's hand was waving. "I saw my mother by the door."

"Well," said the teacher glancing at her watch. "It looks as if our earth clocks tell us it is time to take our make-believe treasures home until next Saturday."

Olive's hand shot up. "Everyone may wear a pair of my ballet shoes home if they'll bring them back next time."

"Olive, how kind of you to share—you with three hundred pairs! Let's each one put on a pair of dancing slippers or slip them into your pocket to wear later," the teacher suggested. "And have a Happy New Year!"

The children enjoyed choosing slippers of different colors. Some of the children danced to the door. Others walked quietly.

"Happy New Year!" several children called as they hurried away together.

WHAT ARE SEVEN- AND EIGHT-YEAR-OLDS LIKE?

Each one of these 16 fun-loving boys and girls is a unique young personality. As a group they have many of the same basic characteristics, needs, interests, and behavior patterns found in most groups of 7- and 8-year-old children.

Physical Characteristics and Needs. Seven- and eight-year-olds appear often to move with jet-propelled speed and action. They often use their entire bodies to express feelings and release energies. They generally move and shift gracefully with more noticeable poise and balance than they did in their earlier more impulsive years. Eights, particularly, enjoy moving freely and forcefully into space, zooming, running, hopping, jumping, galloping. When a child of this age plays hard, he needs to rest often for he tires easily.

Most sevens and eights show evidence of physical development in smaller muscle coördinations, particularly in eye-hand coördinations. For this reason they enjoy pantomiming finer actions such as holding glasses, sipping through straws, putting on ballet slippers, and fastening space suits with emphasis on zipping zippers and snapping snaps.

Mental Characteristics and Needs. Gesell and Ilg have ob-served that "At the age of seven we see new evidences of reason-ableness and of critical capacity. The 7-year-old is more reflective; he takes time to think; he is interested in conclusions and logical ends. . . . He himself uses language more freely and adaptively; not only to establish rapport, but to make running comments on the matter at hand."[3]

About the 8-year-old these authorities have discovered: "There are three traits which characterize the dynamics of his behavior: Speedi-ness, Expansiveness, 'Evaluativeness.'. . . There is a new vein of active curiosity; a mounting energy and a certain robustness which is different from the idyllic sweetness of earlier childhood."[4]

Most sevens and eights are good listeners for short periods of time although restlessness is noticeable among the less mature children in a group. Attention spans are still short, but they are lengthening. This is evident when interest is at a high peak. Children of these ages need and enjoy short discussion periods. They need and en-joy the challenge of solving simple problems. An individual feels highly pleased when he figures out how to do something which at first seems difficult. Likewise a child enjoys the challenge of original and independent thinking. He needs opportunities to share his ideas and express his viewpoints.

Most sevens and eights are eager to explore and venture vicari-ously into new worlds far beyond their immediate horizons. They are eager to get at the heart of an experience and become involved in doing rather than discussing for very long.

Emotional Characteristics and Needs. Sensitiveness seems to

[3] Arnold Gesell and Frances L. Ilg, *The Child from Five to Ten*, Harper & Brothers, 1946.
[4] *Ibid*.

characterize most children of 7 and 8. They are dynamic in a delightful way. They show extremes in experiencing feelings of fear, anger, joy, shyness, heedlessness, and boldness. They are easily motivated, easily excited, and are easily sympathetic with a person, animal, or thing that deserves sympathy. "The 7-year-old projects in terms of feeling as well as of action."[5]

Children of these ages need many vicarious experiences in which they experience courage, bravery, and other strong feelings in make-believe conflicts. This was noticed in Jack's venture with moon monsters and in his desire to report the invasion. In each child's expression of treasure there was a noticeable emphasis on something that aroused his feelings such as "a twirling little angel," "a puppy for my sisters and me," "a ship of flowers with a money tree and a penguin."

Social Characteristics and Needs. Sevens and eights, on the whole, enjoy other children. Approval by one another is beginning to be as necessary as approval by a parent or teacher. It is difficult for many sevens and eights to adjust and function within a group if they are still self-centered. During these years a child needs many experiences in taking turns, and sharing moments of responsibility and importance. A child of this age needs to understand and respect a few simple rules for social behavior. He gets confused if rules are complex and inconsistent.

Boys begin to band with boys, and girls with girls during these years. It is not uncommon to find groupings beginning to form in twosomes. These twosomes frequently shift to new twosomes or develop into threesomes. Because of this natural trend children often enjoy working in pairs or in threes to surprise a group with a creation of their own.

[5] *Ibid.*

Children of 7 and 8 enjoy an opportunity to share information or explain social behavior to others. During these years a child needs opportunities to evaluate himself and to evaluate others. But he needs to be guided carefully, for a child with sensitive feelings is easily offended. A teacher uses care in guiding moments of evaluation so individuals receive recognition, and also recognizes specific ways in which expression may be strengthened. In so doing a feeling of individual and group spirit strengthens.

Sevens and eights need opportunities to organize themselves into functioning groups. Even though individuals become confused in forming single or double lines it is very necessary that they continue to organize in these ways until they are capable of quick and satisfying coöperation.

Spiritual Characteristics and Needs. If a child's creative spirit has been steadily nurtured it reveals itself with naïve freshness during these years. Most 7- and 8-year-olds delight in imagining, pretending, and dramatizing with increased emphasis as compared with their earlier years.

A child's true creative spirit is revealed often in moments of rare humor or in expression that is characterized by a delicate sensitivity. A child needs to have his ideas accepted, respected, and perhaps discussed. Often it is enough for a leader simply to accept with a nod or a smile the beauty of "a fairy in a little blue box," the humor of "Donald Duck to live with us," and the practicality of "building a new house so we won't have to pay rent."

Because each child's creative self is as different and yet as alike as an acorn and a grain of corn, a group needs variety in creative experiences. Children need to fly to the moon to satisfy something within Gene, and Jack, and Georgie, just as much as they need to become puppies, ponies, and penguins to nourish the needs of others.

STRONG INTERESTS OF SEVENS AND EIGHTS

Most sevens and eights seem to have a kinship with Alice-in-Wonderland and Peter Pan. During these years they appear to skip away for moments each day to special places in make-believe land. A noticeable interest in fantasy is evident. Both boys and girls find new wonder and magic in everyday happenings. If a robin flies overhead a child of this age may frequently believe the bird to be a messenger from elves or fairies. An autumn leaf may suddenly become a forest newspaper, and a shadow often becomes a mysterious friendly "Mr. Somebody" come to lure a child to special make-believe adventure. Such commonplace things as sticks, stones, and seed pods hold uncommon enchantment for young wonderers.

Interest in fairy tales is generally high during these years. There is almost as much interest in evil fairy folk such as witches, wizards, and giants as there is in good fairies, elves, and dwarfs. Rhythm and charms hold singular enchantment. Wishbones, stars, rings, four-leaf clovers, forked sticks, and fairy pennies seem especially magic for wishing on at seven and eight. Fantasy often reveals itself in unexpected blendings of romantic and scientific interests in submarine trips to castles in the sea, on helicopter flights to a witch's cave, on sudden discoveries of coke machines inside a rainbow, and in back-yard expeditions with shovels and spoons to try to "dig to China before it gets dark."

Romantic realms hold high appeal for 8-year-olds. Kings, queens, princes, and princesses who reign with striking ceremony are particularly pleasurable. Castle festivities such as christenings, balls, weddings, and birthday celebrations are most inviting to these romantic young dreamers.

Faraway lands where dreams come true, regions where animals

talk and act like human beings, and secret valleys where good always triumphs over evil are among the interests that offer moments of genuine joy to almost every 7- and 8-year-old. Children's desires for "New Year treasures" revealed a noticeable interest in fantasy. Other strong interests were evident in machines that moved with speed, and individual interests in money, food, clothes, building, angels, and beauty.

Many children during these years prefer the enjoyment that comes with real people in faraway places. They prefer to push out vicariously to the fascinating life to be found on a cowboy ranch, an Indian reservation, in an Eskimo hut, or a Mexican village. Many sevens and eights express a desire to go to faraway places that have such pleasant-sounding names as Hawaii, Japan, Scandinavia, and Spain.

Interests in the real world still remain strong. Most sevens and eights reveal wonderings about such things as nature, seasons, home and community happenings, friends and neighbors, grown-up activities, travel and transportation, holidays and birthdays, and heaven and God.

INTRODUCING CREATIVE DRAMATICS TO SEVENS AND EIGHTS

Like Tom the piper's son, 7- and 8-year-olds are eager for experiences that lead them "over the hills and far away." These children are even more ready for group fun than they were when they were younger.

A leader introduces creative dramatics to sevens and eights in much the same way as to younger children. She begins with the fundamentals of drama by stressing the fun of creative playing. She shares a variety of experiences in rhythmic movement, characterization, and dramatic play.

The chief difference in guiding these two age groups lies in the choice of material. Experiences for little children are selected from material based on their interests in the real world. Experiences for 7- and 8-year-olds are selected from material based on their interests in the real world and the world of wonderland and faraway places.

Begin with Rhythmic Movement and Pantomime. The following experiences have been used with 7- and 8-year-olds to invite creative expression in strong rhythmic movement and pantomime. In each experience a mood was first developed. Then the focused question was asked.

Wishing Interest

"Starlight, star bright,
First star I see to-night;
I wish I may, I wish I might,
Have the wish I wish to-night."

When a star shines bright for you,
What one thing do you wish to *do?*

(Fly, dance, play the piano, bat a ball, swim, sing in Sunday School, be on television, win at marbles.)

Nature Interest

Summer days are happy days for having fun.
What was a happy time for you this summer in the sun?

(Picnicking, learning to swim, riding on the train, riding in a parade, building a tent, seeing a fairy ring, going to a ranch, learning to ride a two-wheeler.)

Fairyland Interest

Elves and fairies have fun every day,

With wonderful games they think of to play.
They hide behind clouds and swing on treetops—
Make music with flowers, and jump over dewdrops!

If you went to fairyland today,
What wonderful way would you like to play?

(Fly with a butterfly, swim with a fish, play dandelion tag with fairies, blow bubbles, tiptoe on rocks.)

Imaginative Interest

"Here's a table—just a table," some folks say.
But a table's been a throne for a Queen of May!
A table's been a boat, and a cage in a zoo.
There's magic in a table waiting there for you.

If you could do one magic thing with a table, what would you do? (Make a castle, a playhouse, a cave, a den for robbers, a train engine, a rocket, a lookout station, a fort.)

Faraway Interest

Boots! Boots! Boots!
Shiny magic boots—
I can walk to China—
In three big scoots!

Of all the faraway and wonderful places you've wondered about, where would you like to go today in a pair of magic boots? (To Never-Never Land, to fly, to Texas to ride a bucking horse, to Mt. Rainier to throw snowballs, to heaven to see how pretty it is, to a cloud to float through the sky, to Japan to fly a fish kite.)

Poetry and verse have been used in similar ways to motivate strong rhythmic expression. Unusual creative experiences have developed from the following poems: "I Keep Three Wishes Ready," by Annette Wynne, "Choosing" by Eleanor Farjeon, "Choosing Shoes," Ffrida Wolfe, "Marching Song," by Robert Louis Stevenson, and "Jump—Jump—Jump," and "Oh, Susan Blue," by Kate Greenaway.[6]

Begin with Charades and Guessing Games. Sevens and eights enjoy the fun of simple charades and riddles. One teacher introduced creative dramatics to a class of second grade children by setting a mood for wondering about the many wonderful things there are to do.[7] Then the teacher said, "I have been wondering about something I would like to learn to do, but I haven't told anyone yet." Then, as a transition into pantomime she said:

> "I have a secret, I'll share with you
> If you guess, it's your secret too."

The teacher then pantomimed her desire to play a piano. The children quickly responded to the fun of joining in with her secret, and everyone enjoyed playing an imaginary piano.

One of the boys asked if he could share a secret about something he had been wondering about. He pantomimed with strong feeling for he had been wondering "how loggers cut down great big trees" (Fig. 8.2).

"Secrets" became a favorite game for these second graders. It was frequently used for moments of relaxation during the day, and was correlated with language arts and drawing. The teacher guided the children into creating a melody for the rhyme. When the group sang "Secrets" one child pantomimed to the rhythm of the song. After a few beginning experiences "Secrets" grew to include such desires of 7-year-olds as the following: "My Favorite Game," "The

[6] May Hill Arbuthnot (compiler), *Time for Poetry*, Scott, Foresman and Company, 1952.

[7] Muriel E. Kennedy, Clyde Hill School, Bellevue Public Schools, Bellevue, Washington. Miss Kennedy is now teaching in the Seattle Public Schools, Seattle, Washington.

Most Beautiful Thing in the Woods," "How I Help at Home," "My Christmas Wish," "Something That Scares Me," "A Pet I'd Like to Have," and "When I'm Grown Up" (Fig. 8.3).

FIG. 8.2. "I think this is the way a logger chops a big tree." (*Photograph by Brant Studio; Clyde Hill School, Bellevue Public Schools, Bellevue, Washington*)

FIG. 8.3. "I'm a fireman hosing down the roof after I saved a baby." (*Clyde Hill School, Bellevue Public Schools, Bellevue, Washington*)

Sevens and eights always enjoy pantomiming to action songs and singing games. They enjoy creating from many of the same singing games that they played when they were younger.

Begin with Characterization. "Let's pretend," or "Let's play that . . ." are frequent comments of sevens and eights when they play with friends. Creating a "character" with strong belief is something almost every child discovers for himself during these years. It is natural and fun for him to put strong feeling into his playing and pretending. He frequently speaks spontaneously in character. This was illustrated when Gene became the pilot of the rocket to the moon. He was involved in his characterization and was motivated to give orders. Whenever a leader recognizes that a child is

ready to express with dialogue she encourages him with guidance which keeps an experience organized for an entire group.

The following dramatic play experiences have been enjoyed by 7- and 8-year-olds. Each experience emphasizes characterization in a creative way.

Occupational Interest

> Swishity, swishity, swishity, shwhy!
> I'm grown up! Who am I?

(Cello player, a mother, pitcher for the Brooklyn Dodgers.)

Nature and Fantasy Interest

Suppose you are one of Jack Frost's fairies or elves. What beautiful, frosty picture would you paint, and where would you paint it?

(Roses, trees, mountains, flowers, stars—on the school windows, our big window, on the sidewalk, on a car.)

Holiday Interest

> Halloween, Halloween, strangest night you've ever seen.
> When flying witch waves her magic broom—
> You'll see "spirits" in this room.
> He! He! He! What spooky "spirit" will you be?

(Ghost, owl, jack-o'-lantern, goblin, cat, bat, shadow.)

Fairyland Interest

You're invited to fairyland for the Fairy Queen's party. Fairy Queen says if you think a friendly thought you'll change into a fairy or an elf. "Singing songs together," is such a friendly thought. See how Susie has changed into a fairy. What, for you, is a friendly thought?

(Going to Sunday school, picking flowers, helping mother, having a party for friends, taking care of my baby sister, smiling, sharing a popsicle, giving a marble to Sam, taking turns.)

Animal Interest

The forest is full of friendly little animals who keep it happy with their merry sounds. If you were a little forest animal and were invited to join Mr. Bullfrog's forest band, what animal would you like best to be? How would you help make music?

(Bluebird, cricket, grasshopper, mouse, toad, squirrel.)

Toy Interest

Think of a special toy you have seen in a storybook, a store window or a catalogue. Think of the toy that would make you happiest of all. *Be* that toy in a toy shop, and see how you feel when a fairy waves her magic wand and wakes you up.

(Train, walking doll, dancing doll, baby doll, bride doll, speedboat, electric car, merry-go-round, airplane, helicopter.)

Travel Interest

> Brrr! Toot—Toot! Ding-Dong! Beep—Beep!
> Planes, and trains, and boats, and a jeep.
> If you were going on a journey today,
> How would you *go* so far away?

(Plane, train, boat, jeep, car, truck, horseback.)

Fantasy and Romantic Interest

> Fiddle, dee, dee! Fiddle, dee, dee!
> A million things in the world to see.
> A king, a giant, a lion, a tree!
> Who, in the world, would you like to be?

(King, queen, princess, prince, giant, fairy, animals, Santa.)

Ethel Talbot's "Crab-Apple" is a splendid poem for a creative birthday party for sevens and eights. It introduces children to characterizations of fairies in a rare way which works like magic. Children enjoy figuring out how fairies play "dew-ponds" and deciding about special fairy dances.

"Shadow Dance" by Ivy O. Eastwick always stirs imaginations. Some groups have enjoyed creating from it in a darkened room with a single light source providing sharp shadows. Eight-year-olds have enjoyed playing it in pairs with one child dancing and the other being a shadow doing whatever the dancer does. Shadow play has been heightened by a single question, "What do you think two shadows would like to *play* together?" Ideas for dancing, swinging, playing ball, riding ponies, playing hopscotch, flying to the moon, and other singular interests of sevens and eights have come forth. Strong characterization is always motivated by the question, "If you could be somebody's shadow, whose shadow would you like to be?" Children frequently wish to be shadows of clowns, butterflies, fairies, Davy Crockett and other personages who hold high interest.

Other splendid poems that emphasize creative characterization include the following: "The Little Rose Tree," by Rachel Field, "Halloween," by Harry Behn, "First Snow," by Ivy O. Eastwick and "Snow," by Dorothy Aldis, "A Christmas Folk Song," by Lizette Woodworth Reese, "A Valentine," by Eleanor Hammond, "A Piper," by Seumas O'Sullivan, "The Bagpipe Man" by Nancy Byrd Turner, "Doorbells," by Rachel Field, "Circus Parade" by Olive Beaupre Miller, "Meeting the Easter Bunny," by Rowena Bastin Bennett, "When a Ring's Around the Moon," by Mary Jane Carr, and "Midsummer Magic," by Ivy O. Eastwick.

Introduce Characterization in Conflict. After children have enjoyed creating many different kinds of people and things in pleasant or unusual situations, they are generally ready to create conflict situations. Excellent miniature dramas are to be found in Mother Goose. It is essential for a leader to analyze dramatic elements and to be aware of specific appeals for imaginative 7- and 8-year-olds.

"Humpty Dumpty" is a fine rhyme for a beginning experience.

Humpty Dumpty Falls were the bold headlines that motivated one group of sevens and eights to create an exciting drama. The children were guided to realize that an eggshell needs to be broken before the egg can be used. With this in mind the children decided that the roly-poly Humpty who was a servant was, in reality, a prince under an evil spell. Because of his kindness the princess allowed Humpty to climb the tower wall where he could watch the king's horses and men marching every day. One day when Humpty was on the wall he tried to reach the princess' beautiful white cat which was crawling away. In so doing Humpty fell from the wall, his spell was broken, and he claimed the princess for his bride.

"Who is the fine lady who rides a white horse through the streets of Banbury Cross?" "What kind of musical rings are on her fingers?" "What do the ringing bells on her toes seem to be saying?" "Why does everyone for miles around ride to Banbury to see this mysterious lady?" Such questions always stir wondering minds. Sevens and eights almost always surprise a leader with the exciting drama which they create when they are guided to express "Ride a Cock Horse."

Equally as exciting and beautiful conflicts have been created from other Mother Goose rhymes including "The Queen of Hearts," "Hark, Hark, the Dogs Do Bark," "There Was an Old Woman as I've Heard Tell," "Tom, Tom, the Piper's Son," and "Pussy Cat, Pussy Cat."

An outstanding verse which is a favorite for most 7- and 8-year-olds is Richard Allingham's "The Elf Singing." The conflict centers around a happy dancing elf who is pursued by a wicked wizard. At a crucial moment the elf leaps to a rainbow and is saved while the wizard is snatched up by a mole.

"The Elf and the Dormouse" by Oliver Herford is another favorite for imaginative children. In this situation an elf encounters two conflicts, first a sudden rainstorm with raindrops as large as he is, and then a sleeping dormouse who is twice the elf's size. "Necessity becomes the mother of invention" as the elf figures out what to do to save himself in his exciting crisis.

Other satisfying conflicts, each with limited characterizations, are found in the following verse: "The Monkeys and the Crocodile," by Laura E. Richards, "Some One," by Walter De la Mare, and "A Goblinade" and "There *Once* Was a Puffin," by Florence Page Jaques.

Stories to Begin On. "A Tailor and a Bear," "The Conjure Wives," and "How the Robin's Breast Became Red," meet the basic drama requirements for first stories to create into plays. A favorite beginning story for this age group is "The Peddler and His Caps." Beginning groups have enjoyed creating a short scene in which the peddler and his wife sew beautiful caps. Best of all, however, they enjoy the conflict scene where the peddler encounters unexpected trouble with a family of monkeys. Children delight in playing this story over and over again. Some children enjoy being the peddler to create unusual caps from the most beautiful thing in the forest. Other children enjoy creating songs and rhymes for the peddler's selling. But every child delights in being a monkey to mimic and worry the peddler while he thinks his way out of his unusual predicament.

Wanda Gág's *Millions of Cats* is another choice story for 7- and 8-year-olds to play. It is limited in characterization and rises to an exciting cat-fight in its high moment of conflict. It is especially enjoyed by children who find pleasure in cats. Almost every child who plays this story is intrigued with wondering how to create a believable cat-fight where millions of cats disappear by eating one another up.

A good Halloween story which is limited in characterizations to a teeny-tiny woman and a mysterious choir of teeny-tiny scarecrows or ghosts is the old English folk tale "Teeny Tiny." Another eerie story which may be created at Halloween is "The Strange Visitor." In this old tale an old woman who "wishes for company" is surprised by a visitor who arrives in a most mysterious way. Sevens and eights revel in the creative challenge of becoming such extreme things as "a heavy, heavy shoe" and "a long, long leg."

Longer Stories. After children have created several short stories with enjoyment and satisfaction, they enjoy the challenge of longer stories. An excellent longer story is "The Sorcerer's Apprentice," which may be created with or without dialogue. It is strong in rhythmic movement, conflict, and in its appealing characterizations of brooms, sorcerers, floating wooden objects, and a puff of smoke to transport Fritzl (Fig. 8.4).

Favorite stories which are strong in conflict, with individualized characters who use dialogue are "The Elves and the Shoemaker," "The Little Rabbit Who Wanted Red Wings," "The Wonderful Tar Baby," "The Princess Who Never Laughed," "The Princess Who Could Not Cry," "The Bremen Town Musicians," "Cinderella," "Hansel and Gretel," "Sleeping Beauty," "Jack and the Beanstalk," "Snow-White and the Seven Dwarfs," "Snow-White and Rose-Red," and *Jenny's Birthday Book* by Esther Averill. Episodes from *Peter Pan* and *Pinocchio* have fascinated groups who have asked to play these particular stories.

"Old Man Rabbit's Thanksgiving Dinner," by Carolyn Bailey is an appealing Thanksgiving fantasy for 7- and 8-year-olds if they are ready to play a story this early in a school year.

FIG. 8.4. "Now I know how Willibald makes his telescope magic." (*School of Drama, University of Washington*)

Christmas stories which may be created in pantomime with little if any dialogue include the traditional Nativity story, "The Golden Spider Webs," by Robert Schauffler, "The Story of the First Christmas Tree," by Rose Fyleman, and Clement C. Moore's "The Night Before Christmas," which is a favorite story told in verse. Helen Monsell's "Paddy's Christmas" is liked by groups who are ready to create with dialogue (Fig. 8.5).

FIG. 8.5. "Wake up, folks! I must have some information. What is Christmas?" (*Photograph by Royal C. Crooks; Bryant School, Seattle Public Schools, Seattle, Washington*)

Easter stories which children of these ages have found particularly satisfying are "The Story of the Easter Rabbit," and dramatic episodes in Du Bose Heyward's *The Country Bunny and the Little Gold Shoes.*

Stories with settings in faraway lands hold forcible interest for most 8-year-olds. Some which have been created with marked enchantment include the traditional Japanese stories "Urashima Taro," "The Old Man with a Wen," and "The Dancing Teakettle," and the Chinese stories, "The Wonderful Pear Tree" and *Mai Li*. Stories with settings in Spain and Mexico which have proved their worth for playing are *The Story of Ferdinand* and *Angelo the Naughty One*.

BASIC PRINCIPLES IN GUIDING SEVEN- AND EIGHT-YEAR-OLDS

A leader soon discovers that creative guidance is similar whether she guides younger or older children. Guidance is always keyed to developmental needs and interests. Since children of 7 and 8 years have grown in many ways from their fifth and sixth years new developmental needs are met through careful guidance.

A leader strives to guide in a way that respects the maturity, growth, and needs of a specific group of children. If an 8-year-old group is being introduced to creative dramatics for the first time, a leader may guide in much the same way as she would guide a group of first graders, leading them into experiencing rhythmic action and characterization with the same simplicity, beauty, and fun stressed in autumn leaf play.

On the other hand, if most children in a third grade class have experienced creative dramatics in kindergarten and first and second grades they will be ready for strong experiencing in dramatic and creative challenge. A leader would guide them in a way not unlike the way children were guided to express from "New Year's Treasures."

Because of the characteristic natures of most 7- and 8-year-olds, a leader will find it necessary to emphasize guidance in the following areas: (1) focusing on feelings; (2) respecting individual needs; and (3) encouraging strong participation.

Focus on Feelings. Feeling is vital to creative expression. A child must be in a mood before he expresses from within. To build an initial mood and a mood for each character, a leader strives to focus a child's feelings to a specific area of thought. To arouse feeling she relates a child to an experience.

For example, in sharing "New Year's Treasures," the leader used a subjective, personal approach rather than an objective approach, asking the question: "What did *you do* on New Year's Eve to make you happy?" This question started individuals to thinking and feeling. She then related the children's feeling and thinking to the idea of Japanese customs.

Suppose the leader had used an objective approach without relating the child to the experience. She would probably have stated that they were going to play a Japanese custom. She would probably have asked the initial question without first focusing children's feelings about dreaming of treasure. With this approach it is unlikely that most of the children would have expressed as spontaneously and honestly as they did.

Whenever a leader realizes that children are failing to express true feelings, she should evaluate her guidance closely, analyzing to see how she is relating them to an experience. Feeling is a vital factor in mood-building at all ages, but particularly with sensitive and imaginative 7- and 8-year-olds.

A leader focuses a child's feelings to one idea at a time to free him for strong creative expression. In guiding children to express from "New Year's Treasures," the leader focused children's feelings to three specific areas after an initial mood was built. Each area was

explored, expressed, and enjoyed before moving to a new area. To illustrate, the first question asked was, "If your treasure ship came in and brought you *one thing* to make you happy, what would it be?" The second question was, "How does it feel to have a New Year's milkshake?" The third area was focused with a statement, "See how you feel when you go higher and higher and finally come to the moon."

The leader determines strong group interest in order to focus thinking and feeling to a specific idea. For example, when each child expressed his idea of treasure she was alert to their reactions. She "picked up" Jack's comment about Gene's rocket and referred it to the group. She asked, "How many would like to go to the moon?" The children's response was strong. Later she captured the children's laughter in response to Gary's milkshakes, and focused thinking in this specific direction.

The leader focused feeling by guiding a child to recognize purpose in his expression. For instance she asked, "Why are you going to the moon?" This question caused each child to think and wonder much more than if she had stated, "Let's go to the moon." Purpose was injected in the statement, "This time each one will show how happy you feel doing one thing with your new treasure."

A leader must allow time for a child to focus his feelings. She needs to pause, to refrain from talking and allow quiet moments for children to think and feel. When she respects this need in guidance she will see how vital it is in inducing strong creative expression. A child should not be rushed when he is striving to express; however, he needs to be guided to focus his thinking by guidance in a suggestion such as, "Tell us in one word, or in one clear thought."

Respect Individual Needs. Every individual has his own unique needs. Each one needs to feel important and of worth to others.

During the 50-minute period in which the sevens and eights played "New Year's Treasures" each individual received several moments of individual recognition. Each one was given an opportunity to introduce himself, to express his individual pantomime, to share verbally his idea of treasure, to enjoy a make-believe milkshake, to take a pretend trip to the moon, to share his feelings about the trip, and to wear or take a new pair of pretend slippers home so he could remember this fun all during the week. In addition, Robert received recognition for solving a problem and explaining his idea to the group. Gene and Gary felt particularly important in being able to share their ideas of treasures with the group. Jack's needs were met in several different ways. Patsy, Lillian, Phyllis, Lois, and Chan had brief moments of individual importance.

A leader strives to recognize and meet individual needs during each session. When guiding 7- and 8-year-olds she does this by asking children to solve problems, to figure out creative ways of meeting new situations. She encourages children to work in pairs, to work in groups, to take individual initiative. She makes a constant effort to guide each child into specific moments wherein he feels a sense of responsibility, importance, and friendliness toward the group.

A leader gives children a big responsibility in group planning, group evaluation, and group discipline. With a large group of eager, dynamic, enthusiastic sevens and eights she realizes a strong need to guide for social growth. She must be firm about guiding children to plan social rules, and to enforce them.

Encourage Strong Participation. Child power needs to be both released and channeled. The expansive jet-propelled energy that comes with strong physical growth at seven and eight needs healthy outlets. When a leader guides children to express in rhythmic action she encourages wholehearted expression. She encourages a child to "put his whole self" into whatever he is expressing, to use freely the space available, to create and sustain his creation long enough to meet his needs.

Beginning leaders are sometimes afraid to guide children into strong participation. They fear that they may not be able to control the strong energy release, and consequently guide in ways that hold back rather than release energies. If children's energies are not channeled and released through guidance, individuals will find ways of meeting these natural and basic needs. In these instances discipline problems arise, and the creative atmosphere is threatened. When a leader guides to meet children's basic needs, few if any discipline problems occur, for children's needs are being satisfied in a wholehearted, happy way.

CREATIVE DRAMATICS IN THE SCHOOL PROGRAM

Many second and third grade teachers have found the art of creative dramatics a delightful way to motivate vital and unified learning for children. A second grade teacher says, "Personalities are in the making in childhood. Creative teaching involves children in coöperative planning, playing, and evaluating with a high content of specific learning. It raises children's level of attention, insight, aspiration, endeavor, and achievement. When creative experiences are shared day after day during a school year one can see children gradually grow into thinking, evaluative, responsive individuals— happy, resourceful, and considerate of one another."[8]

In Language Arts. Language is an art the world around. Every child needs to learn to communicate and to enjoy communicating

[8] Bernice L. Rice, View Ridge School, Everett Public Schools, Everett, Washington.

with others by speaking, listening, writing, and reading. Creative dramatics provides a friendly atmosphere where children learn to communicate in situations that closely reflect reality. They learn to speak freely and confidently as they "think on their feet" in discussions and in keeping a story going.

Vocabularies are increased by a variety of creative experiences where children use new words to express strong feelings. Children become aware of words and the power of words when they are asked frequently to "tell in one word how you think this character feels." Vocabularies increase as children dig down deep to find one word "to paint a picture of this person."

Good speech habits are developed from good listening habits. Speech is steadily improved by firsthand experiences in speaking. Constant emphasis is placed on speaking and listening for characters "who speak clearly and loudly enough to be heard." Attention is focused toward a child who "used his voice and spoke so everyone could hear," one who "talked with feeling and used strong words to show how his character really felt," and one who "spoke clearly and said 'get out of my way.'"

Second and third grade teachers have found that creative dramatics contributes directly to growth in reading skills. Because playing is childlike and natural, children often ask to play a story that they have read. Comprehension is tested when the teacher guides them into playing these stories. A child's awareness or lack of awareness of details is revealed when he is guided to pantomime specific actions or characters in a story. Questions such as the following provide a clear gauge of a child's understanding and orderly thinking of what he has read: How did the story begin? What happens next—and next? What character was the first one to speak in the

story? How did he feel? What was he talking about? What do you think that means?

Reading becomes more meaningful to a child who is guided into thinking, feeling, and becoming the very characters he reads about. Not every story a child reads should be played, but after he plays several stories he begins to read with stronger involvement and belief, for he carries himself into his reading. Expression in oral reading is strengthened, for he understands and becomes a part of his reading.

A class of second graders found special enjoyment in reading a story in their readers. They asked if they might play "How The Hen Got Her Speckles." The teacher guided each child to read the story again.[9] Then the group gathered together to make a plan for playing. In an exciting group discussion they worked out a plan of action. Thy were guided to divide the story into three acts with specific scenes in each act. Every day during the next week they created individual characters and short scenes by working together in short 15-minute periods (Fig. 8.6). When they were ready to play the entire story they decided to choose a cast, and each child was chosen to be a character he had enjoyed creating (Fig. 8.7).

After the children had played the story they decided it would be fun for the hen to write a letter to the king. The teacher guided the children into an enjoyable experience in which each child identified with the hen and wrote a creative letter of request. The following letter reveals humor and a liking for the story:

Dear Majesty,
   There should be a law against being noisy around chicken coops. Do you know why? Because I get so scared that I can't lay eggs. But that's only when there's noise. It seems like there's always

[9] Rice, *op. cit.*

Fig. 8.6. "This must be a letter! I'll take it to the king." (*Photograph by Edward A. Gilliland, Everett Junior College; View Ridge School, Everett Public Schools, Everett, Washington*)

Fig. 8.7. "Fire, make yourself small and get into my basket." (*Photograph by Edward A. Gilliland, Everett Junior College; View Ridge School, Everett Public Schools, Everett, Washington*)

noise though. The rest of the hens get just as upset. So make a law
that at laying time everyone must be quiet around chicken coops.

Sincerely,
Miss White Hen[10]

Another letter was created in this way:

Dear Your Majesty,
   I think that our village is just fine and it has nothing to be done.
But we need some paint. We need some money. We need some
food. We need some flowers.

Love,
Mrs. Hen[11]

In Language Arts and Related Arts. Many teachers have been
impressed with a child's unusual creative expression in related arts
after he has experienced creative dramatics. In another second grade
class children created an exciting play from "Jack and the Beanstalk," a story in a second grade reader.[12] During the week in which
the play was created each child was motivated to draw pictures of
the way he "saw each setting," and to write two stories called,
"Once When I Was Brave," and "If I Had a Golden Egg" (Fig.
8.8).

Creative dramatics often motivates integrated learning in creative
rhythms, dancing, and music as well as in writing and drawing.
The third grade class that created a beautiful play from "The Little
Rabbit Who Wanted Red Wings" enjoyed an exciting learning experience.[13] They learned "The Bunny Hop" in physical education
class, and worked in groups of six to create fairy dances around the

---

10 By permission of the 7-year-old author, Glen Anderson.
11 By permission of the 7-year-old author, Kathy Hext.
12 Kennedy, *op. cit.*
13 Polly Jepsen, Bryant School, Seattle Public Schools, Seattle, Washington.

wishing well. Each child painted a picture of the "place in the story which makes you feel the happiest," and each one wrote a revealing

FIG. 8.8. "Hen, Hen! Lay a golden egg!" (*Photograph by Brant Studio; Clyde Hill School, Bellevue Public Schools, Bellevue, Washington*)

story. The story was motivated by a dynamic discussion about the little rabbit and the two following questions: "Have you ever wished you could be or look like someone else?" "If you could, just by wishing, change something about yourself what would you change?"

This same group of children found particular pleasure in creating from music and songs. "Playing Indians" was one of their favorite songs for singing and creating, half of them becoming Indians who sang, while the other half became tribal Indians who created to the rhythm of the song. The singing Indians tapped out drumbeats on desks or on the floor. The tribal Indians became the Crows canoe-ing, the Navajos making pottery, the Sioux riding horses, and the Iroquois shooting arrows for food (Fig. 8.9).

FIG. 8.9. "Let's play Indians!" (*Photograph by Royal C. Crooks; Bryant School, Seattle Public Schools, Seattle, Washington*)

"Fairies' Music" was a special song for the second graders who played "Jack and the Beanstalk."[14] This song kindled a desire for these imaginative 7-year-olds to skip away to fairyland for a few minutes each day (Fig. 8.10). They became fascinated with fairy tales and with Rose Fyleman's lovely fairy poetry. Her "Have You Watched the Fairies?" and "The Best Game the Fairies Play" became choice experiences for playing (Fig. 8.11). While interest was high the children were motivated and guided to write fairy stories and poetry. Each child made his own booklet called "My Fairyland." Among the distinctive ideas which were expressed are the following:

Little Daffodils

Little fairy telephones,
Do you have a message for me?
Maybe from an elf man, or from a tiny bee?
If it is so, I want to know—
And then I'll go skipping home.[15]

Spring

Little golden daffodils
Are you the fairies' telephones
Dancing with the wind?
Do you sing with the wind?
Yes, I dance and sing with the wind.
Will you dance and sing for me?
I will dance, dance, dance,
And sing, sing, sing in the spring.[16]

Make-Believe

I can pretend that I'm a pretty fairy.

[14] Kennedy, *op. cit.*
[15] By permission of the 7-year-old poet, Steven Arnquist.
[16] By permission of the 7-year-old poet, Patricia Matsumoto.

FIG. 8.10. "Look! Grasshoppers are bringing the fairy queen!" (*Photograph by Brant Studio; Clyde Hill School, Bellevue Public Schools, Bellevue, Washington*)

Fig. 8.11. "Sliding down steeples is the most fun for fairies!" (*Photograph by Brant Studio; Clyde Hill School, Bellevue Public Schools, Bellevue, Washington*)

> I can pretend I'm a butterfly.
> Then a green, green hill.
> Yes, I can be anything.[17]

A Fairy Story

If I had a pair of magic shoes I would ask them to take me to fairyland. I would see the elves dancing around. Elves will give you everything you want. They will give you a nice home to live in. They will give you wishes and wishes.

The elves made me into a fairy. They gave me a yellow and red

[17] By permission of the 7-year-old poet, Linda Gordon.

dress. They gave me a wand. A little elf married me. I was the Queen and he was the elf of all the other elves. He gave me a pair of wings. I had a lovely, lovely dress to be married in. I had a wand to touch the fairies with. Then it was time to dance. I said to the fairies, "I am going to go home." They didn't want me to go. So I had to stay. But my mother and father and brother wanted me to come home so I did.[18]

Unified Learning in Social Studies. Creative dramatics offers a vital way for young children to learn about other people by "trying on the lives" of people in faraway places or close at hand. The second graders who enjoyed fairyland found equal enthusiasm in an experience centering around transportation and community helpers.[19] These children discovered how essential transportation is in carrying food and supplies from one part of the country to another. Inspired by James Tippett's "Trains," they became convincing freight and passenger trains which chugged up imaginary mountains, traveled through tunnels, and followed train signals to arrive at different destinations.

One of their most exciting journeys was a creative trip to Texas where they learned how cowboys help the nation. For four days, in 15-minute periods, they played "cowboy," creating thrilling moments in taming wild horses so cowboys could round up cattle from the ranges (Fig. 8.12). They swung lariats, learned to rope steers, rode horses, ate around a cowboy cook wagon, and played imaginary guitars and harmonicas after a day of hard work was over. During these days they wrote cowboy stories and poems and painted cowboy pictures. They read the story of "Cowboy Sam" and learned a new song called "The Cowboy"

The third graders who played Indians and created with enthusi-

---

[18] By permission of the 7-year-old author, Patricia Ward.
[19] Kennedy, *op. cit.*

asm from "The Rabbit Who Wanted Wings" found their most memorable experience to be a creative adventure in Spain.[20] This experience was developed over a six weeks' period, for their interest remained high and learning was vivid and vital.

FIG. 8.12. "Watch this cowboy!" (*Photograph by Brant Studio; Clyde Hill School, Bellevue Public Schools, Bellevue, Washington*)

The teacher who had visited Spain and Palma de Mallorca the year before motivated interest by sharing experiences of her trip and showing articles of beautiful Spanish clothing, toys, jewelry, and snapshots of bullfights. Children were impressed when they realized there was such a colorful country in the world. They located Spain on the map. Resource books were shared, and they worked in groups to discover information about Spanish climate, foods, and customs.

[20] Jepsen, *op. cit.*

The following day a messenger delivered a curious-looking piece of mail to the classroom. It was addressed to the teacher and the third graders. Curiosity ran high. The mail turned out to be a poster from Spain inviting everyone to a bullfight in Madrid. The children became enthusiastic about sharing what information they had about bullfights and matadors. When interest was at a peak, the teacher asked, "Could it be possible that a bull might be as unusual as a famous matador?" After a short discussion the teacher told the story of the most unusual bull in Spain, *The Story of Ferdinand,* by Munro Leaf.

Then the fun began. Because these children had been introduced to creative dramatics on the first day of school, they were experienced and enthusiastic about creating plays. They were guided into making a plan for playing the story in three acts. They recognized a need for learning about Spain and Spanish living so they could make the story convincing. Every day time was spent in research, and then in creating a character or a short scene. The teacher, Polly Jepsen, described the experience in this way:

The children watched an educational television program every Friday afternoon in which a Spanish teacher presented Spanish words, phrases, and sentences. The children followed up with practice. They searched for additional terminology in regard to matadors, toros, and bullfighting. The children learned Spanish words for greetings, comments, questions, and they learned to count in Spanish.

During this experience the children learned four Spanish songs, two dances, and a Spanish game which the children of Spain particularly enjoy. One of the boys suggested the need for creating a Spanish setting in the classroom. This resulted in careful group planning, and the decision to paint a Spanish mural on the board at the back of the room behind the children's desks. Each child created his idea for the mural on a large sheet of newsprint. Ideas from individual murals were chosen

by the children for the big mural. A committee was chosen, and gradually the mural was developed with each child making a contribution.
It was painted in earth colors depicting a bullfight, and was effective in
projecting a Spanish atmosphere into the room [Fig. 8.13].

While the children created *The Story of Ferdinand* several strong dis-

FIG. 8.13. "Ferdinand likes to sit under a cork tree and smell
flowers." (*Photograph by Royal C. Crooks; Bryant School, Seattle
Public Schools, Seattle, Washington*)

cussions arose relative to each distinctive character in the story. After some of the most "heated" discussions children wrote out their viewpoints on such questions as the following:

Why do you suppose Ferdinand was the way he was? [Fig. 8.14].

What is "an understanding mother"?

How do you know his mother understood him?

Who do you think really understands you? Why?

Have you ever felt you were different from others? If so, in what ways?

Have you ever known someone you thought was different? How did you treat this person?

What would you do if you were chosen for some honor, and you realized you weren't ready for it?

What do you think Ferdinand should have done when he was chosen for the bullfight? Should his mother have explained? Why or why not?

If you were at the *corrida* that day would you have cheered Ferdinand, or what would you have done?

How do you think the famous matador felt when he knew Ferdinand didn't want to fight?

Do you think any of the following words describe Ferdinand: brave, silly, afraid, true to himself? Why?

Which character in the story would you most like to have for a friend? Why?

Of all the characters in the story which one would you most enjoy being? Why?

Before the children created the final act of the story they learned about the art of bullfighting, its beautiful ballet movements, its costumes, its famous matadors. They gained an insight into the attitudes of the Spanish people toward bullfighting. They developed an understanding of customs and traditions of the Spanish people who live in the warm, sunny climate. Boys and girls acquired a few signal facts about Spanish history, geography, and products. They gained an awareness of the beauty of Spanish art, costumes, and famous celebrations [Fig. 8.15].

Children did much reading both for information and recreation, silently and orally, but purposefully. Above all, they experienced an ap-

F<small>IG</small>. 8.14. "Can't understand Ferdinand—not wanting to go to a *corrida!*" (*Photograph by Royal C. Crooks; Bryant School, Seattle Public Schools, Seattle, Washington*)

Fig. 8.15. "Olé Olé! He's the great Manolete!" (*Photograph by Royal C. Crooks; Bryant School, Seattle Public Schools, Seattle, Washington*)

preciation for Spanish living, and for all people with individual differences. They learned with enthusiasm and zest. The final creation of *The Story of Ferdinand* was an experience each child will remember. At the end of the school year, after many different kinds of experiences, most of the children expressed a desire someday to take a trip to Spain.

CREATIVE DRAMATICS IN COMMUNITY PROGRAMS

In Brownie and Bluebird Programs. Girl Scout and Campfire leaders are enthusiastic about sharing creative dramatics with children in their programs. Many Den Mothers have found creative dramatics to be a dynamic experience for Cub Scouts as well. When a leader knows and understands the basic guidance principles and philosophy of this art she is ready to share it with children wherever she may meet them. The chief difference lies in selecting material that appeals, meets children's needs, and is related to the specific program. Much of the material used in school programs has found high favor with children when creative dramatics has been shared in leisuretime programs.

In Sunday School and Church School Programs. A child is the same child whether he goes to Sunday school or Monday school. During the past decade there has been a noticeable trend toward sharing creative dramatics with children in church and Sunday school programs. Creative dramatics reaches a child in a natural "play way," and causes him to think and feel from within. In so doing this art teaches little children to "experience" rather than "talk about" basic themes in Christian living.

Teachers in the primary department of Sunday schools generally guide children from lessons focused toward specific themes. Many of the lessons provide specific suggestions for pantomimes from songs, memory verses, and short stories. A leader who understands creative dramatics will recognize many opportunities for teaching basic themes by guiding children to create from Old Testament stories such as "Noah's Ark," "The Baby Moses," and "Elijah and the Ravens." *When Jesus Was a Little Boy* by George Eberling is a story rich in opportunities for creative playing which motivates a young child to understand Jesus in a meaningful way.

A Sunday school superintendent who has shared creative dramatics with children for the past ten years is gratified by the effective way this art contributes to Christian living.[21] During a fall quarter the theme for her entire Sunday school was based on the Second

[21] Nancy Taft Smuck, Superintendent Church School, Richmond Beach Congregational Church, Richmond Beach, Washington.

Commandment, "Thou shalt love thy neighbor as thyself." This teacher shared creative dramatics in two different ways to help children in the primary grades understand this basic theme.

The first approach was in an everyday situation that centered around the kindness of neighbors in sharing. The chief objective was to show how "love goes in a circle." A scene was developed around a situation in which one neighbor who owned an apple orchard shared apples with a neighbor who had no trees. The class decided several children should be apple trees, one person should be the owner of the trees, and one person should be the neighbor. The remainder of the children were chosen to be the audience. The teacher guided the children to create convincing characters, and to weave the neighborly feeling of love into their playing.

When the scene developed into a second playing with dialogue, the neighbor thanked the owner for the apples. The neighbor then went to her house, a space in the room, and baked a huge apple pie and a smaller pie. When the pies were done, the neighbor took the huge pie and shared it with the owner. For a moment it appeared as though this was the end of the "circle of love," but with sudden inspiration the owner carried his pie to the children in the audience, and said with strong feeling, "I'll share this pie with all of my children and my relations." It was a moment of magic! Everyone in the room had suddenly been taken into the "circle of love."

The second approach to this same theme was experienced by guiding the children to play the story of Nehemiah. It was created entirely in pantomime with piano accompaniment. The children created an impressive scene in which the king and queen led a procession of courtiers into a throne room. News was brought to Nehemiah that his friends in Jerusalem needed his help. In the second scene most of the children became builders who worked hard with Nehemiah to rebuild the city wall. In the final scene the people expressed gratitude to Nehemiah for his help as they marched past him through the open gates of the city. The gates were closed and a triumphant group of people went to sleep.

Questions and Activities

1. Bring to class a picture and/or a newspaper clipping that clearly indicates a strong interest of 7- and 8-year-olds. Relate this idea to creative dramatics in a brief statement concerning how the idea therein might be shared in a creative experience.

2. Class members will again work together in two-groups to plan and evaluate a bulletin board display. The bulletin board will center on the basic characteristics, needs, and interests of the 7- and 8-year-olds. It is suggested that members who served previously on the evaluation committee serve on the bulletin board committee and vice versa.

3. Participate in an experience with a group of 7- and 8-year-olds, perhaps a Cub Scout meeting or a Brownie or Bluebird meeting, or observe a creative dramatics class for 7- and 8-year-olds. As a result of one of these experiences, analyze the group in terms of basic characteristics, needs, and interests. Use specific examples including questions, comments, and behavior to substantiate your analysis.

4. At a job interview with an elementary supervisor you are asked, "What five areas of interest appeal to almost every group of 7- and 8-year-olds?" List five such different interest areas. In the same interview you are asked, "What basic needs of 7- and 8-year-olds do you strive to respect in your teaching?" Make a complete statement of at least five basic needs.

5. Select a verse you like which is recommended for creative dramatics for 7- and 8-year-olds. Analyze the dramatic elements of the verse, and underline the chief drama goal you will emphasize when you share this verse. What is its essential mood? Plan and write out a motivation.

6. Select a short story you like which has been recommended for creative dramatics for 7- and 8-year-olds. Analyze the dramatic elements and essential mood of this story. Plan a motivation, and outline a plan for guiding the children to create from this story.

7. Plan to share Oliver Herford's "The Elf and the Dormouse" with a second grade group. Plan a motivation that will cause children to identify with the elf. List focused questions you will ask to guide children to create an elf, raindrops, and a dormouse. Suggest the roles you, as leader, will play as you guide second graders to create each of the above characters. Make a plan to guide the group to create this verse in three short scenes. With your plan in mind guide class members to create from this verse.

8. Divide the class into buzz session groups. Share with each group a song which third grade children enjoy singing. Each group plans how its song may be correlated into a delightful creative experience with creative dramatics. Each group creates from its song to illustrate this correlation for class members.

9. List three social study units which second or third grade children experience. Study and outline one of these units. Show how this unit of study will be vitalized for children by integrating this experience with creative dramatics. List points at which creative dramatics would provide unique teaching and experiencing values. State titles, authors, and sources of materials you would use in connection with this integrated learning experience.

10. If you plan to teach in a church school or Sunday school select a Bible story you like which would interest 7- and 8-year-olds. Analyze the dramatic elements and essential mood of this story. Plan a motivation. Outline a plan for guiding children in the primary department to create from this story.

11. After you have created in class from a story or verse which is strong in appeal for 7- and 8-year-olds, analyze the leader's role in guiding this creative experience. Use a semioutline form.

12. Observe a 7- and 8-year-old class in creative dramatics. Analyze this experience from the leader's role in (a) motivating children into a mood, (b) sharing a story, (c) guiding children to make

plans for each playing, (d) guiding children during playing, (e) praising, and (f) guiding children to praise and evaluate one another's playing.

13. Include in your material file one idea, one verse, and one story which you are convinced would delight sevens and eights for creative dramatics. Recall incidents in your childhood which you experienced when you were 7 and 8 years old. List several of these incidents and include them in your notebook.

CHAPTER 9

Creative Dramatics with Nine-, Ten-, and Eleven-Year-Olds

Afoot and light-hearted, I take to the open road,
Healthy, free, the world before me.
—Walt Whitman

THE MEETING by King Cole[1]

A play in two acts. Inspired by sharing ambitions at our first creative dramatics class.

Act I

Setting: King's Living Room. Time: Ten Years Later. Most of the guests have arrived. Julie enters.

KING: Why hello, Julie! How are you? Are you married yet?

JULIE: Yes. Tommy, I'd like you to meet King. King, this is my husband, Tom.

TOM: Glad to meet you, King. How are you?

KING: Fine. Oh, look at your new car. What did you do—hit an oil well?

[1] By permission of the 11-year-old author.

JULIE: That's exactly what we did.

King looks around the room.

KING: Well, now that everyone is here, let's start the meeting. First, who kept on with what he had planned for a living? *Eleven people talk at once.* "I did." "I didn't." "I did." "So did I." "I changed my plans."

KING: Wait a minute. Let's take this one at a time.

JULIE: Well, I did and dancing pays, too, and I have a lot of fun.

DAVID: Well, same with clowning, only I don't think of the money I make. It's the fun I get out of it.

ANN: I find acting stimulating because I meet interesting people and get acquainted with them.

JULIE: I just knew you were an actress by the way you walked in, Ann. By the way, I saw one of your productions last winter when my Ballerina Group was booked into the Broadway Playhouse. I went backstage but there was such a crowd I couldn't contact you before I was due back for rehearsal.

ANN: I'm sorry to have missed you. Let's be looking for each other whenever we travel. My stage name is Dolores Lane.

KING: Speaking of entertainment, so many of us went into the entertainment field that we could put on our *own* show! That is, if we had time. But say, maybe we could get Joy to play for us—how about it, Joy?

DAVID: Didn't I see where you are scheduled to play a concert at Meany Hall soon?

JOY: Yes, Dave. Why, I'd like to play. Let me see, how about Toselli's "Serenade"?

Everyone speaks at once. "Fine!" "Good!"

FLOYD: Well, I'm due on a flight in 30 minutes so I'll tell you in a hurry. I kept on with flying. I'm a pilot as you can tell, and I'm married. Meet Mary Lou.

Everyone speaks. "Hello, Mary Lou." "Mary Lou!"

FLOYD: Mary Lou, you remember all these old friends. I'm sorry but I do have to hurry, so good-by everybody. Glad to have seen you again. 'By.

Everyone speaks. "Good-by!" "See you, fellow!" "Take it easy." "So long." "Good-by!"

KING: Well, let's hear some more.

MARY LOU: I like being a pilot's wife better than being an African explorer.

TOMMY: I'm studying the old trails of Texas. I find it very interesting.

KING: That does sound mighty interesting, Tom.

CAROL: You know, Tommy, a couple of years ago, I was down in Texas. As you know, we have a lot of horses, and as I was riding my pet horse I was thinking of the way you were studying the San Antonio Trail, and wondering if you had kept on with it. By the way, my occupation is selling horses. Sometimes I haven't the courage to sell some because I like them so well.

SCOTT: I didn't keep up with mountain climbing because when I was climbing Mt. Si I broke my left hip, and I was in the hospital for a long time. Now I am an advisor on *how* to climb. I teach children and adults. Once in a while, I happen to go with them, but not very far because my wife doesn't like to have me climb mountains, so I stay back at camp and cook the food. King, I'm sorry that my wife couldn't make it tonight because she wasn't well. We live in Chicago, you see, and my wife's doctor didn't think she should travel this far.

King goes to front of room.

KING: Well, folks, how about refreshments? We have them in the rec room.

Act II

Setting: King's rec room. Time: One-half hour later.

JULIE: King, where did you get those trophies over there?

KING: Oh, I won them in skating competition. I happen to be in the Ice Follies now, and I practice four times a day. Tonight I had to cancel a practice of a big production number because not all of you people would have been able to attend if the meeting had not been tonight.

King shows trophies.

KING: I won the trophies after I turned "pro"—that is 9 of the 12. (*Smile*) It drives my mom foolish keeping them polished, but I kind of think she figures it is worth it!

DEE-DEE: I'm entering the Northwest swimming contest. I can swim 10 miles in choppy water and 13 and ⅜ in smooth water.

KING: That's pretty far to swim. When is the contest?

DEE-DEE: A week from tomorrow.

KING: Well, I wish you good luck.

MARJORIE: King, I kept up with puppetry. Ann and I are going to put on a puppet show for you, but first I would like you to meet our friend, Donna. Donna, this is King.

MARJORIE: By the way, maybe Tom didn't tell you that I'm his wife?

KING: I guess he wanted you to tell me.

JULIE: King, I'm sorry to interrupt you, but someone is at the front door.

King leaves the room. Soon faint voices are heard from the other room.

KING: Why, hello Helen! How are you? And who are your friends?

HELEN: You don't remember Sally and Joan?

All four arrive back in the rec room.

KING: You all remember Sally and Joan, don't you? Sally, did you keep up with your ambitions?

SALLY: No, I didn't, King. I changed my plans because my husband died four years ago from an auto accident. I am now a taxidermist.

KING: That's mighty interesting being a taxidermist, Sally. What are you now, Joan? Did you keep up *your* ambition?

JOAN: No, I didn't either, King. I'm a secretary now. I've saved up five years' vacation. Now I can have ten weeks' vacation.

HELEN: Ten weeks' vacation! You're lucky!

JOAN: Wait a minute folks. Why not have our next meeting at my

house! I live in New York and have a big enough house for all of us. Let's say two and a half years from now. Is that O.K.?

Everyone speaks. "Sure!" "Fine!" "O.K."

JOAN: Well, let's put our talent to use while we're there. There's a needy hospital near my house and we could put on a benefit show for the children there. King, you get up a committee in a while and we'll put our talent to good use.

KING: O.K. with me. Will do!

JOY: I think I should tell you in case you don't already know. Helen is a doctor at that hospital.

Everyone speaks. "A doctor?" "Are you?" "Great!"

HELEN: Yes, I kept on with my work on cancer. I found a *cure* for it.

Everyone speaks. "Really?" "Wonderful!" "A cure?"

JOY: She cured me of it five years ago.

Everyone speaks. "Joy, that's wonderful!" "You're cured?" "Helen, that's great."

Doorbell rings. King goes to the door.

KING: Well, look who's here!

Mark and Bob enter and say hello.

Everyone speaks. "Hello!" "Mark! Bob!" "Where have you been?" "Come in and join our meeting."

BOB: We belong to the Top Talent Troupe. We just finished putting on a show. I kept on with my trumpet and singing.

MARK: I changed my ambition from a mounted policeman. I'm an entertainer. I do a specialty number in our show. But you should see how Bob can skate.

BOB: If you had any ice here I'd like to skate for you right now if it is all right with my manager, Mark.

MARK: It's fine with me if King knows how we can get some ice.

KING: Leave that to me. I can manage almost everything. We'll have a show right now to celebrate.

Everyone speaks. "Great!" "Wonderful!" "Let's begin!" "This is wonderful!"

The show begins with Mark and King managing everything. Each person shares something. The meeting is lively and gay.

END OF PLAY

WHAT ARE NINE-, TEN-, AND ELEVEN-YEAR-OLDS LIKE?

This happy meeting and the rosy dreams of these boys and girls reveal a cheerful group of aspiring young individualists. Many of the characteristics of these children resemble closely those of other boys and girls who live through these golden years of childhood.

Physical Characteristics and Needs. Even though nines, tens, and elevens experience noticeable changes in growth and development during these years, they have much in common. There is a dynamic relationship between nines and tens, and between tens and elevens. Tens have a balancing effect on a group. They tend to relax the eager active nines, and to stabilize the restless enthusiastic elevens.

These childhood years are active, lively, energetic, often noisy years. They are characterized by energy and power. Most children work hard and play hard. Nines are dynamic and speedy. Tens are active in a smooth exuberant way. Elevens are portraits in everchanging motion; bounding, jumping, springing, lounging, fidgeting, shifting, shrugging, lolling, reclining. Most of them enjoy releasing energies in outdoor games, skills, competitive sports, and large full-body actions. They enjoy the freedom and freshness of the outdoor world. They delight in running, jumping, climbing, leaping, tumbling, and wrestling, with real joy in physical accomplishment. Muscle coördinations are generally well developed. Finer skills offer both enjoyment and challenge, such as working with one's hands to make a model, carve, whittle, paint, sew, play a musical instrument, paint, or draw.

Whenever several children engage in fast-moving, vigorous rhythmic activity they function with noticeable motor control. They seldom bump or collide. They like to be organized in their action.

Mental Characteristics and Needs. *"Self-motivation* is the cardinal characteristic of the 9-year-old. It is the key to understanding him on his progress toward maturity. He has a growing capacity to put his mind to things, on his own initiative or on only slight cues from the environment."[2] Once an idea tickles a child's thinking he generally has a host of ideas which need to be channeled. Above all, he needs an adult to guide him indirectly and keep him pursuing by praise, approval, and questions that keep him on the track.

"Ten is a year of consummation as well as of transition—an amiable, relatively relaxed interlude in which the organism assimilates, consolidates, and balances its attained resources."[3] Life to most tens has a gloriousness about it. Every waking minute seems to bring a certain sense of adventure, be it work, play, or leisurely activity. Ten has a way of accepting life as it happens. He also anticipates with pleasure. He figures out how to meet unexpected happenings. He needs appreciation, and particularly an adult who listens to his many interests.

As a child approaches, completes, or moves through his eleventh year, new growth patterns take place. "The erstwhile complaisant 10-year-old begins to display unaccustomed forms of self-assertion, of curiosity, and of sociability. He is restive, investigative, talkative.

[2] Arnold Gesell and Frances L. Ilg, *The Child from Five to Ten,* Harper & Brothers, 1946.

[3] Arnold Gesell, Frances L. Ilg, and Louise Bates Ames, *Youth: The Years from Ten to Sixteen,* Harper & Brothers, 1956.

He wriggles."[4] It is often difficult for elevens to concentrate, but when they do they become intent and pursue information and details with keen enjoyment. They often think quickly and sharply, and express with sudden philosophic statements such as "I kind of think she figures it is worth it." Tendencies toward an interest in details were noticed throughout "The Meeting" in distances for swimming, in a ten weeks' vacation, and in the reason why Scott became an advisor on mountain climbing.

Although this age group is geared to action, they prefer organization when working in groups. They like discussions that are motivated by purpose. They are capable of discussing for long periods of time. Attention spans, though varying with individuals, have lengthened. It is not uncommon for a group to discuss for an hour at a time when making a plan or discussing a problem that interests them.

Social Characteristics and Needs. These childhood years are social years. Gangs and clubs come into high vogue. Esprit de corps is vital to almost every child, for he values his peers and his place among his companions. Although each child is a strong individualist he needs to belong to a gang, a club, an organization at school or in neighborhood areas. Each one needs opportunities to contribute to a group in specific ways. These needs were revealed in "The Meeting." Each child had status. Sociability revealed itself in the reactions of others toward newly found status, in the pausing for refreshments, in the idea of meeting again in two years, and in the desire to have "a show right now to celebrate."

There is a friendly sense of rivalry, competition, and rather secretive interest in the opposite sex during these middle years. Boys gang with boys and girls with girls. In these smaller groups each child

[4] *Ibid*

needs status. Individuals within a small group want individual responsibility. A child wants to be a chairman, secretary, or a special committee member. In instances such as this, individuals work with high motivation to prove their capabilities and reveal their finer values to one another.

Emotional Characteristics and Needs. These childhood years could be called an I-Can-Take-It age. Individuals, on the whole, are secure, confident, capable, and outgoing. A child, almost but not quite, wants moments wherein he can become heroic. He dreams at length of moments when he does noble acts. In his daydreaming he often rescues others from a burning house, saves someone from drowning, saves a pal from dying from rattlesnake bite as they hike over foothills. A child often dreams of publishing a newspaper, of writing stories and books, of becoming a famous flyer, doctor, nurse, or of contributing in some distinctive or spectacular way to the benefit of mankind. A child frequently dreams of discovering a "cure" or of inventing "something."

The years of nine, ten, and eleven are characterized by strong pursuit in individual achievement. Every child, whether he realizes it or not, makes his individual debut into the world during these years. A child strives for a feeling of independent status and recognition which gives him emotional and social security. He often betrays his need for status by making it known that he can swim farther or stay under water longer than anyone else in his class. Or he may strive to have a bigger collection of rocks or stamps than anyone he knows. Or he may take pride in being the one to read the most books in the classroom, or to be chosen for a solo part in a choir, an orchestra, or a skating exhibition. A child often finds the recognition he seeks in Boy Scout or Girl Scout groups or in Camp

Fire Girl achievement. Each child seeks heroic status in a specific way that satisfies his individuality.

Because of these yearnings and desires children need many vicarious adventures during these years. They need to live the lives of great men and women, and to struggle vicariously against the most difficult odds.

An 11-year-old may reveal marked inconsistencies in emotional living. Because of the many growth changes he experiences, he may resort to noticeable extremes or instability in emotional reactions. For these surging inconsistencies he needs an atmosphere of understanding in which he can grow and work out his new patterns and designs for living.

Spiritual Characteristics and Needs. The unvoiced theme for many a child in these golden years might well be Walt Whitman's "Afoot and light-hearted, I take to the open road." Spiritual qualities reveal themselves in many intangibles. All that most children ask for during these years, not always in words, but in countless other ways, is the outdoor world with space, a dog, a horse, a few companions, and an opportunity to prove themselves. Once proved, a child does not glory for long in his achievements. Rather he rolls up his sleeves, sets new sights, and exerts his energies for reaching the reality of another bright dream.

STRONG INTERESTS OF NINES, TENS, AND ELEVENS

This is an age of adventure—bold, glorious, realistic adventure. Outdoor adventure has top priority with most children during these years. Both boys and girls enjoy sports and outdoor activities such as camping, sleeping out of doors, cooking over open fires, and "roughing it." They relish adventure that has a certain sense of danger, struggle, suspense, and mystery surrounding it. They respond to realistic adventure such as that experienced by early explorers, discoverers, pilgrims, and pioneers. They enjoy adventure that involves intrigue, excitement, and curiosity.

When a teacher asked his fourth graders what the four seasons were, Tommy's eyes flashed with such discernment that he was asked to answer. "Fishing season, deer season, pheasant season," he answered confidently. He was puzzled momentarily by the surprised reactions of his classmates, but as soon as he regained his composure he continued triumphantly, "And out of season!"

Heroes hold high interest for most children during these years—heroes from real life and fiction, animal heroes, and heroes who have risen from "underdog" status to prove their worth.

In one class of nines, tens, and elevens the children created their version of "The Olympic Games." Individuals worked in groups to represent champion participants from countries all over the world. Dean, one of the shorter 10-year-olds, represented "The Champion United States Tumbler." All the children were impressed with his tumbling skills, which he revealed to this group for the first time. Boys and girls clapped and cheered and called out, "Dean, you're good!"

The boy was pleased but a little embarrassed. He flexed his arm muscles and said somewhat humbly, "It's not much, but I am *athletic.*" Julie, one of the sixth graders, completely lost in heroic admiration, spoke out spontaneously and said a little sadly, "I'm not, I'm *Presbyterian.*"

Interest is strong in a new realm of magic, mystery, and codes. Magic interests have moved beyond the fantasy realm for most children of this age into a bolder attitude of magic in such exciting real things as chemistry, electricity, smoke signals, light signals, gravity, and atoms.

Experiences that center around achievement and idealism hold high appeal for most tens and elevens, whereas many nines are still fascinated by fantasy. The suspense of fantasy is satisfying to some children, whereas others demand a struggle in which a hero proves his stature by solving a problem that appears insurmountable. Humor always finds high favor with both boys and girls during these years.

INTRODUCING CREATIVE DRAMATICS TO NINES, TENS, AND ELEVENS

A little child plays for the sheer joy of playing. An older child finds greater enjoyment in playing when he understands whatever he is playing. Whether he is playing a game of cards, in a school band, or a game of baseball, he prefers to know what he is doing. At 7 and 8 a child delights in hitting a ball and running. Now at 9 or 10 he finds himself wanting to play ball as the game is intended to be played, by knowing and respecting its rules and form.

Drama Is Emphasized. So it is with creative dramatics. An older child has a need to know, to understand. He begins to look for the "rules" of the game. He wants to find something as basic in drama as the scale which he has discovered in making music. He wants to play, but through his play he wants to gain a certain understanding of drama. He wants to learn how to express in dramatic form in a way that satisfies him.

In introducing creative dramatics to older children, the same basic approach is used. Children are gradually introduced to the fundamentals of drama through creative play. Drama is introduced with indirection, through playing. In this art a child's creative spirit must find expression through dramatic form. If he pantomimes or characterizes without creating, his expression is empty, lifeless, dull.

Spirit and form must be synchronized in expression. This is the chief challenge of a leader as she guides older children.

A leader motivates a child to create from within in a strong spirit of play. She gradually guides him toward an understanding of how to express himself in rhythmic movement, characterization, dialogue, interaction, and teamwork. A leader "feels her way along" with each new group by considering individual needs and interests. With one group she may recognize a need for children to participate in many enjoyable experiences in rhythmic movement before being introduced to "dramatic terms." With another group she may sense a readiness for children to learn about drama at the outset. In this case she will involve children in the fun of rhythmic play but will indirectly stress drama from the start. Creative dramatics experiences are always based on ideas or literature that holds high appeal for a specific group of children.

Begin with Introduction to Drama. Some leaders prefer to guide children into the fun of expressing in rhythmic movement first and explain creative dramatics afterward. When children have experienced the fun of pantomiming they generally understand an explanation more clearly. In a brief explanation a leader points out that creative dramatics is creating characters, scenes, stories, or situations in such a way as to make them seem real. She explains that each person uses his imagination and his entire self to create. She stresses the need for every child to think, feel, and believe whatever he is creating. She points out that they will have fun creating a play when everyone first learns to have fun creating convincing characters and action. She then proceeds to guide them into many experiences in the freedom and fun of expressing in rhythmic action.

Other leaders prefer to guide children into a brief discussion of creative dramatics by asking them what they believe creative dramatics to be. The leader who guided King Cole and the other nines, tens, and elevens, began in this way. Most children are familiar with drama either from children's theatre plays or from drama on television, radio, or moving pictures. A leader guides children to discuss briefly their ideas of drama. From this discussion she then explains the specific nature of creative dramatics.

A few leaders have introduced children to creative dramatics by first guiding them into a stimulating discussion on creativity before explaining the nature of this art. These leaders have been enthusiastic about the freedom with which children have used their imaginations once they started to express themselves in rhythmic movement and characterizations.

Begin with Rhythmic Movement and Pantomime. The following first and early experiences have been used to introduce older children to creative dramatics. In each experience a mood was created and children introduced themselves to each other. In some instances there was a brief discussion of creative dramatics before the idea was presented.

Outdoor Interest

The best way in the world really to get to know people is to go camping together. Suppose each one gets his duffel ready and we'll hike up the rugged mountain trail to Buck Meadows. We'll rest up there by a mountain spring. Everyone be ready to share the one thing you enjoy doing most when you are camping in the mountains. (Fishing, building a campfire and frying fish, riding a horse, making camp, swimming in a lake, sleeping in a sleeping bag, sitting around the fire and singing.)

Sports Interest

All over the world fine athletes are getting ready for the Olympic Games. When they meet together each one will compete with others to find out the champion sportsmen and sportswomen in the world. Suppose we are having our Olympic Games, and each one of you is a champion in whatever sport you like best. When the trumpets sound and your name is announced, suppose you give a short preview of the sports event in which you are a champion. (Swimming, boxing, baseball, football, tennis, badminton, tumbling, broad jump, running, high jump, golf.)

Seasonal Interest

> Winter, summer, spring, or fall!
> What time do you like best of all?

Show the one thing you find yourself waiting to do all during the year. (Swimming, skiing, picking cherries and eating them, digging for clams, riding horseback on a ranch, fishing, picking wild flowers.)

Music Interest

Suppose today instead of listening to music, we make music.

If you could play an instrument in a band, which instrument would you like to play best of all? (Drum, trumpet, cymbals, trombone, clarinet, tuba, flute.)

Adventure Interest

Welcome adventurers! Every day brings new adventures. Right this minute someone is adventuring on the floor of the ocean. Someone is adventuring high in the sky. Someone is adventuring with a microscope, while someone else is adventuring on television. You have probably dreamed of doing something that would be high adventure for you. What one thing have you dreamed of doing? (Climbing mountains, skiing in Sun Valley, being a doctor, singing on television, dancing in a ballet, being in a wagon train, flying in a rocket, diving down to a treasure ship in the ocean, discovering buried treasure in California.)

Recreational Interest

In last night's paper there was a news story about a boy and girl

in South Africa who wondered what boys and girls in the United States do for fun. If you could send a picture postcard of yourself having fun, what would you be doing? Suppose we send a *moving picture* film and each one will show how he has fun. (Riding a horse, dancing, picnicking, playing football, diving, camping, running in waves, hiking and looking for agates and arrowheads, playing tether ball.)

Poetry and verse which have motivated nines, tens, and elevens into strong creative expression in rhythmic movement include "Beach Fire," by Frances M. Frost, "Maps," by Dorothy Brown Thompson, "Skating," by Herbert Asquith, "Bundles," by John Farrar, and "Happy Thought," by Robert Louis Stevenson.

Charades and guessing games hold high appeal for children of these ages. A large group may be divided into two or four smaller groups. Children within each group are guided to pantomime the same action, but each child is encouraged to express in his own way. Strong spirit and friendly competition generally motivate unusual creative thinking and clear pantomimes. Charades that have proved to be favorites during these years include the traditional "New Orleans," and games based on television programs such as "What's My Line?" and "My Life in Review," and others such as "Ways We Vacationed This Summer," "Ways We Earn Money," and "My Favorite Song."

Introduce Children to Characterization. Characterization is introduced whenever a leader feels that children are ready. During early sessions an alert leader discovers strong individual and group interests. She leads children into characterization based on a variety of experiences which are at the heart of their specific interests. The following experiences in characterization have found strong appeal with different groups of nines, tens, and elevens.

Animal Interest

Have you ever watched a seagull in flight gliding higher and higher with beautiful rhythm in its wings? Have you ever watched a garter snake gliding through the grass in quite a fascinating different rhythm? Have you ever thought how pleasant it would be to change into a bird or an animal for a little while to enjoy its feeling of power and rhythm? Of all the different birds and animals you have watched, which one would you enjoy being most? (Horse, eagle, kangaroo, deer, elk, bear, seagull, snake, monkey, giraffe, lion, hummingbird, owl.)

Invention Interest

Have you ever stopped to think about the number of modern conveniences there are in your kitchen at home? Our great-great-grandparents had kitchens quite different from the ones we have today. Have you ever watched a pressure cooker when it "blows off steam"? Have you ever had days when you felt like "blowing off steam"? Think of the many different kitchen appliances in your kitchen, and decide which one you think it would be fun to be. (Pressure cooker, percolator, refrigerator, toaster, electric clock, water faucet, electric stove, can opener, electric mixer, teakettle.)

Holiday Interest

Halloween is a night of all nights when evil spirits cast spells on someone who has made them angry. A witch gets angry when another witch pushes ahead of her in a witch line. A witch gets angry when a chestnut disappears, and the guilty witch won't "own up" to have eaten it. People as well as witches get angry. How about you? Think of one thing that has made you so angry you still remember it. At the midnight hour each one of us will change into an evil witch. We will each weave a spell on one thing that has made us angry. (A dog that chases my bicycle, my brother, someone who calls me names, my little sister when she tears my books, my brother when he won't let me see my television program, a boy who gets me in trouble.)

Adventure Interest

Years and years ago when the world was new, it was believed that

demons and genii roamed the earth. It is said that powerful kings overpowered the genii and conjured them up in small urns, and buried them deep within the earth. The genii took the forms of strong forces in nature which have the power for good or evil such as fire and wind. If you could take the form of a powerful force in nature, what form would you take? If you were set free after a thousand years, how do you think you would feel as you came out of the urn? What do you think you would do first of all? (Forms of sun rays, wind, water, atoms, a seed, a germ, a lightning spark, thunder.)

Hero Interest

Books bring adventure—storybooks and history books. Wonderful heroes and heroines live inside the pages of books, and do brave and courageous deeds. If you could live inside a book and be your favorite hero or heroine who would you choose to be?

A circus is fun for children of all ages. When nines, tens, and elevens are motivated they enjoy working in groups, and generally create circus acts that are stupendous. After they have created a circus, they are often eager for similar experiences such as a horse show, rodeo, ice follies, aquafollies, and a carnival. Both boys and girls delight in creating such ideas as merry-go-rounds, sword swallowers, strong men, wrestling matches, "lightest and heaviest women in the world," dart-throwing games and other skill games. Water carnivals have resulted in exciting creative experiences for children who have witnessed similar events in reality. Boys and girls have created thrilling hydroplane races, water skiing events, and beautiful exhibitions in swimming and diving.

Parades are always popular with nines, tens, and elevens. Again, they enjoy the challenge of working in groups to create parade units or floats. The patriotic verse, "The Flag Goes By," has motivated striking historical parades. Other parades have been created from specific themes including "Mother Goose Land," "Favorite Songs,"

"Pages from History," "Wonders of the World," "A Century of Progress," "Playground, U.S.A.," and "High Adventure, the World Around."

Some groups have revealed strong interest in pirates, gypsies, and cowboys, and leaders have introduced characterization in these specific areas. Poetry to enrich these interests includes "Being Gypsy," by Barbara Young, "Meg Merrilies," by John Keats, "The Pirate Don Durk of Dowdee," by Mildred Plew Meigs, and "The Cowboy's Life," attributed to James Barton Adams.

Introduce Conflict. When children enjoy and know how to create a character they are ready for situations with strong conflict. Nines, tens, and elevens enjoy creating from some of the same conflict situations that appeal to 7- and 8-year-olds. Beatrice Curtis Brown's "Jonathan Bing" has been a popular conflict for some groups. Other groups have created exciting scenes from Alice Ellison's "Wondering":

> Have you ever wondered what a day may bring
>   With a knock on your door or a telephone ring?
> Or a message that flies across the sky
>   To make you laugh or make you cry?
> If you could choose what today holds in store,
>   Who would you like to come to your door?
> A quaint gypsy maid your fortune to tell—
>   A postman with news you liked so well?
> A great big truck with a prize you'd won
>   For writing a story about the moon and sun?
> A sudden shout from a passerby—
>   That smoke from your roof was puffing high?
> Or, is it more fun with knocks and rings—
>   To listen, and wonder, and see what each brings?[5]

[5] By permission of the poet, Alice Ellison.

"If there was a knock at your door tonight at midnight, and someone special was there to see you, who would you like this person to be?" This question generally arouses a discussion that builds into a strong mood. Children then enjoy working in groups of three or four to create a dramatic scene to share.

Another of Alice Ellison's poems offers a similar challenge for children to create dramatic scenes by working in smaller groups. This poem is called "Earth Folk":

> Away up high in the space of the sky,
>   Lives a wise old man in a mountain on the moon.
> He watches the earth, and ponders on its worth,
>   For he sees the present, the past, and what's to happen soon.
> He laughs, and he cheers—he wonders, and sheds tears,
>   At the way earth folk spend a morning, night, and noon.
> If you could fly to the space of the sky,
>   And spend one day with the man on the moon,
> What would make you cheer as you looked away down here?
>   Would it be a pioneer, or a headline flashed at noon?[6]

"If you could choose to live in any century—in the past, the present, or the future—which century would you prefer?" This question generally stirs 10- and 11-year-olds into a mood that brings exceptional creative thinking. One group believed the most important event in the past was "Columbus discovers America," the most important event in the present was "atomic tests in Nevada," and the most important event in the future "rocket reaches the moon."

Joaquin Miller's "Columbus" and Henry Wadsworth Longfellow's "Paul Revere's Ride" have provided outstanding drama for experienced groups. Mother Goose rhymes have provided challenging conflicts for older children to create in groups.

[6] *Ibid.*

Introduce Short Stories. "The Conjure Wives," "The Sorcerer's Apprentice," and the old myth "Pandora's Box" are excellent beginning stories. Each is strong in conflict and rhythmic movement and limited in characterization and dialogue. Aesop's fables, which have found high favor with some beginning groups, include "The Wind and the Sun," "Mercury and the Woodman," and "The Mice in Council."

After children have created two or three short stories they should enjoy "The Bremen Town Musicians." Fourth and fifth grade groups have reveled in the opportunity to create animal harmony for the musicians, and to create a robber's scene which centers around plundering pirates. "Androcles and the Lion" by Thomas Day is another good beginning story, high in conflict and providing strong opportunities for emotional reaction in mob scenes.

Introduce Longer Stories. When children are ready for the challenge of creating individualized characters with dialogue they should be ready to enjoy thoroughly the whitewashing scene from *The Adventures of Tom Sawyer,* episodes from *The Merry Adventures of Robin Hood,* and scenes from *King Arthur and His Knights of the Round Table.*

If children are still interested in fantasy they may like to create a long play from "Rumpelstiltskin," "Sleeping Beauty," or "The Emperor's New Clothes." Or a group may find unusual challenge in Raymond Alden's "The Knights of the Silver Shield," Louise de la Ramée's *The Nuremberg Stove,* or Robert Browning's "The Pied Piper of Hamelin."

When children are in a mood for myths "The Miraculous Pitcher," "The Three Golden Apples," or "Ceres and Proserpina" should be considered.

Funny stories which groups of nines, tens, and elevens have thoroughly relished include "Mr. and Mrs. Vinegar," "The Three Sillies," "The Wise People of Gotham," *The Story of Ferdinand,* scenes from *Homer Price* by Robert McCloskey, and episodes from *The Story of Doctor Dolittle* by Hugh Lofting.

Bible stories which have been created with spirit and understanding include the Nativity story, "The Good Samaritan," "Joseph and His Brothers," and dramatic episodes centering around the lives of David, Moses, and Jeremiah.

Raymond Alden's *Why the Chimes Rang* is a beautiful Christmas story for a beginning group. It has a noble theme, strong in conflict, many characters, and requires very little dialogue. Experienced groups have created from Menotti's *Amahl and the Night Visitors,* Ruth Sawyer's "The Voyage of the Wee Red Cap," and from scenes in Charles Dickens' *A Christmas Carol.*

From time to time, particularly after children have created a long play, they find fresh challenge in creating from a short verse or from an idea.

BASIC PRINCIPLES IN GUIDING

Guiding Children to Pantomime. There are many different ways to guide children to express in pantomime for a first time. A leader may invite a child to share a pantomime with the group. She may lead the children into a discussion of pantomime by approaching it from a viewpoint of communication which children understand. She may point out ways in which people "speak" entirely with actions such as waving, bowing, gesturing, and signaling. She may invite children to pantomime several different ways of communicating without using words. From this she may lead them to the specific area of pantomime for the session.

Most leaders prefer to introduce children to pantomime by creating a pantomime and guiding them to analyze it. Suppose a group of children has been guided into a strong mood for camping. A leader may heighten the mood with a suggestion that causes the children to visualize the space. She may say, "Here we are in the beautiful outdoor world with tall pine trees, a lake, a stream, mountains, flowers, and time for a real holiday. When I get out to the woods, this is what I like to do first of all." She then pantomimes, with strong feeling and clean-cut actions, fishing, building a camp-fire, roasting wieners, skipping rocks on the water, swinging on a tree branch, or pitching horseshoes. A leader must enjoy a pantomime. She must be involved in whatever she is expressing. If she has never fished, it will be impossible for her to express herself through a convincing pantomime of fishing.

When the pantomime is over, she asks the children to describe what the pantomime told them. "How could you tell I was fishing?" she may ask after several answers are given. "What besides my actions told you I had caught a fish?" A leader focuses the discussion to the three basic aspects of pantomiming—action, feeling, and individuality.

She then guides the entire group into repeating whatever pantomime she has shared, but encourages each child to express this idea in his own way. A child who has never experienced this action in reality is invited to watch the others. After this initial pantomime, children may be encouraged to move out into the open space, each child being guided to "show one thing you like to do best when you've come to the woods for a day."

A leader watches for a child or children who are involved and communicating through pantomime. After everyone has pantomimed, and the spirit of pantomiming is strong, she may invite several children to share their pantomimes for the others in small groups of three or four at a time. She guides children to praise the pantomimes and the ideas. Above all she guides with enthusiasm to keep the spirit of the experience high while she gradually stresses the fundamentals of expression in rhythmic movement and pantomime.

When a leader realizes children are failing to enter wholeheartedly into confident expression in pantomime she may introduce "extremes" to invite fun and emotional freedom. For instance, she may guide them to show in pantomime that they are fishing with the littlest fishing poles in the world. Children almost always respond to the unique, imaginative idea of "extremes." From this idea they are then guided to the opposite extreme—in this instance, fishing with the biggest fishing poles in the world. By proceeding from one extreme to the other in pantomimes such as these almost every child frees himself for confident creative expression.

Guiding Children to Create a Character. Children are guided to create a first characterization in the same way they are guided to create a first pantomime. The leader may guide children to discuss characterization, and then create a convincing characterization for them. She may voice the situation something like this:

We have had fun using our whole selves to swim, skate, fly, hike, and go adventuring.

Now we are going to be someone different from ourselves. We will learn how to create a character, and soon we will be ready to put our characters into plays.

We will experiment and all learn together, each one creating in his own way. It is only as we dig away down deep and bring up our own way of being a character from the inside that a character becomes real and honest. This is the secret to creating a character. When you feel the way a character feels inside, you discover the power inside yourself. You give your character strong feeling, for you create. You feel good because you express in your own way. Every one of us would paint a picture of a character in our own way, and so we expect to create a character in our own way too.

The leader then focuses children's thinking to a specific character. Suppose the children have created a picnic scene in which they are gathered around enjoying an imaginary picnic dinner. The teacher asks a single question, "What might happen which would send all the picnickers scurrying away from this delicious food?" Out of the many replies she focuses children's thinking on one strong suggestion for character, perhaps that of a bear. She guides them to understanding the bear's character by asking focused questions such as the following:

Why do you think the bear is coming toward the picnic?
How does he feel as he smells baked ham and honey?
How do you feel when you're nearly starved and you smell food?
How do you think the bear feels as he gets near the table and sees the people?

After a short discussion the leader may encourage all the children to get up and use their whole selves to create a hungry bear following his nose in search of food. Or she may create a characterization, after which she encourages the children to create. She is alert to characterizations that communicate strong feeling. She encourages individuals to watch one another, and emphasizes feeling and use of the entire body. After many different experiences in characterization a child is guided to create dialogue for his characters.

Guiding Children to Create a Play. Let us examine one leader's guidance as she led a group of 9-, 10-, and 11-year-olds into creating a play from the old myth, "Pandora's Box."[7]

[7] This is a composite condensed account, from students' observation reports, of

Mood Built. A mood for curiosity was developed by sharing a small carved box tied with a worn cord. A parchment scroll secured under the cord read, "Open not."

"Shall we open, or not open?" the leader asked. "Open!" was the unanimous reply. "Why?" asked the leader.

From the replies there came an exciting discussion of curiosity. When the box was opened a message said, "You are like Pandora."

Story Told. This led to the desire to hear the old myth which the leader told with strong appreciation. "This will make a neat play," said one of the boys. "Let's be the evil spirits first."

Thinking Focused to One Character. "Who else has a suggestion of where we should begin?" From the replies the leader sensed that group interest was strongest in the evil spirits and the character of Hope.

"Suppose we take Bill's good suggestion and begin with the evil spirits."

Feeling Aroused and Related to Individuals. "Before we can create an evil spirit we need to get a clear idea of the feeling and appearance of a spirit. Since these spirits are the worst troubles in the world, suppose you think of a time when you've really been worried or in trouble. What causes a sharp sting of trouble for you?"

After thinking, children were ready with these replies:

"War is the worst trouble in the world."

"I think death is worse than war."

"When someone's sick, and suffers, I think that's even worse."

"I think when you suffer from a lie or when somebody else has

a class at the Seattle Public Library under the sponsorship of the School of Drama of the University of Washington.

done something, and they won't own up to it and everyone thinks you're guilty, it's worse than being sick."

"Crimes like murder and kidnaping cause the worst kind of trouble, I think. A murderer is selfish and greedy. He almost always kills for money. I think real greed is about the worst trouble in the world."

"Accidents cause trouble and make people sad."

"When someone is jealous and leaves you out of things, that causes trouble."

"Calling you names and making threats causes a lot of trouble too."

Characterization Focused. "You've certainly thought of some of the terrible troubles that cause worry and sadness. Suppose we first think about the spirit of Greed. Most of us know how a selfish greedy person feels, but if a spirit were greedy from deep inside out to his arms and legs and whole body, how would he look to you? See if you can see Greed clearly enough to describe him in one word."

Children saw Greed as powerful, bold, strong, sly, crooked, bright red, ghostly green, sneaky, pouncing.

"Excellent pictures!" said the leader. "Who is ready to create the character of Greed?"

Clear Statement of Plan. "First, we need an audience to see if we create convincing feelings of Greed. Suppose the audience gathers over here. Everyone who wants to be Greed for the first playing come over into this small space. Each one will be Greed locked up inside the box, waiting for the day when you can force your feelings upon someone. I'll be Pandora. When I open the box, let's see how each one feels when he is set free, and how he feels when he sees Pandora. The audience will watch for interesting characters of

Greed. We will play without talking but with strong greedy feeling."

Leader Reacts to Heighten Feeling. The leader as Pandora pantomimed the opening of the box with a strong feeling of curiosity. She had arranged with one of the children to turn up the volume of a recording of the "Infernal Dance of Kastchei" from Stravinsky's *Firebird Suite.* The surging music provided strong rhythm and feeling for Greeds to bound from the box, and return to pounce upon Pandora. Pandora's reaction provided a strong character for them to work against.

Leader Invites Comments from Audience. "What powerful greedy characters! What did our audience see that made Greed seem real?"

"I liked the way Dick's Greed moved way out with such force before he zoomed toward Pandora. He gave others a turn without crowding around."

"I thought Cathy's Greed was good. Most of the rest came at Pandora from the side, but Cathy's pounced down from above like a big hammer of trouble."

"I thought everybody was feeling sort of wild with feeling. They looked like a swarm of hornets."

Leader Focuses Comments to Drama. "Excellent dramatists in our audience! You liked Dick's use of space. You liked the strong feeling. You liked Cathy's creative idea. Good! Let's keep these three strong points in our next playing."

Leader Guides Evaluation. "Who sees one way we can make our next playing seem more convincing?"

"We could make it more mysterious if we move more like spirits instead of people."

"I think it shouldn't be as noisy and confusing when all the Greeds crowd around Pandora."

Leader Captures These Comments. "You're both right. These are the two ways we will make the next playing stronger. If each spirit is feeling like Greed with much deeper inside feeling, we should be able to weave a mysterious quality in our playing. Who sees how we can avoid the noise and confusion?"

"Each Greed can have his turn at stinging Pandora."

"I know, one of the spirits can be the King of the Troubles. He can be the first one out of the box, and the first one to pounce toward her, and he can sort of signal to each spirit in turn."

Leader Accepts Creative Idea. "A splendid suggestion, Ray. Suppose you be the King of Troubles this time, and we will see how your idea works. We will use dialogue this time, so you may speak to each spirit the way you believe the King of Troubles will speak."

New Cast Is Chosen. One of the children who played in the first playing asked to be Pandora and was chosen for this character. Children who had been in the audience were chosen to be the evil Greeds, and the first Greeds became the audience. The two new goals were stated. The leader guided the cast to begin (Fig. 9.1).

Characters Individualized. After this playing was evaluated and praised, the leader suggested that each child become the Trouble he considered the worst, including such characters as sickness, death, grief, lies, jealousy, accidents, and greed. Each child was guided to picture his character and consider its feeling. A single cast was chosen including the King of Troubles, six Troubles, and Pandora. The scene was played again, with feeling and dialogue being the two goals.

New Character Planned. At the following class meeting the children were eager to create the character of Hope. "What is a hopeful feeling?" the leader asked. The children thought, but no child volunteered an answer. The leader asked the question from a different viewpoint. "When is a time in your life when you have experienced the feeling of hope?"

FIG. 9.1. Greed! Greed! Greed! (*School of Drama, University of Washington*)

Replies came quickly: "When I wanted to be in a Christmas play at school, and I got chosen."

"When we got a telegram saying my dad was flying home from Korea."

"When I passed."

"When my grandmother got better after she was real sick."

Thinking Focused to Character's Appearance. The leader commented on the hopeful feelings, and asked, "If you close your eyes and get a picture of Hope, how do you see her?"

The children responded immediately: "Hope is like a ball of fire with lights flashing out."

"I see Hope like a rose unfolding, like roses all over the world blooming."

"Hope is a golden butterfly."

"I think Hope is like a butterfly who grows into a fair-sized lady."

"I see Hope like a fairy, not just a fairy, but the queen of the fairies, changing into something stronger than a fairy because she's real and full of hope."

New Character Created. In a similar way children were guided to create the character of Hope. Comments and evaluations after each playing encouraged individual expression.

Group Guided to Create One Scene. "Now that we have created strong evil spirits, and the even stronger character of Hope, we are ready to create the closing scene of the story. We will begin where Pandora is alone with the box, and play the story to the end. We have two important places to plan. After the spirits have flown from the box, and each one has stung Pandora and talked with her, what will they do when Pandora hears the voice of Hope?"

Several suggestions were given. The children decided that the evil spirits should move out to the trees and watch Pandora while they wait to pounce on someone else. It was decided the spirits should react to Pandora's actions by reacting with each other to show their feelings rather than speaking their thoughts aloud.

"How will the evil spirits feel when they see Hope?" the leader asked to guide the children to plan this scene.

"They will be mad to think she is out. I think they will cuff and strike out, and maybe fly away."

"If they fly away, it lets the story down. I think they should show that they are afraid when Hope flies near them for she is stronger than the worst trouble in the world, and they should know this."

The leader commented with enthusiasm, "An excellent dramatic idea! Let's choose Troubles who think they understand how to show this feeling."

Cast Is Chosen. A cast was chosen from volunteers. The leader and other members gathered together to be the audience. Two boys were chosen to operate the record player, and to be the stage managers to start and stop the play. The scene was played, evaluated, and replayed, with specific goals stressed—teamwork, reaction, and climax. After a second playing it was again evaluated. In the third playing tempo and strong characterizations were stressed.

Entire Story Created. In a similar way the opening scene was created with the characters of Epimethus and Mercury each being created in turn (Fig. 9.2). The first scene was created and replayed twice. Two casts were chosen to plan the story and create it from beginning to end, each in their own way. Each cast created for the enjoyment of the other and the leader as well as themselves.

CREATIVE DRAMATICS IN THE SCHOOL PROGRAM

In Language Arts. Children go to school to learn and to grow. One of a child's most important learnings lies in his ability to communicate with others. It is a constant challenge for teachers to guide children so they learn to express ideas clearly, correctly, and with enjoyment. Many teachers in the upper elementary school have found creative dramatics an outstanding group experience for fostering learning in language arts.

Creative dramatics by its nature is fun. It includes every child. It provides a friendly, festive, informal atmosphere which invites voluntary individual and group participation. When children gather together to create a play they find real purpose in planning, playing, and evaluating. Individuals communicate freely and clearly in situations that are close to life. Vocabularies increase with each new experience. Children are often motivated to read for information that

FIG. 9.2. "Mercury is mischievous, mysterious, and merry." (*School of Drama, University of Washington*)

contributes directly to the development of a play. Many different creative dramatics experiences broaden a child's interest. He gains a gradual feeling of security with his classmates for he has an increasing variety of interests to talk about. Creative dramatics contributes to personality growth, and every child gains feelings of success in the presence of his classmates.

It must be clearly understood that a teacher cannot expect creative dramatics to "just happen." This art demands careful guidance. It must always be a definitely organized and planned experience. A teacher must guide children in order to set the creative process in motion and to encourage strong participation from every child. A teacher must be alert to the many immediate opportunities that arise in creative dramatics to motivate individuals into strong pursuits in reading, writing, reporting, announcing, and in committee projects.

In Music. Like all arts, singing centers itself in feeling. Many fourth, fifth, and sixth grade teachers have correlated the arts of music, drama, and dance. They have guided children to create a short scene based on the setting and distinctive spirit of a song, guiding them to create and express entirely in pantomime to the rhythm and spirit of a song, while part of the group sings (Fig. 9.3). When-

FIG. 9.3. "With my banjo on my knee." (*Courtesy of Patricia Neal, music teacher, Lake Forest Park School, Shoreline Public Schools, Seattle, Washington*)

ever children create from songs, they increase their appreciation and enjoyment of music, and they sing with deeper feeling and understanding.

"Oh Susannah" and "Sweet Betsy from Pike" were created with

high enthusiasm and sung with noticeable spirit by a class of fifth graders (Fig. 9.4). Other songs that have motivated unusual creative

Fig. 9.4. "Whoa! Steady there with this wagon." (*Courtesy of Patricia Neal, music teacher, Lake Forest Park School, Shoreline Public Schools, Seattle, Washington*)

pantomimes include sea chanteys, mountain ballads, American folk ballads, Negro spirituals, songs of the lumber camps, songs of the railroad builders, and songs of the covered wagon days. A sixth grade class created beautiful pantomimes to "America the Beautiful" and Walt Whitman's "I Hear America Singing."

In Social Studies. Social studies provide a highway of adventure for children in the upper elementary grades. This is especially true when lively, active, enthusiastic boys and girls are guided to understand other peoples by "living their lives" in vivid creative dramatics experiences. Social studies are concerned with people—with people in the past who adventured, dreamed, struggled, and pioneered;

with people in the present who continue to adventure, dream, struggle, and pioneer. How much more meaningful social studies can become when children are guided to create and dramatize scenes from other lands and other eras! They learn with zest when they are guided to create scenes that depict history in the making. They participate with far stronger purpose when they are guided to create and dramatize than they do when they are guided to read and report, day in and day out, for nine months.

A fourth grade class studying the state of Washington decided it would be fun to create an imaginary television program to show distinctive features of the state in which they lived. They planned the program, patterning it after the television program "Wide Wide World." They chose for their theme, "Washington, U.S.A.—a Place to Work, a Place to Play." After creating several pantomimes together they organized into five committees, each representing a distinct geographical area of the state. Each group planned and created pantomimes to show both occupational and recreational opportunities of the area they represented. Considerable reading for specific information was done. Each group was concerned with the authenticity of its sharing.

The group representing the Puget Sound Basin created occupational pantomimes centering around fishing, lumbering, and airplane industries. The group representing the Olympic Peninsula shared thrilling recreational pantomimes by creating scenes showing the fun of mountain climbing, skiing, and hunting for elk and deer.

After several days of committee planning the program was put together. A master of ceremonies was chosen to coördinate the program and children within each group were chosen to be announcers and cameramen. Individuals spent considerable time in planning what they were to say to describe each occupation and recreational pantomime. When they recognized the need for a musical recording to weave the program together they called a class meeting to get suggestions for appropriate music.

The group was unanimous in its approval of the suggestion by one of the boys for the University of Washington Fight Song, "Bow Down to Washington." This boy was given the important position of musical director to weave the music into the show. Enthusiasm ran high. The children created their show with spirit and security. They invited other fourth grade classes and the principal to enjoy their "State of Washington Show."

Near the end of the school year the teacher gave an examination to see how much the children remembered about the social studies areas they had studied during the year. In every instance there was a noticeably high retention of facts and knowledge where children had experienced learning through the art of creative dramatics.

A fifth grade class studying the geographical areas of the Western Hemisphere became interested in the wild life on the continent of North America. In a creative television program this class created a show called "Animal Life of North America." Five different cameramen were stationed in five different natural settings from Alaska to Mexico. Each cameraman, in turn, filmed animal life including shots of American elk, black bear, buffalo, penguins, and marine life on the ocean floor. These 10-year-olds visited the zoo and did considerable research so they were able to create and emphasize unique animal rhythms and peculiar habits of each animal, bird, and fish.

Unified Learning Experiences. Teachers who understand the art of creative dramatics are enthusiastic about the way it motivates integrated learning experiences. One teacher guided a class of sixth graders into a memorable creative experience centering around life in

the medieval days. When this class started a study of the Eastern Hemisphere they began to investigate the early history of Europe and England and became vitally interested in the medieval period. Strong enthusiasm led to a desire to pantomime different aspects of medieval life throughout Europe and England. Pantomimes included developments in customs, cultures, explorations, science, inventions, and entertainment.

A fourth grade teacher motivated an exciting creative adventure into the hot dry lands for her group of 30 fourth graders.[8] This teacher was aware of the children's pleasant reaction to an unexpected hot day in the spring of the year. "How would you like to live in a land that is always hot and dry, just as it is here today?" Most of the children replied positively, but several expressed strong reasons why they wouldn't like hot dry weather all the time. The teacher told about a young boy named Akim who lived in a land that was hot all the time. She said, "I would like to tell you more about Akim, to see if anyone knows just where, in the world, he lives." She then shared a poem she had written called "Akim and I":

> Akim, oh Akim! May I go with you?
> For a year, or a day—matters not.
> Brothers we'll be, brothers we two.
> Travel desert lands, sandy and hot.
>
> We will take out the goats in the cool of the morn.
> We will rest in the heat of the day.
> We'll kneel for our prayers at the sound of the horn.
> Eat our dates as the sun sinks away.
>
> Here comes the wind! A sandstorm—beware!
> Lie down, stubborn camels! Make haste!

[8] Esther Carlson, Ronald School, Shoreline Public Schools, Seattle, Washington.

See the grit swirl! It hurls through the air.
Our turbans will cover our face.

The Night Raiders march; they have plundered and fled.
They have stolen our camels and guide.
The sheik orders, "Mount!"—By his flag we'll be led
Till the enemy's captured and tried.

And then, my brown brother, our camels we'll head
Toward oases when gone our supplies.
To market stalls heaped with grain for our bread;
To palm trees whose arms sweep the skies.

Where the water from wells springs out of the ground
Making gardens and bright flowers grow.
Where bazaars fill the street; hear the barterers sound!
Piles of baskets and jugs—row on row.

Good-by, my brown brother, my stay here is through
At your homeland I've taken a look.
Though never, no never, may all this come true.
I can visit you here in my book.[9]

"He lives somewhere in a desert," a boy quickly volunteered when the poem was finished.

"Could we play we go with this boy the way we do in creative dramatics?" asked another boy who was enthusiastic about creating. "Could we have camel trains and raiders?"

The teacher was enthusiastic too. "Yes," she said. "We'll join Akim as soon as we know on which desert he lives." She shared a large globe of the world. The children located several deserts. When they learned that Akim lived on the Arabian Desert they were eager to start on their trip. "How do you suppose we could get from Seattle to Baghdad?" the teacher asked.

[9] By permission of the poet, Esther Skonnord Carlson.

"If we flew we could get there sooner," one of the girls suggested.

"All right, we'll fly," said the teacher. "Maybe someone will figure out how long it takes to fly from Seattle to Baghdad."

"We'll have to find out what time zone they're in, too," said a boy who enjoyed arithmetic.

The children cleared a space for playing by pushing their desks out to the walls of the room. In a spirit of fun, each one became a transcontinental plane. The planes flew in three groups, and each one landed at an imaginary airport on the edge of the desert.

"Suppose we sit in the shade here at the airport, and take a good look at this interesting country. See what one thing interests you most about Arabia."

The children looked, but each one was a little uncertain in his looking. "I don't know what I am looking for," one of the girls said. She voiced the feeling of the group. This was the moment the teacher had been waiting for. "You know, I think we all feel just as you do, Rosemary. Perhaps we should learn about this hot dry country before we venture out on the desert with Akim. Suppose we decide what we would like to know about this land."

Together the children suggested specific ideas, and the teacher wrote on the airport blackboard "Hot Dry Lands—Things We Want to Know" (Fig. 9.5). After making a plan each child was given a map of the Arabian Desert. Soon the planes took off in high spirit for the Seattle-Tacoma Airport.

During the next week the children read a story about this region called "Two Little Shepherds." They saw films of "Life of Nomad People," "Life in the Sahara," "Ali and His Baby Camel," and "The Arabian Bazaar." The children located the hot dry lands and compared their location to other regions they had learned about before

FIG. 9.5. "An oasis bazaar for the Arabs is something like our supermarkets." (*Ronald School, Shoreline Public Schools, Seattle, Washington*)

They colored the maps, and located specific places and cities they would like to visit (Fig. 9.6).

During this time one of the children brought a newspaper clipping to school telling about King Saud's visit to the United States. The children became interested in the King's young son. They wondered what the boy might see in the United States which would seem strange to him. Each one wrote a short story about this. They wrote stories about what they would like to buy in a bazaar, and they drew pictures of the way they thought a desert looked. Each child made an individual booklet on The Hot Dry Lands.

When it was learned that a student from Baghdad was studying in this country it was arranged for him to visit the group so they could learn firsthand about Akim's country. The children gathered together in buzz session groups to decide on two questions which each group would ask the visitor. It was a memorable experience

FIG. 9.6.   "We learn from pictures, too." (*Ronald School, Shoreline Public Schools, Seattle, Washington*)

when they heard their guest tell about Arabian bazaars, the religion of his people, the customs of eating, sleeping, and living, and a camel train traveling across the desert.

On the following day, when the children wrote letters to thank the visitor for coming, each child recognized the need for making a list of the new words he had learned. Several children used the dictionary to look up words they had heard but did not know for certain how to spell.

After two weeks of intensive learning about Akim's country the children boarded imaginary airplanes again (Fig. 9.7). After arriving at the airport, they moved out into space and created a beautiful

Fɪɢ. 9.7. "Let's fly to Bagdad!" (*Ronald School, Shoreline Public Schools, Seattle, Washington*)

scene of the Arabian Desert. Each child became "the thing you would expect to find on the desert." They became palm trees, the hot warm sun, a sheik, Akim, and hungry goats. The teacher was impressed by the warm feeling which each child carried into his creation. She praised individuals, and together the children evaluated the scene.

In the next playing, the trees, goats, and people reacted to the warm hot sun as it rose high in the sky. The goats, the sheik, Akim, and the men found shelter under the palms. When the sun went down the sheik sounded his horn, and the men knelt for prayer (Fig. 9.8).

At the end of the first day in the desert, the children were ex-

FIG. 9.8. "We stop for daily prayers." (*Ronald School, Shoreline Public Schools, Seattle, Washington*)

cited. During the next four days they created camel trains, sandstorms, raiders, and a bazaar (Fig. 9.9). Creating a convincing camel offered real challenge to these 9-year-olds. Each one had an idea. They decided to work in groups of twos and threes to create a camel "just like a desert camel."

The most exciting scene for them was the raiding scene in the midst of a desert sandstorm. Part of the children created a fierce wind storm with convincing sound effects (Fig. 9.10). Camels and raiders reacted to the stinging biting sands and the forceful wind (Fig. 9.11). The scene reached a climactic height when the camels were goaded to their feet and led away by the desert plunderers. As

FIG. 9.9. "Buy mine! Buy my jar!" (*Ronald School, Shoreline Public Schools, Seattle, Washington*)

FIG. 9.10. "Come, my good beast, we must find shelter." (*Ronald School, Shoreline Public Schools, Seattle, Washington*)

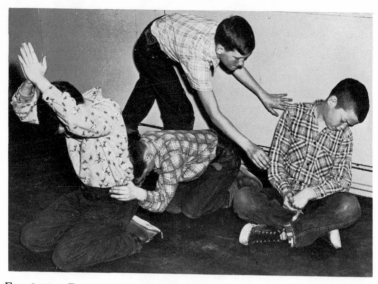

Fɪɢ. 9.11.   Desert raid! (*Ronald School, Shoreline Public Schools, Seattle, Washington*)

a camel was being forced away he nudged the sheik who had slept quietly through the storm. When the sheik awakened and found his camels were gone, he sounded his horn. He and his men made a hasty plan and started in pursuit of the raiders with determination.

When the children journeyed in their planes to Akim's desert land for the last time, they invited the principal and three visitors to join them on their trip. With strong spirit they taxied off in imaginary planes and took the visitors to the desert land which they had learned to know and enjoy.

CREATIVE DRAMATICS IN COMMUNITY PROGRAMS

In Sunday School and Church School. Sunday school teachers, church school leaders, rabbis, priests, and ministers have been earnest in their sharing of creative dramatics with children in religious education programs. One minister says:

Creative dramatics is one of the finest ways of teaching the truths of the Bible. The precepts taught in the sacred scriptures are just as applicable to the lives of children as they are to the lives of adults. The problem that arises in teaching children these truths lies in the didactic method.

Creative dramatics is a dramatic art which overcomes this problem. Many lessons for living are found in dramatic stories and incidents in the Bible. The teachings of Jesus and His matchless parables, the stories of the Hebrew writers, and the lives of many men and women in the Bible offer rich material for creative dramatics and for teaching children the truths of living.[10]

In Recreation Centers. Because creative dramatics is fun and holds such a high appeal for children, it has found its way into many leisuretime programs for children. Community centers which have shared this art include public libraries, museums, creative art centers, Boy and Girl Scout and Campfire Girl groups, summer camps, and park and playground programs. An outstanding creative dramatics leader says, "Recreation leaders have a job which they hold in common with parents and teachers—a job to release, to keep alive, to channel human energies: the physical, the mental, the emotional, the social, and the spiritual."[11] Creative dramatics is an art that provides a fun way for boys and girls to channel energies, ideas, and imaginations in exciting dramatic creations.

CONCLUSION

Children have "awe-fully big" lives to live. Creative dramatics is

[10] Reverend Russel W. Weberg, Resurrection Lutheran School, Redondo Beach, California.

[11] Agnes Haaga and Patricia Randles, *Supplementary Materials for Use in Creative Dramatics with Younger Children,* University of Washington Press, 1952

only one way in which a child's life may be enriched. It is an art that invites a child to play with other children. Every child wants friends, and almost every child wants to play out his dreams and ideas through dramatic pretendings. Creative dramatics offers group experiences which are rich in fun, excitement, problems, struggles, understanding, dreaming, creativity, beauty, and laughter.

Every day, for children all over the world, there is a sunrise. How fortunate is the child who sees in each new day the beauty and gloriousness of real life adventure. And how fortunate indeed, is the child who is guided in everyday living to laugh and to play with others, and to express himself in moments of high creation:

The Sunrise

The clouds are its curtain.

The fading moon tells it soon
  will be time for the performance.

The birds sing the overture
  for the awaiting audience.

Soon everything is still—
  The moon shines no more.

The birds have stopped their singing.

Everything is tense, the trees, the grass, the flowers,
  the animals, the wind. All watch silently.

Soon the pink curtain turns to a pale yellow.
  It begins to rise, slowly at first.

Then all of a sudden there is a burst of light,
  like music in the air!

The sun! The sun!
  Oh, 'tis the marvelous sun.

The day is beginning—
For the Sun has risen![12]

Questions and Activities

1. You have just arrived in Rainbow Valley where you are to share creative dramatics in a summer program for children. These children, like all children, have played at make-believe, but they have never heard of creative dramatics. Make a list of ideas that will appeal to children of 9, 10, and 11 during the summer months. List characteristics and needs that are basic to this age group. With these two lists before you sketch out an idea for a poster or dodger to invite, inform, and motivate boys and girls to attend a first meeting in creative dramatics.

2. The children of Rainbow Valley are enthusiastic about creative dramatics; the parents are curious. Write an open letter to parents to inform them concerning (a) what creative dramatics is, (b) values it may bring to children, and (c) reasons why this art is being included in school and community programs for children.

3. You have just received a contract to teach a fifth grade class at Rainbow Valley. The school superintendent has asked you to introduce creative dramatics in the fifth grade curriculum. Outline a brief overview plan from introducing the simplest form of dramatic expression to the point at which you believe the class will be ready to create plays from stories. In your outline indicate the five areas of drama you will include. List, tentatively, three specific suggestions for material in each area.

4. Read again King Cole's "The Meeting." List the variety of childhood interests revealed in this play. Categorize these interests into basic areas of interest that hold appeal for almost every group of nines, tens, and elevens. List the basic growth characteristics revealed through this play and categorize them into basic areas. Indicate the degree with which they compare to basic characteristics of most groups of children during these years.

12 By permission of the 11-year-old poet. Marilyn Cook.

5. Observe a creative dramatics class for children of 9, 10, and 11 years. Analyze this class from the viewpoint of group characteristics, needs, and interests. Use a semioutline form, and include comments, questions, and specific actions and interactions of children to strengthen your analysis and verify understanding.

6. List five ideas strong in appeal for nines, tens, and elevens which would lend themselves to dramatic expression in rhythmic movement. List five ideas strong in appeal to this age group which would lend themselves to dramatic expression in characterization. List five ideas which would appeal to this age group for developing into conflict situations—ideas different from those suggested in the text.

7. Select a short story you like which has been recommended for creative dramatics for nines, tens, and elevens; analyze the dramatic elements in this story. Make a plan of guidance for sharing this story with children.

8. Observe a creative dramatics class for children of 9, 10, and 11 years. Analyze this creative experience from the viewpoint of the creative process. Use a semioutline form to analyze the leader's role in (a) motivating children into a mood, (b) sharing a story, (c) guiding children to make a plan for each playing, (d) guiding children during playing, and (e) guiding children to praise and evaluate.

9. Select a social studies unit which is to be shared with a fourth, fifth, or sixth grade class. Study this unit of work. Prepare a list of specific ways in which creative dramatics may integrate this learning into a vital experience for children. Indicate titles, authors, and sources of specific material you suggest for integration.

10. Include in your creative dramatics material file one idea, one verse, and one story which you are convinced would appeal to nines, tens, and elevens. Recall incidents in your childhood which you experienced when you were nine, ten, and eleven. List several of these incidents, and include in your notebook.

Review Questions and Activities

1. Divide into buzz session groups. Discuss (a) what has been the

most meaningful creative dramatics experience in class participation, (b) in children's observation classes, and (c) in this text. Select two spokesmen from each group to report the findings to the group.

2. List at least seven examples from children's observations, from your class participation, and from your reading which you may cite to those individuals who don't know whether or not they favor creative dramatics or with those who are "on the fence" in respect to including creative dramatics in school and community programs for children.

3. Outline a two-page article you are going to write for an educational, recreational, religious, or parents' magazine. Select one of the following titles for your article.

"Creative Teaching in the Classroom."

"School Environment Comes to Life through Creative Dramatics."

"Creative Dramatics Contributes to Child Growth and Personality Development."

"Watch Your Child's Imagination Grow."

"The Play's the Thing Wherein Children Take Wing."

"Growing and Learning Through the Art of Creative Dramatics."

"Where There Is No Vision the People Perish."

"Social Studies—a Highway of Creative Adventure for Children."

"Creativity—the Cornerstone of Civilization."

"Arts Are a Necessity, Not a Luxury."

4. List the quotations at the beginning of each chapter. Plan to give a five-minute speech to class members in which you relate one quotation to creative dramatics.

5. Bring one excerpt from your creative dramatics notebook. Be prepared to share the essence of your contribution in one or two minutes so it motivates class members to a strong interest in this contribution.

6. What one "hyacinth" or awareness have you been most grateful for during the development of this class? Write out a brief reply.

7. If a school superintendent, recreational director, minister, or parent asked you to explain briefly the philosophy of the art of creative dramatics, how would you explain it in a way which would cause

him to understand the true significance of this art? Write out a brief explanation.

8. In a buzz session consider the following question: What do you believe is the best way for creative dramatics to find its place in the school curriculum along with music and the other arts?

9. Think about the community in which you live. How do you see a program of creative dramatics being launched for children in this community? Outline your plan.

10. Why do you think a child needs drama experiences? Discuss with class members.

APPENDIX A

Bibliography

The best books available in the field of creative dramatics and related creative arts have been included in this bibliography. Others have been selected to stimulate imagination and to provide a good representative background in a study of the art of drama. Books in children's literature, education, and religious education have been included because of background information, philosophies, or specific suggestions and techniques.

This is a selective rather than comprehensive list of books for the creative dramatics leader. The bibliography has been classified to correspond with the chapter discussions. It should be understood that categories are flexible. For instance, books listed under education may serve to stimulate imagination and inspire creative leadership.

Creative Dramatics and Related Arts for Children

Andrews, Gladys, *Creative Rhythmic Movement for Children*, Prentice-Hall, Inc., 1954.

Brown, Corrine, *Creative Drama in the Lower School*, Appleton-Century-Crofts, Inc., 1929.

Burger, Isabel B., *Creative Play Acting*, A. S. Barnes and Company, 1950.

Cole, Natalie R., *The Arts in the Classroom*, The John Day Company, Inc., 1942.

Dixon, C. Madeleine, *The Power of the Dance*, The John Day Company, Inc., 1939.

Durland, Frances Caldwell, *Creative Dramatics for Children*, The Antioch Press, 1952.

Fitzgerald, Burdette S., *Let's Act the Story*, Fearon Publishers, 1957.

Gillies, Emily P., "Crosses and Knives," *Childhood Education*, May, 1946, pp. 435 ff.; April, 1947, pp. 382 ff.

Gillies, Emily P., "Therapy Dramatics for the Public Schoolroom," *The Nervous Child*, July, 1948, pp. 328 ff.

Haaga, Agnes, and Randles, Patricia, *Supplementary Materials for Use in Creative Dramatics with Younger Children*, University of Washington Press, 1952.

Lease, Ruth, and Siks, Geraldine Brain, *Creative Dramatics in Home, School, and Community*, Harper & Brothers, 1952.

Merrill, John, and Fleming, Martha, *Play-Making and Plays*, The Macmillan Company, 1930.

Slade, Peter, *Child Drama*, University of London Press, Ltd., 1954.

Ward, Winifred, *Creative Dramatics*, Appleton-Century-Crofts, Inc., 1930.

Ward, Winifred, *Playmaking with Children*, 2d ed., Appleton-Century-Crofts, Inc., 1957.

Creative Imagination

Cox, Doris E., and Weismann, Barbara W., *Creative Hands*, John Wiley & Sons, Inc., 1945.

Forbes, R. J., *Man the Maker*, Henry Schuman, Inc., Publishers, 1950.

Frazer, Sir James George, *The Golden Bough*, The Macmillan Company, 1951.

Hartman, Gertrude, and Shumaker, Ann (eds.), Progressive Education Association, *Creative Expression*, The John Day Company, Inc., 1932.

Lowenfeld, Viktor, *The Nature of Creative Activity*, Harcourt, Brace and Company, Inc., 1939.

Lowenfeld, Viktor, *Creative and Mental Growth*, The Macmillan Company, 1947.

Mearns, Hughes, *Creative Youth*, Doubleday & Company, Inc., 1928.

Mearns, Hughes, *Creative Power*, Doubleday & Company, Inc., 1929.

Mearns, Hughes, *The Creative Adult*, Doubleday & Company, Inc., 1940.

Mirsky, Jeannette, and Nevins, Allan, *The World of Eli Whitney*, The Macmillan Company, 1952.

Musselman, Morris McNeil, *Wheels in His Head*, McGraw-Hill Book Company, Inc., 1945.

Osborn, Alex F., *Applied Imagination*, Charles Scribner's Sons, 1953.

Osborn, Alex F., *Your Creative Power*, Charles Scribner's Sons, 1948.

Osborn, Alex F., *Wake Up Your Mind*, Charles Scribner's Sons, 1952.

Poston, Richard W., *Small Town Renaissance*, Harper & Brothers, 1950.

Woollcott, Alexander, *The Story of Irving Berlin*, G. P. Putnam's Sons, 1925.

The Art of Drama

Chambers, E. K., *The Elizabethan Stage*, 4 vols., Oxford University Press, 1923.

Chekov, Michael, *To the Actor*, Harper & Brothers, 1953.

Cheney, Sheldon, *The Theatre: 3000 Years of Drama, Acting, and Stagecraft*, Longmans, Green & Co., Inc., 1930

Chorpenning, Charlotte B., *Twenty-One Years with Children's Theatre*, The Children's Theatre Press, 1954.

Clark, Barrett H., and Freedley, George (eds.), *A History of Modern Drama*, Appleton-Century-Crofts, Inc., 1947.

Clark, William George, and Wright, Willam Aldis (eds.), *The Complete Works of William Shakespeare*, Grosset & Dunlap, Inc., 1911.

Dean, Alexander, *Fundamentals of Play Directing*, Farrar & Rinehart, Inc., 1941.

Dolman, John, *The Art of Acting*, Harper & Brothers, 1949.

Flickinger, Roy C., *The Greek Theatre and Its Drama*, University of Chicago Press, 1918.

Freedley, George, and Reeves, John A., *A History of the Theatre*, Crown Publishers, Inc., 1941.

Gassner, John, *Producing the Play*, The Dryden Press, Inc., 1941.

Hughes, Glenn, *The Story of the Theatre*, Samuel French, Inc., 1928.

Huizinga, Johan, *Homo Ludens: A Study of the Play Element in Culture*, The Beacon Press, 1950.

Jones, Robert Edmond, *The Dramatic Imagination*, Theatre Arts Books, 1941.

Nicoll, Allardyce, *The Development of the Theatre*, 3d rev. ed., Harcourt, Brace and Company, Inc., 1946.

Ommanney, Katherine A., and Ommanney, Pierce C., *The Stage and the School*, 2d rev. ed., McGraw-Hill Book Company, Inc., 1950.

Stanislavski, Constantin, *An Actor Prepares*, Theatre Arts Books, 1952.

Ward, Winifred, *Theatre for Children*, rev. ed., The Children's Theatre Press, 1950.

Whiting, Frank M., *An Introduction to the Theatre*, Harper & Brothers, 1954.

Creative Leader

Barrie, J. M., "Peter Pan," *The Plays of J. M. Barrie*, Charles Scribner's Sons, 1935.

Carroll, Lewis (pseud. of Dodgson, Charles Lutwidge), *Alice's Adventures in Wonderland*, and *Through the Looking Glass*, in 1 vol., Heritage Press, 1944.

Emerson, Ralph Waldo, *The Complete Essays and Other Writings of Ralph Waldo Emerson*, Random House, Inc., 1940.

Grahame, Kenneth, *The Wind in the Willows*, Charles Scribner's Sons, 1908.

Highet, Gilbert, *The Art of Teaching*, Alfred A. Knopf, Inc., 1950.

Hughes, Langston, *The First Book of Rhythms*, Franklin Watts, Inc., 1954.

Liebman, Joshua Loth, *Peace of Mind*, Simon and Schuster, Inc., 1946.

Lindberg, Anne Morrow, *Gift from the Sea*, Pantheon Books, Inc., 1955.

Milne, A. A., *Winnie-the-Pooh*, E. P. Dutton & Co., Inc., 1926.

Pratt, Caroline, *I Learn from Children*, Simon and Schuster, Inc., 1948.

Sawyer, Ruth, *The Way of the Storyteller*, The Viking Press, Inc., 1947.

Shedlock, Marie L., *The Art of the Story-Teller*, rev. ed., Appleton-Century-Crofts, Inc., 1936.

Stephens, James, *The Crock of Gold*, The Macmillan Company, 1936.

Thompson, Francis, *The Works of Francis Thompson*, Vol. III: Prose, Burns, Oates & Washburne Ltd., 1913.

Thoreau, Henry D., *Walden*, Houghton Mifflin Company, 1929.

Travers, P. L., *Mary Poppins*, Reynal & Hitchcock, Inc., 1934.

Twain, Mark (pseud. of Clemens, Samuel), *The Adventures of Huckleberry Finn*, Heritage Press, 1944.

Walton, Izaak, *The Complete Angler*, T. N. Foulis, Ltd., 1925.

Weber, Julia, *My Country School Diary*, Harper & Brothers, 1946.

Weill, Blanche C., *Through Children's Eyes*, Island Workshop Press, 1940.

Yutang, Lin, *The Importance of Living*, The John Day Company, Inc., 1937.

Children's Literature

Andersen, Hans Christian, *Fairy Tales*, Coward-McCann, Inc., 1933.

Arbuthnot, May H., *Children and Books*, rev. ed., Scott, Foresman and Company, 1957.

Arbuthnot, May H. (compiler), *The Arbuthnot Anthology*, Scott, Foresman and Company, 1954.

Becker, May L., *Adventures in Reading*, rev. ed., J. B. Lippincott, 1946.

Curry, Charles, and Clippinger, Erle Elsworth, *Children's Literature*, Rand McNally & Company, 1920.

Duff, Annis, *Bequest of Wings*, The Viking Press, Inc., 1940.

Eaton, Anne T., *Reading with Children*, The Viking Press, Inc., 1940.

Frank, Josette, *Your Child's Reading Today*, Doubleday & Company, Inc., 1954.

Grimm's Fairy Tales, Pantheon Books, Inc., 1944.

Hartman, Gertrude, *Medieval Days and Ways*, The Macmillan Company, 1937.

Hazard, Paul, *Books, Children and Men,* 2d ed., The Horn Book, 1947.

Hollowell, Lillian (ed.), *A Book of Children's Literature,* 2d ed., Farrar & Rinehart, Inc., 1950.

Huber, Miriam B., *Story and Verse for Children,* The Macmillan Company, 1940.

Johnson, Edna, Scott, Carrie E., and Sickels, Evelyn R. (compilers), *Anthology of Children's Literature,* 2d ed., Houghton Mifflin Company, 1948.

Moore, Anne C., *My Roads to Childhood,* Doubleday & Company, Inc., 1939.

The Tenggren Mother Goose, illustrated by Gustaf Tenggren, Little, Brown & Company, 1940.

Ward, Winifred, *Stories to Dramatize,* The Children's Theatre Press, 1952.

Creative Dramatics in Education

American Association of School Administrators, *Educating for American Citizenship,* Thirty-Second Yearbook, National Education Association, 1954.

Applegate, Mauree, *Everybody's Business—Our Children,* Row, Peterson & Company, 1952.

Association for Supervision and Curriculum Development, *Organizing the Elementary School for Living and Learning,* 1947 Yearbook, National Education Association, 1947.

Baruch, Dorothy, *New Ways in Discipline,* McGraw-Hill Book Company, Inc., 1949.

D'Amico, Victor E., *Creative Teaching in Art,* rev. ed., International Textbook Company, 1953.

Dewey, John, *Art As Experience,* Minton, Balch & Co., 1934.

Dewey, John, *Experience and Education,* The Macmillan Company, 1938.

Dewey, John, *Art and Education,* 2d ed., The Barnes Foundation Press, 1947.

Dixon, Clarice M., *High, Wide, and Deep,* The John Day Company, Inc., 1938.

Gesell, Arnold, and Ilg, Frances L., *Infant and Child in the Culture of Today,* Harper & Brothers, 1943.

Gesell, Arnold, and Ilg, Frances L., *The Child from Five to Ten,* Harper & Brothers, 1946.

Gesell, Arnold, Ilg, Frances L., and Ames, Louise Bates, *Youth: The Years from Ten to Sixteen,* Harper & Brothers, 1956.

Havighurst, Robert J., *Developmental Tasks and Education,* 2d ed., Longmans, Green and Co., Inc., 1952.

Kelley, Earl C., *Education and the Nature of Man,* Harper & Brothers, 1952.

Klausmeier, Herbert J., Dresden, Katherine, Davis, Helen C., and Wittich, Walter Arno, *Teaching in the Elementary School,* Harper & Brothers, 1956.

Lee, J. Murray, and Lee, Doris M., *The Child and His Curriculum,* 2d ed., Appleton-Century-Crofts, Inc., 1950.

Lowenfeld, Viktor, *Your Child and His Art,* The Macmillan Company, 1954.

National Society for the Study of Education, *Early Childhood Education,* Forty-Sixth Yearbook, Part II, University of Chicago Press, 1947.

Ogilvie, Mardel, *Speech in the Elementary School,* McGraw-Hill Book Company, Inc., 1954.

Rasmussen, Carrie, *Speech Methods in the Elementary School,* The Ronald Press Company, 1949.

Shane, Harold G. (ed.), *The American Elementary School,* Thirteenth Yearbook of the John Dewey Society, Harper & Brothers, 1953.

Sheehy, Emma D., *Fives and Sixes Go to School,* Henry Holt and Company, Inc., 1954.

The Laura Zirbes Recordings on Teaching and Learning, Teaching Aids Laboratory, Ohio State University, 1957.

Van Riper, Charles, and Butler, Katharine G., *Speech in the Elementary Classroom,* Harper & Brothers, 1955.

Ward, Muriel, *Young Minds Need Something to Grow On,* Row, Peterson & Company, 1957.

Creative Dramatics in Religious Education

Doane, Pelagie, *A Small Child's Bible,* Oxford University Press, 1946.

Eberling, Georgia Moore, *When Jesus Was a Little Boy,* Children's Press, Inc., 1954.

Fitch, Florence Mary, *A Book About God,* Lothrop, Lee, & Shepard Co., 1954.

Hill, Dorothy LaCroix, *Working with Juniors at Church,* Abingdon Press, 1955.

Keiser, Armilda B., *Here's How and When,* Friendship Press, 1952.

Ligon, Ernest M., *A Greater Generation,* The Macmillan Company, 1948.

Manwell, Elizabeth M., and Fahs, Sophia L., *Consider the Children— How They Grow,* The Beacon Press, 1946.

Morsch, Vivian Sharp, *The Use of Music in Christian Education,* The Westminster Press, 1956.

Petersham, Maud, and Petersham, Miska, illustrators, *The Christ Child, as Told by Matthew and Luke,* Doubleday & Company, Inc., 1931.

Roorbach, Rosemary K., *Religion in the Kindergarten,* Harper & Brothers, 1949.

Sayer, Dorothy, *The Mind of the Maker,* Harcourt, Brace and Company, Inc., 1941.

Shields, Elizabeth McE., *Guiding Kindergarten Children in the Church School,* rev. ed., John Knox Press, 1955.

Smither, Ethel L., *The Use of the Bible with Children,* Abingdon Press, 1937.

Smither, Ethel L., *Primary Children Learn At Church,* Abingdon Press, 1944.

The Holy Bible, King James Version, John Dickson Publishing Company, 1946.

Material for Creative Dramatics

The following suggestions of poetry, songs, stories, and ideas have been selected to correspond with the discussion of material in each of the three age level chapters. Material has been categorized to meet children's basic interests and needs, and to correlate with school curricula. It should be understood that suggestions listed under *Material for Little Children* may appeal and satisfy children who are seven and eight years old and older. Older children in beginning groups may enjoy creating from material which has been suggested for younger children.

This is a selective list. Only material which has been tested and proved worthy for creative dramatics has been included. It is hoped that these suggestions will motivate the leader to search for new ideas and dramatic literature which appeal to specific groups of children.

Numbers after each suggestion refer to their sources, as listed in the *Bibliography of Material* immediately following.

Material for Little Children

RHYTHMIC MOVEMENT AND PANTOMIME

FUN THE YEAR ROUND

FALL

"When the Sun Shines" (53)

Children enjoy walking, running, rolling, jumping, swinging, and resting to the variety of rhythms in this recording. Children often think of many different ways to play on a sunshiny day.

"The Swing," by Robert Louis Stevenson (*11*) (*40*) (*47*)

Swinging in a make-believe swing is almost as much fun as swinging in a real one. "Swing in the swing you like best of all" generally motivates pantomimes of swinging in park swings, rope swings, chain swings, swings with one rope, tire-swings, and swinging on tree branches. Children like to pump high and "look far and wide" to see one special thing to share when the swings come to a rest.

"The Parade" (*2*)

It's fun to parade to the gay rhythm of this song, particularly to march in time, blow a horn, and beat a drum.

"Happiness," by A. A. Milne (*11*) (*47*)

On a rainy day children enjoy pretending to dress like John with "great big waterproof boots, mackintoshes, and hats." They enjoy walking to the rain-drop rhythm of this verse, and of thinking of other delightful things to do in the rain such as splashing in rain puddles, skipping, hopping, throwing rocks, wading in puddles, and sailing sticks and leaves.

"The Rain," by an Unknown Author (*11*) (*47*)

It is fun to go walking in the rain under an umbrella too.

"Down, Down," by Eleanor Farjeon (*11*) (*42*) (*47*)

On an autumn day children like to pretend they are walking and scrunching in leaves. After this initial play other ideas are generally suggested such as rolling in leaves, throwing leaves into the air, running after dancing leaves, raking leaves, and building a leaf bonfire.

A Halloween Parade

When Halloween is in the air little children enjoy tiptoeing with make-believe jack-o'-lanterns to the homes of other children for the fun of scaring others into "trick and treating."

Preparing for Thanksgiving

"What do you do to help mother get ready for Thanksgiving Day?"

brings a variety of pantomimes. Children think of ideas such as making a cake, shining apples, chasing a turkey, driving to grandmother's house, picking flowers, gathering around the table, singing and sharing Thanksgiving thoughts and prayers.

"The Mulberry Bush" (2)

Little children delight in playing this traditional pantomime game and in thinking of a variety of ways to work and play on each of the days of the week.

WINTER

A Snowy Day

A first snowfall motivates a variety of fun for dramatic play such as throwing snowballs, building a snowman or snow lady, sliding, sledding, making angels and other snow designs.

"Galoshes," by Rhoda Bacmeister (11) (47)

It's fun to pretend that everyone has new galoshes to "make splishes and sploshes" when they join Susie to walk in the rain.

"Jingle Bells" (2)

A favorite song for singing, especially when going for a gay sleigh ride.

"The Christmas Pudding," by an Unknown Author (11) (47)

Little children enjoy making a make-believe pudding, particularly when they are guided to stir in a Christmas wish to make someone happy. Pantomimes generally include mixing, stirring, baking, decorating, and eating pudding.

Bringing In a Christmas Tree

Dramatic play is exciting when little children decide where to get the Christmas tree. Some groups ride in a car to the forest or to a Christmas tree lot while others go for a sleigh ride to the forest. Trimming the tree is equally exciting when each child decorates it with "one thing to make it beautiful."

Finding Christmas Presents

It is always fun when each child finds one present under a Christ-

mas tree, and shows in pantomime what he has found to make him happy.

"Jack Be Nimble," by Mother Goose (*11*) (*15*) (*40*) (*47*)

A pretend candle stick may be short or tall. It is fun for children to take turns jumping over a candle stick especially when they decide why they, like Jack, are jumping. Some groups jump because they are happy it is "Billy's birthday," and others have jumped because "the snowflakes came."

SPRING

It's a Warm Spring Day.

"What would you like to do best of all on this first warm day of spring?" This question generally motivates a panorama of movement in such pleasant activities as shooting marbles, riding tricycles, roller-skating, swinging, riding imaginary ponies, see-sawing at the park, and planting a garden.

"New Shoes," by Alice Wilkins (*11*) (*42*) (*47*)

A child always enjoys going to an imaginary shoe shop to buy the kind of shoes he likes best. Each child enjoys showing how his new shoes make him feel. Popular new shoes include cowboy boots, hiking boots, ballet slippers, dancing slippers, squeaking oxfords, patrol boots, and bedroom slippers.

"Hippity-Hop To The Barber Shop," by Mother Goose (*11*) (*47*)

When each child is given a make-believe penny he hippity-hops with joy to a special Barber Shop to spend it.

On Easter Day in the Morning

"How might we have a happy Easter service?" generally leads little children to action and expression which is strong in feeling and creativity.

SUMMER

"Merry-Go-Round," by Dorothy Baruch (*11*) (*47*)

To the gay rhythm of merry-go-round music children enjoy riding up and down and around and around. After one active ride children generally have many suggestions such as including a merry-go-round man, riding on a motor boat, sliding down a slide, riding in a little train or on an airplane.

"At the Sea-Side," by Robert Louis Stevenson (11) (40) (42) (47)

The seaside brings delightful pantomimes when children are motivated to feel the wet sand and dig with make-believe spades and shovels. Ideas generally include building sand hills and rivers for boats, running through waves, wading out together into deep water, finding shells and surprises, digging for clams, and listening to seaside sounds.

"Mud," by Polly Boyden (11) (47)

It's gay fun to pretend to walk in mud "All squishy-squash between the toes." After this experience children generally share other pleasant sensory pleasures.

Going Camping:

Camping trips with families generally motivate strong expression in hiking, building a fire, cooking, eating, fishing, and exploring to "find one new thing" in the forest.

CHARACTERIZATION

ANIMALS

"Jump or Jiggle," by Evelyn Beyer (11) (47)

It is exciting for a child to discover that each animal has his own unique way of moving such as "Frogs jump, caterpillars hump. . . . Lions stalk, but—I walk."

"Mrs. Peck Pigeon," by Eleanor Farjeon (11) (42) (47)

Children who have seen and enjoyed pigeons delight in becoming Mrs. Peck Pigeon especially when this verse is chanted.

"The Seals," by Dorothy Aldis (11) (47)

On a circus day this verse never fails to motivate unusual ideas for expression when children become lively seals "flapping flips," and "bouncing balls on nosey tips."

"Fuzzy, Wuzzy, Creepy, Crawly," by Lillian Schultz Vanada (*11*) (*47*)

Little children find special wonder in being crawling caterpillars who change into beautiful butterflies.

"Over in the Meadow" (*2*)

There's special joy when mother animals or insects in the meadow teach their young. Mother Toadie teaches her little toadie to hop while all the meadow watches. Then Mother Bird teaches her little bluebirds to fly while the toads find satisfaction in watching.

"Rabbits," by Dorothy Baruch (*11*) (*47*)

A lovely surprise is experienced when a child follows two "humping, hopping" rabbits and discovers a special "something shivering under the leaves." Children enjoy playing this over and over again.

"Little Charlie Chipmunk," by Helen Cowles Le Cron (*11*) (*47*)

A favorite verse for playing when children are familiar with chipmunks. Little children generally decide that Charlie has several brothers and sisters and mother chipmunk takes them to visit their wise uncle or grandfather.

"The Animal Story," by Rachel Field (*11*) (*47*)

To visit an animal store with one hundred imaginary dollars is an experience most children ask to play again and again. A child finds enjoyment in buying, but most children prefer to create "the animal you would like best to buy in an animal store."

WONDERS IN THE WORLD

"Baby Seeds" (*2*)

The rhythm of this song provides gentle swinging for a milkweed cradle filled with baby seeds cuddled together "snug and warm." A special feeling is experienced when Mr. Wind comes with his helpers to send the baby seeds flying to a "special place" out in the world where each one will sleep during the winter.

"Fly Away, Fly Away," by Christina Rossetti (42)

On a cold autumn day little children empathize with the birds and outdoor creatures. Children find strong expression when they become swallows flying "away over the sea."

"Twinkle, Twinkle, Little Star," by Jane Taylor (11) (47)

It is a special experience to become a twinkling star high up in the nighttime sky. Children enjoy sharing one reason why they are twinkling.

"First Snow," by Marie Louise Allen (11) (47)

A child experiences a quiet and wonderful feeling when he creates a snowflake and when he becomes bushes or trees that look like snowy popcorn balls.

"Who Has Seen the Wind?" by Christina Rossetti (11) (42) (47)

A windy day offers strong motivation for expression in becoming the wind and trees. This verse never fails to arouse beauty and wonder.

"Windy Wash Day," by Dorothy Aldis (11) (47)

There is delightful fun in creating simple things like clothes on the line, especially when the wind causes them to skip, and trip, and dance.

"A Kite," by an Unknown Author (11) (47)

When kites are flying a little child identifies with the freedom of movement and enjoys becoming a kite being blown high in the sky.

SPECIAL PEOPLE

"Brownies and Witches" (2)

When Halloween is in the air witches and brownies come lurking out of secret places to scare folks who are about. The rhythm of this song heightens the mysterious mood which motivates strong expression and fun.

"Ten Little Indians" (2)

This old song interests almost every group of little children. They like to decide where the Indians are when they appear so suddenly, and where they go when they disappear as quietly and suddenly as they have come.

"My Policeman," by Rose Fyleman (11) (47)

A traffic scene with cars, people, and special policeman is always exciting. It requires organization as carefully planned as it is in a busy city intersection.

THINGS-THAT-GO

"Boats," by Rowena Bennett (11) (47)

Steamboats, sailboats, and speed boats each require a different rhythm and feeling as they move out of the harbor. Children like to decide where so many boats are going—perhaps to a speed boat race, a parade, or a fishing derby.

"Stop-Go," by Dorothy Baruch (11) (47)

It is satisfying to many children when they are guided to become an automobile, a truck, a motorcycle, or a big trailer. It is even more fun when a policeman directs traffic and each vehicle knows where and why he is going.

"Taking Off," by Mary McB. Green (11) (47)

There is always a reason when many airplanes taxi "down the field/And head into the breeze." Young pilots are eager to decide, and then to soar into the sky.

"Trains," by James S. Tippett (11) (42) (47)

The rhythm of this verse fairly invites children to become trains chugging down a track. A child enjoys becoming a freight car to decide what he will carry from one place to another.

BEGINNING CONFLICTS

"Little Miss Muffett," by Mother Goose (11) (40) (47)

Being Miss Muffetts and spiders to frighten her provides exciting drama for little children. Leaders find it wise to guide children to identify with a curious spider who crawls silently in a way which really surprises a little girl.

"Little Bo Peep," by Mother Goose (11) (40) (47)

Animals, and especially sheep, interest most children. Boys and girls find delight in becoming sheep who wander away while Bo Peep is sleeping. A joyous celebration generally occurs when the sheep are found again.

"Little Boy Blue," by Mother Goose (11) (40) (47)

A boy who "goes to sleep on the job," a herd of hungry cows, a flock of hungry sheep, and an angry farmer provide strong characterizations in this conflict. Children should be guided to understand how hungry animals feel when they find such fine fresh food. When feeling is strong animals are convincing rather than noisy.

"The North Wind Doth Blow," by Mother Goose (15) (40)

A fierce north wind, snowflakes, and hungry robins experience a situation which provides a brief but touching drama.

"Humpty Dumpty," by Mother Goose (11) (15) (40) (47)

Little children enjoy the simplicity and fun of this "tragedy." They like to decide why Humpty Dumpty fell from the wall, but they find even more satisfaction in becoming king's horses and king's men who gallop or march to the "scene of the accident," and try to help.

"Seagull and the Fish," by Elizabeth Coatsworth (11) (47)

Excitement always results when children become seagulls flying and swooping after families of fish. It is always more fun when there are "near escapes."

"The Little Turtle," by Vachel Lindsay (11) (42) (47)

This is a favorite conflict for little children. They delight in becoming a turtle to snap at a family of mosquitoes, a family of fleas, and a family of minnows. It is always fun when the turtle catches one of his prey, but it is even more fun when he fails to catch a boy or girl.

"The Snow Man," by an Untraced Author (*39*)

Little children delight in creating from this verse and ask to play it again and again. The appeal comes in being snowmen who are blown into a warm house by the cold North Wind. A warm fire soon melts the snowmen and they become "puddles on the floor."

STORIES TO BEGIN ON

A Book About God (*12*)

The beauty and simplicity of this colorful picture book motivate a variety of characterizations which cause little children to understand that the sun, moon, stars, and the beauties of the outdoor world are like God for He made them.

The Boy and the Billy Goats (A Song Story) (*2*)

Children always enjoy playing this story after they learn the song. Drama centers around the conflict a young boy experiences when he goes to sleep and his billy goats get into a corn patch. A rabbit and fox try to help him get the goats, but it is the gay honey bee who finally finds a way.

Goldilocks and the Three Bears (*15*) (*39*) (*46*)

Most children hear this thrilling story for the first time when they are three or four years old, but it is quite a different experience to play it. Beginning groups prefer to play the story over and over using only the characters of Goldilocks and the Three Bears in the conflict scene. Children with more experience may wish to add forest creatures such as birds, butterflies, and rabbits to warn Goldilocks not to enter the bear's house, and to react as they watch her actions through the windows.

The Lion and the Mouse (*15*) (*46*)

Drama is strong in this story, particularly when the lion wakes and claps his paw over the mouse. Most children prefer to have a family of mice venture near the sleeping lion and to have at least two mice get caught.

Little Black Sambo (39) (40)

Almost every child dreams of finding himself in a heroic position where he works his way out of danger, but Little Black Sambo's experience is not a dream. It is real. Beginning groups prefer to create only the Jungle Scene where Black Sambo encounters the tigers, finds a way to save himself from each one, witnesses the striking tiger fight, and returns home triumphantly. Children with more experience prefer to play this story in three scenes, including the Home Scene where Sambo receives his presents, The Jungle Scene, and the Homecoming Scene where Black Sambo, Black Mumbo, and Black Jumbo celebrate by eating pancakes.

The Peddler and His Caps (4) (39)

This is a favorite for beginning groups when the action is limited to the Monkey Scene. Children delight in being monkeys to find new caps, to dance, to hide when the peddler awakens, and to mimic the actions of the worried peddler. In a large group children like to take turns being a monkey and a tall palm tree for a monkey to hide behind.

The Tale of Peter Rabbit (15) (39)

One of the best stories for beginning groups with exciting drama and a happy ending. Characterizations are generally limited to Peter Rabbits and Mr. McGregor for first playings. An occasional group finds enjoyment in being rows of cabbages, lettuce, and radish plants to provide interference for the rabbit chase. Children with considerable experience enjoy creating individualized characters such as birds, cats, and scarecrows to react to Peter's predicament. Some groups like to create the opening scene as well as the final scene, but most groups prefer to play the Chase Scene again and again for it is here that excitement and emotion are strong.

The Three Billy Goats Gruff (15) (39) (40) (46)

A favorite with almost every group. Children find strong sympathy for the hungry goats who are determined to overcome the problem by "putting an end to the old troll." Beginning groups prefer to create the conflict scene over and over again. Children with more experience enjoy creating other hungry goat families to warn and react to the dangerous actions of the three Billy Goats Gruff.

Teeny Tiny (15) (39) (46)

Children thoroughly enjoy this story when played near Halloween. Most groups decide that the teeny tiny scarecrows in all the nearby gardens join the teeny tiny scarecrow when she goes to ask the teeny tiny woman to return the teeny tiny bonnet and teeny tiny dress which she took for herself. Children generally have unusual ideas about the way scarecrows walk, talk, and feel in this situation.

When Jesus Was a Little Boy (51)

A variety of splendid opportunities for dramatic play are provided here when children experience the activities of home, outdoor fun, special days, camel trains at night and market days.

Why the Bear is Stumpy Tailed (11) (15) (40)

A fun story for a beginning group to play during the winter. A family of bears and a family of sly foxes enjoy a conflict on a cold wintry day. The story is short and humorous, and invites unusual discussion.

LONGER STORIES

Andy and the Lion (8)

A delightful version of the old tale of Androcles and the lion. This story provides a strong conflict between Andy and the lion ending in a gay circus parade in which Andy receives a medal for bravery.

Another Day (10)

It's a special day when children become individualized forest animals "having a confab." Old Elephant is in charge of having each animal show what he can do, but he asks a little boy to blow a horn to help him get the confab started. Giraffe, lion, monkeys, bears, hippopotamus, duck, mouse, snake, and elephant show what they can do, but the boy is the only one who can do something that every animal wishes he could do.

Ask Mr. Bear (*39*) (*40*)

A favorite story for little children who are ready to create dialogue. The conflict centers around Danny's desire to give his mother a birthday present. His barnyard friends offer to help, but Danny realizes his mother has every present they suggest. The surprise ending holds high suspense. Children generally play this story by increasing the animal characters to two of each so children may create in pairs.

The Big Turnip (*38*)

A delightful story which appeals to almost every group when children are ready to create individualized characters. The problem of pulling the big turnip from the garden offers strong suspense to the little old man, the little old woman, Katrinka, the dog, the cat, and even the mouse. The surprise ending brings unexpected fun.

Brownies—Hush! (*13*)

A delightful and simplified version of the old tale, "The Elves and the Shoemaker."

Chee-Chee and Keeko (*14*)

An exciting plot centers around the conflict which is experienced by an Indian boy and Chee Chee, his bird scout. Papa Moose and his son Little Moose are involved in the forest excitement.

The Christ Child (*16*)

A beautiful picture story of the Nativity which motivates almost every group of children to create this story with reverence, beauty, and understanding.

Henny-Penny (*15*) Chicken Licken (*46*)

A delightfully humorous story in which Cocky-locky, Ducky-daddles, Goosey-poosey, Turkey-lurkey join Henny-penny as they hurry to tell the king that the "sky's a-falling." A feeling of fear enters the story with the entrance of sly Foxy-woxy who outwits his farmyard friends except for Cocky-locky and Henny-penny.

Little Duckling Tries His Voice (*49*)

A humorous but touching story of a little duck who tries to talk like a kitty, a dog, a bird, and a cow until he realizes that his mother has the most beautiful voice in all the world, and he finds that he too can talk like her.

The Little Engine That Could (30)

Children enjoy creating little engines, haughty engines, tired engines, selfish engines, and little engines who help. Characterizations are strong when children identify with the little engine and his problem on Christmas eve. Some children prefer to create Christmas toys who help to flag the engines as they come down the track.

The Little Pink Rose (39)

A lovely story for springtime. The beauty and wonder which a child experiences when he discovers the first flower of spring is experienced by most children when they create from this story. Children enjoy creating little pink rosebuds, rain, and sunshine. Experienced groups enjoy creating "beautiful sights" for Rosebud to see when she "pokes her head through the garden" to see the world.

The Little Red Hen (39) (46)

Another good story for children to play in the spring. When they are ready to create dialogue as well as action this is always a favorite. Children identify strongly with little Red Hen and with the animals who refuse to help her.

Make Way For Ducklings (32)

Children find strong enjoyment in creating the dramatic scene where Mrs. Mallard takes her baby ducks to the park. The traffic scene with Michael the policeman calling police cars is always exciting. Children play in three groups—the ducks, the traffic, and the policemen.

The Three Little Pigs (15) (40) (46)

A favorite story for most groups. Most children prefer to play only the scenes where the wolf "huffs and puffs" at each little pig's house, and finally comes to an end when he jumps down the chimney. An occasional group prefers to play the story in sequence including all of the scenes from beginning to end.

The Noisy Book (36)
The little dog Muffin who gets a cinder in his eye listens and hears familiar sounds. He recognizes cars, a train, galloping horses, snow-flakes, and something very special.

Surprise For Mrs. Bunny (43)
Eight little bunnies surprise their mother with beautiful Easter eggs on Easter day in the morning.

Why The Bear Sleeps All Winter (21)
Children find excitement and fun in becoming Brothers Rabbit, Frog, Squirrel, Mole, and Fox to play a trick on mean old Brother Bear.

Material for Seven- and Eight-Year-Olds

RHYTHMIC MOVEMENT AND PANTOMIME

The Year Around

FALL

"Autumn Woods," by James S. Tippett (11) (42) (47)
On an autumn day when the "wind sweeps by with a lonesome rushing sound" children create with strong expression. When they pretend they are in a park or wooded area such pantomimes as the following are generally expressed: walking through leaves, skipping after a single leaf, making a pile of leaves and rolling in it, following a leaf to a special place.

"O Dear Me!" by Walter de la Mare (11) (47)
This verse invites children to work in four groups to create an activity which symbolizes each of the four seasons. The verse suggests such ideas as "picking crocuses," gathering blackberries, walking in leaves, and playing in snow.

"Choosing," by Eleanor Farjeon (11) (47)
This verse tickles imaginations and provides for expressive pan-

tomimes when children choose such special things as a ball, a cake, a kitty, a rose. These objects always motivate new ideas for strong pantomimes.

"Different Bicycles," by Dorothy Baruch (11) (47)

A bicycle parade is always fun. It offers strong creative expression when children share different ways of riding such as pumping up a steep hill, coasting, riding in a circle, riding two abreast, and "without holding on to the handle bars."

"Our Orchestra" (4)

This gay song invites children to form an orchestra. An imaginary orchestra in pantomime is the next best thing to playing in a real one. Sometimes it is even more fun.

WINTER

"White Fields," by James Stephens (42)

This verse about winter snow motivates children to create unusual "footprints" and pantomimes in imaginary snow. Children think of "angels," flowers, stars, crystals, and unexpected loveliness to express with their hands, feet, and entire selves.

"In the Week When Christmas Comes," by Eleanor Farjeon (11) (47)

Children enjoy working in groups to create a special activity for this holiday season. Ideas suggested in the verse include baking puddings, trimming trees, decorating halls, singing carols on doorsteps.

"For Christmas Day," by Eleanor Farjeon (11) (47)

Unusual pantomimes are expressed when children pretend it is Christmas day, and each one shares a custom which is observed in his home.

"Skating Away" (4)

There is always excitement and fun when children sing and skate. This song provides a gay rhythm and invites children to skate in a circle with partners.

"Choosing Shoes," by Ffrida Wolfe (*11*) (*42*) (*47*)

Children like to show in pantomime the kind of shoes they would choose if they could buy "a pair of special shoes." Creative expression results when children buy such shoes as fairy slippers, cowboy boots, dancing shoes, hopping shoes, and ballet slippers. One teacher became a "Seller of Shoes" with a quaint shop inside a mountain. Children came to buy "seven-league boots," "running shoes," "flying slippers," "Jack Frost boots," "giant sandals," and "Cinderella's glass slippers."

"Jump-Jump-Jump," by Kate Greenaway (*11*) (*47*)

There's joy in jumping, but particularly when one may jump "to the next town," "to the moon," "over the sea," and "far away for wonders to see." After the fun of vigorous rhythmic expression children enjoy sharing the "special place" each one has found.

"Skipping Ropes," by Dorothy Aldis (*40*)

The rhythm of skipping with a rope is always inviting, but there is a special delight in jumping with a rope made of rainbows. After skipping with rainbows, alone, together, and to jumping rope rhymes, children like to share ideas for other special ropes.

"Timothy Boon," by Ivy O. Eastwick (*11*) (*47*)

Children express with free pleasant movement when each one pretends he is flying with a balloon up to the moon. After the fun of flying children like to sit on the moon and look for one "special sight" on the moon or in the world below.

"Marching Song," by Robert Louis Stevenson (*11*) (*47*)

Everyone likes a parade, but to be in one brings an even stronger feeling of enjoyment. Children enjoy marching, playing in a make-believe band, and thinking of ways to make a parade spectacular.

"Shore," by Mary Britton Miller (*11*) (*42*) (*47*)

"Play on the seashore and gather up shells" is a pleasant way to begin this play. Sevens and eights like to listen to a seashell, and share messages which a seashell brings.

"The Picnic," by Dorothy Aldis (*11*) (*47*)

This verse motivates the fun of picnic pantomimes, and invites each child to show one thing that is fun to do on a picnic.

"I Keep Three Wishes Ready," by Annette Wynne (*11*) (*47*)

A favorite for sevens and eights who enjoy showing what they would wish "to do," "to have," or "to be" if a fairy should happen by.

CHARACTERIZATION

WONDERS IN THE WORLD

"Autumn Chorus" (*4*)

This song stirs imaginations. It invites children to create lovely autumn choirs for birds, insects, and children to sing together when autumn comes with its bright beauty.

"Trees," by Harry Behn (*11*) (*47*)

The beauty of this verse motivates children to create beautiful trees, for, as the poet says, "Trees are the kindest things I know."

"Rain," by Robert Louis Stevenson (*11*) (*15*) (*42*) (*47*)

A rainy day sets a strong mood for children to become convincing raindrops raining on trees, boats, or on umbrellas.

"Mary, Mary Quite Contrary," by Mother Goose (*11*) (*47*)

Sevens and eights find delight in creating Mary's garden. They like to work in groups to create rows of silver bells which make special music, cockle shells which whisper secrets, and "pretty little maids" who think of lovely things to do in such an unusual garden.

"The Little Rose Tree," by Rachel Field (*11*) (*42*) (*47*)

It is a special day when children create flowers with personalities. Roses and pansies with their "different faces" enjoy the fun of coming alive to talk about "summer parties," "garden visitors," and "fairy secrets."

"First Snow," by Ivy O. Eastwick and "Snow," by Dorothy Aldis (11) (47)

Every child finds creative expression when he becomes a snowflake "lighter that thistledown blown by a fairy." Children enjoy working in groups to become snowflakes, fairies, fenceposts, bushes and trees "kneeling down to pray," or others "who want to dance away."

FAIRY FOLK AND SPECIAL PEOPLE

"Hallowe'en," by Harry Behn (11) (47)

A gay Halloween dance "round their queen" is exciting for children who transform themselves into witches, spirits, gnomes, spooks, trolls, and pumpkins.

"The Witch" (3)

When mystery is in the sky witches fly. This song arouses imaginations and motivates children into becoming witches with black cats who soar through the clouds and frighten folk on this mysterious night.

"A Piper," by Seuman O'Sullivan (11) (47)

"All the world goes gay, goes gay" when a merry piper sets up, tunes, and starts to play. Excellent opportunity for children to create a gay piper and villagers of all ages.

"The Bagpipe Man," by Nancy Byrd Turner (11) (47)

Unusual creative expression is motivated by this verse. Children like to create a quaint Bagpipe Man who comes over the hill "with a whirl and a skirl, a toot and a trill." In the queer bagpipe music children hear and become marching men, "fairies down in a dusky glen," an unusual river, a bird in June, and wonderful things that are heard in the music.

"Have You Watched the Fairies?" by Rose Fyleman (11) (47)

When the sun shines after a rain children delight in becoming fairies "spreading out their little wings to dry them in the sun" and "dancing and singing to a fairy orchestra."

"The Best Game the Fairies Play," by Rose Fyleman *(11)* *(47)*

When one has magically become a fairy or an elf there is nothing quite so inviting as sliding down steeples, catching clouds, flying to weathercocks, and mixing mud. Fairies and elves always think of other games which are especially magic after playing these favorites.

"Twenty Foolish Fairies," by Nancy Byrd Turner *(42)*

What a joke! Twenty robins watch and chuckle when twenty fairies skate and dance in the moonlight on a shiny mirror which they believe to be an ice pond.

"A Fairy Went A-Marketing," by Rose Fyleman *(42)*

Fairies have markets which sell such lovely things as colored birds, magic fish, gossamer gowns of thistledown, messenger mice and a hundred other things which boys and girls who enjoy fairies are sure to think of. This verse offers opportunities for children to work in groups to create market scenes and to become fairies who go "a-marketing."

"Fairies" (Scherzo by Schubert) *(37)*

The delightful rhythm of this recording sets a strong mood for fairyland dancing, playing, and marketing.

"Shadow Dance," by Ivy O. Eastwick *(11)* *(47)*

Children create wonderful shadows for shadows themselves are wonderful.

"What the Toys Are Thinking," by Ffrida Wolfe *(11)* *(47)*

Sevens and eights like to believe that toys have feelings. A toy-shop shelf offers splendid opportunities for creative characterizations.

"The Cowboy" *(3)*

The gay Texan tune for this song invites cowboys to ride and enjoy a day and a night on the prairie.

ANIMALS, CREATURES, AND SUCH

"Hey, Diddle, Diddle," by Mother Goose *(11)* *(15)* *(47)*

A cats' violin ensemble, a jumping cow, and a laughing dog celebrate with spirit. Sevens and eights enjoy wondering and deciding just why the animals are having such a celebration.

"Is A Caterpillar Ticklish?" by Monica Shannon (*11*) (*47*)
It's fun to create caterpillars when each one wiggles, giggles, inches along, and rests to share a dream or song.

"The Cat," by Mary Britton Miller (*11*) (*40*) (*42*) (*47*)
An outstanding verse for motivating children into creating a variety of unusual cats.

"The Mysterious Cat," by Vachel Lindsay (*11*) (*40*) (*47*)
Many groups of children have created unusual mysterious cats who are served by slaves in a far away castle. Some groups have created a brief plot which reveals the mystery behind the cats.

"Frogs At School," by George Cooper (*40*)
It's a happy day when children become frogs being taught by Master Bullfrog. Frogs learn to leap, dive, sing "Ker-chog," and dodge blows. Frogs enjoy the fun of "frog-recess."

"Elephants" (*3*) "Holding Hands," by Lenore Link (*11*) (*47*)
"Elephants walking along the trails/Are holding hands by holding tails." This verse and song always motivate a gay elephant parade which may lead straight to a circus.

"The Friendly Beasts" (*4*)
When children have learned this beautiful old song they find unusual expression as they become animals in the stable where the Christ Child was born.

THINGS-THAT-GO

"I Saw a Ship A-Sailing," by Mother Goose (*11*) (*15*) (*40*) (*47*)
A rare adventure awaits boys and girls who sail on this ship. It is captained by a duck and manned by mice-sailors. The ship sails for

a destination which appeals to the imaginations of sevens and eights as they decide just where and why.

"Ferry Boats," by James S. Tippett (*11*) (*42*) (*47*)

Playing ferry-boats is satisfying fun for children who have enjoyed this experience in reality. This gay rhythmic verse motivates children to become passengers boarding the ferry, giving tickets to the boatmen, listening to the engineer give orders, moving out to watch sea-gulls and small boats out on the water.

HAPPY, HAPPY DAYS

"Crab-Apple," by Ethel Talbot (*11*) (*47*)

When children spend a birth night with fairies, it is an experience never to be forgotten.

"Thanksgiving Magic," by Rowena Bennett (*11*) (*47*)

Sevens and eights find fun in becoming cooks to create one special treat for a Thanksgiving dinner.

"Cradle Hymn," by Martin Luther (*4*) (*11*) (*47*)

A beautiful experience when children know this old song. While a part of this group sings others create the "Manger Scene" of the Nativity with beauty and depth of feeling.

"A Valentine," by Eleanor Hammond (*11*) (*47*)

An "Outdoor Valentine" tickles the imaginations of seven and eight-year-olds. Each child enjoys pantomiming "one valentine" such as "frost flowers," "hopping chickadees," "bending elm trees," and "flitting lacy snowflakes."

"Meeting the Easter Bunny," by Rowena Bennett (*11*) (*42*) (*47*)

This verse always motivates strong expression when half of the children become Easter bunnies to surprise the others with "a special Easter surprise" from the forest. "What is the loveliest thing an Easter Rabbit might find in the forest?" generally brings such delightful expression as a basket full of "dewdrops," "a rainbow," "a bluebird's song," and "a pet grasshopper."

BEGINNING CONFLICTS

ANIMALS

"How Doth the Little Crocodile," by Lewis Carroll (*11*) (*47*)

A sly little crocodile enjoys luring little fish into his gentle smiling jaws in a spirit of fun. Sevens and eights delight in deciding how to create a crocodile and to show how many little fish he has captured.

"The Monkeys and the Crocodile," by Laura E. Richards (*11*) (*42*) (*47*)

A gay time is experienced when children become convincing monkeys to tease Uncle Crocodile. Quite a contrast develops when Uncle Crocodile "eats a little monkey brother." Some groups have heightened the drama by creating wise old monkeys in nearby trees who warn the little monkeys when they become daring with their teasing antics.

"There Once Was a Puffin," by Florence Page Jaques (*11*) (*47*)

An exciting conflict is provided here between puffin and fish on the high seas. The scene starts with a problem in which puffin skim after fish and catch them. The fish solve the problem in an unexpected and satisfying way.

ANIMALS AND SPECIAL PEOPLE

"The Elf and the Dormouse," by Oliver Herford (*11*) (*39*) (*47*)

A favorite verse for playing. Conflict is strong when elves get caught in a rain storm, hide under toadstools only to discover sleeping dormice. "Necessity becomes the mother of invention" when elves decide how to solve this frightening situation.

"The Elf Singing," by Richard Allingham (*39*) (*40*)

A strong conflict develops between singing elves and wicked wizards. The situation is solved in a delightful way by an unexpected rainbow and a family of moles.

"A Goblinade," by Florence Page Jaques (*11*) (*39*) (*47*)

It is fun for children to become goblins who try to frighten maidens and beetles out in the forest. When the goblins realize that they fail to frighten others they decide to become elves and "dance all day and enjoy themselves."

"Hark, Hark! The Dogs Do Bark," by Mother Goose (11) (15) (47)

A strong conflict is created when children decide who the beggars are and why they are coming to town.

"Momotara" (Japanese) by Rose Fyleman (11) (47)

Children like to become giants fighting among themselves for possession of jewels and gems. An exciting scene develops when Momotara goes forth bravely with his dog, pheasant, and monkey to silence the giants.

"Pussy Cat, Pussy Cat," by Mother Goose (11) (15) (40) (47)

A pussy cat who solves the mystery of the castle by discovering a little mouse is honored by the queen and her court in a gay castle ceremony.

"The Queen of Hearts," by Mother Goose (15)

A castle ceremony centering around the conflict over the disappearing tarts appeals to most groups of sevens and eights.

"Ride A Cock Horse to Banbury Cross," by Mother Goose (11) (15) (40) (47)

Excitement is high when villagers ride from far and near to witness the striking happening in Banbury Cross. Sevens and eights have unusual ideas about "the fine lady upon a white horse" who rides through the roads leading to Banbury Cross.

"Someone," by Walter de la Mare (11) (40) (42) (47)

Mystery and wonder are strong when "someone" comes "knocking at a wee small door." Children enjoy deciding where the door is, and who comes knocking "in the still dark night."

"A Visit from St. Nicholas," by Clement V. Moore (11) (40) (47)

Children always delight in being St. Nick, reindeer, Papa, Mama, children, mice, and toys on this wonderful night of the year.

"The Basket House" (*3*)

This song, with its gay tune and quick conflict, offers a good beginning story experience for children. They enjoy creating convincing mice, rabbits, and a big bear who sits on the basket house and always surprises everyone, including himself.

"The Sleeping Princess" (*3*)

A delightful, simplified version of the old fairy tale. Characterizations and pantomimes are well defined in this song. Children should be encouraged to create each character rather than being allowed to imitate each other's actions as they play.

STORIES TO BEGIN ON

The Elves and the Shoemaker (*15*) (*39*) (*40*)

A favorite for many groups who delight in being elves to surprise and puzzle the poor cobbler and his wife. The story requires little dialogue, but offers strong suspense and a delightful ending.

How the Robin's Breast Became Red (*39*)

This story may be played entirely in pantomime. It offers strong conflict between a bear, a robin, and northland villagers. Sevens and eights find strong expression in creating clumps of frozen grass which change to flaming fires by the help of the brave little robin.

Millions of Cats (*34*)

A favorite story for playing. It is limited in characterization to an old man, an old woman, and "millions" of cats.

The Nativity Story (*24*) (*39*)

The Shepherd Scene, the Inn Scene, and the Manger Scene are the scenes which most groups enjoy creating when they play this beautiful story either in pantomime or with dialogue.

Old Man Rabbit's Thanksgiving Dinner (*23*)

Sevens and eights enjoy creating the characters of Old Man Rabbit, hungry squirrels, birds, and mice. It is always a dramatic moment when the animals cheer Old Man Rabbit, and he suddenly realizes he shared a Thanksgiving Dinner without realizing it was a special day for sharing.

The Strange Visitor (26)

An eerie ghost story which provides suspense and creative fun on Halloween. An old woman who wishes for company is visited by a stranger who arrives in pieces. Children enjoy working in pairs to create such fascinating characters as long, long arms, a round, round body, and other pieces who enter silently and mysteriously.

LONGER STORIES

HOLIDAY STORIES

The Country Bunny and the Little Gold Shoes (17)

A story every child should hear. Most groups create this story in three scenes including the Home Scene where each of the 21 bunnies helps Mother Bunny; the Castle Scene in which Mother Bunny becomes the Easter Bunny; and the Hilltop Scene where Mother Bunny struggles against ice and snow to deliver an Easter egg to a little boy at the top of the mountain. An experienced group generally requires four sessions to create this story with satisfaction.

The First Thanksgiving (27)

A strong feeling is experienced when Pilgrims and Indians gather together to feast, to give thanks, and to enjoy songs and games.

Jenny's Birthday Book (28)

A delightful birthday story in which children become cats to celebrate the birthday of a shy little cat named Jenny Linsky. Cats enjoy a picnic, sharing gifts, playing in an orchestra, and dancing in the moonlight before they ride home on a fire engine, and listen quietly to Jenny's birthday prayer.

Paddy's Christmas (39)

A favorite story for groups who are ready for dialogue. Experienced groups enjoy creating two scenes where action alternates from the

SPAIN

he Naughty One (9)

xican boy who dislikes water and baths must have one on the
his sister's wedding. Angelo tries his best to escape his bath
happy afterward that he did get ready, for never has he seen
y festivity as a Mexican wedding brings.

ory of Ferdinand (41)

inand, the bull who "likes to sit quietly and smell flowers,"
unexpected experience when he encounters a bee and is chosen
bullfight in Madrid. Gay dances and celebrations take place pre-
g the bullfight, but an even greater surprise is in store for the
dors and people who have come to see Ferdinand the Fierce.

Material for Nine-, Ten-, and Eleven-Year-Olds

RHYTHMIC MOVEMENT AND PANTOMIME

The Year Around

ports Parade and Rally:

Children like to parade to the gay music of a school song or
pirited band recording. A parade provides for strong rhythmic expression when children are guided to plan different ways to parade.
Drills, cheers, and a band are generally suggested.

"The American Way" (5)

When children know and enjoy this song they like to sing while
they parade. Emphasis on patriotic feeling brings forth strong expression and often motivates a variety of pantomimes.

Sports Pantomimes:

To the mood and rhythm of a school song, cheering, or a recording
boys and girls enjoy "warm-up" pantomimes of football, baseball,
soccer, tennis, badminton, and basketball.

bear's cave on the hillside to the family's Christmas celebrations in a
forest cabin.

The Story of the First Christmas Tree (45)

A strong conflict occurs on Christmas eve when a kind woodcutter
is lost in the snow. His daughter Annis who is a friend of the fairies
and woodland creatures becomes worried until she sees how her
special friends have helped to light the father's way.

FOLK AND FAIRY TALES

Hansel and Gretel (11) (39) (40)

Many leaders prefer the Humperdinck version for creative playing.
It offers strong motivation for the stepmother to send the children
into the forest, and it provides unusual characters in a Sand Man,
Dew Man, Guardian Angels, as well as the Wicked Witch who is
always a favorite. Recordings from the Humperdinck opera heighten
the mood for strong expression. (29:4)

Jack and the Beanstalk (15) (40)

A favorite for almost every group. Strong scenes include the following: the Home Scene in which Jack sells the cow and his mother
throws the seeds from the window; the Beanstalk Scene in which
Jack meets the good Fairy; the Castle Scene in which Jack outwits
the Giant; and the Beanstalk Scene which brings the play to a
triumphant ending. Strong characterizations are offered in the characters of Jack, his mother, the mysterious man with the beans, the
cow, the fairies, the giant, his wife, the magic harp, money bags,
golden hen, and climbing beanstalk.

The Princess Who Could Not Cry (39) (48)

Two dramatic scenes are provided by this story: a Castle Scene in
which the problem is revealed when the king and queen consult a
wise fairy, and a later Castle Scene in which unusual people arrive
to try to cause the princess to laugh.

The Rabbit Who Wanted Red Wings (23)

A little rabbit, a red bird, a groundhog, a duck, an owl, and the rabbit's family become involved in the conflict which arises when the little rabbit wishes he could be like a little red bird with red wings.

Sleeping Beauty (39)

A beautiful story for children to create in springtime. An experienced group generally creates this story in three acts including the Christening Scene, the Sixteenth Birthday Scene, and the Awakening Scene 100 years later. Four or five sessions are generally required to create this story with strong satisfaction.

Snow White and Rose Red (11) (15) (40)

This old story offers strong conflict and an opportunity for children to become Snow White, Rose Red, an unusual bear, an angry dwarf, a fish, an eagle, and a handsome prince. The surprise ending provides a striking dramatic scene.

Snow White and the Seven Dwarfs (11) (39) (40)

Another favorite for many groups of children. Characters of the wicked queen, the seven dwarfs, Snow White, and the prince hold high appeal and creative challenge.

The Wonderful Tar Baby (11) (39)

Children who enjoy hearing the Uncle Remus tales usually enjoy playing them. This is a favorite for children to create not only the strong animal characters, but the appealing tar baby as well.

STORIES FROM FARAWAY TIMES AND PLACES

JAPAN

The Dancing Kettle (18)

An old priest and his three young pupils are frightened by what they believe to be a bewitched teakettle. They sell the kettle to a Junkman who makes a fortune from this Teakettle of Good Luck, for it has the power to dance, sing, and do extraordinary tricks. The Junkman returns the kettle and half his fortune to the Priest, who, in turn, treats the kettle with due respect.

The Old Man With the Bump

A traditional Japanese tale in on his cheek encounters a frigh spirits, and unusual dancing out i bump disappears. When the old m bor learns of this experience and quite a different happening.

Urashima Taro and the Princess of t

This old Japanese tale has a charm ages. Children enjoy creating a tortois of the Sea, unusual servants, and the The mystery of the jewel box and its s a strong opportunity for creative expressi

The Wedding of the Mouse (18)

A humorous tale with delightful charac looks for "the greatest being in this whole Chuko to marry. Father Mouse goes to greatest being in the world." Mr. Sun send Cloud who in turn sends him to Mr. Wind, to Mr. Wall, who in turn sends him to the lit holes." An unusual wedding takes place when little mouse is "the greatest being on earth."

CHINA

Mai Li (31)

A story with a conflict which centers around a of the new year. Customs, traditions, and unusua provided.

The Wonderful Pear Tree (44)

A selfish fruit peddler, an unusual tree, and curious along a roadside near a Chinese village to experience mysterious happening.

Angelo
A Me
day of
but is
such g

The S
Fer
has a
for a
cedin
mata

FALL

S

"Can You Play?" (5)

After children have learned this song they generally ask to create an orchestra of their own. After creating to the rhythm of the song, recordings should be used. Recordings should offer variety in spirit, tempo, and mood. (37)

"Fall," by Aileen L. Fisher (11) (47)

Fall activities and harvest time provide strong pantomimes when "Everything is put away before it starts to snow."

"Hallowe'en," by Dorothy Brown Thompson (11) (47)

Bobbing for make-believe apples, scooping out jack-o'-lanterns, pulling taffy, and walking through the town on Halloween night offer strong and friendly pantomimes.

"Thanksgiving Day," by Lydia Maria Child (40)

Children enjoy working together in groups of four or five to become families riding in sleighs to Grandmother's house. Pantomimes and strong expression are found in the riding, stopping in the country to enjoy snow activities, and arriving at Grandmother's for feasting and giving thanks.

WINTER

"Winter Sports" (5)

Skating and sledding on the millpond to the pleasant rhythm of this song provides a variety of creative expression. After skating alone children enjoy thinking of ways in which they may skate together such as skating in pairs, in a train, in circles, in designs, and in formation for "crack-the-whip." Ideas for a campfire and singing are often suggested when a leader asks, "What might be fun to do while we rest for awhile?"

Indoor Sports:

Children enjoy sharing pantomimes which reveal favorite indoor sports including basketball, volley ball, ping-pong, tumbling, chess, checkers, and other ideas which provide pleasant surprises.

"Bundles," by John Farrar (*11*) (*47*)

Children enjoy opening imaginary bundles and pantomiming whatever they find inside. The bundle may be a present they would like to receive, a present for a friend, or a bundle they are preparing to send to children in another land.

"Here We Come A-Wassailing" (*6*)

There's special joy in walking and singing carols in the weeks before Christmas.

SPRING

"Spring is Showery, Flowery, Bowery," by Mother Goose (*11*) (*47*)

To create from single words provides a strong challenge for older children. This verse has four lines, each of which describes a season in three words. Children have enjoyed working in four groups to create seasonal pantomimes. They may be divided according to the season in which birthdays occur.

"January Brings the Snow," by Mother Goose (*11*) (*47*)

An idea similar to that presented above, but generally used with a large group which may be better divided into twelve divisions by months. Each group creates a pantomime which reveals an activity, holiday, or characteristic of a specific month.

Springtime Fun:

Spring fun brings unusual pantomimes in such ideas as bicycling, hopscotching, horseback riding, playing baseball, hiking, flying kites, and canoeing.

Springtime Work:

Spring work brings pantomimes equal to the season in spirit. Children are guided to show how they do "one thing to make ready for spring."

"My Shadow and I" (*5*)

After children have learned this song they enjoy creating shadow pantomimes. While part of the group sings others work in pairs, one being the child and the other the shadow.

"Wings and Wheels," by Nancy Byrd Turner (*11*) (*47*)

Roller skating pantomimes are generally spirited—particularly when a musical accompaniment is provided. After an initial pantomime of free rhythmic movement, children enjoy thinking of different ways to skate: skating on one foot, skating while squatting, coasting, skating backward, in circles, with partners, skating four abreast, and skating in figures.

SUMMER

"Row Your Boat" (*5*)

After children know this traditional song they enjoy working in pairs or groups and pretending they are rowing in a stream, a lake, or a canal. Spirit and feeling are emphasized when the children decide where and why they are rowing.

"America The Beautiful" (*7*)

Children have enjoyed working in groups to create work and play activities throughout America. Some groups have created from this song in the nature of a television show. Others have taken a visitor from another land in an airplane trip across the country to give him a bird's eye view of the recreational and occupational opportunities of America.

"Careers" (*6*)

After singing this song, children like to work together in groups to share the careers they think they will follow. The song suggests ideas such as magicians, policemen, flyers, and sailors. Children always think of others which are surprising and revealing.

CHARACTERIZATION

PEOPLE—HERE, THERE, EVERYWHERE

"African Dance," by Langston Hughes (*11*) (*47*)

Many children find strong appeal in becoming natives of another land and experiencing one of its customs or cultures. In this verse boys are generally motivated to beat on drums to provide a rhythm while girls dance slowly and gracefully "like a wisp of smoke." Children create with stronger feeling when they first decide why the dancers are dancing.

"The Cowboy's Life," attributed to James Barton Adams (*11*) (*47*) and "Goodby, Old Paint" (*5*)

Almost every group of children finds a strong sense of adventure and expression when they are guided to become American cowboys in the early days of exploring and settling our country. The leisurely, plaintive rhythm of this old cowboy ballad and the ideas in the verse motivate children to become cowboys gathered around a campfire enjoying a cowboy's life. Pantomimes generally include strumming on guitars, singing, riding, and eating.

"The Circus Parade," by Olive Beaupré Miller (*11*) (*47*)

When a circus comes to town this verse heightens the mood for creating a colorful parade and circus acts.

"Doorbells," by Rachel Field (*11*) (*39*) (*47*)

Unusual characters including witches, pirates, and sailors are generally created after hearing and planning to create from this verse. Beginning groups should be guided in keeping characterizations clear and convincing rather than getting involved in the complexities of creating a plot.

"The Flag Goes By," by Henry Holcomb Bennett (*11*) (*47*)

Famous people from history hold high appeal for children during these adventurous years. This verse generally motivates children to work in groups to create floats or scenes which reveal historical episodes in our country's development.

"Being Gypsy," by Barbara Young (*11*) (*47*) and "A Gypsy Song" (*5*)

This verse and song motivate unusual experiences for children to create gypsies. The song is based on Brahms' *Hungarian Dance* and provides a gay rhythm for gypsies to dance. The verse invites such pantomimes as "listening to stars and dawn, learning tunes of wind and rain, and talking to the fox and faun."

"Meg Merrilies," by John Keats (*11*) (*47*)

This verse presents the powerful character of Old Gypsy Meg, and provides an unusual opportunity for dramatic play centered around gypsy life for a group who becomes fascinated with the life of gypsies.

"Blow the Man Down" (*5*)

Many groups enjoy the fun of becoming sailors. This old halyard chantey was a work song which was used for hoisting sails. It is a popular song and provides spirit and rhythm for sailor pantomimes.

"If You Want to Know" (*5*)

When children are studying South America they find strong enjoyment in learning this song and becoming cowboys. Pantomimes which provide strong rhythmic expression include riding broncos, lassoing, and enjoying the *cueca,* the national dance of Chile.

"Oh! Susanna" (*5*)

This favorite song provides excellent motivation for children to become early day settlers gathered around a covered wagon along a trail. Feeling is always stressed when settlers strum on banjos, fry buckwheat cakes, gather around a fire, rock a baby to sleep, bring water from a nearby stream, or ride out to guard the wagon train.

"Ho for California!" (*6*)

In a similar way children are motivated to become "Forty-Niners" after they sing this song.

"The Prairie Schooner" (*6*)

This song motivates strong identification with homesteaders as they rode over the trails in prairie schooners.

"The Pirate Don Durk of Dowdee," by Mildred Plew Meigs (*11*) (*47*)

Most children delight in becoming pirates, especially wicked pirates who join the crew and sail with the wicked Don Durk. Strong characterizations result when each pirate is challenged to "show one thing he can do" to prove his worth to old Don Durk. Ideas for revealing skill with knives, daggers, ropes, or entertaining are generally created.

ANIMALS, CREATURES, AND SUCH

"Beach Fire," by Frances Frost (*11*) (*47*)

This verse motivates unusual expression for children who have experienced the beauty and fun of being at a beach. Some children prefer to create seagulls, twinkling stars, a brand new moon, or jumping
fish, while others prefer to create people who enjoy the beauty of the
beach while they sing and watch, and wish wishes.

"Fog," by Carl Sandburg (*11*) (*47*)

This verse motivates unusual characterizations of fog. Some children create catlike characters; others create fog in the form of
ghostlike characterizations with strong characteristics, feeling, and
movement. A conflict generally arises when children are asked, "What
trouble or danger might fog cause to people in a city, in the country,
or out at sea?"

"Hallowe'en" (*5*)

This song invites strong characterizations of witches, ghosts, and
goblins who move about mysteriously and with purpose.

"Macavity: The Mystery Cat," by T. S. Eliot (*11*) (*47*)

Children who enjoy cats find strong creative challenge in creating
Macavity. Most groups create catlike characterizations in the form
of two-legged cats with distinct personality traits. After characterizations are created Macavity enjoys deciding whether he will "loot a
larder or rifle a jewel case." Other cats enjoy strolling in the moonlight until the alarm is sounded, and cats come from everywhere to
offer advice and evidence.

"Mr. Bullfrog" (*5*)

After singing this song children frequently ask to create frogs.
They enjoy the fun of rehearsing in a frog chorus and croaking
"brek-a-brek" to create unusual frog renditions.

"Polar Bear" (*5*)

The power and rhythm of the polar bear is felt in this song. Some
children enjoy creating powerful bears stalking for seal, birds, or
fish.

"Silver," by Walter de la Mare (*11*) (*47*)

The recording of "Claire de Lune" (*29:5*) motivates strong expression when children are guided to create from this verse. Children enjoy working in groups to create trees, bushes, and forest creatures while a stately moon walks slowly and silently to "peer and see" the beauties of the moonlit world.

"Something Told the Wild Geese," by Rachel Field (*11*) (*47*) (*50*)

This verse and the beauty of wild geese often motivate children into unusual creative expression. Creating wild geese offers free expression in flying. Some groups like to create orchard trees moving in cold autumn winds even though branches are heavy with fruit. Boys frequently ask to create coyotes or wolves with taunting sounds to heighten the fear of the geese as they circle near the orchard trees.

"Winter Winds" (*5*)

After children have learned this song they enjoy being snowflakes to the rhythm of the winter wind. Groups have asked to create from this song again and again.

"Wind-Wolves," by William D. Sargent (*11*) (*47*)

A night scene in a forest with frightened deer and other forest creatures is motivated by this verse. Forest creatures find strong expression as they flee from weird wind wolves. A high wind and a gray day heighten the mood for creativity.

BEGINNING CONFLICTS

"Columbus," by Joaquin Miller (*11*) (*47*)

A strong scene at sea between the courageous Columbus and his fearful crew is powerfully presented in this verse. Some groups have created it as a play entirely in pantomime, others have used words, and still others have created in pantomime while a part of the group shares the verse in choral speaking.

"The Duet" (*6*)

A humorous contest between a cuckoo and a donkey results when

each one sings to see who "sings best." Some children have increased
the characters to include many donkeys and many cuckoos, while
other children have introduced barnyard animals and birds who become judges who listen and reach a conclusion.

"Great Ideas" (20)

Scenes behind "Great Ideas" provide outstanding short scenes in
conflict. When children become motivated by the many ideas and inventions which have contributed to the growth and progress of civilization they enjoy working in groups to share scenes. Episodes from
the life of Thomas Edison, Clara Barton, Alexander Graham Bell, the
Wright Brothers, and others have provided exciting conflicts for short
creative scenes.

"Jonathan Bing," by Beatrice Curtis Brown (11) (47)

This verse offers strong motivation for creative playing. Children
enjoy and yet sympathize with poor Old Jonathan Bing who is
forgetful and does not realize the significance of social graces. In
addition to Jonathan, children like to create characterizations of
guards, Archbishop, and curious visitors at the castle gate who comment and react to Jonathan's plight.

"Paul Revere's Ride," by Henry Wadsworth Longfellow (11) (47)

A highly dramatic episode which may be created entirely in pantomime. Children generally work in three groups including Paul
Revere, the villagers, and the British soldiers.

"The Wonderful Weaver," by George Cooper (39)

On a snowy day children enjoy becoming a "wonderful weaver
high up in the air, weaving a white mantle for cold earth to wear."
A conflict in nature arises when the sun comes forth to undo the
unusual weaving of the weaver. Splendid expression results when
children become weavers, snowflakes, trees, bushes, and the sun.

BEGINNING STORIES IN SONG

"The Arkansas Traveler" (7)

A favorite for playing with its delightful rhythm and gay mood.

Old Fiddlin' Dan plays gay music for a grizzly bear who dances in the light of the moon. Soon the forest is gay with the coon, porcupine, bobcat, bear, and all the critters from the countryside dancing reels and sets—and "somewhere in the hills they are dancin' yet."

"Daniel Boone" (6)

An exciting adventure to create in pantomime while part of the group sings. Daniel Boone follows the trail of a grizzly bear, decides to "sleep all winter through," but is tracked by a band of Indians. An exciting battle ends in a settlement between Daniel and the Indians.

"Father Rumble" (6)

The humorous traditional tale of the old man who said he "could do more work in a day than his wife could do in three." Strong characterizations are provided in the characters of the man, his wife, the speckled hen, the cow, and the pig.

"The Mermaid" (7)

A sailor's chantey in which the captain and crew spy a pretty mermaid who weaves them under her spell. After sailing three times round, the ship sinks to the bottom of the sea where the mermaid dwells.

"The Piper of Hamelin" (6)

The song is based on the old folk tale, and offers a gay tune for the piper, the rats, the children, and the councilmen.

"The Wedding of the Fleas" (6)

A gay and nonsensical time is had when a lion, bear, monkey, canary, and frog join together to conduct the wedding for Miss and Mister Flea.

"Wraggle Taggle Gypsies" (7)

Three gypsies sing to a fair lady who joins them and rides away to revel in their gay gypsy dances. When her good lord returns home and finds her gone he rides after her. He finds her gaily dancing and asks her to return. She dances and calls, "What care I for my new-wedded lord, I'm off with the wraggle, taggle gypsies, O."

STORIES TO BEGIN ON

FOLK AND FAIRY TALES

The Conjure Wives (26) (39)
An outstanding story in which children create individualized characters of wicked witches or wives, enchanted dough, and a mysterious voice. Little dialogue is required.

Chanticleer and the Fox (48)
Little dialogue is required to present the conflict, which arises when the proud Chanticleer is stolen away by a fox. He is chased by cackling hens, farmer and his wife, several farm animals, and wasps and crows, but it is Chanticleer himself who outwits the fox and saves himself.

Danse Macabre (19)
At the hour of midnight on Hallowe'en, Death tunes his fiddle. Spirits and ghosts gather together for a gay, wild dance which grows wilder with the arrival of each new ghost and skeleton. A merry, pleasant spirit pervades the wild dance until a cock crows announcing the approach of dawn, and the ghostly dancers fade away to become silent for another year.

King Peramund's Wish (48)
A humorous story for children to create when they are interested in kings, queens, witches, and spells. A delightful opportunity is provided here when the king is put under a spell which causes him to fly.

Mercury and the Woodsman (15)
Children who enjoy myths find special challenge in creating the mysterious, mischievous character of Mercury. Other characters in this story include a woodsman, his curious companions, and a greedy follower.

Mice in Council (15)
A mice convention provides a humorous situation for children to create.

Musicians of Bremen (15) (39)

A favorite story for groups who enjoy creating animals. Unusual creative challenge is provided for creating animal music. Most groups enjoy an opportunity to create a "band of robbers."

A Night on Bald Mountain (35)

An exciting witch story in which all the evil sisters in the world assemble on Bald Mountain. The Wicked Black Spirit is pleased with their evil and he dances and celebrates in their honor. A gay dance follows until dawn breaks and church bells in the distance send the evil spirits away for another year.

Pandora (15) (50)

An excellent story to create in spring. It may be created entirely in pantomime or with dialogue if children are ready. Outstanding characterizations are offered in the variety of evil spirits, Hope, Mercury, and the characters of Epimetheus and Pandora.

Seven Dancing Stars (48)

A mysterious Indian legend which describes the origin of the seven dancing stars in the sky. An Indian tribe follows the setting sun to a plentiful land. Little Eagle and his seven brothers wander deep into the forest and find an enchanted place for dancing. They are warned by a mysterious stranger to leave this secret place. When they refuse they are changed into seven dancing stars. When Little Eagle looks back to the earth he changes into a falling star, but his brothers rise to the sky to dance forever.

The Sorcerer's Apprentice (39)

One of the favorite stories for almost every group. This story may be played with little or extensive dialogue. Characterizations include the characters of Willibald, the sorcerer, Fritzl, the brooms, puffs of smoke, visiting sorcerers, and floating wooden objects which bounce and float merrily as the water rises high.

Wind and the Sun (15)

An old fable which holds high appeal for many children. Children

work in groups to create the sun, the wind, and travelers reacting to the powers of these two who have decided to solve an argument.

HERO AND ADVENTURE TALES

Androcles and the Lion (*15*)

This story offers strong suspense and characterizations of Androcles, the lion, soldiers, cruel master, guards and spectators. It may be created with dialogue or in pantomime with strong feeling.

The Good Samaritan (*24*) (*39*)

Beginning groups in church school have created this dramatic Biblical story with very little dialogue. Characters include the man who is traveling, his heavily laden donkeys, thieves, priest, Levite, and the Good Samaritan.

Story of Johnny Appleseed (*39*) (*50*)

Some groups have created this story entirely in pantomime. Others have used dialogue to create Johnny's experiences with the villagers, the Indians, and the outdoor creatures.

Story of the First Thanksgiving (*20*)

A strong and reverent feeling is experienced when children identify with the Pilgrims and Indians who join together in this first feast of Thanksgiving in a new land.

Why the Chimes Rang (*52*)

An excellent story for beginning or experienced groups. It is a Christmas story with the underlying theme of self-sacrifice. Character opportunities include Pedro, Little Brother, the Old Woman, and the passers-by who include the people who attend the church services. Such passers-by often include an artist, an author, lords and ladies, wealthy villagers, king and queen and servants, the church organist, and members of the choir.

LONGER STORIES

HOLIDAY STORIES

Amahl And The Night Visitors (*1*)

A beautiful Christmas story for an experienced group. It is based on the visit of the Three Kings, who stop for shelter at the home of Amahl, a crippled shepherd boy. While they rest a scene of high emotion takes place. When the visitors prepare to continue their journey to find the Christ Child, Amahl asks the Kings to carry his humble gift to the Child. It is decided that he may join the Kings. A miraculous happening takes place which builds this story to a beautiful ending.

A Christmas Carol (39)

The Counting House Scene is a favorite with many sixth grade groups. Children enjoy creating the characters of Scrooge, Bob Cratchit, Marley, and the unusual ghosts which come to haunt the selfish Scrooge.

The Voyage of the Wee Red Cap (39)

A delightful Christmas story which leads children into creating Christmas customs in many different lands. The character of old Tieg appeals to children for he closely resembles Scrooge in disposition and attitude. Favorite characters are the wee Good People who "clap on their caps," and take Tieg throughout the world on the eve of Christmas. A dramatic scene brings this story to a surprise ending. Five or six sessions are required to create this entire story with satisfaction.

HERO AND ADVENTURE TALES

A Boy Who Loved the Sea (20)

The dramatic story of Columbus is a favorite with some groups. This story may be created in four scenes including the Wharf Scene, the Shop Scene, the Court Scene, and the Voyage Scene ending in the triumphant and reverent episode where Columbus kneels in prayer and claims the new land for Spain.

David the Shepherd Boy (25) (48)

Strong episodes for playing include David's experience with the restless King Saul; David's encounter with a lion and a bear who attack the flocks of sheep; and David's experience with the giant Goliath.

Homemade Fiddle (50)

Irby, a likeable young lad, plays his one-string fiddle in a fiddlin' contest. His tune, which he made up from scraps of tunes he heard in the mountain, brings the village folk to their feet in a gay dance and wins a new fiddle for Irby. Gay music and square dances make this story a favorite one for playing.

Joan of Arc (50)

An excellent story for a group who expresses a desire to create from this beautiful story. Dramatic scenes include the Garden Scene, where Joan hears voices; the Battle Scene, where Joan rides forth with her warriors; the Crowning Scene, where King Charles is crowned King of France; and the final scene, where Joan triumphs when she is burned as a witch.

Joseph and His Brothers (25) (48)

A dramatic story for many groups. Strong scenes include the Dream Scenes; the Coat Scene, the Pit Scene, and the Palace Scene.

The Knights of the Silver Shield (15)

An excellent story for an experienced group. Some groups have started the action with a Knighting Scene where Sir Roland is knighted. The ceremony is interrupted by the announcement that the giants are surrounding the castle. The Bridge Scene offers strong conflict in the characterizations of Sir Roland, the three disguised giants, and servants and bridge tenders who react to the unusual situations. A final courtroom scene builds to an unexpected and astonishing climax.

Robin Hood Adventures (33) (39) (50)

Robin Hood's Merry Adventures should be selected according to the interests of the children. Some groups prefer to create the opening episode, How Robin Became an Outlaw. Others enjoy the following: Robin Meets Little John, Robin and the Sheriff of Nottingham, and Robin's Adventures with Midge the Miller.

William Tell (39) (50)

A dramatic story for children who are ready to create strong characterizations and dialogue. Stirring episodes which are based on Swiss history include a Village Scene, an Arrow-Shooting Scene, a Storm Scene, and an Escape Scene. The underlying theme of courage and faith is closely woven into each dramatic episode.

FOLK AND FAIRY TALES

Ali Baba and the Forty Thieves (15)

In this old tale there is strong opportunity for rhythmic expression when children become wicked thieves commanded by the Robber Chief. Characters of Ali Baba, Cassim, Mustapha the tailor, and Morgiana offer strong creative challenge to both boys and girls. Several sessions are required to create this story with conviction and satisfaction.

Beauty and the Beast (11) (15)

A favorite fairy tale which may be created in four scenes. It is best suited for an experienced group ready to create strong characterizations with dialogue. The character of the beast and the magical happenings in this story challenge most children.

The Emperor's New Clothes (11) (15) (39)

A favorite story for a group that enjoys creating dialogue. Three dramatic scenes include a Palace Scene where the Emperor reveals his selfish vanity for clothes; a Weaving Scene in which the two gay rogues create exquisite descriptions of cloth for the Minister and other trusted servants; and a Procession Scene which ends dramatically and unexpectedly for the Emperor and everyone in the village.

The Flying Carpet (22)

A delightful *Arabian Nights' Tale* in a colorful picture book. Children enjoy creating a flying carpet, a spying tube, and a magic apple. Three strong scenes are rich in oriental ceremonies and customs. An interesting underlying conflict runs through the plot.

King Midas and the Golden Touch (39)

When children ask for Greek myths this story generally satisfies. It offers an unusual creative opportunity for flowers, bushes, birds, and other living things to become transformed into golden statues.

The Miraculous Pitcher (15)

Another old Greek myth which is popular with some groups of children. Character opportunities are provided in the old couple, Baucis and Philemon, the two mysterious visitors Jupiter and Mercury, and in the curious crowd of villagers including children and dogs.

The Nuremberg Stove (39)

An experienced group often finds this story an exciting challenge. The Curiosity Shop where objects of art come to life provides strong expression both in dialogue and in dancing rhythm. A strong plot arouses suspense throughout the story as August goes with his beautiful stove Hirschvogel which his father has sold.

Rumpelstiltskin (11) (39) (48)

Many groups of older children ask to play this exciting old fairy tale. It is strong in characterizations, suspense, and humor.

Story of Mr. Vinegar (15)

A gay nonsense story which challenges the imaginations of children as they create the characters of Mr. and Mrs. Vinegar, thieves, a farmer with a cow, a quaint bagpipe man, an unusual man with unusual gloves, a man with a good stout stick, and a talking parrot.

Three Sillies (15) (46)

Children find special delight in creating with serious intent three episodes which are sillier than a crying family. Unusual opportunities are found for children to work in groups to create the following scenes: Villagers fishing the moon out of a pond; A Gentleman trying his best to jump into his trousers; and a Peasant Woman trying to get her cow to the roof of her hut.

Bibliography of Material Cited in Appendix B

1. *Amahl and the Night Visitors,* Gian-Carlo Menotti, McGraw-Hill Book Company, Inc., 1953.
2. *The American Singer,* sec. ed., Book One, John W. Beattie, Jose-

phine Wolverton, Grace V. Wilson, and Howard Hinga, American Book Company, 1954.

3. *The American Singer,* sec. ed., Book Two, John W. Beattie, Josephine Wolverton, Grace V. Wilson, and Howard Hinga, American Book Company, 1954.

4. *The American Singer,* sec. ed., Book Three, John W. Beattie, Josephine Wolverton, Grace V. Wilson, and Howard Hinga, American Book Company, 1954.

5. *The American Singer,* sec. ed., Book Four, John W. Beattie, Josephine Wolverton, Grace V. Wilson, and Howard Hinga, American Book Company, 1954.

6. *The American Singer,* sec. ed., Book Five, John W. Beattie, Josephine Wolverton, Grace V. Wilson, and Howard Hinga, American Book Company, 1955.

7. *The American Singer,* sec. ed., Book Six, John W. Beattie, Josephine Wolverton, Grace V. Wilson, and Howard Hinga, American Book Company, 1955.

8. *Andy and the Lion,* James Daugherty, The Viking Press, 1938.

9. *Angelo the Naughty One,* Helen Garrett (illustrator), Leo Politi, E. M. Hale and Company, 1944.

10. *Another Day,* Marie Hall Ets, The Viking Press, 1953.

11. *The Arbuthnot Anthology,* May Hill Arbuthnot, Scott, Foresman and Company, 1954.

12. *A Book About God,* Florence Mary Fitch, Lothrop, Lee and Shepard Company, Inc., 1953.

13. *Brownies—Hush!* Gladys L. Adshead, Oxford University Press, 1938.

14. *Chee-Chee and Keeko,* Charles Thorson, Wilcox and Follett Co., 1952.

15. *Children's Literature,* C. M. Curry and E. E. Clippinger, Rand McNally and Company, 1920.

16. *The Christ Child,* Illus., Maud and Miska Petersham, Doubleday and Company, Inc., 1931.

17. *The Country Bunny and the Little Gold Shoes,* DuBose Heyward, Houghton Mifflin Company, 1939.

18. *The Dancing Kettle and Other Japanese Folk Tales,* retold by Yoshiko Uchida, Harcourt, Brace and Company, 1949.

19. *Danse Macabre,* Op. 40, Camille Saint-Saens, Capitol Long Playing Recordings.

20. *Exploring Our Country,* O. Stuart Hamer, Dwight W. Follett, Ben F. Ahlschwede, and Herbert H. Gross, Follett Publishing Company, 1953.

21. *Firelight Stories,* Carolyn S. Bailey, Milton Bradley Company, 1917.

22. *The Flying Carpet,* Marcia Brown, Charles Scribner's Sons, 1956.

23. *For the Story Teller,* Carolyn S. Bailey, Milton Bradley Company, 1913.

24. *The Golden Bible for Children: The New Testament,* Elsa Jane Werner, Simon and Schuster, 1953.

25. *The Golden Bible for Children: The Old Testament,* Elsa Jane Werner, Simon and Schuster, 1946.

26. *Heigh Ho For Hallowe'en,* Elizabeth Sechrist, Macrae Smith Company, 1948.

27. *Holiday Storybook,* Child Study Association of America (compiler), Thomas Y. Crowell Company, 1952.

28. *Jenny's Birthday Book,* Esther Averill, Harper & Brothers, 1954.

29. *Listening Activities,* A Library of RCA Victor Records for Elementary Schools, Radio Corporation of America, RCA Victor Division, 1947.

30. *The Little Engine That Could,* retold by Watty Piper, The Platt and Munk Co., Inc., 1954.

31. *Mai Li,* Thomas Handforth, Doubleday and Company, 1938.

32. *Make Way for Ducklings,* Robert McCloskey, The Viking Press, 1941.

33. *The Merry Adventures of Robin Hood,* Howard Pyle, Charles Scribner's Sons, 1946.

34. *Millions of Cats,* Wanda Gág, Coward McCann, Inc., 1928.

35. *A Night on Bald Mountain,* Modest Mussorgsky, Capitol Long Playing Recordings.

36. *The Noisy Book,* Margaret Wise Brown, Harper & Brothers, 1939.

37. *Rhythmic Activities,* A Library of RCA Victor Records for Elemen-

tary Schools, Radio Corporation of America, RCA Victor Division, 1947.

38. *Russian Tales For Children,* Alexei Tolstoy, E. P. Dutton Company, 1947.

39. *Stories To Dramatize,* Winifred Ward, The Children's Theatre Press, 1952.

40. *Story and Verse for Children,* Miriam Blanton Huber, The Macmillan Company, 1940.

41. *The Story of Ferdinand,* Munro Leaf, The Viking Press, 1936.

42. *Sung Under the Silver Umbrella,* Literature Committee of the Association for Childhood Education (compiler), The Macmillan Company, 1945.

43. *A Surprise For Mrs. Bunny,* Charlotte Steiner, Grossett and Dunlap, Inc., 1945.

44. *Tales of a Chinese Grandmother,* Frances Carpenter (ed.), Doubleday and Company, Inc., 1937.

45. *The Tall Book of Christmas,* Dorothy Hall Smith (ed.), Harper & Brothers, 1954.

46. *The Tall Book of Nursery Tales,* Artists and Writers Guild, Inc., Harper & Brothers, 1943.

47. *Time For Poetry,* May Hill Arbuthnot, Scott, Foresman and Company, 1952.

48. *Times and Places,* William S. Gray and May Hill Arbuthnot, Scott, Foresman and Company, 1942.

49. *Told Under the Magic Umbrella,* Literature Committee of the Association for Childhood Education (compiler), The Macmillan Company, 1939.

50. *Trails To Treasure,* David H. Russel, Constance M. McCullough, and Doris Gates, Ginn and Company, 1949.

51. *When Jesus Was a Little Boy,* Georgia Moore Eberling, Children's Press, 1954.

52. *Why the Chimes Rang,* Raymond M. Alden, The Bobbs-Merrill Company, Inc., 1954.

53. *Young People's Records,* Young People's Records, Inc., 1947.

Index